Randomised Controlled Trials and Multi-Centre Research

D1493747

MASTER CLASSES IN PRIMARY CARE RESEARCH

Edited by Yvonne Carter, Sara Shaw and Cathryn Thomas

Randomised Controlled Trials and Multi-Centre Research

MARTIN UNDERWOOD, PHILIP HANNAFORD, ANNE SLOWTHER

Martin Underwood MD FRCGP
Senior Lecturer
Department of General Practice and Primary Care
NHS R&D Primary Care Career Scientist
Queen Mary and Westfield College

Philip Hannaford MD FRCGP
Grampian Health Board Professor of Primary Care
Director, RCGP Centre for Primary Care Research and Epidemiology
University of Aberdeen

Anne Slowther MA MRCGP
Research Fellow in Ethics
Oxford Institute for Ethics and Communication Skills in Health Care Practice
Division of Public Health and Primary Care University of Oxford

Published by
The Royal College of General Practitioners
2000

The Royal College of General Practitioners
was founded in 1952 with this object:

"To encourage, foster and maintain the highest possible standards in general practice and for that purpose to take or join with others in taking steps consistent with the charitable nature of that object which may assist towards the same."

Among its responsibilities under its Royal Charter
the College is entitled to:

"Encourage the publication by general medical practitioners of research into medical or scientific subjects with a view to the improvement of general medical practice in any field and to undertake or assist others in undertaking such research.

Diffuse information on all matters affecting general practice and establish, print, publish, issue and circulate such papers, journals, magazines, books, periodicals, and publications and hold such meetings, conferences, seminars and instructional courses as may assist the object of the College."

© Royal College of General Practitioners

First impression 2000

Published by the Royal College of General Practitioners
14 Princes Gate
Hyde Park
London, SW7 1PU

All rights reserved. No part of this publication may be reproduced, stored in a retrieval system, or transmitted, in any form or by any means, electronic, mechanical, photocopying, recording or otherwise without the prior permission of the Royal College of General Practitioners.

Printed and bound by BSC Print Ltd, Wimbledon

ISBN 0 85084 251 4

CONTENTS

Plan your study meticulously
- Box 9: The different phases of your study
Develop a manual of study procedures
Quality assurance
Think about technological assistance
Pilot, pilot and pilot again
- Box 10: If possible, pilot all aspects of your study
Launch your study
Initial response
Maintain the study
Keep stakeholders on board
See the study through to the end
Remember the potential spin-offs
Have fun!
Further reading

5. PRACTICAL EXERCISES

Exercise 1: Trial design
Learning objective
- A randomised controlled trial to demonstrate that the RCGP
     back pain guidelines and/or *The Back Book* improve the outcome
     for back pain sufferers
- Suggested figures to use in the cost estimation
Exercise 2: Implementing the proposal
Learning objective
- 1. How will you recruit practices?
- 2. How will you recruit patients?
- 3. What studies will you do for the trial?
- 4. How will you maintain quality?

6. SOLUTIONS TO EXERCISES

Sample solutions to Exercise 1
Sample solutions to Exercise 2

INTRODUCTION

Martin Underwood

Primary care practitioners participating in multi-centred research are usually involved in a randomised controlled trial (RCT), a cohort, a case-control study, or a cross-sectional survey. The focus of this workbook is the design and implementation of multi-centre studies with particular reference to RCTs. Although RCTs usually provide the highest quality of evidence for assessing the effectiveness of different interventions, they are not always the best way of answering important research questions – another quantitative, or a qualitative, approach may be better. Before designing any study, therefore, you should consider carefully which approach would answer best your particular research question.

This workbook deals with some of the issues involved in the design and implementation of RCTs and multi-centre studies. Since most multi-centre research relates principally to quantitative research, we have focused on this methodology in the workbook. It is assumed that you are already familiar with the basic scientific principles of quantitative research. If you aren't then, before you start this workbook, it is recommended that you read a basic text on research methods in primary care that covers medical statistics. Recommended books include workbook 3 in this Master Class series, or one of the following: Carter and Thomas 1997; Crombie and Davies, 1995; Polgar and Thomas, 1995.

This workbook has been developed from course material from a master class in randomised-controlled trials and multi-centre research run by the Royal College of General Practitioners. It is not intended to be a definitive textbook. Readers are advised to consult other texts as appropriate. Other workbooks in this series that may be useful include:

No 3: *Statistical Concepts*
No 5: *Patient Participation and Ethical Considerations*
No 6: *Funding for Primary Care Research*
No 7: *Issues in Primary Care Epidemiology*

In addition, a number of detailed texts are available covering the theory and practice of randomised controlled trials. One or more of these will provide a firm foundation for developing your own research proposal.

The underlying principles involved in designing an RCT are the same in any health care system. Perhaps inevitably, however, the workbook is orientated towards issues involved in performing research in primary care within Britain. Nonetheless, we believe that overseas readers will find that many of the issues discussed are relevant to other primary care systems. Many of the issues are operational; such matters are inadequately covered in conventional texts.

Back pain has been used as our exemplar, as researching this common clinical problem reveals important lessons that can be applied to many other clinical topics in primary care. The practical exercises provide readers with experience of the type of information that researchers need when planning a randomised controlled trial. We have provided some solutions to the practical problems but it is recognised that many other questions and solutions could emerge from the same data. We have also included in the resource material other information that you may find useful when designing your research project.

· 1 ·

BACKGROUND

Martin Underwood

Learning objectives: *To become familiar with the historical perspective of multi-centre research in primary care, and with the changing context of multi-centre research in primary care*

A BRIEF HISTORY OF MULTI-CENTRE RESEARCH IN PRIMARY CARE

Multi-centre research in primary care dates back at least to the 1960s, when the Royal College of General Practitioners (RCGP) co-ordinated the first case-control study of venous thrombosis and use of combined oral contraceptives (RCGP, 1967). This led, in 1968, to the RCGP oral contraception study (RCGP, 1974), a continuing cohort study that has involved more than 1,400 GPs throughout the UK. This study continues to influence practice today (See Hannaford and Kay in Additional Resource Material section)

During the 1970s, a GPs research club began (Mant, 1998). A collaborative study of induced abortion between the RCGP and the Royal College of Obstetricians and Gynaecologists, involving more than 1,000 practices and 800 gynaecologists, started in 1976 (Kay and Frank, 1981). In 1973, the Medical Research Council (MRC) recruited 176 practices to carry out a study of the treatment of mild hypertension (MRC working party, 1985). These practices subsequently went on to become the MRC General Practice Research Framework (GPRF). During the 1980s a small number of locally based research networks emerged, with a bottom-up approach to developing research rather than the top-down approach of the large RCGP studies and the GPRF. During the 1990s, there has been a rapid expansion of local research networks and the GPRF has grown to over 1,000 practices. The GPRF is now recognised as a national research resource that is available to any researcher with an appropriate proposal.

MULTI-CENTRE STUDIES IN PRIMARY CARE?

Current changes in the NHS, in particular the development of evidence-based practice and clinical governance, require robust evidence that will inform the management of common primary care problems. Much of this evidence will need to come from RCTs, cross-sectional surveys, cohort studies and case-control studies performed in primary care. By performing these studies in British primary care we can ensure that the questions

asked are those most appropriate to our work, and that hypotheses are tested in the correct population, our patients and in our practices. RCTs will provide the 'gold standard' evidence needed to avoid the potential biases that can be introduced from observational and uncontrolled studies. Advice on choosing the most appropriate research design is beyond the scope of this workbook. For further information on issues of choice of design see Black (1996) and Kliejnen (1997) in Additional Resource Material.

There has been a growth industry in recent years of using meta-analysis to pool the results from smaller studies. Although meta-analysis is a useful tool for combining results from studies that are, in themselves, inconclusive, they are not a substitute for large original studies. One review of 30 meta-analyses found that 18 disagreed with subsequent definitive studies, either in direction of difference or its significance (Villar et al., 1995). There are occasions when meta-analyses disagree with each other, when analysing the same basic data set (Koes et al., 1966, Shekelle et al., 1992). Also they can produce results that many may find difficult to believe, for example one rigorous meta-analysis produced results that support the conclusion that homeopathy is effective (Linde et al., 1997).

There is a continuing need to develop large scale studies answering the research questions important to those working in primary care, producing results that are generalisable across the UK and more widely to other countries.

WHAT IS STOPPING US?

Historically there has been relatively poor infrastructure for carrying out multi-centre research in primary care. This is changing:

- the GPRF is open to any researcher with a good proposal
- there are many research networks
- there are increasing numbers of recognised research practices
- an RCGP initiative in the South and West region is piloting the accreditation of research practices.

The problems of poor research training are being addressed by the local research networks, the increased availability and uptake of Masters Degrees, and the availability of more research training fellowships.

Following the publication of the Mant Report (Mant, 1998) and the Culyer Report (Department of Health, 1994) it is likely that sufficient funding for more large scale studies will be available.

FUNDING TERMINOLOGY

The focus of this workbook is not on the financing of studies, readers are recommended to consult workbook 6 in this Master Class series.

It is likely that the details of how financial support for research in primary care will change in the future. However, it is worth being aware of a few current funding terms.

Culyer Budget One: This is support for NHS providers (trusts and GPs). This covers the cost of hosting research and development (R&D) funded by the MRC and other external funding bodies, as well as research and development which providers conduct themselves. This money is allocated nationally.

Culyer Budget Two: This is the funding that supports the NHS Research and Development Programme. It is largely used for funding research projects and is commissioned regionally.

Budget One is divided into treatment costs and service support costs. These are defined (NHS Executive, 1997) as:

> '*Treatment costs* are the patient care costs which would continue to be incurred if the patient care service in question continued to be provided after the R&D activity has stopped. If patient care is to be provided that differs from the normal, standard treatment for that condition (either an experimental treatment or a service in a different location from where it would normally be given), the difference between total treatment cost and the cost of the 'standard alternative' (if any) can be termed *excess treatment costs*.
> *Service support costs* are the additional patient care costs associated with the research, which would end once the R&D activity in question had stopped, even if the same patient care service continued to be provided. This might cover things like extra blood tests, extra in-patient days and extra nursing attention.'

For studies where research costs are provided by a large funding organisation such as the MRC, or some medical charities, the NHS will meet all the treatment and service support costs as a matter of policy.

RANDOMISED CONTROLLED TRIALS

Martin Underwood

Learning objective: *To provide sufficient theoretical background to allow readers to tackle the trial design exercise*

Double blind randomised controlled trials are the only research design that can eliminate the biases that affect any other form of research. Using an appropriate randomisation procedure and blinding is crucial to the elimination of bias. However, blinding participants to their treatment allocation is not always possible in trials of important primary care questions. For example, if the practical exercise was to design a trial to assess the effect of spinal manipulation, it would be impossible to blind the participants to their treatment allocation. A randomisation procedure should be used that ensures that neither the researcher, or the research subject, can predict their allocated treatment before randomisation. Standard texts on statistics or trial design should be consulted for advice on these issues.

STATISTICAL REVISION

For detailed explanations of statistical concepts a standard statistics book, or workbook 3 in this series, should be consulted. Two of the commonest statistical questions asked are:

- what sample size do I need?
- do the results support the hypothesis?

The general answer to both of these questions is 'ask a statistician'. The importance of getting statistical advice early in the design of any trial or study cannot be emphasised strongly enough. This should ensure that an appropriate sample size is chosen, and that the results can be analysed in a meaningful manner.

When calculating a sample size a statistician will ask for some basic information.

For a prevalence or incidence study:
- an estimate of prevalence
- the accuracy or precision required.

For example: What sample size do I need to be able to estimate the point prevalence to a certain degree of accuracy, say *within five percentage points*, given that the prevalence is about 14%?

For a comparative study:
- the required significance, usually 5% [sometimes given as $\alpha = 0.05$]. If a significance of 5% is chosen then there is a 1:20 chance that the results may show a significant difference when no such difference actually exists in the population
- the power required is usually between 80% and 95% [sometimes given as $\beta = 0.2$ or $\beta = 0.05$, Power = $(1- \beta) \times 100\%$]. A study with a power of 80% will fail to show a difference between two groups, when such a difference is present in the population on one in five occasions
- what is a clinically important difference between the two groups?

For a categorical variable (e.g. do you have back pain today? Yes/No) this is the difference in proportion between the two groups.
- An estimate of the prevalence or incidence is also required.

For example: What sample size do I need to show that physical therapy reduces the proportion of patients who consult their GP with back pain who are significantly disabled one year later from 10% to 5% with a significance of 5% and power of 80%?

For a continuous variable (e.g. height or weight) a clinically important difference needs to be defined as a difference in means and an estimate of the population Standard Deviation (SD) is required. The SD can be obtained from previous studies or from pilot work.

For example: What sample size do I need to show that physical therapy reduces the mean Roland Morris Disability Questionnaire Score (a back pain outcome measure) one year after treatment by 2.5 points with a significance of 5% and a power of 80%? The population standard deviation is 4.0.

Sample size estimation is not an exact science. Final sample sizes are often affected by the likely availability of research subjects and funding. It is sometimes worthwhile to slightly overestimate the number of subjects needed to account for unexpected events. It is up to the researchers to decide what accuracy is required or what is a clinically important difference. This cannot be calculated by statisticians. Remember to allow for those who do not respond to surveys or are lost to follow up. The number of people you approach or randomise will need to be increased to allow for this. If you want to recruit patients consulting with a particular condition, it is highly likely that the number of patients seen will be much less than the pre-trial estimate. Allow for this in your calculations. A number of computerised sample size calculators are available. A trial version of one statistical package, Arcus Quickstat, which is available on the Internet (www.camcode.com) includes a sample size calculator. Alternatively books of tables can be used, for example Machin and Campbell (1997). A useful exercise, before seeing your statistician, is to examine how changing the assumptions you have made about your study affects the required sample size. For the two examples of comparative studies above the numbers are 946 for the comparison of proportions and 82 if the Roland Morris score is used.

CLUSTER RANDOMISATION

A cluster randomised trial is one that tests the effect of introducing an intervention at, for example, a practice or primary care group level rather than at an individual patient level. This would be appropriate if the trial was testing a change in the practice's approach to a condition or for some educational initiatives. Statistical analyses assume that the behaviour of all individuals studied is totally independent. If a cluster randomisation is used this assumption is no longer robust, since there may be factors about belonging to a particular practice that may affect outcome. This effect is quantified using the Intra-cluster Correlation Co-efficient (ICC), also known as ρ (pronounced 'rho').

- If $\rho = 0.00$ all individuals behave independently
- If $\rho = 1.00$ all individuals from one cluster behave identically

Typically values of ρ are between $0.01 - 0.05$ for studies randomising by practice although this can be much higher. The increase in sample size required is given by the formula:

$$1 + (\bar{n} - 1)\rho$$

Where $\bar{n}$ is cluster size and ρ is the ICC. An additional correction is required if the clusters are of different sizes.

An additional calculation is required if the clusters vary in size. See Kerry and Bland (1998), and Underwood et al (1998) in Additional Resource Material. If you are considering performing an RCT using cluster randomisation you are strongly advised to consult an experienced statistician for advice.

DATA ANALYSIS

At the end of your study or trial the data will need to be analysed. A successful study is one that collects, analyses and reports all of the relevant data, not one that supports the original hypothesis. Whatever the results, even if they disagree with your strong prior belief, they should be published. Only by doing this will you prevent others going down the same blind alley and also help others reach a consensus on the best way forward. If the study fails for methodological reasons, it should still be published as it will help others to design their studies.

CONSORT STATEMENT

The editors of several major journals have signed up to the CONSORT statement, which lays down precise rules about the presentation of trial results. Not all of these rules apply to the sorts of trials done in primary care. Many of these rules also apply to observational studies.

See Altman D (1996) in Additional Resource Material. Designing your trial or study with these in mind will make writing up easier and will help ensure you are published in a major journal.

BOX 1

Examples of the effect of cluster randomisation

- In a trial of chlamydia screening guidelines, where $\rho = 0.29$ (Oakeshott and Kerry, 1999) that wanted to recruit 50 participants per practice the inflation factor is given by the calculation:

$$1+(50-1)0.29 = 15.21$$

Thus, over 15 times as many participants would be required compared to randomising by individual participant.

- In a trial of childhood injury prevention, where $\rho = 0.017$ (Kendrick et al., 1999) that wanted to recruit 200 individuals per practice the inflation factor is given by the calculation:

$$1+(200-1)0.017 = 4.38$$

Thus, nearly four and a half times as many participants would be required compared to randomising by individual.

OTHER ADVANCED TRIAL DESIGNS

There are a number of more advanced trial techniques that can sometimes be useful. These include:

Factorial trials

Two interventions (factors) are tested on the same population. This can be very cost effective as long as one can be confident that the two interventions do not interact with each other.

Equivalence studies

Rather than wishing to show that two treatments are different, one wishes to show that they are equally effective.

Patient preference studies

An element of patient choice in the treatment they receive is allowed. These may be appropriate in a situation where outside the trial an element of patient choice in selecting treatment is usual.

Multiple comparisons

It is possible to do an RCT where three or more treatments are compared. If this is done there can be quite large effects on the sample size required because of the increased risk of finding a difference by pure chance.

Zelen studies

Participants are told that they are in a study only after randomisation.

A number of texts that relate to these issues are included in the Additional Resource Material: Edwards et al. 1998; Jones et al., 1999; Silverman and Altman, 1996; Torgerson and Roland, 1998; Torgerson and Sibbald, 1998. If you are considering these types of trials consult a specialist text and a colleague with previous experience.

CONCLUSION

Finally, two points to remember in designing your trial:
1. Clear questions have clear answers
2. Keep it simple; make it big (KISMIB).*

*Attributed to Richard Peto

· 3 ·

GETTING IT APPROVED

Anne Slowther

Learning objective: *To become familiar with the process of gaining ethical approval for multi-centre research*

Once you have planned your study, and before it can be implemented, it will need to be approved by a research ethics committee. Depending on the size of the study, you must submit your proposal to either all of the Local Research Ethics Committees (LRECs) covering the centres that you plan to use or, if it will involve more than five LRECs, to a Multi-centre Research Ethics Committee (MREC). As this workbook concentrates on large quantitative multi-centre trials the MREC procedure will be discussed in detail, but the process of considering research proposals, and the ethical principles involved will be essentially the same for LRECs.

BACKGROUND OF MRECS

For many years it has been necessary to consult a research ethics committee about any research that is health related and involves:

- NHS patients (subjects recruited by virtue of their past or present treatment by the NHS), foetal material and the recently dead
- access to records and names of past and present NHS patients
- the use of, or potential access to, NHS premises or facilities. (MREC, 1999)

Before July 1997 research ethics committees were local; that is, situated in and accountable to, a local health authority. These committees reviewed all research carried out within their geographical boundary. Thus, it was necessary for researchers conducting multi-centre studies to submit their proposal to all LRECs that covered their study population. As any researcher who has been through this procedure will attest, it is both time-consuming and frustrating. Ethics, like medicine, is not an exact science and different ethics committees may give different opinions, or suggest different changes to the study protocol. In response to the concerns voiced by researchers, in particular the large pharmaceutical companies, MRECs were established to facilitate the process of ethical review of multi-centre studies. There is one MREC for each region in England and one each for Scotland, Wales and Northern Ireland. In Northern Ireland there is a single NHS research ethics committee combining MREC and LREC functions.

The primary objective of all research ethics committees is to facilitate research of high ethical standard. It is not, contrary to some researchers' beliefs, to obstruct worthwhile research. It is the role of the research ethics committee to balance the merits of the research against the potential harm to the research subjects and to ensure that the autonomy of the research subject is respected.

BOX 2

Process of application to an MREC

Application forms and guidance for applicants can be obtained from the appropriate MREC administrator or from the MREC website (http://dspace.dial.pipex.com/mrec). Tips for ensuring a smooth passage for your application include:

1. Make sure that you answer all appropriate sections of the form.

2. Obtain a scientific critique of your proposal if possible, and include any referees reports with your application.

3. Make sure that the background and outline of your proposal is explained clearly and simply so that it can be understood by someone not familiar with your area of research.

4. Give some thought to the ethical issues which may need to be considered in your study. Do **not** write "not applicable" in this section of the application form.

5. Make sure your patient information sheet covers the areas specified in the checklist provided with the guidance for applicants.

An application should be submitted three weeks before the meeting at which it is to be considered. You may be asked to attend the meeting at which your project is discussed, but how likely this is will depend on the particular committee. The committee makes a decision about each proposal considered at the meeting, and you will be notified of the decision within ten working days of the meeting. There are three possible decisions that the committee can make about each proposal. It can:

- approve the proposal
- reject the proposal
- defer the proposal with requests for amendments.

The committee's response must explain the reasons for deferral or rejection of the proposal. A member of the committee may contact you before the meeting to discuss your proposal or to ask for clarification of a point. If your proposal is deferred, you should be able to discuss the requested amendments with the administrator and, if appropriate, a member of the committee. If your proposal is rejected you may resubmit it to the same committee after making appropriate changes, taking into account the committee's reasons for rejection. If you disagree with the committee's decision and you are unable to resolve the issue, it is possible that your proposal could be considered by another MREC. The decision of the second MREC is final with no right of appeal.

MEMBERSHIP OF THE MREC

The MREC requires a broad spectrum of expertise to ensure effective and impartial consideration of research proposals.

BOX 3

**The MREC constitution
suggested membership list**

1 statistician
2 GPs
2 nurses
1 senior research/information pharmacist
1 clinical pharmacologist
4 consultants
1 public health physician or epidemiologist
1 social scientist currently doing research
4 additional lay members
1 professional allied to medicine

Either the chairman or the vice-chairman must be a lay member.

RELATIONSHIP BETWEEN THE MREC AND LRECs

Once your proposal has been approved by the MREC you will need to submit the endorsed proposal and letter of approval to all LRECs covering your study area. LRECs may only refuse an application, or request amendments on local issues. For example, they may refuse an application because of the unsuitability of the local researcher, or they may request that an information sheet should be produced in languages other than English. The LREC is not required to consider the protocol other than for local issues. If it has general ethical concerns it can make these known to the MREC chairman, but it **cannot** delay the research on these grounds (NHSE, 1998).

ETHICAL ISSUES CONSIDERED BY THE MREC

There are three main ethical principles which ethics committees need to consider when assessing research proposals.

1. They must consider the benefits of the proposed research to present or future patients, or to society in general.

This will entail assessing the scientific merit of the research and the MREC is expected to advise on the 'science and general ethics of multi-centre research proposals' (Department of Health, 1997). If a study is not scientifically robust, then it will not be able to answer the research question and research subjects will have been inconvenienced or put at risk to no purpose. From an ethical point of view, the standard for scientific rigour will, to some extent, depend on the nature of the study. For example, a trial of a new drug or physical treatment will need to meet strict criteria for ensuring a clear and clinically significant result than a simple questionnaire study of patients' attitudes to mammography. The potential harm to the research subject must be balanced with the potential benefit of the research.

BOX 4

**Possible reasons for an ethics committee
rejecting a proposal on scientific grounds**

- in an RCT, the sample size is too small to detect a significant difference
- the expected difference will be statistically significant but not clinically important
- the study population has been chosen in such a way that the results will not be generalisable

(This list is by no means exhaustive)

---

2. The committee must consider the harm likely to occur to the research subject and to what degree, if any, this can be justified.

This will include considering: risks of new treatment or of withholding conventional treatment; psychological harm, for example mental health questionnaires in vulnerable patients; discovery of potentially harmful information, as in genetic research; or the risks of additional investigations. The issue of compensation should be addressed and the committee will want to know what arrangements have been made for this. For pharmaceutical company research, the company will include an assurance that they are insured to compensate research subjects for non-negligent harm in accordance with ABPI guidelines. For other research it is the responsibility of the researcher to ensure that provision is made for appropriate compensation, and if this is not possible then it must be absolutely clear in the patient information sheet that no compensation for non-negligent harm will be available. The ethics committee will require clear information on this point in your proposal.

Non-negligent harm is that harm suffered by a research subject because of their participation in the research which is not caused by the negligent action of the researcher or others.

BOX 5

Points worth remembering when considering compensation to research subjects

• Medical defence bodies will not accept liability for claims for compensation due to non-negligent harm

• NHS indemnity does not cover non-negligent harm arising from research carried out by NHS employees, or on NHS premises

- The NHS, and other publicly funded bodies such as the Medical Research Council (MRC), may not offer advance indemnities or take out insurance for non-negligent harm.

- In exceptional circumstances (within a designated limit of around £50,000) the NHS may offer an ex gratia payment. The MRC will usually issue a statement saying that claims will be considered and payment is met by the MRC.

- Independent sector sponsors of research (e.g. universities and research charities) may take out insurance to cover compensation for research subjects, but you will need to check that they are willing to do so.   (NHSE, 1996)

BOX 6

Examples of harm to research subjects

• Invasive procedures which would not normally be part of the patient's clinical care
• Screening for conditions for which there is no recognised treatment
• Questions likely to cause distress in vulnerable subjects
• Risk to patients of withdrawal of current treatment

(*This list is by no means exhaustive*)

Subjects could also be harmed by a breach of confidentiality (see Box 6). The committee will want to know what measures will be taken to ensure confidentiality of patient's records and any specimens relating to the research. An assurance of confidentiality should be included in the information sheet, in addition to a statement saying whether persons outside the NHS will have access to patient information.

3. The issue of respect for the autonomy of the research subject must be addressed. This involves ensuring that the subject is able to make an informed judgement about whether to take part in the research. When considering this ethical issue the committee will concentrate on the patient information sheet and consent form.

For consent to be valid it must be:

• competent
• voluntary
• informed.

Competence
Most research will involve competent adult research subjects. In some instances it will be necessary to carry out research on subjects who are not legally competent, for example children or some mentally impaired adults. If your research will include such subjects you must pay particular attention to the consent procedures. The legal definition of competence is laid down in the judgement of the High Court in the case Re C (1994). For a consent, or refusal, to be competent, the subject must be able to:

• believe the information given to them
• understand the information
• evaluate the information and make a choice.

The assessment of competence relates to the decision being made. It may be that a person who is not competent to make an informed consent to take part in a complicated drug trial, could be competent to consent to a study comparing two bath aids. Mentally impaired adults are not deemed incompetent as a group, but the ethics committee will want to know that you are aware of the potential problem in gaining consent to research from such subjects, and how you will deal with it.

Non-competent research subjects
Adults: Research should only be carried out on non-competent adults if it is in the best interests of the patient and / or the research can only be carried out on that particular group of patients, for example a trial of a new drug for Alzheimer's disease. Non-competent adults cannot give consent and legally no one can give consent on their behalf. However, in such circumstances the ethics committee would expect consent to be obtained from a patient's close relative or carer and for this to be witnessed by an independent person.
Children: Research should only be carried out on children if it is in their best interests and the research cannot be carried out on adults. Non-therapeutic research can occasionally be carried out on children if the risk and discomfort to the child is minimal and the research cannot be carried out on adults. The issue of consent in children aged between 16 and 18 is a legal grey area. In Scotland they can consent to any medical procedure, which could include research. However, in England and Wales section 8(1) of the Family Law

Reform Act (1969) states that they can give consent to any "surgical, medical or dental **treatment**". It is not clear that this would cover consent to research. Similarly the Gillick judgement (1986) relating to consent of children less than 16 years also specifies treatment and may not relate to research. The MREC information for researchers, while acknowledging that children under 16 **may** give consent to research, advises that it would be unwise to allow participation of such a child in research where parental consent was not forthcoming (MREC, 1999). You are less likely to run into problems with the ethics committee if you confine your recruitment to persons over 18, unless the research needs to be done on children and adolescents. If your research subjects include children, you will need to provide a patient information sheet appropriate to the child's level of understanding, and obtain the child's assent as well as obtaining informed consent from the parent.

Voluntariness

It is often the case in medical research that the researcher is also the person who normally provides health care for the patient. This can lead to conflict for the researcher who is anxious to recruit for their study, but also has a duty of care to their patient to provide the best management possible. The patient may feel under pressure to consent to participate in the study because of a wish to please their doctor, or because of an assumption that the doctor (or other health care professional) will ensure that they get the best treatment. This is especially true in primary care research because of the close relationship that often builds up between patient and health professional. Patients recruited for medical research are often unwell and as such are vulnerable to persuasion from people they perceive as experts, thus unwitting coercion can be a danger. An information sheet must therefore make it clear that participation in the research is entirely voluntary, and refusal will not in any way compromise the future care of the patient. In addition, adequate time must be given to allow the patient to consider the information, ask questions and discuss the research with others. Usually the ethics committee will expect at least 24 hours to be given unless there is a good reason why this is not possible. If less time is given you may wish to consider the use of an independent witness to the consent.

Information

The patient information sheet should be written clearly and easily understood by a lay person. It should be appropriate to the level of understanding of the subjects (for example, separate sheets for children). A checklist for patient information sheets is included in the MREC guidance for researchers which is part of your resource pack. Some MRECs may include their own checklist. The South and West MREC checklist is also included in your resource pack. The European Directive on Good Clinical Practice came into effect in 1999. This will adopt the ICH guidelines for clinical trials that relate to pharmaceutical research. These guidelines have specific requirements for patient information and a copy of the guidelines is contained in your resource pack. Although these guidelines relate to pharmaceutical research, the ethical principles underlying them relate to all research, and there is a move to ensure that all research is compliant with these guidelines. The MRC guidelines for good clinical practice state that the underlying principles are the same as those of ICH guidelines. A Department of Health working party has produced guidelines for patient information sheets which are now an integral part of the MREC documentation (since April 1999). These guidelines are intended to be ICH compatible.*

BOX 7

Points to remember when developing information sheets and consent forms

- The wording must be appropriate to the research subjects' age, ethnicity and intellectual level
- Children must give assent as well as their parents giving consent to the research
- In cases of vulnerable patients, have an independent witness to the consent
- Comply with the guidelines accompanying the MREC application form

---

Every issue discussed above will not be relevant to your particular study but if you are able to demonstrate that you have considered all the issues, and addressed those relevant to your proposal, you are more likely to achieve a favourable decision from the MREC at your first attempt.

*Personal communication Palmer, A

· 4 ·

PRACTICAL ISSUES

Philip Hannaford

Learning objective: *To understand some of the practical issues involved in doing multi-centre research*

IMPLEMENTING THE RESEARCH PROPOSAL

Many of the issues discussed in this chapter are the same whether you are undertaking a small single centre study of a few patients or a large national (or international) multi-centred project; and whether the study is of a quantitative or qualitative nature. The main difference with multi-centred research is the scale. Since many individuals are involved, there is great potential for problems to emerge and small problems can very rapidly develop into major difficulties. The following advice does not guarantee that your project will succeed. Consideration of each point, however, may help you avoid common problems and may make the task less daunting. It is assumed that you will be the principal investigator for your study.

GETTING THE STAKEHOLDERS ON BOARD

In order to convert your research question into a successful multi-centred project, you need to get a number of stakeholders on board (see Box 8). Since some of the stakeholders may be reluctant participants in your work, this phase of the work often requires considerable skills in negotiation and motivation.

BOX 8

Stakeholders of a successful multi-centred research project in primary care

- you
- funding body
- ethics committee
- your research team
- key opinion leaders
- participating practices / users of services

First of all, you need to convince yourself that you are addressing an important issue that is worth the considerable amount of time and effort that good research requires. Pioneering research can be

controversial, and as principal investigator you may be the focus of attention of detractors and critics of your work. You need to strike a balance between being able to answer any criticisms confidently with robust scientific arguments and not becoming so emotionally involved that you become deaf to valid outside comment.

Before you can secure funding for your work, you need to demonstrate to a funding body that your research question:

1. is important
2. will be answered in a scientifically valid way
3. cannot be addressed in another way (at least not as efficiently)
4. has not been addressed before (or needs replicating in your particular setting)
5. justifies the resources requested
6. is best answered by your research team because it has the necessary combination of skills and experience.

The appropriate ethics committee(s) will need to be convinced that your study is scientifically valid and ethical. Confidence in your project will help you to respond to any questions that arise in an appropriate manner (sometimes robustness is required).

Your research team will be crucial to the success of your project. Ideally, all members of the team should be inspired to believe that they are working on one of the best studies around, addressing an important research question. Time spent explaining the rationale for the project, giving background information and discussing current controversies in the field is a good investment in motivating your team. This information also helps team members who are asked questions about the project by participating practitioners or patients.

Identify local or national key opinion leaders (KOLs) who may assist, or hinder, the successful completion of your project. These individuals may be influential primary care practitioners, members of medico-political, managerial or professional organisations, colleagues in the secondary care sector or recognised authoritative figures working in the research area. Having identified likely KOLs, develop a dialogue with them at an early stage. The discussions may reveal issues that could affect your work, such as other research projects that will reduce the pool of patients available for recruitment, local political problems or previous attempts to answer the same research question. Support from a respected KOL might assist patient recruitment, although a badly chosen KOL might have the opposite effect! A sympathetic KOL may provide much needed support when critics appear. Conversely, failure to get KOLs on board may result in covert (or overt) sabotage of your research. It is not always possible to reach total agreement that your proposal is worthwhile, or even ethical, but it is useful to be aware of criticisms as soon as possible so that you can develop strategies for minimising the effects of adverse comment.

Multi-centred research requires participating practices or primary health care teams who need to be told why you would like them to be involved and what you would like them to do. Even if a practice that you approach cannot participate, you want to generate general support for your work. Practitioners may talk about your project when they meet together; you do not want non-participating practices to undermine your efforts at such occasions.

As well as participating practices, you need participating patients. These individuals also need to be motivated into contributing to your work. In business, marketing campaigns often involve the priming of the market before the launch of a product. It is worth thinking about whether you can generate support for your work by informing special interest groups and/or the media about the project prior to its launch.

PLAN YOUR STUDY METICULOUSLY

Research requires careful attention to detail. Allow plenty of time for the careful planning of each stage of your study (see Box 9). Time is needed for obtaining ethical approval for your study and the pilot work. Ideally, this planning stage should be adequately funded.

BOX 9

The different phases of your study

- identification of practices who might participate
- invitation to practices to participate
- identification of patients who might participate
- getting informed consent
- recruitment procedure
- recruitment packs
- returning of documents and/or samples from the practices
- receipt of documents and/or samples in the research office
- replenishing stocks in participating practices
- follow-up procedures
- stock control
- data entry of returned documents
- data analysis
- archiving of documents and/or specimens.

When planning the study, minimise the workload of participating practices and patients, even if this results in more work for you. Consider potential problems in identifying patients for recruitment. If your study involves asking general practitioners to identify patients during routine surgery consultations consider aide-mémoires to facilitate good recruitment rates. Consider whether some procedures can be done outside the consulting room. Think about mechanisms for identifying patients who were seen in the surgery but who were not asked to participate in the study, perhaps because the doctor forgot.

Make adequate allowance in your budgets for: slower recruitment than expected; chasing up slow recruiters; correcting errors and omissions on study documentation (perhaps 10-20% of all forms); extra work resulting from changes in the study protocol that arise. Provide reply-paid envelopes for any forms or blood samples that have to be returned and consider reimbursement of expenses for extra staffing, telephone use etc. Provide any consumables needed for the study, such as syringes, blood tubes etc. Consider whether you need to provide travelling costs for patients.

DEVELOP A MANUAL OF STUDY PROCEDURES

After considering the different phases of your project, develop a written manual of study procedures. This document is very different from the study protocol that you submitted to the funding body and ethics committee(s). The manual of study procedures details the operational aspects of your study: what will be done at each stage, when and by whom. The manual should include details of your day-to-day study management group, the project's steering group, data monitoring committee and any other group that you wish to establish to ensure the success of the project. The remit, composition and frequency of meeting of each group should be agreed before the study starts. Think carefully about whom you invite to be on each group, although for some groups (such as the data monitoring committee) you may have little say in the matter. If interim analyses are planned make sure that these are documented in the manual of study procedures beforehand.

A manual of study procedures helps maintain consistency among your research team, thus facilitating quality control. It also helps ensure the successful completion of the study even if key members of your team leave. The manual needs continuous revision so that changes made as the project progresses are incorporated.

QUALITY ASSURANCE

Build quality assurance into your study from the start. How will you assess that the right patients have been recruited? How you will assess the completeness and accuracy of collected data? You may want to check a sample of completed forms against original medical records – is this feasible, especially if practices are widely distributed throughout the country? Do you want to enter data twice (i.e. double data entry, a system commonly used to minimise data entry errors) or can you manage with the checking of a random sample of entered forms? If important, how can you ensure the blinding of investigators, office staff and / or data analysts to the interventions given? How will study end-points be defined? Does an independent end-point committee need to be established?

THINK ABOUT TECHNOLOGICAL ASSISTANCE

Technology can (but not always) reduce the administrative burden of a study. It might also improve quality. For example, bar codes on forms can speed up data processing and reduce errors during data input. Similar benefits can be achieved by using questionnaires that can be optically scanned into a computer. Machines that fill envelopes and frank envelopes reduce mailing workload. Technological advances have reduced the cost of much office equipment. Sometimes it is possible to rent rather than buy this type of machinery. Local academic departments, and some health authorities, may have access to this type of equipment; they may be amenable to requests that you use it for your project.

PILOT, PILOT AND PILOT AGAIN

Assume that anything that can be misread, misinterpreted, ignored or forgotten will be. Doctors are often the worse culprits in this respect. Piloting (see Box 10) does not mean that you won't get any problems in your main study but it should help to minimise them.

BOX 10

If possible, pilot all aspects of your study

- letters of invitation to doctors
- letters of invitation to patients
- identification of potential participants
- recruitment procedures
- forms to be used
- mailing procedures
- office procedures

There are no hard and fast rules about how many practices or patients to include in pilot work. Enough need to be recruited to reveal as many of the problems that might arise in the main study as possible. Think carefully about where you do the pilot work. Sites need to be representative of those that you intend to use in the main study. Some studies start with an initial phase in which a small number of test-bed sites are used in order to learn about problems with the main study. Patients recruited during this phase can be included in

the final dataset provided that there are no major changes in the protocol. However, important changes often occur during this initial phase, in which case information collected from patients recruited at this time cannot be included in the main study.

LAUNCH YOUR STUDY

Consider publicity when launching your study. If your project is funded by a charity, it may wish to use the launch to publicise its charitable activities. Consider this carefully. Media interest may affect your recruitment, perhaps by leading to the recruitment of individuals with a particular interest in your research question; are these participants representative of those you wish to include in your project? If you have a big launch and the project subsequently fails, how will you (and your funding body) react? If your study is particularly controversial you may not want to have a public launch; could you be accused at a later stage of being secretive?

Avoid notoriously difficult recruiting times, such as Christmas and the summer holidays. Remember school holidays vary around the country (notably, summer holidays start and finish earlier in Scotland than England). If a flu epidemic strikes, you may wish to delay launching your study although other pressures, such as funding issues, may make this impossible.

INITIAL RESPONSE

Respond immediately to questions about, or agreements to participate in, your study. Enthusiasm wanes fast. Busy practitioners are likely to show interest in your study for only a limited period of time before their attention moves elsewhere. You are more likely to sustain their interest if you follow up initial responses quickly with additional information and recruitment packs. This means that you have to have everything ready *before* the launch.

Be prepared for negative comments. Depending on the nature of your study, this may come from patients receiving unsolicited mailings; busy health care professionals feeling that you are harassing them or conducting unethical work; professional groupings annoyed that you are (actually or perceived to be) encroaching on their territory. However hard you try to avoid such criticism it will probably occur to some degree. You need to develop a thick skin and remember the importance of your study. If possible, follow up all messages of complaint. An apology to recently bereaved relatives upset because you have inadvertently sent a questionnaire to a deceased loved one will usually reduce the distress caused. Developing a dialogue with your critics can lead to new understandings and even subsequent support for your work. If nothing else, you will have the opportunity to put your side of the argument and hopefully minimise the impact of any adverse comments that your critics might continue to make.

MAINTAIN THE STUDY

Chase up slow recruiters. Did they get the recruitment materials? Did they read them? Where are the materials now located? Feedback from these potential participants may reveal problems that you had not anticipated. Respond immediately to any problems encountered, or concerns expressed, by recruiting practices. Again, this shows interest in the practices. The first few patients entered into a study are usually the most difficult; appearing to understand and support practices at this stage will encourage them to continue recruitment.

If your study is based on a postal questionnaire try to have a minimum of three mailings. As a general rule of thumb you should expect a return rate of 50% at the first, 20% at the second and 10% at the third mailing.

Keep on top of data processing and queries. Backlogs of work are depressing and demoralising, clearing them often seems to take a disproportionate amount of effort. If you are recruiting hundreds or thousands of patients, a small proportion of queries still represents a large number of people. Regular meetings of your management group should help to ensure problems are dealt with promptly.

KEEP STAKEHOLDERS ON BOARD

Newsletters and reprints maintain interest and provide a reminder of why the study is worth doing. Ethics committees and funding bodies usually like, and some expect, an annual report of progress. During the recruitment phase, details of recruitment rates can encourage hesitant practitioners to start recruiting. Newsletters also provide an opportunity to thank everyone for their work. Other ways of recognising the work of participating practices include financial rewards, books or perhaps provision of no-cost PGEA approved courses. Think carefully about paying participating practices. You can rarely offer the true rate of pay and you may cause offence by offering what may be perceived to be a derisory amount of money. On the other hand, many practitioners do value a token payment as it recognises that their time and effort is valuable.

Be aware of new developments in your research area. New research can suddenly make your study unethical, or make it even more imperative that you continue. Someone, somewhere, will read the same papers. Their sudden appearance may upset your project, especially if the individual has already expressed concerns about the ethics of your work.

SEE THE STUDY THROUGH TO THE END

Even if you have to finish your study before the pre-defined time, finish data entry and publish your results. You may no longer have statistical power to detect effects that really exist but the data will be in the public domain, available for future systematic reviewers. It is especially important that you publish negative results, thereby reducing opportunity for publication bias. Some would argue that failure to publish constitutes scientific misconduct.

REMEMBER THE POTENTIAL SPIN-OFFS

During the difficult times it is helpful to remember the potential spin-offs. New research questions are likely to arise from your work, leading to new projects possibly requiring new approaches. Your research may result in new collaborations and networking with others. Participating practices may be inspired by your efforts to develop their own questions and research projects.

HAVE FUN !

Life is too short to be filled with dull, monotonous work. If this is how you experience research to be, stop doing it – you won't do it well. On the other hand, if you enjoy research, try to secure resources that allow you protected time to engage in this activity. Workbook 6 in this series discusses funding issues.

Further reading
Carter Y, Shaw S, Thomas C (eds). *Master Classes in Primary Care Research No. 6: Funding for Primary Care Research*. London, RCGP. *In Press*.

5

PRACTICAL EXERCISES

Resource material for these exercises can be found at the back of this workbook

EXERCISE 1: TRIAL DESIGN

Learning objective: *To understand the process of designing a controlled trial*

You have been provided with material to allow you to start designing an RCT. In the outline, there is most of the information that is needed to design the trial. Resource material is provided that includes a selection of the important reference material that you would have available if you were designing a trial in this area. The design of trials for the treatment of back pain is complex. There are no right answers as to how this should be done. This example has been chosen as it illustrates many of the problems you might face in designing trials in primary care.

More data have been provided than is needed to design a trial. Part of designing any trial is deciding which existing information is essential to the trial design and which is not. There are many possible solutions to the problem. Two worked examples are provided but many more are possible.

In your outline proposal, please cover the following areas:

1. What outcome measure or measures are to be used?
2. What are clinically important differences in the principal outcome measures?
3. How is/are the intervention or interventions to be delivered?
4. What is the unit of randomisation?
5. What is the sample size?
6. How long will it take?
7. What ethical or legal problems might be encountered?
8. What problems do you forsee?
9. How will it be co-ordinated?
10. Roughly how much will it cost?
11. Should it be funded?

You may wish to present your outline in the following headings:

Study population; Intervention; Outcome; Follow up; Sample size; Randomisation; Recruitment; Duration; Ethical considerations; Potential problems; Co-ordination; Cost estimate.

A randomised controlled trial to demonstrate that the RCGP back pain guidelines and / or *The Back Book* improve the outcome for back pain sufferers

In April 1999, the RCGP published its revised low back pain guidelines for the management of acute low back pain. The advice in these guidelines is presented for patients in the form of *The Back Book*. You have been invited by a major grant giving agency to submit a proposal to demonstrate, in a randomised controlled trial, that using these in primary care will improve the outcome for back pain sufferers. One of your colleagues has produced a background for the bid and provided you with some key information. Your task is to outline the method you would use to tackle this problem, including an estimate of the research costs. You are not expected in this exercise to estimate the cost of providing the intervention or providing service support for practices. For the right study, this funding body would be prepared to provide about £1,000,000 to cover research costs.

Low back pain is a common problem. Typically a GP would expect about 5% of patients on their list to consult annually with low back pain. Of these about a third will consult again with back pain in the following three months (Croft et al., 1999).

Traditionally, it is said that the majority of those with back pain will improve rapidly. More recent observational evidence suggests that 'back pain has an untidy pattern of grumbling symptoms and periods of relative freedom from pain and disability interspersed with acute episodes, exacerbations, and recurrences' (Croft et al., 1999). It is likely that around 5-10% of those who consult their GP with acute low back pain will be significantly disabled at one year (Underwood and Morgan, 1998).

Less than 1% of those who consult with low back pain will be referred for a consultant opinion (CSAG, 1994).

The prevalence of low back pain in the community is:

(GPRF unpublished data)

Lifetime	66%
Annual	50%
Three month	33%
One month	25%
One week	20%
Today	15%

Some suggested figures to use in the cost estimation

(These are indicative figures based on 1999 costs for use in this example only)

Printing one questionnaire	25p
Posting one letter (Letter, envelope, reply envelope & stamp)	
Assume it is the same for a participant and a practice	25p
Cost of one returned reply paid envelope	22p
Response rate to postal questionnaire	50% on each posting
Research nurse time	£15.00/hour
Receptionist time	£10.00/hour
GP time	£20.00/hour
One computer	£1,500
Time to complete any pre-randomisation assessment	45 minutes
Time to complete any search of GP computer for the first time	1 hour
Time to complete any repeat computer search	15 minutes
Time to search individual patient's records	20 minutes
Cost of one form for use by research team	10p
Ethics committees	
To cover preparation, printing and posting of applications	£1,000 for MREC and £100 for LREC

Specimen annual salary costs including on costs (N.I. and superannuation) and university overheads @ 46%

Trial Manager	£50,000	IT officer	£50,000
Trial statistician	£50,000	Secretary	£20,000
Administrative assistant	£17,500	Clinical senior lecturer	£100,000

Of those who are issued with a sick note for back pain the proportion who remain off work is: (CSAG, 1994)

One week	33%
One month	16%
Three months	6.5%
Six months	4.3%
One year	3.0%
Two years	2.0%

Although the back pain guidelines have been produced by the RCGP the evidence base underlying them is weak (Underwood, 1995) and they only apply to acute back pain.

The cost of low back pain disability has increased dramatically over recent decades. However, there is no evidence that its prevalence has increased. The main burden of disability payments is for chronic disability. Over 90% of the costs of low back pain disability are for sickness absences of more than one year (CSAG, 1994).

Back pain and disability are difficult to measure. For the purposes of this exercise the Roland Morris Disability Questionnaire (RMDQ) will be considered the patient-completed measure of choice. This consists of 24 questions about back pain disability. The score is the number of positive responses that patients give (Roland and Morris, 1983). Many other scales are available; it is beyond the scope of this exercise to decide between competing measures. For this exercise, consider a score of four or more to represent significant disability and a difference of 2.5 points to be a clinically important difference.

In a previous study treating patients referred from primary care RMDQ scores were:

	Baseline	Six weeks	Six months	One year
RMDQ 4 or more	67%	38%	35%	28%
Mean RMDQ	6.08	3.56	3.48	3.35
SD	4.00	3.69	4.07	4.01
Mean change RMDQ from baseline	-	-2.38	-2.27	-2.46
SD	-	3.76	4.73	4.44

(With thanks to Jennifer Klaber Moffett and Amanda Farrin of the York Back Pain Study)

It is known from previous studies in primary care that the ICC is likely to be in the range 0.01 to 0.05 (Underwood et al., 1998).

Typically one might expect to recruit 1.5 participants per year for each 1,000 individuals on a GP's list.

Recruitment of participants to trials during routine consultations tends to be poor.

If cluster randomisation is used there is a risk that recruitment will be much less in control practices and that the characteristics of those recruited will be significantly different in the two groups of practices. (Lamers et al., 1998; Farrin, 1999)

It is believed that guideline dissemination is more effective if there is local ownership and if the whole team is involved in applying them (RCGP, 1999).

EXERCISE 2: IMPLEMENTING THE PROPOSAL

Learning objective: *To become familiar with some of the practical issues involved in implementing multi-centre research.*

Having managed to persuade the grant giving body to fund your project now you have to implement it. In this exercise we want to consider four aspects of implementation:

You may wish to use the sample solutions provided for Exercise 1 as a basis (see page 24).

1. How will you recruit practices?

Consider: sampling strategy
               letter of invitation to the study
               possible incentives

2. How will you recruit patients?

Consider: recruitment procedures
               getting informed consent
               study information sheet

3. What pilot studies will you do for the trial?

Consider: where to do the piloting
               number of patients
               what to pilot

4. How will you maintain quality?

Consider: quality assurance within recruiting practices
               quality assurance within the office

SOLUTIONS TO EXERCISES

SAMPLE SOLUTIONS TO EXERCISE 1

Back pain trial one
The Back Book implementation (BABI) trial

A randomised controlled trial of the effect of nurse advice and provision of educational material on the outcome for patients seen by their GP with acute or sub-acute back pain.

Study population
Patients aged 18-65 consulting with back pain of any severity of less than six months duration.

Intervention
The Back Book and advice from practice nurse on the active management of back pain.

Outcome
Primary outcome measure
Acute / subacute back pain (< 6 months) has a generally good prognosis. Many patients will have few if any symptoms one year after presentation. Absolute values in a disability scale may not be distributed normally. For this reason, the difference in change since baseline has been used for the principal outcome measure. A 2.5 point difference in the change in RMDQ is considered to be a clinically important difference.
Secondary outcome measure
Health service activity for economic analysis (questionnaires and record examination).
Patient beliefs about back pain.
Satisfaction with treatment.

Sample size
Previous studies have found the mean improvement in RMDQ at one year to be 2.5 points (SD 4.44). To show a 2.5 point difference in RMDQ between intervention and control, with an α of 0.05 and a β of 0.1, 150 evaluable participants are required. Assuming a 25% drop out rate, 200 participants need to be recruited.

Randomisation
The unit of randomisation will be the individual. Randomisation will be stratified by severity and duration.

Recruitment
Potential participants referred by GP to practice nurse for assessment. Participants randomised after assessment. Assuming 1.5 participants are recruited for each 1,000 on the GP's list a population base of 133,333 will be needed. With a typical practice size of around 7,000 patients 19-20 practices need to participate in the trial.

Duration
Months 1-6	Set up procedures, recruit practices, develop intervention, obtain ethical approvals. (Pilot performed previously.)
Months 7-18	Recruit participants. (Assume all practices start on the same day.)
Months 19-33	Collect follow up data. (May be up to three months after the end of the study before all follow up data is available.)
Months 34-36	Analysis and writing.

Ethical considerations
Participants in the control arm are not being told that they are part of a trial. This is a 'Zelen Study'. It is acceptable to do this because explaining the treatment to the control group would mean that they received part of the intervention.

Some patients with back pain due to a 'serious cause' may be falsely reassured that there is no serious problem with their back. This may delay them receiving appropriate investigations.

Participants do not have time to consider between being asked to join the study and being randomised.

Potential problems
Failure of GPs to notify the study team of patients with back pain, thus failing to meet recruitment targets. Contamination between control and intervention groups.
Ensuring high response rate to follow up questionnaires.

Co-ordination
The study will be co-ordinated by a full-time study manager and administrative assistant. Supervised by a part-time senior lecturer working with a part-time statistician and part-time secretary.

BABI cost estimate

Research staff

Whole time trial manager, three years @ £50,000	£150,000
Whole time administrative assistant, three years @ £17,500	£52,500
0.20 clinical senior lecturer, three years @ £20,000	£60,000
0.1 statistician, three years @ £5,000	£15,000
0.25 secretary, three years @ £5,000	£15,000
Research staff costs	**£292,500**

Field staff

Receptionist time

Half an hour per week in each of 20 practices for one year
to identify individuals who consult with back pain.
0.5 x 20 x 52 = 520 hours in total @ £10.00 per hour £5,250

Nurse time:

One hour per participant randomised @ £15.00	£5,000
Four hours training for each of 20 nurses @ £60.00	£1,200
Record examination 200 @ 20 mins nurse time	£1,000
Field staff costs	**£12,450**

Consumables

Screening questionnaires, assume 1:10 of those approached enter
the trial. 2,000 individuals screened. If one reminder is sent 3,000
questionnaires will be needed. Each one will cost 50p to send. Half
will be returned at a cost of 22p. Thus the cost of each questionnaire
sent is 61p. 3,000 questionnaires @ 61p £1,830

Potential participant record sheet 2,000 @ 10p	£200
Participant medical record extraction sheet 200 @10p	£20

Baseline assessment questionnaires. Not all of those sent to practices
will be used. Print 300 @ 25p £75

Follow up questionnaires. Unit cost of posting 61p. Allow two
reminders thus 350 needed for each of three follow up cycles. 1,050 in total £641

Ethical committee approvals. Assume 1 MREC @ £1,000 and
10 LRECs @ £100 £2,000

Telephone calls co-ordinating centre to practice etc	£1,000
Fax, stationery and sundries	£1,000
Consumables cost	**£6,766**

Equipment

Computers 3 @ £1,500	£4,500
Back books 100 @ £1.20	£120
Equipment costs	**£4,620**

Travel and subsistence

Practice visits by co-ordinating centre staff. One recruitment and one
quality control. Estimate travel at £50 per trip £2,000

Conferences	£1,000
	£3,000

Overall cost estimate	*£319,336*

This overall cost estimate does not include inflation, service support costs, or staff increments. It is indicative of likely cost, not an exact estimate

Back pain trial two
Cluster randomised active management (CRAM) trial.

Study population
All individuals consulting GPs in study practices with back pain during the study period.

Intervention
Training of the whole practice team in the principles of active management of back pain, backed up with provision of *The Back Book* in the waiting room and during consultations.

Outcome
Primary outcome
Reduction in the re-consultation rate for back pain in the three months after the first consultation during the study period from 33% to 25%.
Secondary outcomes
Patient satisfaction and current back pain disability, assessed by questionnaire three months after the end of the study.

Sample size
To show a difference between a re-consultation rate of 33.3% and 25% with an α of 0.05 and a β of 0.1 requires 699 subjects in each group, 1,400 in total. There will be minimal loss to follow up in the three month follow up period. A typical practice of 7,000 patients would expect 5% of their list, 350 individuals to consult with back pain annually; assume that 300 are actually identified and that this is the mean cluster size. Erring on the side of caution, assume ρ is 0.05. The inflation factor for cluster randomisation is given by $1+(300-1) \times 0.05$. Thus the sample size would need to be increased – 15.95 times. The total sample needed is 22,400 subjects and 75 practices should be recruited. *(Note that if cluster size varies the inflation factor is further increased.)*

Randomisation
Randomisation will be at practice level stratified by size, training status and presence of practice based physical therapy.

Recruitment
The identification of subjects will be from Read coded consultations for back pain. Only fully computerised practices will participate to reduce recruitment bias. The patient identification data and re-consultation rate will be identified from the practice computer. All subjects identified will be sent follow up questionnaires. *(One might choose to follow up a proportion of the subjects only to reduce costs. For simplicity, for this example they are all going to be followed.)*

Duration
Months 1-6	Set up procedures, recruit practices, develop intervention, obtain ethical approvals. (Pilot performed previously.)
Months 7-18	Recruit participants. (Assume all practices start on the same day.)
Months 19-24	Collect follow up data. (May be up to three months after the end of the study before all follow up data is available.)
Months 25-27	Analysis and writing.

Ethical considerations
No individual consent is obtained.
Records are being examined for research purposes.

Potential problems
GPs in the two groups of practices may record different proportions of their back pain patients.
Control practices may apply elements of the active management programme.
Few data on individual subjects.
Large number of follow up questionnaires may be needed.
Only three months follow up.
Principal outcome not patient centred.

Co-ordination
The study will be co-ordinated by a full-time study manager and administrative assistant. Supervised by a part-time senior lecturer working with a part-time statistician and full-time secretary.

CRAM cost estimate

Research staff

Whole time trial manager, 27/12 @ £50,000	£112,500
Whole time administrative assistant, 27/12 @ £17,500	£39,375
0.20 clinical senior lecturer, 27/12 @ £20,000	£45,000
0.2 statistician, 27/12 @ £5,000	£11,250
Whole time secretary, 27/12 @ £15,000	£33,750
Research staff costs	**£241,875**

Field staff

Computerised data extraction fee @ £100 in each of 75 practices	£7,500
Staff training in active management. Assume two hour session attended by	
4 doctors, 4 x 20 x 2 = £160	
8 receptionists, 8 x 10 x 2 = £160	
2 nurses, 2 x 15 x 2 = £60	
(assume study team do practice based training, assume no charge for intervention)	
Cost per practice = £380	£28,500
Field staff costs	**£36,000**

Consumables

Each questionnaire will cost 50p to send. Half will be returned, at each	
of three postings at a cost of 22p. Thus cost of each questionnaire sent is 61p	
22,400 x 1.75 questionnaires will be sent @ 61p each	£23,912
Ethical committee approvals. Assume 1 MREC @ £1,000 and 10	
LRECs @ £100	£2,000
Telephone calls co-ordinating centre to practice etc	£1,000
Fax, stationery and sundries	£1,000
Consumables cost	**£27,912**

Equipment

Computers 4 @ £1,500	£6,000
Back books 25,000 @ 60p (assume 50% discount)	£15,000
Equipment costs	**£21,000**

Travel and subsistence

Practice visits by co-ordinating centre staff. One recruitment (one person)	
and one training (two people). Estimate travel at £50 per trip	£11,250
Conferences	£1,000
	£12,250

Overall cost estimate	*£339,037*

This overall cost estimate does not include inflation, service support costs, or staff increments. It is indicative of likely cost, not an exact estimate.

For studies with large numbers of questionnaires, consider automatic envelope filler and scanning systems to read questionnaires rather than secretarial time to post questionnaires and enter data.

SAMPLE SOLUTIONS TO EXERCISE 2

There are no right or wrong answers. The following illustrates some possibilities.

1. How will you recruit practices?

All GPs in an area (local, regional or national) could be invited by post. In this case you will need to start everything from scratch. The wider the geographical distribution the more generalisible the trial's findings tend to be, but the logistics of the exercise become more complex. It can also be harder to maintain quality. An established research network (local or national such as the MRC GPRF) will have the infrastructure in place, but it may already be committed, it may be expensive to access and you may feel a loss of control and ownership of your project. A group of GPs with a particular interest (e.g. a primary care back pain association) may be a useful compromise, but this may be a select group of interested doctors, raising questions about how generalisible the trial's findings are.

The letter of invitation should be short (less than one side of A4) and friendly. It needs to include details of the importance of the study (e.g. costs to the nation, workload issues etc); what is expected of the practice; the number of patients and practices needed; the workload involved; any incentives; what to do if the doctor is interested; and a contact name and number for further enquiries.

Consider incentives carefully. It is unlikely that you can pay the proper rate for the job and to pay too little may insult all concerned. There can also be considerable costs involved in issuing cheques for small amounts to many individuals. On the other hand it is important to recognise the work that the doctors are undertaking on your behalf. You may wish to consider providing opportunities to attend PGEA approved workshops (with attendance at no cost), training opportunities, free books etc. In general, if the research question is right (i.e. important and relevant) it is more likely that you will be able to recruit practices without an incentive.

2. How will you recruit patients?

Trials that aim to recruit patients during routine consultations need to be very simple. The doctors need to be reminded to recruit patients with aide memoires (e.g. trial mouse mats, prompts on the computer that appear if the condition is typed in etc). Patients will be missed either because the doctor forgot, or because other things happened in the consultation which made the doctor feel that mentioning the trial was inappropriate. Even if patients are missed it is important to try and identify the characteristics of these individuals so that an assessment can be made of the generalisibility of patients entered into the study. Recruitment outside the consultation room can be more leisurely but relies on good systems for identifying potential recruits. There is also the ethical consideration of approaching patients once they have left the surgery, some of whom may not want further contact. The practicalities of doing so also need to be considered (e.g. telephone contacts will exclude those without a telephone and one can encounter problems if someone else answers the telephone).

Informed consent must be obtained before entering the trial. Depending on the nature of the intervention there should (ideally) be a period of time between informing the patient about the trial and obtaining consent. This allows patients to discuss the trial with relatives or friends and allows them time to consider their participation. Informed consent should be written in almost all cases.

The study information sheet should be concise, understandable by most readers (many of whom have a low reading age) and written so that it can be taken away for future reference. The type of information that needs to be included is detailed in the checklist included in the research material.

3. What pilot studies will you do for the trial?

Piloting needs to be undertaken in similar practices to those who will recruit in the main study. The practices may be the same as those who will recruit in the main study, but this may seriously reduce the pool of patients available for the main trial. Other convenient practices, such as those of friends or colleagues, may not give you a true picture of the problems involved with the trial (they may be too nice and say everything is fine even when there are huge problems). The pilot practices certainly need to serve the same group of patients that you intend to recruit in the main trial (a study of a new treatment for heart failure is unlikely to be successfully piloted in a student health centre!).

Try to pilot the study procedures on as many patients as possible. This allows you to gain a picture of the full range of responses, misunderstandings and problems that might be encountered during the main trial. The first few patients entered into any study (pilot or main) are often unusual and can give you a skewed picture of the final outcome. On the other hand, if you recruit too many pilot patients you might run into ethical problems as the data are rarely suitable for inclusion in the main trial and so patients will be providing information for which there is limited scientific value. This may be a particularly important consideration if blood samples or other invasive interventions are done as part of the piloting.

Pilot everything if possible: likely doctor and patient interest in the study; letter of invitation to GPs; information sheets for doctors and patients; recruitment procedures; aide memoires, data collection forms; log books for participating doctors; follow-up procedures; and office procedures. Modifications should be re-piloted if possible. Questionnaires need particular attention; the apparently simple, straightforward question often has a surprisingly large number of different interpretations.

4. How will you maintain quality?

Quality assurance has to be built in at all stages of the trial; identifying practices that are committed and likely to be active participants; ensuring that the correct recruitment procedures are followed; getting proper informed consent; making sure recruitment forms are completed accurately and comprehensively (and returned); and correct adoption of follow-up procedures. Recruitment rates from each practice need to be monitored (to detect those who recruit too many as well as too few). Data from the recruiting studies has to be assessed regularly for obvious discrepancies. Some data collection sheets may need to be checked against the medical records held by the practice. A key to maintaining quality is to emphasise its importance to participating practices (and patients where necessary). This requires regular communications via newsletters etc. This may provide an opportunity to highlight current problems that have been encountered elsewhere, and ways of addressing these problems.

Quality assurance also needs to be built into all office procedures from day one. Every aspect of the office procedures needs to be considered, tested, modified where necessary and documented. A detailed manual of study procedures allows for inconsistent human memory, and unfortunate mishaps such as the principal investigator falling under a bus! The MRC Code of good practice guidelines, included in the Resource Material, provides a useful start for establishing good office quality assurance. Problems will arise at most stages of a trial – become aware of them as soon as possible so that they can be rectified early thereby reducing subsequent problems.

REFERENCES

Carter Y, Shaw S, Thomas C (eds) (2000). *Master Classes in Primary Care Research No 3: Statistical Concepts.* London, Royal College of General Practitioners.

Carter Y, Shaw S, Thomas C (eds). *Master Classes in Primary Care Research No 5: Patient Participation and Ethical Considerations.* London, Royal College of General Practitioners. *In press.*

Carter Y, Shaw S, Thomas C (eds). *Master Classes in Primary Care Research No 6: Funding for Primary Care Research.* London, Royal College of General Practitioners. *In press.*

Carter Y, Shaw S, Thomas C (eds). *Master Classes in Primary Care Research No 7: Issues in Primary Care Epidemiology.* London, Royal College of General Practitioners. *In press.*

Carter YH, Thomas C (eds) (1997). *Research Methods in Primary Care.* Abingdon, Radcliffe.

Clinical Guidelines Working Group (1995). *The development and implementation of clinical guidelines: report of the Clinical Guidelines Working Group.* Exeter, RCGP.

Clinical Standards Advisory Group (1994). *Epidemiological review: the epidemiology and cost of back pain.* The annex to the Clinical Standards Advisory Group's report on back pain. London, HMSO.

Croft PR, Macfarlane GJ, Papageorgiou AC et al. (1998). Outcome of low back pain in general practice: a prospective study. *British Medical Journal* **316**, 1356-9.

Crombie IK, Davies HTO (eds) (1996). *Research in Health Care.* Chichester, J Wiley & Sons.

Farrin AJ (on behalf of the UK BEAM Trial Team)(1999). Lessons learnt from a cluster randomised trial in primary care – the UK Back Pain, Exercise, Active Management and Manipulation (UK BEAM) feasibility study. Whirlow Grange, University of Sheffield Cluster Trials Workshop.

Health Service Guidelines (1996). *NHS Indemnity: arrangements for handling clinical negligence claims against NHS staff.* HSG(96)48.

Health Service Guidelines (1997). *Ethics Committee Review of Multi-Centre Research. Establishment of Multi-Centre Research Ethics Committees.* HSG(97)23.

Kay CR, Frank PI (1981). Characteristics of women recruited to a long-term study of the sequelae of induced abortion: report from a joint RCGP/RCOG study co-ordinated by the RCGP's Manchester Research Unit. *Journal of the Royal College of General Practitioners* **31**, 473-477.

Kendrick D, Marsh P, Fielding K et al. (1999). Preventing injuries in children: cluster randomised controlled trial in primary care. *British Medical Journal* **318**, 980-983.

Koes BW, Assendelft WJ, Van der Heijden GJ, et al. (1996). Spinal manipulation for low back pain. An updated systematic review of randomised clinical trials. *Spine* **21**, 2860-73.

Lamers HJ, Jamin RH, Zaat JO et al. (1998). Dietary advice for acute diarrhoea in general practice: a pilot study. *British Journal of General Practice* **48**, 1819-23.

Linde K, Clausius N, Ramirez G et al. (1997). Are the clinical effects of homeopathy placebo effects? A meta-analysis of placebo-controlled trials. *Lancet* **350**, 834-43.

Machin D, Campbell MJ, Fayers P et al. (1997). *Sample size table for clinical studies.* Oxford, Blackwell Science.

Mant Report (1997). *R&D in primary care: National Working Group Report.* Leeds, Department of Health.

MRC Working Party (1985). MRC trial of mild hypertension. *British Medical Journal* **291**, 97-104.

Multi-Centre Research Ethics Committees (1999). Application Form and General Guidance for researchers. Plymouth, NHS Executive South and West Research and Development Directorate.

National Health Service Research and Development Task Force (1994). *Supporting Research and Development in the NHS (Culyer Report).* London, HMSO.

NHS Executive (1997). EL (97) 77. Leeds.

NHS Executive Research and Development Directorate (1998). *Ethical Appraisal of Multi-centre research and the CMO's review: Interim guidance.* NHS Executive.

Oakeshott P, Kerry S (1999). Development of Clinical Guidelines. *Lancet* **353**, 412.

Polgar S, Thomas SA(eds) (1995). *Introduction to Research in the Health Sciences.* London, Churchill Livingstone.

Re C (adult: refusal of medical treatment) (1994) NLJR p290.

Roland M, Morris R (1983). A study of the natural history of back pain. Part 1: development of a reliable and sensitive measure of disability in low-back pain. *Spine* **8**: 141-44.

Royal College of General Practitioners (1974). *Oral Contraceptives and Health.* London, Pitman Medical.

Royal College of General Practitioners, Records Unit and Research Advisory Service (1967). Oral Contraception and thrombo-embolic disease. *Journal of the Royal College of General Practitioners* **13**, 267-279.

Shekelle PG, Adams AH, Chassin MR, et al. (1992). Spinal manipulation for low back pain. *Annals of International Medicine* **117**, 590-597.

Underwood M (1995). Randomised controlled trials of treatment needed. *British Medical Journal* **311**: 569.

Underwood MR, Barnett AG, Hajioff S (1998). Cluster randomisation; A trap for the unwary. *British Journal of General Practice* **48**:1089-90.

Underwood MR, Morgan J (1998). The use of a back class teaching extension exercises in the treatment of acute low back pain in primary care. *Family Practice* **15**: 9-15.

Villar J, Carroli G, Belizán JM (1995). Predictive ability of meta-analyses of randomised controlled trials. *Lancet* **345**, 772-776.

SUGGESTED FURTHER READING

Department of Health website http://www.doh.gov.uk

Foster C (1997). *Manual for Research Ethics Committees.* London, King's College.

MREC website http://dspace.dial.pipex.com/mrec

Pocock SJ (1983). *Clinical trials: a practical approach.* Chichester, Wiley.

RESOURCE MATERIAL FOR EXERCISE 1

Croft PR, Macfarlane GJ, Papageorgiou AC et al. (1998). Outcome of low back pain in general practice: a prospective study. *British Medical Journal* **316**, 1356-9.

Deyo RA, Battié M, Beurskens AJHM et al. (1998). Outcome measures for low back pain research: A proposal for standardized use. *Spine* **23**, 2003-13.

Grimshaw J, Russell I (1994). Achieving health gain through clinical guidelines: II ensuring that guidelines change medical practice. *Quality in Health Care* **3**, 45-52.

Hoffman R, Turner JA, Cherkin DC et al. (1994). Therapeutic trials for low back pain. *Spine* **19**, 2068S-75S.

Klaber Moffett J, Torgerson D, Bell-Sayer S et al. (1999). Randomised controlled trial of exercise for low back pain: clinical outcomes, costs, and preferences. *British Medical Journal* **319**, 279-83.

Koes BW, Bouter LM, Mameren H et al. (1992). Randomised clinical trial of manipulative therapy and physiotherapy for persistent back and neck complaints: results of a one-year follow up. *British Medical Journal* **304**, 601-605.

Roland M, Waddell G, Moffett J et al. (1996). *The Back Book.* The Stationery Office, London.

Royal College of General Practitioners, Chartered Society of Physiotherapy, Osteopathic Association of Great Britain et al. (1996). *Clinical Guidelines for the management of acute low back pain.* Royal College of General Practitioners, London.

1

2

3

4

5

6

7

8

ADDITIONAL RESOURCE MATERIAL

Altman D (1996). Better reporting of randomised controlled trials: the CONSORT statement *British Medical Journal* **313**, 570-1.

Archibald CP, Lee HP (1995). Sample size estimation for clinicians. *Annals of Academic Medicine* Singapore **24**, 328-32.

Black N (1996). Why we need observational studies to evaluate the effectiveness of health care. *British Medical Journal* **312**, 1215-18.

Department of Health NHS Indemnity (1997). *Arrangements for clinical negligence claims in the NHS.* London, HMSO.

Edwards SJL, Lilford RJ, Hewison J (1998). The ethics of randomised controlled trials from the perspectives of patients, the public, and healthcare professionals. *British Medical Journal* **317**, 1209-12.

Hannaford P, 1999. The RCGP Centre for Primary Care Research and Epidemiology. In: Carter Y Thomas C (eds) *Research Methods in Primary Care*. Abingdon, Radcliffe Medical Press.

Hannaford P, Kay C (1998). The risk of serious illness among oral contraceptive users: evidence from the RCGP's oral contraceptive study. *British Journal of General Practice* **48**, 1657-62.

ICH Harmonised Tripartite Guideline for good clinical practice (1997). Richmond, Brookwood Medical Publications Ltd.

Jones B, Jarvis P, Lewis JA et al. (1999). Trials to assess equivalence: the importance of rigorous methods. *British Medical Journal* **313**, 36-39.

Kerry SM, Bland JM (1998). Sample size in cluster randomisation. *British Medical Journal* **316**, 549.

Kliejnen J, Gotzsche P, Kunz RH et al. (1997). So what's so special about randomisation? In: Maynard A, Chalmers I (eds). *Non-random reflections on health services research: on the 25th anniversary of Archie Cochrane's Effectiveness and Efficiency*. 93-106. London, BMJ Publishing Group.

Medical Research Council (1998). MRC Guidelines for good practice in clinical trials. London, MRC.

Multi-Centre Research Ethics Committees (1999). MREC Application form and General Guidance for Researchers. Plymouth, NHS Executive South and East Research and Development Directorate.

Silverman WA, Altman DG (1996). Patients' preferences and randomised trials. *Lancet* **347**, 171-174.

South and East Research and Development Directorate (1999). Patient Information Sheet Checklist. Plymouth, NHS Executive South and East Research and Development Directorate.

The standards of reporting trials group (1994). A proposal for structuring reporting of randomized controlled trials. *JAMA* **272**, 1926-31.

Torgerson D, Roland M (1998). Understanding controlled trials: what is Zelen's design? *British Medical Journal* **316**, 606.

Torgerson D, Sibbald B (1998). Understanding controlled trial: what is a patient preference trial? *British Medical Journal* **316**, 360.

Underwood MR, Barnett AG, Hajioff S (1998). Cluster randomization; A trap for the unwary. *British Journal of General Practice* **48,** 1089-90.

Ward E, King M, Lloyd M et al. (1999). Conducting randomized trials in general practice: methodological and practical issues. *British Journal of General Practice* **49**, 919.

This article was first published in the BMJ *and is reproduced by permission of the* BMJ

OUTCOME OF LOW BACK PAIN IN GENERAL PRACTICE: A PROSPECTIVE STUDY

Peter R Croft *professor*, University of Keele, School of Postgraduate Medicine, Industrial and Community Health Research Centre, Hartshill, Stoke on Trent, ST4 7QB

Gary J Macfarlane *senior lecturer,* Ann C Papageorgiou *studies coordinator,* Elaine Thomas *research statistician,* Alan J Silman *director.* ARC Epidemiology Research Unit, School of Epidemiology and Health Sciences, University, of Manchester, Stopford Building, Manchester M13 9PT

Correspondence to: Dr Macfarlane

G.Macfarlane@man.ac.uk

BMJ 1998;**316**:1356-9

ABSTRACT

Objectives: To investigate the claim that 90% of episodes of low back pain that present to general practice have resolved within one month.

Design: Prospective study of all adults consulting in general practice because of low back pain over 12 months with follow up at 1 week, 3 months, and 12 months after consultation.

Setting: Two general practices in south Manchester.

Subjects: 490 subjects (203 men, 287 women) aged 18-75 years.

Main outcome measures: Proportion of patients who have ceased to consult with low back pain after 3 months; proportion of patients who are free of pain and back related disability at 3 and 12 months.

Results: Annual cumulative consultation rate among adults in the practices was 6.4%. Of the 463 patients who consulted with a new episode of low back pain, 275 (59%) had only a single consultation, and 150 (32%) had repeat consultations confined to the 3 months after initial consultation. However, of those interviewed at 3 and 12 months follow up, only 39/188 (21%) and 42/170 (251%) respectively had completely recovered in terms of pain and disability.

Conclusions: The results are consistent with the interpretation that 90% of patients with low back pain in primary care will have stopped consulting with symptoms within three months. However most will still be experiencing low back pain and related disability one year after consultation.

INTRODUCTION

Low back pain contributes substantially to the workload of general practice. During any 12 month period, 7% of the adult population will consult with this problem.[1] However, it is generally believed that most of these episodes will be short lived and that "80-90% of attacks of low back pain recover in about six weeks, irrespective of the administration or type of treatment:"[2]

In two separate surveys of the British general population, 38% of adults reported a significant episode of low back pain in one year, and a third of these experienced the symptom for longer than four weeks.[3,4] During the past 20 years in Britain, the prevalence of disabling low back pain for which benefits are paid has risen exponentially.[5] It is difficult to reconcile these observations with the notion that most patients seen primary care are completely better within a month.

We investigated the claim that 90% of episodes resolve within a month by determining the outcome of unselected episodes of low back pain in general practice. The two outcomes evaluated were the proportion of patients who ceased to consult about the problem three months later and the proportion of patients who were free of pain and back related disability after three and 12 months.

SUBJECTS AND METHODS

The study population consisted of all patients aged 18-75 years in two general practices in south Manchester who consulted their general practitioner about low back pain at least once in a 12 month period. In both practices doctors routinely recorded each consultation on computer, enabling us to identify all patients with low back pain recorded as a reason for consultation. We obtained ethical approval from the local health authority.

We defined the first consultation for low back pain by any patient during the 12 months as the "index" consultation. This was not necessarily the patient's first consultation in an episode of back pain. All those who had not visited their general practitioner because of low back pain in the three months before this index consultation were defined as experiencing a "new consulting episode" of low back pain. Those who had consulted in the three months before the index consultation were excluded.

We checked practices' computer records weekly for home visits and call outs at night to identify any visits to patients with low back pain, and, at the end of the recruitment year, made a further computer search to ensure that no consultation for low back pain had been missed. We excluded patients with pain limited to the

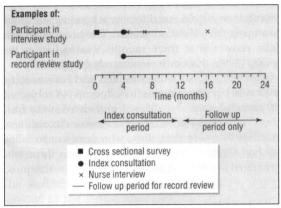

Design of study for evaluating patients' consultations with their general practitioner about low back pain

thoracic region of the back or with pain associated with gynaecological problems or urinary tract infection but recruited those with generalised pain that included pain in the lower back.

Interviewees

The practices had also participated in a cross sectional survey at the start of the study to determine factors that might predict the outcome of a subsequent episode of low back pain. All registered adults aged 18-75 years had been invited to take part, and 59% had done so.

The survey responders formed a subgroup in the cohort study who, if prospectively identified as having a new consulting episode of low back pain during the study year, were followed up by research nurses to determine the nature and outcome of the episode.

Outcome measures

We evaluated the outcome of each new consulting episode by means of two approaches (see figure). Firstly, we reviewed the patients' records for subsequent consultations up to six months after the index consultation and classified patients into three groups:

• Those who had no further consultations about low back pain
• Those who consulted again with back pain within three months, but not subsequently
• Those whose further consultations about their pain extended beyond three months.

Secondly, we evaluated outcome from follow up visits among the subgroup of survey responders. These patients were visited by a research nurse and interviewed within a week of their index consultation, and then again after three and 12 months. Subjects were asked about the presence of low back pain on the day of interview and to mark the severity of any pain on a visual analogue scale from 0 to 10; a score of 0 or 1 was defined as no pain. The subjects were also asked to complete the Hanover back pain daily activity schedule, which asks about the ease of performing 12 everyday activities in the previous week.[6] The items are scored and summed to a percentage value, with 100%

representing no restriction in any activity. We categorised subjects as having no disability (summed score >90%) or having disability (£90%). For this study, we classified patients into three groups according to the level of pain and disability recorded at each interview:

• No pain and no disability.
• Pain or disability (but not both)
• Both pain and disability.

RESULTS

Consultations

During the 12 month recruitment period 490 people (203 men and 287 women) consulted at least once because of pain in the lower back. This represents an annual cumulative incidence in the adult practice populations of 6.4%. Figures for the two study, practices were similar (6.3% and 6.4%). Table 1 shows the proportion of men and women consulting in each age group. Women were more likely, than men to consult because of low back pain, and in both sexes consultation rates were highest in those aged 45-59. Based on medical records, 463 (94%) of the 490 consulters had not visited their general practitioner because of low back pain in the three months before their index consultation and were therefore considered to have a new consulting episode of low back pain. We excluded the remaining 27 patients from all further analyses.

Of the 463 patients, 275 (59%) did not consult again about the problem in the six months after their index visit (table 2). These patients were younger than the other consulters (median age 40 *v* 47 years). Of the 188 patients who did consult again, 150 (32% of all new episode consulters) did so only within the first three months after their index visit. The remaining 38 people (8%) had consultations or sickness certification related to low back pain that extended for more than three months after the index consultation.

Although women had a higher initial consultation rate then men, there was no difference in the proportions with repeated consultations: 80 (42%) men and 108 (40%) women had two or more. Patients aged

Table 1

Annual cumulative rate of consultation for low back pain of patients aged 18-75 years registered in practices

Age group (years)	Men Total population	Men No (%) of patients who consulted	Women Total population	Women No (%) of patients who consulted
18-29	906	34 (4)	994	55 (6)
30-44	1180	68 (6)	1194	93 (8)
45-59	760	61 (8)	791	78 (10)
≥60	772	40 (5)	1072	61 (6)
Total	3618	203 (6)	4051	287 (7)

Table 2

Consultation patterns of 463 patients who visited their general practitioner with a new episode of low back pain. Values are numbers (percentages) of patients

Consultation pattern	Patients' age (years)								
	Men				Women				
	18-29	30-44	45-59	60-75	18-29	30-44	45-59	60-75	Total
One only*	26 (76)	33 (52)	31 (53)	21 (60)	46 (85)	56 (62)	34 (48)	28 (50)	275 (59)
Repeat within 3 months†	7 (21)	21 (33)	21 (36)	12 (34)	8 (15)	28 (31)	29 (41)	24 (43)	150 (32)
Repeat beyond 3 months‡	1 (3)	10 (16)	6 (10)	2 (6)	0	7 (8)	8 (11)	4 (7)	38 (8)

*Subjects who did not consult again after index consultation.
†Subjects who consulted again only within 3 months of index consultation.
‡Subjects who consulted again beyond 3 months after index consultation.

over 30 were three times more likely to have repeat consultations than younger consulters (risk ratio 2.5, 95% confidence interval 1.6 to 4.0).

Pain and disability at interview

Of the 463 patients who consulted with a new episode of low back pain, 218 (47%) were included in the interview study and were visited by the research nurses one to two weeks after their index consultation (table 3). Of the 212 patients with available data, five (2%) had completely, recovered by the time of the first interview. This had increased to 39/188 (21%) by the three month interview and to 42/170 (25%) by 12 months. Follow up information was incomplete for 48 subjects.

Table 3

Outcome in patients who consulted their general practitioner with a new episode of low back pain and were followed up by interview at three and 12 months. Values are numbers (percentages) of patients

Follow up period	Outcome*		
	No pain and no disability	Pain or disability	Pain and disability
Main sample (n=218)			
Initial interview (n=212†)	5 (2)	53 (25)	154 (73)
3 month interview (n=188†)	39 (21)	55 (29)	94 (50)
12 month interview (n=170†)	42 (25)	43 (25)	85 (50)
Validation sample (n=44)			
Initial interview (n=43†)	3 (7)	11 (26)	29 (67)
3 month interview (n=36†)	12 (33)	6 (17)	18 (50)
12 month interview (n=31†)	11 (35)	6 (19)	14 (45)

* No pain and no disability: visual analogue score for pain=0 or 1, Hanover disability score >90%. Pain or disability: either pain score=2-10 or disability score <90%, not both. Pain and disability: pain score=2-10 and disability score <90%.
†Data missing for some subjects interviewed.

Table 4 shows change in reported pain and disability, during the study year. Eighteen (44%) of 41 patients with either pain or disability at first interview had fully recovered by 12 months. Of those with both pain and disability initially, the proportion who had fully recovered by 12 months was much lower (23/126 (18%)).

Patients' pain and disability status at interview was related to the likelihood of repeat consultation during the recruitment year. The proportion of interviewees who reported complete recovery at three months was higher among those who had not consulted again after their initial visit. By 12 months, those who had continued to consult for longer than three months after the index visit had lower levels of reported recovery than those who had stopped consulting before three months.

The median duration of symptoms as recalled at initial interview was three weeks (interquartile range 2-9 weeks). Table 5 shows the proportion of patients who reported recovery by reported duration of symptoms.

Table 4

Outcome in 170 patients who consulted their general practitioner with a new episode of low back pain and were followed up at 12 month interview by their status at initial interview. Values are numbers (percentages) of patients

Status at initial interview	12 month outcome*		
	No pain and no disability	Pain or disability	Pain and disability
No pain and no disability (n=3)	1 (33)	2 (67)	0
Pain or disability (n=41)	18 (44)	14 (34)	9 (22)
Pain and disability (n=126)	23 (18)	27 (21)	76 (60)

* No pain and no disability: visual analogue score for pain=0 or 1, Hanover disability score >90%. Pain or disability: either pain score=2-10 or disability score <90%, not both. Pain and disability. pain score=2-10 and disability score <90%.

Most subjects who reported a duration of less than two weeks had recovered by 12 months, whereas those consulting about episodes of longer duration were less likely to have recovered.

Non-participation in interview study

There were two main sources of potential selection bias. Firstly, only patients who had responded to the earlier survey and agreed to be interviewed were potentially followed up. The remaining 245 patients who consulted about low back pain may have been different in initial severity and subsequent rates of recovery. A sample of 44 such consulters with a new episode of low back pain were followed up by interview to estimate the size of any such bias. Table 3 shows the distribution of pain and disability at baseline and at follow up in this validation sample. The proportion who fully recovered at three months was higher in this group (33%) than in the main study group (21%).

Secondly, those who consulted and had an initial interview but who were lost to follow up (48 subjects at 12 months) may have differed in their recovery from those who remained under observation. According to baseline interview data, those who were lost to follow up had slightly lower disability levels than those who remained under observation.

DISCUSSION

By three months after the index consultation with their general practitioner, only a minority of patients with low back pain had recovered. There was little increase in the proportion who reported recovery by 12 months, emphasising the recurrent and persistent nature of this problem. However most patients with low back pain did not return to their doctor about their pain within three months of their initial consultation, and only 8% continued to consult for more than three months.

The mean number of consultations per person recorded in this study, (1.7) is similar to that in a national survey of general practice consultations (1.6 per person).[7] This suggests that our identification of all consultations for low back pain was relatively complete and that although consultation rates (and hence case mix and outcome) may vary between practices, the practices in, this study were generally representative.

Potential bias

Of the total of 463 patients who consulted with a new episode of low back pain in the recruitment year, 218 (47%) were interviewed, after having agreed to the interview and responded to the earlier survey. Selection bias might have resulted in the data from our follow up interviews underestimating the recovery of all patients presenting with low back pain in primary care. In a sample of non-participants who were followed up, recovery at three months was indeed higher than that of the main interview group. However, even if this higher rate of improvement applied to all non-participants, the overall recovery at three months after consultation for a new episode of back pain. would still be low (about 27%).

Table 5

Outcome in patients who consulted their general practitioner with a new episode of low back pain and were followed up by interview according to duration of pain at first consultation. Values are numbers (percentages) of patients

Outcome*	Duration of pain at time of first contact (weeks)		
	0-1	2-3	≥4
Initial interview (n=212)			
No pain and no disability	1 (5)	1 (1)	3 (3)
Pain or disability	8 (36)	25 (29)	20 (19)
Pain and disability	13 (59)	60 (70)	81 (78)
3 month interview (n=188)			
No pain and no disability	6 (38)	20 (25)	13 (14)
Pain or disability	6 (38)	27 (34)	22 (24)
Pain and disability	4 (25)	33 (41)	57 (62)
12 month interview (n=170)			
No pain and no disability	10 (67)	21 (29)	11 (13)
Pain or disability	2 (13)	20 (28)	21 (25)
Pain and disability	3 (20)	31 (43)	51 (61)

*No pain and no disability: visual analogue score for pain=0 or 1, Hanover disability score >90%. Pain or disability: either pain score=2-10 or disability score <90%, not both. Pain and disability: pain score=2-10 and disability score <90%.

In addition, those patients who were lost to follow up from within the interview group had slightly milder disease at baseline than those who remained under observation for the whole year. The effect of this on our estimates of recovery is likely to have been small, but again indicates a degree of underestimation.

Comparison with other studies

The findings of our interview study are in sharp contrast to the frequently repeated assumption that 90% of episodes of low back pain seen in primary care will have resolved within a month. However, the results of our consultation figures are consistent with the interpretation that 90% of patients presenting in primary care with an episode of low back pain will have stopped consulting about this problem within three months of their initial visit. The original article to which the statement of "90% recovery" can be traced[8] drew on a record review in one general practice. If no further consultation within an episode is taken as the measure of "recovery," then record review is a valid measure of this. However, the inference that the patients have completely recovered is clearly not supported by, our data. General practice records cannot be used to draw such conclusions.

Such an explanation does not apply to the study of Coste et al, who followed up patients independently of consultation and reported that 90% were without pain or disability two weeks after first presentation to their general practitioner.[9] However, the patients recruited were restricted to those who presented to their general practitioner within three days of low back pain starting and who had previously been free of pain for at least three months. The meticulous follow up in this French study provided a clear description of the short term natural course of such episodes, and 90% were indeed better within a month. However, our study confirms that such patients are a select minority of all low back sufferers seen in primary care.

Conclusions

Our study has shown that consulting a doctor is not a direct measure of the presence of pain and disability. Many patients seeing their general practitioner for the first time in an episode of back pain will have had symptoms for a month or more. Although their symptoms will improve, most will still have some pain or disability 12 months later but not be consulting their doctor about it. Deyo has written of the need to describe and measure low back pain in terms of an individual's lifetime experience.[10]

We should stop characterising low back pain in terms of a multiplicity of acute problems, most of which get better, and a small number of chronic long term problems. Low back pain should be viewed as a chronic problem with an untidy pattern of grumbling symptoms and periods of relative freedom from pain and disability interspersed with acute episodes, exacerbations, and recurrences. This takes account of two consistent observations about low back pain: firstly, a previous episode of low back pain is the strongest risk factor for a new episode,[11,12] and, secondly, by the age of 30 years almost half the population will have experienced a substantive episode of low back pain.[13] These figures simply do not fit with claims that 90% of episodes of low back pain end in complete recovery.

Finally, the observation from our study that most patients continue to get some degree of pain and disability after consulting about low back pain raises an important question of whether early treatment can improve this picture and, hence, reduce the cumulative prevalence of low back pain and its accompanying social, economic, and medical consequences.

> ### KEY MESSAGES
>
> - It is widely believed that 90% of episodes of low back pain seen in general practice resolve within one month
> - In a large population based study we examined the outcome of episodes of low back pain in general practice with respect to both consultation behaviour and self reported pain and disability
> - While 90% of subjects consulting general practice with low back pain ceased to consult about the symptoms within three months, most still had substantial low back pain and related disability
> - Only 25% of the patients who consulted about low back pain had fully recovered 12 months later
> - Since most consulters continue to have long term low back pain and disability, effective early treatment could reduce the burden of these symptoms and their social, economic, and medical impact

Contributors: PRC, AJS, and ACP designed the study protocol, discussed core ideas, coordinated the study, and participated in analysis and interpretation of data and writing the paper. GJM and ET discussed core ideas and participated in data analysis and interpretation and writing the paper. Malcolm Jayson participated in the design and development of the study. Margaret Carrington, Jane Barnett, and Hannah Chambers carried out the study interviews. The authors thank the partners, staff, and patients of the Brooklands and Bowland Medical Practices, Manchester, for help with conducting the study and Lesley Jordan for typing the manuscript. All the authors are guarantors for the paper.

Funding: This study was supported by the Arthritis Research Campaign, the National Back Pain Association, and the Department of Health in the United Kingdom.

Conflict of interest: None.

References

1. McCormick A, Fleming D, Charlton J. *Morbidity statistics from general practice. Fourth national study 1991-1992. Office of Population Censuses and Surveys.* London: HMSO, 1995. (Series MB5 No 3.)
2. Waddell G. A new clinical model for the treatment of low-back pain. *Spine* 1987; 12:632-44.
3. Walsh K, Cruddas M, Coggon D. Low back pain in eight areas of Britain. *J Epidemiol Community Health* 1992;46:227-30.
4. Mason V. *The prevalence of back pain in Great Britain. Office of Population Censuses and Surveys. Social Survey Division.* London: HMSO, 1994.
5. Clinical Standards Advisory Group. *Epidemiology review: the epidemiology and cost of back pain.* London: HMSO, 1994.
6. Kohlmann T, Raspe H. Der Funktionsfragebogen Hannover zur alltagsnahen Diagnostik der Funktionsbeeintrachtigung durch Rucken-schmerzen (FFbH-R). *Rehabilitation* 1996;35:I-VIII.
7. Office of Population Censuses and Surveys. *OPCS Monitor MB5 94/1. Morbidity Statistics from General Practice 1991/2 (MSGP4).* London: HMSO, 1994.
8. Dixon AStJ. Progress and problems in back pain research. Rheumatol Rehabil 1973;12(4):165-75.
9. Coste J, Delecoeuillerie G, Cohen de Lara A, le Parc JM, Paolaggi JB. Clinical course and prognostic factors in acute low back pain: an inception cohort study in primary care practice. *BMJ* 1994;308:577-80.
10. Deyo RA. Practice variations, treatment fads, rising disability. *Spine* 1993;18:2153-62.
11. Roland MO, Morrell DC, Morris RW. Can general practitioners predict the outcome of episodes of back pain? *BMJ* 1983;286:523-5.
12. Papageorgiou A, Croft P, Thomas E, Ferry S, Jayson M, Silman A. Influence of previous pain experience on the episode incidence of low back pain. *Pain* 1996;66:181-5.
13. Papageorgiou A, Croft P, Ferry S, Jayson MIV, Silman A. Estimating the prevalence of low back pain in the general population. *Spine* 1995;20:1889-94.

(Accepted 29 January 1998)

This article was first published in Spine *and is reproduced by permission of Lippincott Williams and Williams*

OUTCOME MEASURES FOR LOW BACK PAIN RESEARCH

A Proposal for Standardized Use

Richard A. Deyo, MD, MPH; Michele Battle, PhD, PT; A.J.H.M. Beurskens, PhD, PT; Claire Bombardier, MD; Peter Croft, MD; Bart Koes, PhD; Antti Malmivaara, MD, PhD; Martin Roland, MD; Michael Von Korff PhD; Gordon Waddell, DSc, MD

Study Design. An international group of back pain researchers considered recommendations for standardized measures in clinical outcomes research in patients with back pain.

Objectives. To promote more standardization of outcome measurement in clinical trials and other types of outcomes research, including meta-analyses, cost-effectiveness analyses, and multicenter studies.

Summary of Background Data. Better standardization of outcome measurement would facilitate comparison of results among studies, and more complete reporting of relevant outcomes. Because back pain is rarely fatal or completely cured, outcome assessment is complex and involves multiple dimensions. These include symptoms, function, general well-being, work disability, and satisfaction with care.

Methods. The panel considered several factors in recommending a standard battery of outcome measures. These included reliability, validity, responsiveness, and practicality of the measures. In addition, compatibility with widely used and promoted batteries such as the American Academy of Orthopaedic Surgeons Lumbar Cluster were considered to minimize the need for changes when these instruments are used.

Results. First, a six-item set was proposed, which is sufficiently brief that it could be used in routine care settings for quality improvement and for research purposes. An expanded outcome set, which would provide more precise measurement for research purposes. includes measures of severity and frequency of symptoms, either the Roland or the Oswestry Disability Scale, either the SFA 2 or the EuroQol measure of general health status, a question about satisfaction with symptoms, three types of "disability days," and an optional single item on overall satisfaction with medical care.

Conclusion. Standardized measurement of outcomes would facilitate scientific advances in clinical care. A short, 6-item questionnaire and a somewhat expanded, more precise battery of questionnaires can be recommended. Although many considerations support such recommendations, more data on responsiveness and the minimally important change in scores are needed for most of the instruments. [Key words: back pain, clinical research, disability, health status, outcomes] **Spine 1998;23:2003-2013**

The measurement of patient outcomes in clinical studies of low back pain has been vexing for many investigators. Traditionally, in an effort to achieve objectivity, physiologic measures such as range of motion and muscle strength were widely used. However, in many cases, such measures are only weakly associated with outcomes that are more relevant to patients and to society, such as symptom relief, daily functioning, and work status.[7] In recent years, social science methods and clinical expertise have been fused in the creation of a series of questionnaire measures that seek to capture this broader range of relevant outcomes.[7,8] However, there is little standardization of use of these instruments, and comparisons among studies are therefore difficult or impossible. New questionnaires seem constantly to emerge. As a result, there is little shared understanding of what certain results mean, what their clinical relevance may be, or how the patient populations and results of different studies may compare.

A multinational group of investigators met as part of an international program on primary care research on back pain held in The Hague, The Netherlands, in May 1997. The group considered the question of whether a

---

Table 1

Advantages of a Standardized Set of Outcome Measures

Improve comparability of results among clinical studies

Improve comparability of baseline patient characteristics among clinical studies

Facilitate meta-analysis (pooling of results from multiple studies)

Facilitate cost-effectiveness analysis by creating an accepted metric for effectiveness (would also facilitate comparison of cost-effectiveness with treatments for other medical conditions)

Encourage more complete reporting of relevant outcomes

Facilitate conduct of multicenter studies

Facilitate design and review of manuscripts, publications, research proposals

Avoid "reinventing the wheel"

relatively standardized set of outcome measures could be recommended, based on published studies and the group's assessment of the important domains. This report summarizes the discussion and provides initial recommendations for investigators in this field.

A standardized "core" set of questions and questionnaires would have many advantages for clinicians and investigators. Such a core would facilitate many types of comparison and pooling of data, while leaving investigators free to augment the core with a wide variety of measures of their own choice. Thus, the effort to develop a standardized set of instruments is not intended to force investigators into a straitjacket, but to provide a common yardstick that is appropriate for use in many types of studies. For individual investigations, it may be important to augment this core with measures of specific clinical effects or to experiment with new measures of the constructs included in the standardized core. Thus, it should be anticipated that the "core" measures may change somewhat with time but that change may be gradual enough to maintain some standardization within the field.

It seems clear that the traditional surgical outcome measure of a single rating scale (excellent, good, fair, and poor) is no longer sufficient. Howe and Frymoyer [13] demonstrated that different definitions of these terms could result in widely differing conclusions about the success of a given surgical procedure. Furthermore, such a rating scale fails to indicate, for example, how many patients are employed at the beginning of a study and how many are employed at the end of a study. It also combines multiple dimensions of outcome, such as symptoms, function, and work disability, which may be relatively unrelated in their clinical trajectory after a treatment intervention. For example, it has been shown that among patients undergoing discectomy for sciatica, surgery offers substantial advantages in symptom and functional outcomes at 1 year, but that return to work is equivalent for surgical and nonsurgical treatments.[1] Thus, a standardized set of instruments should measure various outcomes in different dimensions and keep them relatively distinct.

ADVANTAGES OF STANDARDIZED OUTCOME MEASUREMENT

A standardized set of clinical outcome measures would make it easier to compare the results of clinical studies of similar treatments. Presently, this is almost impossible, even when outcome ratings are superficially similar (such as the excellent–good–fair–poor scale). Even when studies are concordant in demonstrating benefit for a given treatment, differences in outcome measures may make it difficult to assess the relative magnitude of treatment effects among various studies. This may make it difficult or impossible to pool the results of multiple studies in the form of a meta-analysis. Such pooling of results may be important when there are multiple small studies in which results show a treatment benefit, but the individual studies are too

Table 2
Factors to Consider in Choosing "Standardized" Outcome Measures

Breadth of coverage

Demonstrated validity and reproducibility

Demonstrated responsiveness

Practicality (brevity and low cost)

Compatibility with widely promoted instruments or batteries (e.g., SF-36, AAOS, NASS)

Importance to patient

Importance to society

AAOS = American Academy of Orthopaedic Surgeons; NASS = North American Spine Society; SF-36 = Short Form, 36 items (from Medical Outcomes Study [16]).

small to show statistical significance; when clinical subgroup analyses may be important, but studies must be combined to achieve adequate numbers of patients; and when a single assessment of the magnitude of treatment effects is sought for purposes of cost effectiveness analyses. Because cost-effectiveness analysis is always a ratio of cost to treatment effectiveness, the denominator must be a valid estimate of the magnitude of treatment effects, along with confidence intervals. If the outcome measures can be integrated with an assessment of patient preferences or weighting of the outcomes (utilities) the effectiveness and cost-effectiveness measures can be transferred into a standardized metric that permits comparison with many other treatments for other medical conditions. This may be important for resource allocation purposes.

The availability of a standardized outcome measurement set should also improve the quality of the medical literature. It would encourage more complete reporting of relevant outcomes, so that investigators do not simply report a single dimension of outcome while ignoring others. Having a common set of measures that are widely used would also encourage development of cooperative multicenter studies, which offers the prospect of large, rapid, and generalizable efficacy and effectiveness studies. If various centers were familiar with a core set of measures, had the instruments readily available, and were familiar with their administration and manipulation, the design and conduct of such cooperative studies would be facilitated. Finally, having some standardized measures of outcome would simplify the process of designing and reviewing research proposals, manuscripts, and published studies.

DIMENSIONS OF OUTCOME

Some have previously argued for measuring the outcomes of low back pain in terms of symptoms, functional status, overall well-being, and work disability.[14] Valid measures of all of these constructs are available, and such dimensions have been incorporated

Table 3.

A Proposed "Core Set" of Six Questions, Practical for Routine Clinical Use, Quality Improvement, and as a Component of More Formal Research*

Domain	Specific Question	Source, References	Where Used
Pain symptoms	During the past week, how bothersome have the following symptoms been? a) low back pain b) leg pain (sciatica)	From back pain PORT; Patrick et al, [14] Atlas et al[1]	MLSS AAOS NASS TyPE
	or		
	Conventional visual analog pain scales		
Function	During the past week, how much did pain interfere with your normal work (including both work outside the home and housework?	SF-36 and SF-12[16,17]	AAOS MLSS TyPE
Well-being	If you had to spend the rest of your life with the symptoms you have right now, how would you feel about it?	From back Pain PORT; Cherkin et al[4]	AAOS MLSS
Disability	During the past 4 weeks, about how many days did you cut down on the things you usually do for more than half of the day because of back pain or leg pain (sciatica)?	Adapted from Questions in NHIS; Patrick et al [14]	MLSS TyPE
Disability (social role)	During the past 4 weeks, how many days did low back pain or leg pain (sciatica) keep you from going to work or school?		
Satisfaction with care	Over the course of treatment for your low back pain or leg pain (sciatica), how would you rate your overall medical care? (optional)		TyPE

* The exact questions and response options are listed in Appendix 1.
PORT = patient outcome research team; MLSS = Maine Lumbar Spine Study; AAOS = American Academy of Orthopaedic Surgeons; NASS = North American Spine Society; NHIS = National Health Interview Survey; TyPE = typology of patient experience; SF = Short Form.

into the outcome instruments of the American Academy of Orthopaedic Surgeons (AAOS) and the North American Spine Society (NASS). Thus, there seems to be a growing consensus that these are appropriate dimensions of outcome for patients with back pain.

There is substantial evidence that symptoms and functional status change fairly readily among patients with acute low back pain and that these aspects of outcome can be influenced by various treatments. In contrast, results in some studies show that affecting work disability or employment status may be very difficult.[1] Although work status has the advantage that it is easily assessed, objective, and highly relevant, it is usually a function of many factors, among which medical intervention may be only minor. For example, physical job demands, job satisfaction, relationships with fellow employees, supervisor ratings, income, regional job availability, closeness to retirement age, or the availability of another breadwinner in the family all influence the likelihood of return to work. Thus, although return to work is an outcome of great social and personal importance, it may also be one that is less responsive to clinical treatment than symptoms or daily

functioning. In considering a core set of outcome measures, it seems appropriate to consider outcomes that are highly responsive to treatment and those that are of major social importance, even though some outcome measures do not have both traits.

For many purposes, physiologic outcomes such as neurologic function, range of motion, or muscle strength are important outcomes to measure as well. However, the wide range of methods for measuring such physiologic functions and the extensive literature on the reliability and validity of such measures is beyond the scope of this article. Furthermore, there are many examples in which measures such as electromyogram activity, spine mobility, or straight leg raising results were poorly associated with pain relief, functional status, or use of health care resources.[7] Thus, the current group chose to focus on questionnaire measures that could be easily administered in multiple settings and by a wide variety of personnel.

Finally, health care use may be considered an important outcome domain, because hospitalization, use of imaging, surgery, and health care costs are important considerations in studying therapy. However, these are measures of the process of care, rather than outcomes.

Table 4

A Proposed "Core Set" of Instruments for Clinical Researchers

Domain	Source References	Specific Instrument
Pain symptoms	Bothersomeness or severity and frequency of low back pain and leg pain (sciatica)	From LBP TyPE, used in AAOS and NASS instruments. Patrick et al,[14] Atlas et al,[1] Daltroy et al[5]
Back-related function	Roland and Morris Disability Scale (or adaptations)	Roland et al,[15] Fairbank et al, [11] Dltroy et al,[5] Patrick et al,[14] Modified Oswestry used in NASS and AAOS
or	Oswestry Disability questionnaire (or adaptations)	
Generic well- being	SF-12 or EuroQoL; also, "If you had to spend the rest of your life with the symptoms you have right now, how would you feel about it?	From SIF-36[16] Ware et al,[17] Patrick et al, [14] Used in AAOS., EuroQoL Group
Disability (social role)	Days of work absenteeism, cut down activities, bed rest	"Cut down days" from NHIS, Patrick et al[14]
Satisfaction with care	Single question on overall satisfaction (optional)	TyPE

NHIS = National Health Interview Survey; TyPE = typology of patient experience. LBP = low back pain; AAOS = American Academy of Orthopaedic Surgeons; NASS = North American Spine Society; SF-36 = Short Form, 36 items.

They do not necessarily reflect health status and are not easily measured with a brief, uniform set of items. Again, measures of cost or health care use could easily be added by individual investigators, depending on the goals of their research.

FACTORS TO CONSIDER IN RECOMMENDING A STANDARD BATTERY OF OUTCOME MEASURES

Many factors could be considered in selecting questions or questionnaires for standardized use. The recommendations made here were drawn up primarily in consideration of the demonstrated validity of instruments, their responsiveness to change with time, and their practicality. For validity, the major concern was whether the items selected had evidence of construct validity — that is, associations with different but related measures in a predictable direction and of moderate magnitude. Construct validation is necessary, because for symptoms, function, and well-being, there is no widely accepted gold standard for measurement.

Responsiveness refers to the ability to detect true changes in patient status beyond the random variability that is expected on repeat measurement of any sort. All measures of responsiveness are in some way measures of "signal" to "noise:" The signal is the true change in patient status and the noise is the random variability of measures. Several indicators of responsiveness have been proposed, including effect size, the standardized response mean, and variations of these statistics. Some

investigators have also examined score changes as they relate to other external measures of improvement or deterioration, using either correlation analysis or receiver operating characteristic (ROC) curves.[9] For an instrument designed to measure change in longitudinal studies, such measures of responsiveness may be more important than cross-sectional reliability, in which the signal-to-noise ratio represents differences between patients (rather than longitudinal change for a single patient) related to cross-sectional score variability.

The major concern regarding practicality was the length of the questionnaires. To be practical, they should be as brief as possible, minimizing response burden and the costs of data collection and management. Furthermore, the core data set should be brief if investigators are to feel free to add other measures to the battery.

A final consideration was the compatibility of questions with widely promoted instruments or batteries, such as the Lumbar Cluster developed by the AAOS, the NASS Lumbar Spine Outcome Assessment Instrument, or the typology of patient experience (TyPE) originally developed by InterStudy (later reverting to the Health Outcomes Institute, Bloomington, Minnesota, now a part of Stratis Health, Bloomington). Thus, it would be desirable for the core items to be included in commonly used instruments so that practitioners or health care systems that have already implemented one of these batteries would not have to make changes (or could make minor changes) to include the core battery.

A VERY PARSIMONIOUS SIX-ITEM CORE SET

A proposed core set of just six questions was developed (Table 3 and Appendix I) that would be practical for use in a wide variety of settings, including routine clinical care, quality improvement efforts, and more formal research. It is so brief that even lengthy supplemental measures (e.g., physiologic measures, detailed questionnaires) could be added and still be practical, retaining a core set of multidimensional measures that would assure comparability with results in a wide variety of other studies. Most investigators would want to collect other demographic and clinical information for baseline description, and this set focuses strictly on outcomes of care. However, many investigators would also want to measure each of these constructs at a baseline time, or before some intervention. This set has the advantage of measuring several dimensions of outcome, each with a single item. Even this short set of measures would be a substantial improvement compared with simply measuring pain severity, or excellent–good–fair–poor outcomes.

Each of the questions in this short set has been studied and validated elsewhere and is already incorporated into other widely promulgated questionnaires. For example, the questions on bothersomeness of back and leg pain, function, and well-being are all included in the Lumbar Cluster of the AAOS and the NASS outcome questionnaire.[5] However, some of the questions (*e.g.*, those concerning the "bother" of symptoms) have not been transated into languages other than English or tested outside the United States.

The first item in this core set is a measure of pain symptoms that have been divided into low back symptoms and leg symptoms. For this purpose, the current suggestion is that pain severity be measured in one of two ways at the discretion of the investigator. First, a set of questions could be used to determine how bothersome pain symptoms have been, as was reported in the Maine Lumbar Spine Study and is incorporated in the AAOS, NASS, and TyPE instruments. This question is shown in Appendix I. A-1 week time frame for these symptoms is suggested because it allows the patient to integrate recent experience of a long enough interval to be meaningful, but short enough that memory is not likely to be a problem and short-term improvements are apparent.[5] The severity of low back and leg pain could also be measured using conventional visual analog scales, a type of measure more familiar to some investigators. Guyatt et al [12] demonstrated nearly identical statistical measures of responsiveness for 7-point Likert Scales and Visual Analog Scales. However, they found that the Likert format with verbal descriptors (such as the "bothersome" question) was easier to understand for patients and required less instruction. This is likely to be especially important with elderly patients, such as those with spinal stenosis.

Although some investigators may wish to ask much more extensive pain questions, such as the most severe pain, the duration of pain, or other aspects of pain symptomatology, the current investigators recommend these items on pain severity for the past week as a minimum set of core questions. The questions on "bothersomeness" of pain symptoms have been validated in patients with sciatica by demonstrating highly significant associations with measures of functional status, absence from work, reflex changes, straight leg raising, and use of opioid analgesics.[1,14] Similarly, visual analog pain scales have enjoyed wide use, and similar evidence of construct validity has accrued.

Regarding function, the parsimonious set includes a single question about how much pain interfered with normal work. This question is derived from the widely used Short Form 36 (SF-36) [16] and its derivative shorter version, the SF-12, developed by Ware and colleagues.[17] It is also incorporated into the Lumbar Cluster of the AAOS and was a part of the Maine Lumbar Spine Study.[1]

The current proposal is that a single item be used to measure overall well-being by asking, "If you had to spend the rest of your life with the symptoms you have right now, how would you feel about it?" This item was used by the low back pain Patient Outcome Research Team at the University of Washington, and was also used by the initial Patient Outcome Research Teams for studies in coronary heart disease, prostate disease, and cataract disease that were funded by the Agency for Health Care Policy and Research. This item was also adopted as part of the Lumbar Cluster of the AAOS and was incorporated into the Maine Lumbar Spine Study. The performance of this particular question has been studied in relation to Roland Disability Scores, symptom bothersomeness, and the presence of symptoms and depression.[4] In the Maine Lumbar Spine Study, it was highly responsive to differences in treatment outcomes.[14]

Two items on disability related to social role are included in the core set. Both are derived from the U. S. National Health Interview Survey, and have been validated by identifying significant associations with compensation status, use of opioid analgesics, abnormal lower extremity strength, symptom frequency and severity, and changes in symptoms.[14] The first item asks on how many days patients have had to cut down on their normal activities, an item that is applicable even for retired or nonworking people. The second question asks about days lost from usual work or school because of leg or back pain. Although this item is not as responsive to changes occurring after therapy as direct measures of symptoms or functional status, it reflects significant differences in treatment outcomes for surgical *versus* nonsurgical patients in the Maine Lumbar Spine Study.[1,14] For the working-age population, specific time of absence from work was thought to be a key outcome measure. This question is also a part of the Low Back Pain TyPE questionnaire.

Finally, the parsimonious core set includes an optional question regarding patient satisfaction with care. Although this is not a measure of health outcome, it is an important concern in many types of interventions and in quality improvement applications. As ineffective treatments are used less frequently and as efforts are made to reduce unnecessary imaging, it may be important to measure and maintain patient satisfaction with care.

PROPOSED CORE INSTRUMENTS FOR CLINICAL RESEARCHERS

For many clinical research purposes, greater precision in measurement than is achievable with a single question is desirable. Thus, a somewhat expanded set of core instruments is recommended for investigators who have sufficient resources to collect and analyze such data. It is still a brief set of instruments, designed with the intent that other specific measures could be added at an investigator's discretion. This modestly expanded set of outcome measures is listed in Table 4. Some of the actual instruments are included as Appendices II–IV.

The same dimensions of outcome used in the parsimonious six-item set are preserved. The same measures of pain severity or bothersomeness are recommended as are used in the parsimonious core set. This includes separate measures of back pain severity and leg pain severity. In this expanded set, however, the determination of symptom frequency is also recommended.

With regard to functional status, the use of either the Roland and Morris Disability Scale [15] (or its adaptations [14]) or the Oswestry Disability Questionnaire [11] (and its adaptations) is recommended. These are among the most widely used and well validated of functional status questionnaires, and both would be highly acceptable. The Roland and Morris Scale, which was derived from the longer Sickness Impact Profile,[6,15] is well suited to administration by telephone, which may be important when seeking high follow-up rates at low cost. The Oswestry Scale would be tedious at best to administer by telephone. The Roland and Morris Disability Scale may be most useful in primary care settings, or in any situation in which the anticipated level of dysfunction at the end of a trial is small. The Oswestry Disability Questionnaire may be most useful in specialty care settings or in situations in which the disability level is likely to remain relatively high throughout a trial (e.g., chronic severe low back pain).[2] A modest adaptation of the Roland and Morris Disability Scale has been studied and validated with the intent of producing a more responsive instrument, although head-to-head comparisons are unavailable.[14] The original version is reproduced in Appendix II. This instrument is now available in eight non-English languages (French, Dutch, Flemish, Spanish, Romanian, Italian, Portuguese, Polish, and Czech). These translations are available from Dr. Sandra Sinclair (e-mail address: ssinclair@wh,on.ca) or from the MAPI Research Institute (27 Rue de la Villette, 69003 Lyon, France). In addition, a modest adaptation of the Oswestry Disability Questionnaire has been developed and

validated for use in the AAOS and NASS outcome questionnaires [5] (Appendix III).

With regard to generic well-being, inclusion of either the SF-12 (adapted from the SF-36 [16]) or the EuroQoL (Appendix IV) is tentatively recommended.[10,17] Both are measures of general health that are not disease specific and that provide an assessment of a patient's overall health status. The SF-12 has been incorporated into the Lumbar Cluster of the AAOS and is widely used in a variety of settings within the United States. Translations are available in several languages. The EuroQoL instrument has the advantage that it produces a preference-weighted score that is necessary for use in formal decision analysis and cost-effectiveness analysis. That is, it measures a patient's "utility" for various health states in the manner that is theoretically necessary for these forms of analysis. Unfortunately, there is little evidence regarding the responsiveness of either the SF-12 or the EuroQoL instrument, although the larger SF-36 has been found to be responsive.[3,14] In general, such generic measures have proved to be less responsive than disease-specific questionnaires. In addition, the use of the single item from the parsimonious set that asks "if you had to spend the rest of your life with the symptoms you have right now, how would you feel about it?" is recommended.

Regarding disability from social role, the questions about days of work absenteeism and days in which the patient had to cut down on normal activities are recommended, but days spent in bed for at least half a day should also be determined. Again, these questions have been adapted from the National Health Interview Survey, validated for use in patients with back problems, and shown to discriminate between surgical and nonsurgical outcomes in the Maine Lumbar Spine Study.[1,14] Finally, the optional inclusion of a single item on overall patient satisfaction with care is again recommended.

The SF-12 includes questions related to mental health and, depression, but the battery proposed here does not include a more extensive or formal measure of depression or mental health. Depending on the goal of a particular study, such measures might be added to this battery, but in many studies of back problems, measures of mental health are not as responsive to treatment effects as measures of physical health.[1]

INTERPRETING CHANGES OR DIFFERENCES IN OUTCOME MEASURES

In some cases there are sufficient data to make recommendations for the smallest clinically relevant change or difference in outcome measures. For example, data from the Maine Lumbar Spine Study show that the minimum change that is of clinical importance in Roland Scale Score is between 2 and 3 points and in the SF-36 Physical Function subscale, it is approximately 7 points.[14] Effect sizes for many of the outcome measures listed here have been published among a cohort of patients with sciatica who demonstrated general improvements in 3 months.[14] These effect sizes could be used for purposes of calculating sample sizes for clinical trials. Nonetheless, there is a general need for more data on the responsiveness and the minimal changes of clinical importance in these outcome measures.

In summary, there are several scientific advantages to the use of a standardized set of measures for most clinical trials of treatment for low back pain. There are well-validated measures available that capture the many dimensions of outcome that are important for most patients with back pain, including symptoms, daily functioning, well-being, work disability, and satisfaction. The current group of investigators has prepared a core set of six items for extensive use and a modestly larger set of instruments that could be widely used by investigators with sufficient resources. There can be no illusion that either of these standardized sets will be sufficient for all research studies, and it is anticipated that most investigators will want to add specific and more detailed measures of outcomes that are particularly important for their individual settings or particular forms of treatment. In addition, it is hoped that the battery of questionnaires proposed here will undergo further evaluation, and it is anticipated that it will be continually refined and updated. To the extent that research on back pain incorporates this standardized set, however, it will facilitate comparability among studies, formal pooling of data, and an increase in large, multicenter studies.

References

1 Atlas SJ, Deyo RA, Keller RB, et al. The Maine Lumbar Spine Study, II: One year outcomes of surgical and non-surgical management of sciatica. Spine 1996;21:1777-86.

2 Baker CD, Pynsent PB, Fairbank JCT. The Oswestry Disability Index revisited: Its reliability, repeatability, and validity, and a comparison with the St. Thomas's Disability Index. In: Roland MO, Jenner JR, eds. Back Pain: New Approaches to Education and Rehabilitation. Manchester, UK: Manchester University Press, 1989:174-86.

3 Beaton DE, Hogg-Johnson S, Bombardier C. Evaluating changes in health status: Reliability and responsiveness of five generic health status measures in workers with musculoskeletal disorders. J Clin Epidemiol 1997;50:79-93.

4 Cherkin DC, Deyo RA, Street JH, Barlow W. Predicting poor outcomes for back pain seen in primary care using patient's own criteria. Spine 1996;21:2900-7.

5 Daltroy LH, Cats-Baril WL, Katz JN, Fossel AH, Liang MH. The North American Spine Society Lumbar Spine Outcome Assessment Instrument: Reliability and validity tests. Spine 1996;21:741-9.

6 Deyo RA. Comparative validity of the Sickness Impact Profile and Shorter Scales for Functional Assessment in low back pain. Spine 1986;11:951-4.

7 Deyo RA. Measuring the functional status of patients with low back pain. Arch Phys Med Rehabil 1988;69:1044-53.

8 Deyo RA, Andersson G, Bombardier C, et al.. Outcome measures for studying patients with low back pain. Spine 1994; 19(Suppl):S2032-6.

9 Deyo RA, Centor RM. Assessing the responsiveness of functional scales to clinical change: An analogy to diagnostic test performance. J Chronic Dis 1986;39:897-906.

10 EuroQoL Group. EuroQoL: A new facility for the measurement of health-related quality-of-life. Health Policy 1990;16:199-208.

11 Fairbank JCT, Davies JB, Mbaot JC, O'Brien JT. The Oswestry Low Back Pain Disability Questionnaire. Physiotherapy 1980;66:271-3.

12 Guyatt GH, Townsend M, Berman LB, Keller JL. A comparison of Likert and visual analogue scales for measuring change in function. J Chronic Dis 1987;40:1129-233.

13 Howe J, Frymoyer JW. Effects of questionnaire design on determination of end results in lumbar spine surgery. Spine 1985;10:804-5.

14 Patrick DL, Deyo RA, Atlas SJ, Singer DE, Chapin A, Keller RB. Assessing health related quality of life in patients with sciatica. Spine 1995;20:1899-909.

15 Roland M, Morris R. A study of the natural history of back pain. I: Development of a reliable and sensitive measure of disability in low back pain. Spine 1983;8:141-4.

16 Ware JE, Sherbourne C. The MOS 36-item short-form survey (SF-36): I. Conceptual framework and item selection. Med Care 1992;30:473-83.

17 Ware JE, Kosinski, Keller SD. A 12-item short form health survey. Med Care 1996;34:220-33.

Richard A. Deyo Center for Cost and Outcomes Research, the Department of Medicine, and the Department of Health Services, University of Washington, Seattle, Washington
Michele Battie University of Alberta, Edmonton, Alberta, Canada
A. J. H. M. Beurskens The Department of Epidemiology, Maastricht University, Maastricht, The Netherlands
Claire Bombardier The Institute for Work and Health, Toronto, Ontario, Canada
Peter Croft Keele University School of Postgraduate Medicine, Stoke-on-Trent, United Kingdom
Bart Koes EMGO Institute, Vrije University, Amsterdam, The Netherlands
Antti Malmivaara Finnish Institute of Occupational Health, Helsinki, Finland
Martin Roland National Primary, Care Research and Development Centre, University of Manchester, Manchester, United Kingdom
Michael Von Kort Group Health Cooperative, Seattle, Washington
Gordon Waddell The Glasgow Nuffield Hospital, Glasgow, Scotland

Supported in part by a grant (HS-08194) from the Agency for Health Care Policy and Research, Washington DC.

Presented in part at the Second International Forum for Primary Care Research on Low Back Pain, The Hague, The Netherlands, May 30-31, 1997.
Acknowledgment date: August 14, 1997.
First revision date: January 30, 1998.
Acceptance date: February 11, 1998.
Device status category: 1.

Address reprint requests to
Richard A. Deyo, MD, MPH
Division of General Internal Medicine
University of Washington
Box 356429
Seattle, WA 98195
E-mail: deyo@u.washington.edu

This article was first published in Quality in Health Care *and is reproduced by permission of the BMJ Publishing Group*

ACHIEVING HEALTH GAIN THROUGH CLINICAL GUIDELINES

II: Ensuring guidelines change medical practice

Jeremy M Grimshaw, Ian T Russell

Quality in Health Care 1994;**3**: 45-52

"Clinical guidelines are proliferating on both sides of the Atlantic."[1] Nevertheless there is considerable uncertainty whether this will improve clinical practice.[2] We therefore systematically reviewed published evaluations of clinical guidelines.[3] We identified 59 rigorous evaluations covering a wide range of clinical activities, all but four of which detected statistically significant improvements in the process of medical care and all but two of the 11 that also measured the outcome of care reported statistically significant improvements in outcome. We concluded that guidelines improve clinical practice and achieve health gains when introduced in the context of rigorous evaluations.

Within the United Kingdom, clinical guidelines are likely to be incorporated into contracts between purchasers and providers.[4] However, if these guidelines are to achieve the health gains reported in our review,[3] two things are needed. Firstly, purchasers and providers should identify scientifically valid guidelines in the sense that, when followed, they lead to the health gains projected for them.[5] To this end we have proposed a classification of factors influencing the validity of guidelines, designed to inform choice about which guidelines should be integrated into contracts. Greater validity is likely to follow from the use of systematic literature reviews, of independent guideline development groups including representatives of all key disciplines, and of explicit links between recommendations and scientific evidence.[5] Secondly, purchasers and providers should ensure that these scientifically valid guidelines are successfully introduced, in the sense that medical practice is significantly changed in the direction proposed by the guidelines, thus leading to health gain. The successful introduction of guidelines is dependent on many factors, including the clinical context and the methods by which they are developed, disseminated, and implemented.[6] Different methods are appropriate in different contexts. In this paper we tabulate the methods adopted by the studies identified by our review (tables 1-3)[3] and propose a framework for successful introduction of guidelines, covering development, dissemination, and implementation strategies. We use the term "dissemination strategy" to describe educational interventions that aim at influencing targeted clinicians' attitudes to, and awareness, knowledge, and understanding of, a set of guidelines and we use "implementation strategy" to describe interventions that aim at improving targeted clinicians' compliance with guideline recommendations (that is, to turn changes in attitudes and knowledge into changes in medical practice). Although this distinction is helpful in exploring the process of introduction of guidelines, we recognise that some interventions influence both dissemination and implementation.

DEVELOPMENT STRATEGIES

In developing clinical guidelines the aim is to produce explicit recommendations that are both scientifically valid and helpful in clinical practice. We previously discussed factors that may influence the development of scientifically valid guidelines.[5] We now consider factors associated with the successful introduction of guidelines, including who develops them, how they are developed, and how they are presented.

Who Should Develop Guidelines?

Guidelines can be developed by internal groups (composed entirely of the clinicians who will use them), intermediate groups (including some of the clinicians who will use them), or external groups (none of whom will use them).[5] Studies evaluating internal, intermediate, or external guidelines all observed significant changes in clinical behaviour. Three studies directly compared the success of internal guidelines and local external guidelines (table 1). Sommers *et al*, evaluating guidelines for managing unexplained anaemia in four community hospitals in the United States, observed that, though the introduction of internal guidelines had no effect on compliance, that of local external guidelines increased compliance.[16] In contrast, Putnam and Curry reported a greater increase in compliance when Canadian family physicians developed their own guidelines for five common conditions than when they received guidelines developed by others.[19] Similarly, in the North of England Study of Standards and Performance in General Practice, which compared the success of internal guidelines and local external guidelines for five common paediatric conditions, significant changes in process and in outcome were apparent only when general practitioners developed their own guidelines.[28]

Although fewer resources are needed to disseminate and implement internal guidelines than intermediate or external guidelines,[3] internal guidelines are less likely to be scientifically valid [5,68] because local groups lack the

Table 1
Development, dissemination, and implementation strategies adopted by rigorous evaluations of guidelines for clinical care[5]

Year	Authors	Subject	Type of guideline	Method of dissemination	Method of implementation	Effect on process	Effect on outcome
1976	McDonald[7]	Diabetes and various medical conditions	External local	None reported	Computer generated reminder in notes	+++	-
1976	McDonald[8]	Various medical conditions	External local	None reported	Computer generated reminder in note	+++	-
1978	Barnett et al[9]	Streptococcal sore throat	Intermediate	Guidelines "determined" by medical and nursing staff	Failure to comply caused computer generated reminder following consultation	++	-
1978	Sanazaro and Worth[10]	Various medical, surgical, and paediatric conditions	External national	Guidelines approved by medical staff	Guidelines inserted in patients' notes	+	0
1980	Hopkins et al[11]	Hypotensive shock	External local	Residents instructed in use of guidelines for 30 minutes	Copy of guidelines carried by residents	++++	++
1980	Linn[12]	Management of burns	External national	Seminar lasting 4 hours focusing on guidelines	Copy of guidelines kept in emergency department	+	++
1980	McDonald[13]	Various medical conditions	External local	Supporting publications available on request	Computer generated reminder (+/- bibliographic citation) in notes	++	-
1983	Barnett et al[14]	Hypertension	External local	None reported	Failure to comply caused computer generated reminder following consultation	++++	++
1983	Thomas et al[15]	Diabetes	External local	None reported	Computer generated reminder in notes	++	0
1984	Sommers et al[16]	Unexplained anaemia	Internal and external	Internal post	Phase 1 – feedback on baseline compliance	++	-
					Phase 2 – failure to comply caused computer generated reminder after consultation	++++	
1985	Norton and Dempsey[17]	Cystitis and vaginitis	Internal	None reported	Feedback on baseline compliance	+++	-
1985	Palmer et al[18]	Various medical and paediatric conditions	Intermediate	Guidelines discussed, assessed, and then posted	Feedback on baseline compliance discussed then posted	++	-
1985	Putnam and Curry[19]	Various medical conditions	Two internal, three external	External guidelines posted	Interview with feedback on baseline compliance, subsequent personal education package	++++	-
1986	Brownbridge et al[20]	Hypertension	Intermediate	Guidelines discussed with participants	Paper or computerised protocol as part of medical record	++	-
1986	McAlister et al[21]	Hypertension	External provincial	Guidelines posted to all participants	Computer generated reminder in notes	0	++
1986	Wirtschafter et al[22]	Neonatal respiratory distress syndrome	External local	Lectures lasting 3 hours with/without training in protocol use	Protocol embedded within medical record	+	-
1987	Kosecoff et al[23]	Breast cancer, caesarean section, coronary artery bypass grafting	External national	Published in medical press posted to relevant professionals	None	0	-
1989	Lomas et al[24]	Caesarean section	External national	Published in medical press posted to relevant professionals	None	+	-
1991	Lomas et al[25]	Caesarean section	External national	(A) Education programme led by opinion leader	(A) None	++	-
				(B) Local guideline adaptation	(B) Aggregated feedback and discussion of hospital compliance	0	-
1992	Durand-Zaleski et al[26]	Hypovolaemia	External national	Internal post to all doctors, meetings for all prescribers	Monthly feedback on total albumin use and cost to all prescribers	++++	-
1992	Margolis et al[27]	Six paediatric conditions	External local	Clinicians adapted guidelines for local use	Protocol within computerised medical record	+++	-
1992	North of England Study of Standards and Performance in General Practice[28]	Five paediatric conditions	Internal and external	External guidelines posted	Feedback on baseline compliance	+	++++
1992	Sherman et al[29]	Localised prostatic carcinoma	External national	Published in medical press, posted to relevant professionals	None	0	-
1993	Emslie et al[30]	Infertility	Intermediate	Posted to relevant professionals	Protocol embedded within medical record	++++	-

-   Outcome not measured.
0   No significant improvement.
+   Significant improvement<10% in absolute terms.

++   Significant improvement 10-19.9% in absolute terms.
+++   Significant improvement 20-29.9% in absolute terms.
++++   Significant improvement $\geq$ 30% in absolute terms.

Table 2
Development, dissemination, and implementation strategies adopted by rigorous evaluations of guidelines for preventative care[5]

Year	Authors	Subject	Type of guideline	Method of dissemination	Method of implementation	Effect on process	Effect on outcome
1978	Morgan et al[31]	Antenatal care	External national	Guidelines discussed at departmental meetings	Failure to comply caused computer generated reminder after consultation	++	-
1982	Cohen et al[32]	Preventive care	External local	Five seminars on preventive medicine	Copy of guidelines attached to patients' notes	++++	-
1983	Rodney et al[33]	2 Adult immunisations	External local	Education programme on preventive medicine	Medical record redesigned to highlight health maintenance (including tetanus and pneumococcal vaccinations)	++	-
1983	Thompson et al[34]	Investigations in "routine" physical examinations	Intermediate	Extensive educational programme over 2 years	2X aggregated feedback	+++	-
1984	McDonald et al[35]	9 Preventive tasks and six laboratory tests	External local	None reported	Computer generated reminder in notes	+++	*
1984	Winickoff et al[36]	Colorectal cancer screening	Internal	Regular meetings of Department of Internal Medicine	Feedback of group and individual compliance	++	-
1985	Cohen et al[37]	13 Preventive tasks	External local	Internal post	Credit at university bookshop after reading guidelines	†	-
1986	McDowell et al[38]	Influenza vaccination	External national	None reported	Computer generated reminder in notes	++	-
1986	Prislin et al[39]	2 Preventive tasks	External local	Conference on preventive care and use of flowsheet	Flowsheet in patients' notes	++++	-
1986	Tierney et al[40]	11 Preventive tasks	External local	Internal post	(A) Computer generated reminder in notes (B) Computer generated monthly feedback on patient specific non-compliance	++ +	-
1987	Cheney and Ramsdell[41]	12 Preventive tasks	External national	None reported	Checklist placed in patients' notes	++	-
1987 1989	Cohen et al[42 43]	Smoking cessation	External national	1 hour lecture and booklet on smoking cessation	Two types of reminders in patients' notes	++++	-
1988	Robie[44]	3 Preventive tasks	External national	Lecture on cancer screening	Reminder in notes	+++	-
1988	Schreiner et al[45]	4 Preventive tasks	External national	None reported	Reminder in notes	+	-
1988	Wilson et al[46]	Smoking cessation	External national	4 hour training in smoking cessation	Patients recruited by receptionist	++++	+
1989	Becker et al[47]	9 Preventive tasks	External national	None reported	Reminder in notes	+	-
1989	Chambers et al[48]	Mammography	External national	None reported	Computer generated reminder in notes	++	-
1989	Cummings et al[49]	Smoking cessation	National external	3 hour continuing medical education programme	Reminder in notes	++	+
1989	McDowell et al[50]	Blood pressure screening	External national	None reported	Computer generated reminder in notes	++	-
1989	McDowell et al[51]	Cervical screening	External national	None reported	Computer generated reminder in notes	0	-
1989	McPhee et al[52]	7 Preventive tasks	External national	None reported	(A) Computer generated reminder in notes (B) Aggregated feedback	+++ ++	-
1991	McPhee et al[53]	11 Preventive tasks	External national	None reported	Computer generated reminder in notes	++	-
1991	Rosser et al[54]	Smoking cessation	External national	None reported	Computer generated reminder in notes	+++	-
1992	Cowan et al[55]	7 Preventive tasks	External national	None	Guidelines placed in patients' notes	+	-
1992	Headrick et al[56]	Cholesterol	External national	Lecture	(A) Computer generated reminder in notes (B) Guidelines placed in patients' notes	++ +	-
1992	Lilford et al[57]	Antenatal care	Intermediate	None reported	New paper record or computerised questionnaire	+	-
1992	Rosser et al[58]	Tetanus vaccination	National external	None reported	Computer generated reminder in notes	++	-

-	Outcome not measured.
0	No significant improvement.
+	Significant improvement <10% in absolute terms.
++	Significant improvement 10-19.9% in absolute terms.
+++	Significant improvement 20-20.9% in absolute terms.

++++	Significant improvement ≥ 30% in absolute terms.
*	Authors report significantly fewer emergency room visits by patients treated in study group during influenza epidemic.
†	Authors report "modest" increase in compliance.

clinical, managerial, and technical skills needed to develop guidelines.[69,70-72] Furthermore, greater resources in total are needed to develop internal guidelines.[68] In Scotland the Clinical Resource and Audit Group has recently proposed an attractive solution to the potentially conflicting demands of developing a guideline that is both scientifically valid and likely to change medical practice.[5,73] It suggests that resources should be devoted to the development of national scientifically valid guidelines which can be modified locally to reflect context and resources. Nevertheless, further research is required to identity the most effective forum for developing guidelines, whether national or local.

How Should Guidelines Be Developed?

The methods used to develop guidelines include consensus conferences, peer groups, and the Delphi technique (in which consensus is achieved by successive circulation of a postal questionnaire); we have described these methods in detail elsewhere.[71] Although all evaluated methods were successful in at least two studies,[3] it is difficult to draw conclusions about which method is best in given circumstances. In many studies the method of development was not explicitly stated, in others the potential of a method of development is difficult to judge in the face of unsatisfactory dissemination and implementation strategies. For example, three studies evaluating guidelines developed by consensus conference found little change in medical practice (table 1).[23,24,29] However, the guidelines were disseminated with little effort and without any attempt at implementation. In contrast, Lomas et al identified substantial improvements in performance when such guidelines on caesarean section were disseminated by a local "opinion leader",[25] and Durand-Zaleski et al reported even greater improvements when guidelines on hypovolaemia were disseminated at local meetings and implemented through monthly feedback.[26] From these five studies we can conclude that the successful introduction of guidelines developed by consensus conference is very dependent on the choice of appropriate dissemination and implementation strategies. The studies also serve to illustrate why there is general uncertainty over whether clinical guidelines change medical practice.

How Should Guidelines Be Presented?

There is little published information on the effect of the style and format of guidelines on their adoption. In the North of England study, peer groups of general practitioners showed considerable diversity in the style of their internal standards,[69] but this did not prevent substantial improvements in process and outcome (table 1).[28] In contrast, the Harvard Community Health Plan has established a quality assurance programme based exclusively upon algorithms,[74] building on their successful use as a method of information transfer in educational settings.[75] However, doctors are often reluctant to use algorithms in everyday practice because of their apparent complexity and lack of flexibility.[76,77] A recent guideline for urinary incontinence sponsored by the Agency for Health Care Policy and Research[78] has responded to these criticisms by adopting an annotated algorithmic format incorporating literature citations and patient counselling notes.

Kahan et al analysed the content of 24 consensus statements by the National Institutes of Health (NIH) and suggested that variations in style may affect their acceptance by clinicians.[79] Subsequently, the national institutes encouraged consensus development conferences to produce guidelines which were concrete (making specific recommendations), didactic (offering practical advice to the clinician), and differentiating (dividing patients into specific subclasses). Whatever format is chosen, it is important that the guideline is both reader friendly and comprehensive.[80] To meet these potentially conflicting demands many institutions now produce guidelines containing a short summary of the principal recommendations (which can be consulted in clinical practice), underpinned by detailed documentation about the process of guideline development and the scientific basis. Although more research is needed, it is reassuring to note that rigorously evaluated guidelines have achieved success with a wide range of styles and formats.[3]

DISSEMINATION STRATEGIES

Dissemination strategies aim at influencing targeted clinicians' awareness, attitudes, knowledge, and understanding of a set of guidelines. These strategies include publication in professional journals, postal distribution to relevant groups, incorporation within continuing medical education, and educational initiatives that focus specifically on the guidelines. Unfortunately, in many of the studies we reviewed, the method of dissemination was not explicitly stated.

Of the six studies that reported on guidelines disseminated without concurrent implementation strategies, three were consensus conferences that generated little or no change in clinical practice (table 1).[23,24,29] Yet, one reported moderate success in reaching the appropriate target audience[23] and another found that 90% of doctors were "aware of the guidelines" and concluded that dissemination of "guidelines may predispose physicians to consider changing their behaviour but may not effect rapid change in the absence of other incentives."[24]

Rodney et al were able to observe the effect of an educational programme on adult immunisation before the institution of implementation strategies; they observed little improvement in compliance before implementation (redesigning the medical records to highlight health maintenance activities including immunisation) but a significant improvement thereafter (table 2).[33] Only two studies observed significant changes in clinical practice after the dissemination of guidelines without an explicit implementation strategy (table 3).[66,67]

3

Table 3

Development, dissemination, and implementation strategies adopted by rigorous evaluations of guidelines for prescribing and ancillary services[5]

Year	Authors	Subject	Type of guideline	Method of dissemination	Method of implementation	Effect on process
1976	Brook and Williams[59]	Prescribing of injectable antibiotic	Intermediate	Guidelines posted to all doctors and visits to doctors not complying with guidelines	Payment denied for Medicaid claims not complying with guidelines	++++
1980	Lohr and Brook[60]					
1984	Fowkes et al[61]	Skull x ray examinations for patients with head injuries	National external	Guidelines approved by senior staff, two seminars on guidelines	Structured head injury casualty card	++++
1986	Fowkes et al[62]	Preoperative chest x ray examinations	National external	Guidelines approved by senior staff and sent to all consultants	(A) Utilisation review committee	++
					(B) Feedback on individual compliance	++
					(C) New chest x ray examination forms	+
					(D) Review of requests by radiographers	++
1988	Landgren et al[63]	Antibiotic prophylaxis in surgery	Intermediate	Educational marketing programme	Feedback on and discussion of baseline compliance	+++
1990	Bareford and Hayling[64]	Haematological tests	External local	Postal distributing and introductory lecture to junior medical staff	Monthly comparative feedback and inappropriate expensive tests cancelled	+++
1990	Clarke and Adams[65]	Skull x ray examinations for patients with head injuries	Intermediate	Posters and lectures to new casualty doctors	Copy of guidelines distributed to casualty officers	+++
1990	De Vos Meiring and Wells[66]	9 Radiological investigations	External local	Guidelines approved by local medical committee and sent to all general practitioners	None	+++
1992	Cama et al[67]	Cardiac enzyme tests	Intermediate	Presentation to department	None	++++

+	Significant improvement < 10% in absolute terms.	+++	Significant improvement 20-29.9% in absolute terms.
++	Significant improvement 10-19.9% in absolute terms.	++++	Significant improvement ≥ 30% in absolute terms.

In contrast, all the other successful studies we reviewed undertook implementation very soon after dissemination. Our review also suggests that the more overtly educational the dissemination strategy, the greater the likelihood that the guidelines will be adopted within clinical practice, provided that dissemination of guidelines is reinforced by an appropriate implementation strategy.

IMPLEMENTATION STRATEGIES

Implementation strategies are intended to encourage clinicians to change their own clinical practice in line with guidelines, and they may be divided into those that operate during or outside the doctor-patient consultation.

Strategies Operating During Consultation

Implementation strategies operating within the doctor-patient consultation include general reminders of the guidelines, feedback specific to the previous care of individual patients, changes in medical records, and patient specific reminders at the time of consultation.

The simplest strategy is to provide clinicians with easily accessible copies of the guidelines; successful studies have used posters (tables 1, 3)[12,65] or guidelines packaged in a format that can be easily carried.[11,63] Feedback specific to individual patients was successfully used in five studies (tables 1, 2).[9,14,16,31,40] Successful changes to medical records have introduced computerised history taking [20,27,57] or focused on a defined activity or condition (tables 1, 3).[33,61,62]

Several different methods have been used to provide patient specific reminders at the time of consultation. The simplest strategy is to place a copy of the guidelines in the patient's notes (tables 1, 2).[10,32,55,56] For example, Cowan et al who did this with preventive care guidelines (without any further attempt at dissemination) observed significant improvements in the provision of preventive care (table 2).[55] Other studies have placed a checklist, flowsheet, or reminder based on the guidelines in patient's notes.[39,41-45,47,49] In some studies guidelines were embedded in a supplementary medical record or investigation request form. For example, Wirtschafter et al provided Canadian community hospitals with medical record cards containing embedded protocols for specific neonatal emergencies, and they reported significant improvements in managing neonatal respiratory distress syndrome (table 1).[22] Emslie et al reported improvements in general practice management and referral of infertile couples when guidelines were embedded within an infertility management package.[30] Many studies have reminded doctors about previous non-compliance with guidelines at the time of consultation: patients' notes are screened before the consultation, either by a trained health care professional or more often by a computer, and reminders are placed only in those notes not complying with the guidelines (tables 1, 2).[7,8,11,13,15,21,35,38,40,48,50-54,56,58]

Strategies Operating Outside Consultation

Strategies operating outside the consultation that have been rigorously evaluated include aggregated feedback on compliance with guidelines, introducing financial incentives, explicit marketing, and peer review organisations. Feedback of aggregated data on performance is commonly used in medical audit but varies in its evaluated success.[25,26,34,36,52,62,64] Reporting on a direct financial incentive, Brook et al observed a dramatic reduction in the prescription of injectable antibiotics when payment was denied for claims not complying with the guidelines (table 3)[59,60]; reporting on an indirect financial incentive, Cohen et al observed that residents who were offered a credit at the university bookshop showed improved knowledge of the guidelines but only a "modest" increase in compliance (table 2).[37] Several studies have used advertising campaigns to implement guidelines: for example, Landgren et al mounted a successful "educational marketing campaign" to implement guidelines for prophylactic antibiotic use in 12 Australian hospitals (table 3).[63] Although the use of peer review organisations to stimulate change is mostly associated with the United States, the only two rigorous evaluations are British: Fowkes et al showed that a utilisation review committee successfully discouraged chest X ray examinations [62] and Bareford and Hayling that professional monitoring reduced inappropriate laboratory testing.[64]

Relative Effectiveness Of Implementation Strategies

Several studies have compared different implementation strategies. Fowkes et al compared four strategies to promote guidelines for routine preoperative chest x ray examinations — namely, utilisation review committee feedback on individual compliance, introduction of a new x ray examination request form, and review of requests for x ray examinations by radiologists: all were moderately successful, none more so than the other three (table 3).[62] In a sequential study Sommers et al compared the effect on managing unexplained low haemoglobin concentration of two different types of feedback — aggregated versus patient specific feedback: they found that both strategies improved compliance but patient specific feedback was better (table 1).[16] Lomas et al compared the effects of the traditional audit cycle with continuing education led by a local "opinion

leader": they observed significant improvements in compliance with guidelines for caesarean sections only for the opinion leader.[25] MePhee et al compared computer generated reminders placed in patients' notes with aggregated feedback to promote cancer screening, both strategies were successful but reminders were better (table 2).[52] Headrick et al, comparing two strategies to improve compliance with National Cholesterol Education Program guidelines namely, copies of the guidelines and computer generated reminders, both placed in patients' notes – showed that both strategies improved compliance but that reminders were better.[56] Tierney et al compared the effects of two strategies on compliance with preventive care protocols — monthly patient specific feedback and patient specific reminders at the time of consultation — and they found that both strategies improved compliance but that reminders were better.[40]

In summary, implementation strategies operating within the consultation that focus on the management of individual patients are more likely to lead to changes in medical practice. Although there is little evidence on the relative effectiveness of strategies operating outside the consultation, they seem to have contributed substantially to the success of guidelines when they have been used.

DISCUSSION

Clinical guidelines can change medical practice and achieve health gains.[3] However, if guidelines are to achieve health gain through the contracting process purchasers and providers need to identify successful strategies for introducing them into clinical practice. Although literature reviews have begun to identify effective techniques for introducing clinical guidelines and to propose an agenda for future research,[81-83] they have not attempted to quantify the relative effectiveness of different strategies.

In this paper we have shown that the introduction of clinical guidelines is a complex process with three crucial stages: creating a guideline (development), assimilation

Table 4			
Factors influencing the successful introduction of guidelines[6]			
Relative probability of being effective	*Development strategy*	*Dissemination strategy*	*Implementation strategy*
High	Internal	Specific educational intervention	Patient specific reminder at time of consultation
Above average	Intermediate	Continuing medical education	Patient specific feedback
Below average	External local	Posting targeted groups	General feedback
Low	External national	Publication in professional journal	General reminder of guidelines

3

of the guideline by clinicians (dissemination), and ensuring clinicians act on the guideline (implementation). By examining the strategies adopted in rigorous evaluations of clinical guidelines we have previously identified those most likely to change medical practice.[6] This review has reinforced our previous conclusions[6] — namely, that if guidelines are developed internally by the clinicians who are to use them few resources are needed to disseminate or implement them whereas successful introduction of guidelines developed externally needs much more emphasis on dissemination and implementation. Table 4 provides a basic framework for those using guidelines, but the evidence available on the relative effectiveness and efficiency of different strategies is still sparse.

Furthermore, only 10 of the studies reviewed were conducted in the United Kingdom; four of these were concerned with radiological investigations. It is therefore timely to explore this classification more thoroughly in the context of the restructured NHS. The challenge to those who evaluate guidelines in future is to provide rigorous evidence on the relative merits of different combinations of development, dissemination, and implementation strategies.

Despite this call for further research, three conclusions can be drawn. Firstly, clinical guidelines cannot achieve health gains unless they are scientifically valid (in the sense that they are rigorously developed and thus consistent with the available scientific evidence or, without such evidence, best clinical judgement.[5] Secondly, clinical guidelines can achieve health gains if

appropriate development, dissemination, and implementation strategies are adopted during their introduction. Thirdly, implementation strategies provide the key to the successful introduction of intermediate or external which are potentially more valid[5]; in particular, implementation strategies that use information technology to focus on consultations with individual patients rather than general performance are very likely to change practice. This suggests that major advances will stem from the development of real time information systems in both hospital and general practice.

Finally, if guidelines are to achieve maximum benefit within the multidisciplinary NHS[84] careful attention should be given in their introduction to the principles of change management[85]; in particular, successful introduction needs leadership; energy; avoidance of unnecessary uncertainty; good communication, and, above all, time.[72]

We thank Sheila Wallace for help with the literature review, the anonymous reviewer who provided helpful comments, and the Wellcome Trust and Chief Scientist Office of the Home and Health Department of the Scottish Office for funding JMG and ITR. The opinions expressed in this paper are those of the authors and not of the funding bodies.

University of Aberdeen, Foresterhill, Aberdeen AB9 2ZD
Jeremy M Grimshaw, senior lecturer, department of general practice
Ian T Russell, director, health services research unit
Correspondence to: Dr J M Grimshaw, Department of General Practice, University, of Aberdeen, Foresterhill Health Centre, Westburn Road, Aberdeen AB9 2ZD

Accepted for publication 24 March 1994

References

1. Haines A, Feder G. Guidance on guidelines: writing them is easier than making them work. *BMJ* 1992;**305**:785-6.
2. Anonymous. Guidelines for doctors in the new world. *Lancet* 1992;**339**:1197-8
3. Grimshaw JM, Russell IT. Effects of clinical guidelines of medical practice. A systematic review of rigorous evaluations. *Lancet* 1993;**342**;1317-22.
4. NHS Management Executive. *Improving clinical effectiveness.* Leeds: Department of Health, 1993. (EL(93) 115.)
5. Grimshaw JM, Russell IT. Achieving health gain through clinical guidelines: I. Developing scientifically valid guidelines. *Quality in Health Care* 1993;**2**:243-8.
6. Russell IT, Grimshaw JM. The effectiveness of referral guidelines: a review of the methods and findings of published evaluations. In: Roland MO, Coulter A, eds. *Hospital referrals.* Oxford: Oxford University Press, 1992:179-211.
7. McDonald CJ. Use of a computer to detect and respond to clinical events: its effect on clinician behaviour. *Ann Intern Med* 1976;**84**:162-7.
8. McDonald CJ. Protocol-based computer reminders, the quality of care and the non-perfectability of man. *N Engl J Med* 1976;**295**:1351-5.
9. Barnett GO, Winickoff R, Dorsey JL, Morgan M, Lurie RS. Quality assurance through automated monitoring and concurrent feedback using a computer-based medical information system. *Med Care* 1978;**16**:962-70.
10. Sanazaro PJ, Worth RM. Concurrent quality assurance in hospital care. *N Engl J Med* 1978;**298**:1171-7.
11. Hopkins JA, Shoemaker WC, Greenfield S, Chang PC, McAuliffe T, Sproat RW. Treatment of surgical emergencies with and without algorithm. *Arch Surg* 1980;**115**:745-50.
12. Linn BS. Continuing medical education: impact on emergency room burn care. *JAMA* 1980;**244**:565-70.
13. McDonald CJ, Wilson GA, McCabe GP. Physician response to computer reminders. *JAMA* 1980;**244**:1579-81.
14. Barnett GO, Winickoff RN, Morgan MM, Zielstorff RD. A computer-based monitoring system for follow-up of elevated blood pressure. *Med Care* 1983;**21**:400-9.
15. Thomas JC, Moore A, Qualls PE. The effect on cost of medical care for patients treated with an automated clinical audit system. *J Med Syst* 1983;**7**:307-13.
16. Sommers LS, Scholtz R, Shepherd RM, Starkweather DB. Physician involvement in quality assurance. *Med Care* 1984;**22**:1115-38.
17. Norton PG, Dempsey LJ. Self-audit: its effect on quality of care. *J Fam Pract* 1985;**21**:289-91.
18. Palmer RH, Louis TA, Hsu L-N, *et al.* A randomised controlled trial of quality assurance in sixteen ambulatory care practices. *Med Care* 1985;**23**:751-70.
19. Putnam RW, Curry L. Impact of patient care appraisal on physician behaviour in the office setting. *Can Med Assoc J* 1985;**132**:1025-9.
20. Brownbridge G, Evans A, Fitter M, Platts M. An interactive computerised protocol for the management of hypertension: effects on general practitioner's clinical behaviour. *JR Coll Gen Pract* 1986;**36**:198-202.

3

21 McAlister NH, Covvey HD, Tong C, Lee A, Wigle ED. Randomised controlled trial of computer assisted management of hypertension in primary care. *BMJ* 1986;**293**:670-4.

22 Wirtschafter DD, Sumners J, Jackson JR, Brooks CM, Turner M. Continuing medical education using clinical algorithms: a controlled-trial assessment of effect on neonatal care. *Am J Dis Child* 1986;**140**:791-7.

23 Kosecoff J, Kanouse DE, Rogers WH, McCloskey L, Winslow CM, Brook RH. Effects of the National Institutes of Health consensus development program on physician practice. *JAMA* 1987;**258**:2708-13.

24 Lomas J, Anderson GN, Domnick-Pierre K, Vayda E, Enkin MW, Hannah WJ. Do practice guidelines guide practice? The effect of a consensus statement on the practice of physicians. *N Engl J Med* 1989;**321**:1306-11.

25 Lomas J, Enkin M, Anderson GN, Hannah WJ, Vayda E, Singer J. Opinion leaders vs audit and feedback to implement practice guidelines: delivery after previous caesarean section. *JAMA* 1991;**265**:2202-7.

26 Durand-Zaleski I, Bonnet F, Rochant H, Bierling P, Lemaire F. Usefulness of consensus conferences: the case of albumin. *Lancet* 1992;**340**:1388-90.

27 Margolis CZ, Warshawsky SS, Goldman L, Dagan O, Wirtschafter D, Pliskin JS. Computerised algorithms and paediatricians' management of common problems in a community clinic. *Acad Med* 1992;**67**:282-4.

28 North of England Study of Standards and Performance in General Practice. Medical audit in general practice: effects on doctors' clinical behaviour and the health of patients with common childhood conditions. *BMJ* 1992;**304**:1480-8.

29 Sherman CR, Potosky AL, Weis KA, Ferguson JH. The consensus development programme: detecting changes in medical practice following a consensus conference on the treatment of prostate cancer. *Int J Tech Assess in Health Care* 1992;**8**:683-93.

30 Emslie CJ, Grimshaw J, Templeton A. Do clinical guidelines improve general practice management and referral of infertile couples? *BMJ* 1993;**306**:1728-31.

31 Morgan M, Studney DR, Barnett GO, Winickoff RN. Computerised concurrent review of prenatal care. *Qual Rev Bull* 1978;**4**:33-6.

32 Cohen DI, Littenberg B, Wetzel C, Neuhauser DB. Improving physician compliance with preventive medicine guidelines. *Med Care* 1982;**20**:1040-5.

33 Rodney WM, Chopivsky P, Quan M. Adult immunisation: the medical record design as a factor for physician compliance. *J Med Educ* 1983;**58**:576-80.

34 Thompson RS, Kirz HL, Gold RA. Changes in physician behaviour and cost savings associated with organisational recommendations on the use of routine chest x-rays and multichannel blood tests. *Prev Med* 1983;**12**:385-96.

35 McDonald CJ, Hui SJ, Smith DM, *et al.* Reminders to physicians from an introspective computer medical record: a two year randomised trial. *Ann Intern Med* 1984;**100**:130-8.

36 Winickoff RN, Coltin KL, Morgan M, Buxbaum RC, Barnett GO. Improving physician performance through peer comparison feedback. *Med Care* 1984;**22**:527-34.

37 Cohen SJ, Weinberger M, Hui SL, Tierney WM, McDonald CJ. The impact of reading on physicians' non-adherence to recommended standards of medical care. *Soc Sci Med* 1985;**21**:909-14.

38 McDowell I, Newell C, Rosser W. Comparison of three methods of recalling patients for influenza vaccination. *Can Med Assoc J* 1986;**135**:991-7.

39 Prislin MD, Vandenbark MS, Clarkson QC. The impact of health screening flow sheet on the performance and documentation of health screening procedures. *Fam Med* 1986;**18**:290-2.

40 Tierney WM, Hui SL, McDonald CJ. Delayed feedback of physician performance versus immediate reminders to perform preventive care. *Med Care* 1986;**24**:659-66.

41 Cheney C, Ramsdell JW. Effect of medical records' checklists on implementation of period health measures. *Am J Med* 1987;**83**:129-36.

42 Cohen SJ, Christen AG, Katz BP, *et al.* Counselling medical and dental patients about cigarette smoking: the impact of nicotine gum and chart reminders. *Am J Public Health* 1987;**77**:313-6.

43 Cohen SJ, Stookey GK, Katz BP, Drook CA, Smith DM. Encouraging primary care physicians to help smokers quit: a randomised controlled trial. *Ann Intern Med* 1989;**110**:648-52.

44 Robie PW. Improving and sustaining outpatient cancer screening by medicine residents. *South Med J* 1988;**81**:902-5.

45 Schreiner DT, Petrusa ER, Rettie CS, Kluge RM. Improving compliance with preventive medicine procedures in a house staff training program. *South Med J* 1988;**81**:1553-7.

46 Wilson DM, Taylor DW, Gilbert JR, *et al.* A randomised trial of a family physician intervention for smoking cessation. *JAMA* 1988;**260**:1570-4.

47 Becker DM, Gomez EB, Kaiser DL, Yoshihasi A, Hodge RH. Improving preventive care at a medical clinic: how can the patient help? *Am J Prev Med* 1989;**5**:353-9.

48 Chambers CV, Balaban DJ, Carlson BL, Ungemack JA, Grasberger DM. Microcomputer-generated reminders: improving the compliance of primary care physicians with mammography screening guidelines. *J Fam Pract* 1989;**29**:273-80.

49 Cummings SR, Coates TJ, Richard RJ, *et al.* Training physicians in counselling about smoking cessation: a randomised trial of the "Quit for life" program. *Ann Intern Med* 1989;**110**:640-7.

50 McDowell I, Newell C, Rosser W. A randomized trial of computerised reminders for blood pressure screening in primary care. *Med Care* 1989;**27**:297-305.

51 McDowell I, Newell C, Rosser W. Computerized reminders to encourage cervical screening in family practice. *J Fam Pract* 1989;**28**:420-4.

52 McPhee SJ, Bird JA, Fordham D, Rodnick JE, Osborn EH. Promoting cancer screening: a randomized controlled trial of three interventions. *Arch Intern Med* 1989;**149**:1866-72.

53 McPhee SJ, Bird JA, Fordham D, Rodnick JE, Osborn EH. Promoting cancer prevention activities by primary care physicians: results of a randomized controlled trial. *JAMA* 1991;**266**:538-44.

54 Rosser WW, McDowell I, Newell C. Use of reminders for preventive procedures in family medicine. *Can Med Assoc J* 1991;**145**:807-14.

55 Cowan JA, Heckerling PS, Parker JB. Effect of a fact sheet reminder on performance of the periodic health examination: a randomized controlled trial. *Am J Prev Med* 1992;**8**:104-9.

56 Headrick LA, Speroff T, Pelecanos HI, Cebul RD. Efforts to improve compliance with national cholesterol program guidelines: results of a randomized controlled trial. *Arch Intern Med* 1992;**152**:2490-6.

57 Liford RJ, Kelly M, Baines A, *et al.* Effect of using protocols on medical care: randomised trial of there methods of taking an antenatal history. *BMJ* 1992;**305**:1181-4.

58 Rosser WW, Hutchison BG, McDowell I, Newell C. Use of reminders to increase compliance with tetanus booster vaccination. *Can Med Assoc J* 1992;**146**:911-7.

59 Brook RH, Williams KN. Effect of medical care review on the use of injections: a study of the New Mexico Experimental Care Review Organisation. *Ann Intern Med* 1976;**85**:509-15.

60 Lohr KN, Brook RH. Quality of care in episode of respiratory illness among Medicaid patients in New Mexico. *Ann Intern Med* 1980;**92**:99-106.

61 Fowkes FGR, Williams LA, Cooke BRB, Evans RC, Gehlbach SH, Roberts CJ. Implementation of guidelines for the use of skull radiographs in patients with head injuries. *Lancet* 1984;**ii**:795-7.

62 Fowkes FGR, Davies ER, Evans KT, *et al.* Multicentre trial of four strategies to reduce use of a radiological test. *Lancet* 1986;**i**:367-70.

63 Landgren FT, Harvey KJ, Mashford ML, Moulds RFW, Guthrie B, Hemming M. Changing antibiotic prescribing by educational marketing. *Med J Aust* 1988;**149**:595-9.

64 Bareford D, Hayling A. Inappropriate use of laboratory services: long term combined approach to modify request patterns. *BMJ* 1990;**301**:1305-7.

65 Clarke JA, Adams JE. The application of clinical guidelines for skull radiography in the accident and emergency department: theory and practice. *Clin Radiology* 1990;**41**:152-5.

66 De Vos Meiring P, Wells IP. The effect of radiology guidelines for general practitioners. *Journal of Clinical Radiology* 1990;**42**;327-9.

67 Gama R, Nightingale PG, Ratcliffe JG. Effect of educational feedback on clinicians' requesting of cardiac enzymes. *Ann Clin Biochem* 1992;**29**:224-5.

68 Brook RH. Practice guidelines and practising medicine: are they compatible? *JAMA* 1989;**262**:3027-30.

69 Grol R. Quality assurance: approaches to standard setting, assessment and change. *Atencion Primari* 1990;**7**:737-41.

70 North of England Study of Standards and Performance in General Practice. *An overview of the study.* Newcastle upon Tyne: Centre for Health Services Research, 1991. (Report 50.)

71 Newton JC, Hutchinson A, Steen IN, Russell IT, Haines EV. Educational potential of medical audit: observations from a study of small groups setting standards. *Quality in Health Care* 1992;**1**:256-9.

72 Russell IT, Grimshaw JM, Wilson BJ. Scientific and methodological issues in quality assurance. In: Beck JS, Bouchier IAD, Russell IT, eds. Quality assurance in medical care. *Proceedings of the Royal Society of Edinburgh* 1993;**101B**:77-103.

73 Clinical resource and Audit Group. *Clinical guidelines.* Edinburgh: Scottish Office Home and Health Department, 1993.

74 Schoenbaum SC, Gottieb LK. Algorithm based improvement of clinical quality. *BMJ* 1990;**301**:1374-6.

75 Margolis CZ, Cook CD, Barak N, Adler A, Geertsma A. Clinical algorithms teach paediatric decision making more effectively than prose. *Med Care* 1989;**27**:576-92.

76 North of England Study of Standards and Performance in General Practice. *Final Report: I – setting clinical standards in small groups.* Newcastle upon Tyne: Health Care Research Unit, 1990. (Report 40.)

77 Institute of Medicine. *Guidelines for clinical practice: from development to use.* Washington, DC: National Academy Press, 1992:248-9.

78 Hadorn DC, McCormick K, Diokno A. An annotated algorithm approach to clinical guideline development. *JAMA* 1992;**267**:3311-4.

79 Kahan JP, Kanouse DE, Winkler JD. Stylistic variations in National Institutes of Health consensus statements, 1979-1983. *Int J Technol Assess Health Care* 1988;**4**:289-304.

80 Kanouse DE, Jacoby I. When does information change practitioners' behaviour? *Int J Technol Assess Health Care* 1988;**4**:27-33.

81 Lomas J, Haynes RB. A taxonomy and critical review of tested strategies for the application of clinical practice recommendations: from "official" to "individual" clinical policy. *Am J Prev Med* 1987;**4**:77-94.

82 Grol R. Implementing guidelines in general practice care. *Quality in Health Care* 1992;**1**:184-91.

83 Mittman BS, Tonesk X, Jacobson PD. Implementing clinical practice guidelines: social influence strategies and practitioner behaviour change. *Qual Rev Bull* 1992;**18**:413-22.

84 McNicol M, Layton A, Morgan G. Team working: the key to implementing guidelines. *Quality in Health Care* 1993;**2**:215-6.

85 Bechard R, Harris J. *Organisational transitions: managing complex change.* 2nd ed. London: Addison-Wesley, 1989.

This article was first published in Spine *and is reproduced by permission of Lippincott Williams and Williams*

THERAPEUTIC TRIALS FOR LOW BACK PAIN

Spine 1994;**19**:2068S–2075S

Richard M. Hoffman, MD, MPH, Judith A. Turner, PhD, Daniel C. Cherkin, PhD,
Richard A. Deyo, MD, MPH, and Larry D. Herron, MD

4

Little consensus exists regarding the indications for and effectiveness of many back pain treatments. This clinical uncertainty arises because most back pain research has been flawed by poor methodology. The authors discuss strategies for improving the quality of back pain research on treatment efficacy. Design features, including randomized treatment allocation, independent outcome assessors, comprehensive outcome, measures, appropriate statistical analyses, and close patient follow-up can increase study validity. Complete descriptions of enrollment criteria, patient characteristics, and clinical interventions can increase the generalizability of results. Although large scale trials often involve university centers, community-based researchers can collaborate on randomized trials or conduct valuable cohort studies. [Key words: low back pain, spine surgery, randomized trials, health status measures, study design]
Spine 1994;19:2068S–2075S

Numerous treatments are available for patients with low back pain, but there is often only modest consensus on their indications or effectiveness.[11,18,33] Despite an extensive literature, most therapies lack scientific evidence for efficacy because much of the published research is flawed by poor design and suboptimal outcome measures (Table 1).[11,22,42,43] Additionally, substantial deficits in data reporting limit the applicability of study findings for clinical practice.[11]

Improving the quality of clinical back pain research is crucial to resolving uncertainty surrounding the treatment of back pain. This paper discusses features of study design and data reporting that are important for valid research. The first section presents strategies to increase a study's validity, defined as the extent to which its results are accurate. The second section discusses methods to increase a study's generalizability, defined as the extent to which its conclusions are applicable to clinical practice. Throughout, we highlight specific difficulties inherent in studying low back pain and propose solutions.

VALIDITY

Validity implies that study results are accurate because systematic errors, or biases, have been minimized (Table 2). Bias can occur in patient selection, study methods

and treatments, and in outcome assessment. In the following section, we discuss important sources of bias, their effects on study validity and how to avoid them.

Cohort Assembly

The first step in a therapeutic trial is deciding which population to study. This is not an easy decision because the syndrome of low back pain encompasses a wide spectrum of etiologies and severity. Explicit inclusion and exclusion criteria are necessary to select an appropriate population; otherwise, even a well-designed study of an effective intervention may produce inconclusive results. For example, investigators studying a treatment directed at relieving acute lumbar strain would want to exclude patients with vertebral fractures or neurologic deficits.

Study Design

The most valid research designs for evaluating treatments are cohort, or follow-up, studies and randomized controlled trials. A cohort study can compare outcomes between subjects receiving the study intervention and a comparison group receiving alternative treatments or a placebo. These cohort studies can be retrospective, selecting subjects treated in the past and following them to the present, or prospective, beginning in the present and following subjects into the future. Comparison groups in cohort studies can be either concurrent or historical. In any event, the assignment to treatment groups is naturalistic and not controlled by the investigators. In contrast, the randomized controlled trial, or experimental design, is always prospective, investigators assign treatments, and experimental subjects are compared with concurrent controls.

The weakest study design, but perhaps the most prevalent in the back pain literature, is the case series. A case series is a cohort study without a comparison group. Although the case series can provide useful information on technique, costs, and complications, efficacy data are of uncertain meaning because there is no comparison with results from an alternative control treatment. In a case series, there is no way to determine the extent that patient outcomes reflect treatment effects, placebo effects, or natural history.[2,18]

Retrospective studies with comparison groups, either concurrent or historical, are also flawed. Evidence from

Table 1

Methodologic Flaws in Back Pain Literature: Literature Synthesis of Discectomy for Herniated Lumbar Discs (81 total studies)[22]

Study Design Feature	N (%) Studies with Feature
Random allocation to treatment group	2(2)
Comparison group	19(23)
Prospective design	14(17)
Inclusion or exclusion criteria described	57(70)
Statistical analysis	22(27)
Independent outcome assessment	5(6)
Comprehensive outcome assessment (symptoms, activity and/or employment)	27(40)*†
Uniform follow-up evaluations	19(28)*
Standard follow-up intervals	13(19)*

* Excluding 11 studies with only complication data.
† Excluding 3 studies with only reoperation data.

a lumbar spinal-fusion literature review suggests that retrospective studies may overestimate treatment benefits, reporting significantly more satisfactory outcomes (mean, 72.6%) than prospective studies (mean, 54.1%).[42] In retrospective studies, decisions about patient selection and treatment allocation are unlikely to have produced completely equivalent groups, and uniform collection of relevant data is unlikely since subjects were not part of a study protocol.[19,33,37] A study using historical comparison groups is further susceptible to biases arising from temporal changes in the demographics and clinical characteristics of patients chosen for therapy, in patient management strategies, and in overall health care.[33] A well-designed prospective study has the advantage of determining, in advance, patient inclusion criteria, the type of data to be collected, treatment algorithms, specific outcome measures, and follow-up schedules.[8,37]

Despite these advantages, even prospective follow-up studies cannot provide definitive evidence of treatment efficacy, because biases may arise when patient groups are dissimilar at baseline.[11,33,37] For instance, if one treatment group has more patients at risk for poor outcomes, perhaps due to past failed back surgeries or unresolved litigation or compensation claims, patients in that group are less likely to have good outcomes regardless of the specific treatment. Non-randomized comparisons of surgical and medical treatments often lead to biased treatment assignments because high risk patients are unlikely to be considered for surgery.[5] The strength of the randomized controlled trial is that both known and unknown risk factors are balanced across treatment groups, so that any differences in outcomes are more likely to be attributable to the specific interventions.[3,19,37,38]

The impact of bias from dissimilar patient groups is evident from comparing results of randomized and non-randomized trials. Smaller treatment benefits are

consistently found in the randomized trials.[7,11,27,28] Further, while reported rates of successful outcomes from non-randomized studies of back pain treatments such as chymopapain, traction, and facet injections have varied, the results from randomized trials have been more con cordant.[6,10,16,23,25,26,29,31,44,47,48]

Nonrandomized designs are not the only threat to internal validity. When investigators both provide the treatment and evaluate the outcome, their knowledge, beliefs, or self-interest may influence the intensity and result of the search for particular outcomes.[11,18,19,27,30,33,37] Readers should be skeptical when the only reported assessment is the investigator's subjective rating of treatment effectiveness. These biases can be avoided by using an independent observer to assess outcomes. Patient assessments are also useful, but surgical patients

Table 2

Study Features that Minimize Methodologic Bias

1. **Explicit inclusion and exclusion criteria.** The investigators should clearly establish that an appropriate population has been selected
2. **Random allocation of treatment.** Randomization is the best way to equally distribute prognostic factors between the treatment and control groups, and minimize biases due to baseline differences
3. **Independent outcome assessment.** Blinding investigators to treatment status reduces bias in measuring outcomes; in surgical trials an independent observer is required to rate outcomes.
4. **Equal co-treatments.** Many back pain therapies are available for study patients; if these co-treatments are not applied equally then study results are biased.
5. **Minimal contamination.** Study results are also biased when subjects intentionally or inadvertently use the alternative treatment, either in addition to or instead of the one assigned.
6. **Compliance.** Therapy is not effective if not received. Investigators should encourage compliance, particularly with physical treatments and behavioral modification, and assess the level of patient compliance to avoid misinterpreting study results.
7. **Outcome measurements.** Back pain is rarely completely cured; comprehensive patient outcomes should be assessed, including quality of life, functional ability, and work status, as well as relief of symptoms.
8. **Adequate follow-up duration.** Enough time should be allowed to accomodate the natural history of the disease, at least two years are recommended following surgical back procedures.
9. **Minimal patient attrition.** High attrition rates in back pain studies may be due to either very good or very bad outcomes; drop-outs bias the remaining sample.
10. **Appropriate statistical analyses.** Investigators should report the statistical significance of their results, and estimate the statistical power for negative studies.

may be reluctant to report poor outcomes. These patients may not want to admit that they underwent an unhelpful procedure or to risk displeasing their surgeon. When patient assessments are used, the patients should be assured that their individual responses will be kept confidential.

The "gold-standard" study design, offering the strongest evidence for treatment effectiveness, is the double-blind, randomized placebo-controlled trial. In this design, patients, treating clinicians, and outcome assessors are blinded to the actual treatment that each patient receives. This study design is the standard for drug trials and has been successfully adapted for interventions such as transcutaneous electrical nerve stimulation units, biofeedback, intradiscal injections of chymopapain, facet joint injections, and traction.[13,23]

Obviously, such study designs are not readily applicable to surgical treatments. Placebo surgery is considered unethical, and double blinding is impossible. Randomized comparisons between surgery and nonsurgical treatments are feasible, however, as are randomized comparisons of different surgical procedures. Treatment outcomes can be evaluated by independent raters. Nonetheless, few orthopedic procedures have been subjected to randomized comparisons.[2,19,33] Only seven randomized trials of surgery for herniated discs have been published,[10,16,29,34,41,44,46] and none have been reported for spinal fusion or spinal stenosis.[42,43]

A major barrier to performing experimental trials comparing surgical procedures is the need for random treatment allocation. Typically, subjects are referred to a physician and then randomly allocated to either an experimental or control procedure. This raises a number of troublesome issues for surgeons, who may be more skilled and comfortable with one procedure than with another. With random treatment allocation, the surgeon is expected to perform both procedures with equal skill, but when the level of skill is not equal, a bias emerges favoring operations that are in wider use or technically simpler.[19,37,45] Further, conducting a randomized controlled trial during the evolutionary phase of a new technology is difficult because the learning curve is steep. As techniques are further refined and surgeons become more experienced, fewer complications and better outcomes may be expected.[3,15,37,45] Thus, early results from a new procedure may underestimate its potential effectiveness.

Surgeons also have ethical concerns about enrolling patients in randomized controlled trials. The risks and irreversibility of surgery demand that the surgeon be convinced of the effectiveness of both alternative operations (or treatments). When a surgeon has doubts about performing one of the assigned procedures, obtaining informed consent becomes problematic. Other troublesome issues raised by surgeons include concerns about assuming legal liability and personal responsibility for a poor outcome, appearing unsure and indecisive to patients, disliking to openly discuss

uncertainty, having practical difficulties in following study protocols and feeling conflict between the roles of clinician and scientist.[8,20,37,40]

Fortunately, many of the technical and ethical concerns about random allocation can be overcome by an alternative randomization scheme. In the randomized surgeon clinical trial, patients are randomly allocated to two groups of surgeons, each group specializing in a different procedure. The surgeons in each group are thus offering only one procedure, which they can perform adeptly and with conviction. The study must ensure, though, that the skill levels are comparable between the competing surgical groups.[19,37,45]

Other designs that may facilitate randomized trials of surgical interventions include the technique "prerandomization" in which patients are randomly allocated to standard therapy or experimental therapy before seeking consent. This design poses ethical problems and can produce statistical inefficiencies that must be accounted for in sample size planning, but may enhance the feasibility of surgical randomized trials.[8] Still another design would involve randomly allocating entire groups of physicians, clinics, or hospitals to alternative treatment interventions. Again, such a design requires specialized statistical techniques for sample size planning and data analysis but can still help to reduce bias in treatment assignment.[14]

These designs can make randomized trials more attractive to surgeons. Encouraging further randomized surgical trials is important because most current treatments for low back pain lack empirical support for benefits beyond improvements associated with natural history or nonspecific treatment effects.[2,18,21,33,37] When there is uncertainty about the optimal treatment and more than one procedure can be clinically justified, a randomized trial is both ethical and necessary.[37]

The Design of Treatment Interventions

Even randomized, blinded trials may be flawed by treatment biases. The presence of co-treatments, contamination of the study groups, or noncompliance can bias results, making it difficult to determine whether clinical outcomes are due to the assigned treatments alone. Co-treatments, or therapies not included in the study protocol, are readily available for back pain and include nonprescription medications, various psychotherapies, corsets, physical therapists, chiropractic treatment, and acupuncturists. Co-treatments can potentially interact with the study treatments, and/or may not be uniformly applied to all patients. Contamination occurs in comparative studies when patients intentionally or inadvertently use the alternative treatment, either in addition to or instead of the one assigned. Another source of bias arises when patients are poorly compliant with assigned treatments. In this case, poor outcomes may reflect either an ineffective treatment or poor compliance with an effective treatment.

These sources of treatment bias are difficult to control. Co-treatments and contamination should be

4

explicitly prohibited, but investigators also should be prepared to carefully document their occurrence to allow for statistical adjustments.[6,11] Extensive investigator efforts may be needed to enhance patient compliance, particularly with physical treatments and behavioral modification. Carefully instructing patients on performing the intervention, discussing treatment benefits, positively reinforcing patient participation, using patient diaries and scheduling frequent follow-up may help ensure patient compliance. Investigators should assess and report on compliance, particularly for nonsurgical treatments. With drug trials, investigators can count pills and measure drug blood levels. Measuring compliance with physical treatments and behavioral interventions is difficult, but can be estimated from diaries and family reports, patient demonstrations of exercise performance, and appointment keeping.[11]

A final related issue is treatment performance bias. In surgical comparison trials, investigators should use comparably skilled surgeons in each assigned treatment group and also ensure that all subjects are receiving the best available technology and supportive care.[37] When using a nonsurgical comparison group, the investigators should ensure that the comparison treatment is appropriate for the clinical condition and that it is being performed properly. By avoiding any "undertreatment" of the comparison group, investigators minimize the chance of unfairly favoring the experimental intervention.

Outcome Measurements

Determining and measuring appropriate outcomes for back pain treatment is challenging. Back pain is rarely due to a fatal disease and rarely permanently cured. Few physiologic tests of spine function, including laboratory and physical measurements, are clinically meaningful to patients. A variety of other outcomes are more relevant, including relief of specific symptoms (back pain, leg pain), improvement in functional ability, work status (including type of work), improvements on psychosocial measures, and use of health care resources and medication. The overall utility of a given treatment can be fully characterized only when its effects on health-related quality of life are assessed.[11,27]

Quality of life may be difficult to measure, and many investigators consider it a "soft" endpoint. However, if "hardness" is defined by a high level of measurement reproducibility, then well-constructed scales to quantify symptoms and daily functioning may be equal to more traditional measures.[11] A number of objective, psychometrically valid, and reliable outcome assessment measures are available to back pain researchers, including the Sickness Impact Profile, and the Roland-Morris and Oswestry scales.[1,17,35] The North American Spine Society is also developing an outcome questionnaire for clinical studies of back pain treatments that may soon become widely available. These or similar outcome measurements should be used consistently pre- and post-intervention and at regular intervals during

long-term follow-up. This increases study validity and allows comparisons across studies.[11,30,37,42]

Patient Follow-up

Inadequate follow-up time can be a major problem in therapeutic trials. Although there is no hard rule for length of follow-up, enough time should be allowed to accommodate the natural history of the disease and to assess all clinically relevant outcomes.[2,33] Interventions for acute low back pain may require frequent, early follow-ups because the natural history is so favorable.[11] Surgery, however, is performed with the intention of relieving pain, increasing function, and improving quality of life. Long-term results are the most relevant to both the study subjects and the surgeon.[37] Shorter surgical follow-up will underestimate the rate of reoperations and will not accurately reflect the long-term course of complications and outcomes. For example, national Medicare claims data show a crossover in reoperation rates after lumbar spine surgery. Initially, higher rates were observed among laminectomy or discectomy patients not receiving fusion than among patients receiving fusion. However, by two years of follow-up, reoperation rates were similar, and thereafter patients who had fusions were more likely to undergo reoperation.[12] Editors of several leading orthopedic journals recommend a minimum follow-up of 2 years for published reports of treatment for chronic symptoms.[9,30]

Another challenge for back-pain treatment trials is achieving an adequate follow-up rate.[18] When substantial numbers of study subjects are unavailable for follow-up, interpreting outcomes becomes difficult. Although there is no specific drop-out rate that automatically threatens validity, attrition of more than 15% is troubling.[11] A further problem occurs when the treatment outcome itself, either good or bad, creates a differential loss to follow-up across study groups. For example, many acute back pain patients may improve rapidly and lose interest in the study, failing to continue with their treatments or not returning for follow-up. Chronic pain patients may drop out of a study if they feel that the treatment is not helpful.[11] As a result of the differential loss to follow-up, any conclusions about effectiveness may be unreliable.[18] Retrospective studies, in which patients are selected by virtue of being available for follow-up, are especially susceptible to this form of bias.

When a study has a high attrition rate or a differential loss to follow-up, investigators should assess whether outcomes were biased. Evaluating for bias requires recording accurate and complete information for all patients lost to follow-up, including their initial characteristics, status when last seen, and reason for loss.[18] If no significant differences emerge between patients lost to follow-up and those remaining in the study, then the investigators may be somewhat reassured that bias from attrition was minimal.[19,30,37] Another safeguard against misinterpreting results is performing a worst-case analysis. This analysis assumes that all subjects lost to follow-up are unimproved, regardless of their treatment group. Conclusions about treatment effectiveness are more convincing if they persist after a worst-case analysis.[30]

An example of a worst-case analysis comes from a surgical case series evaluating discectomy for herniated lumbar discs. Questionnaires were sent to 886 patients. Overall, 344 of 695 responding patients were considered "cured," and the authors concluded that 56% of patients were improved by surgery. However, data were unavailable from 266 patients; if none of these patients were improved, then the overall "cure" rate was only 39%.[39] Obviously, without data from these missing patients, the treatment results are uninterpretable.

Ultimately, the best way to avoid follow-up bias is by keeping the patients in the study. Strategies for this include using monetary reimbursements and telephoning or sending written reminders. Aggressive attempts at locating patients and flexibility in accommodating to their schedules are also helpful for achieving high rates of follow-up.[11]

Statistical Analysis

Selecting appropriate statistical tests is often overlooked in designing back pain treatment trials. To maximize the validity of a study, we recommend having a biostatistician participate in study planning and data analysis. Investigators should always report their statistical methods and discuss the statistical significance (or confidence limits) of their results.

Statistical significance is described in terms of the "α-level" and the "statistical power" of the study. The α-level is the probability (P) that an observed outcome difference could be due to chance alone. Conventionally, the α-level is set at 0.05, which means that the risk of obtaining a false-positive result, or a type 1 error, is less than 1 in 20. If a study reports a positive treatment effect with a p value, or the risk of a type 1 error, less than 0.05, then the effect is considered statistically significant.

The power of a statistical test refers to whether an adequate sample size has been enrolled to avoid a type II error. This error occurs when small sample sizes prevent a study from demonstrating a statistically significant difference between treatment outcomes even though a clinically important difference actually exists. Often, a power of 80% is used for estimating sample size requirements, implying that the risk of a type II error (false-negative result) is no greater than 20%.[3,18,27,33] Calculations of statistical power depends not only on sample size, but also on the magnitude of treatment effects and on the extent of variability in outcomes. Power calculations should be done in the study planning phase, before subject enrollment begins. This allows investigators to develop strategies for ensuring that a sufficient number of subjects are enrolled to address the objectives of the study. Statistical textbooks and software programs are available for power calculations.[4,24] An adequate sample size (generally ≥ 30) is also necessary for case series to ensure that the point estimates for

---

Table 3

Study Features to Enhance Generalizability

1. **Cohort assembly.** The clinical spectrum of back pain is vast; investigators must describe the study's source of patients and eligibility criteria.
2. **Demographics and clinical characteristics.** Data should be provided on age, gender, employment and litigation status, symptoms, physical findings, and past medical history, particularly previous back surgery.
3. **Diagnostic testing and treatments.** Techniques, application, and findings of diagnostic tests should be reported. Treatment descriptions should be clear enough to allow replication by others.
4. **Outcomes.** Criteria for outcome assessments should be described, and all relevant clinical outcomes and important complications reported.

---

outcomes (e.g., the percentage of patients with the given outcome or complication) have small confidence intervals, implying reasonable accuracy.

Statistical tests of significance are most valid in randomized trials where there are no important differences between the groups in baseline characteristics, study participation, and follow-up rates. Under these conditions, differences in outcomes between groups can be attributed directly to treatment effects. These outcome differences then can be further described by a probability distribution that can be tested for statistical significance. In nonexperimental studies, outcomes are dependent on both treatment effects and known and unknown prognostic factors. In these studies, statistical analyses can be used to determine whether significant changes occurred after treatment, but not whether these changes can be attributed directly to the treatment. Predictor variables for specific outcomes can be identified in nonexperimental studies by using correlation and regression analyses.[5]

GENERALIZABILITY

Generalizability refers to whether trial estimates of treatment effectiveness and safety can be extrapolated to broader clinical practice (Table 3).[33,36] Even though rigorous methodologic design can minimize bias, valid results are not necessarily generalizable ones. To increase external validity, investigators should select patients representative of an appropriate clinical population, and include all (or a random sample of) eligible subjects.[2,18] Choosing a representative study sample, however, is not the only criterion for generalizability. Investigators also need to define the study subjects and treatments clearly enough that readers can determine whether the subjects are recognizable and the interventions feasible in their practice.[30]

The complexity of diagnosing back pain and assessing treatments provides additional challenges to

Table 4

Quebec Task Force Classification of Spinal Disorders*

Class	Symptom	Duration	Work Status
1.	LBP, no radiation	<7 days	Working, not working
2.	LBP, radiation to thigh	7 days-7 weeks	
3.	LBP, radiation to calf foot	>7 weeks	
4.	LBP, radiation to leg, + neuro deficit		
5.	Presumed radicular compression on plain x-ray (spinal instability or fracture)		
6.	Confirmed radicular compression (CT, myelogram, or MRI)		
7.	Spinal stenosis		
8.	Postsurgical status, <6 months		
9.	Postsurgical status, >6 months a. Asymptomatic b. Symptomatic		
10.	Chronic pain syndrome		Working, not working
11.	Other diagnoses		

Adapted from reference 32.
LBP = low back pain.

clinical practice, and they also provide prognostic information. For example, the adverse effects of disability compensation or litigation on back treatment outcomes are well documented, as are higher surgical complication rates among older patients.[11]

Clinical Description

Because low back pain is a nonspecific complaint, clinical data should include relevant physical signs, especially neurologic deficits (motor, sensory, and reflexes) and abnormal straight leg raising. Symptoms of back pain, sciatica, and neurologic deficits should be reported separately, and characterized by severity and time course. These signs and symptoms are important prognostic indicators for back pain. Previous back surgery should be reported, as should medical comorbidity (because it may significantly affect quality of life measurements). One symptom-based classification scheme incorporating many of these elements has been developed by the Quebec Task Force (Table 4).[32] Despite the obvious importance of reporting detailed baseline data, a literature synthesis of surgery for herniated lumbar discs found that only 5 of 81 studies reported age, sex, specific symptoms and duration, and whether patients were involved in litigation or compensation claims or had a history of previous back surgery.[22]

Diagnostic Testing

Back pain can be evaluated by clinical examination, anatomic imaging, and physiologic testing. The reproducibility and accuracy of these diagnostic approaches vary considerably. Consequently, investigators should specify which diagnostic tests were used in the study, the number of subjects undergoing each test, criteria for abnormality, and the number of patients with abnormal tests.

generalizability. The differential diagnosis for back pain is lengthy with poor agreement on classification criteria, and diagnostic test findings and clinical symptoms are often discordant. Even though a definitive diagnosis may be unattainable, investigators should establish reasonable exclusion criteria, and provide an adequate description of patient characteristics, including known clinical classifications and prognostic features.[11] Generalizability is also increased by selecting measures of health status that assess symptoms, functional ability, and work status.

Cohort Assembly

Because the clinical spectrum of back pain is vast, a study's source of subjects and eligibility criteria must be explicitly defined.[18,27,33] The source of patients, whether ambulatory care clinics, emergency rooms, specialists' offices, or hospitals, needs to be described. Furthermore, the clinical symptoms, physical findings, and diagnostic test results necessary for study inclusion should be listed. The investigators should describe how many patients were approached to participate in the study, how many accepted study enrollment, and how many actually began treatment. Documentation on all ineligible patients, and the reasons for their exclusion helps the reader evaluate the results.[33]

Demographics

The description of study subjects should include age, gender, education level, ethnicity, and employment and litigation status. These data are crucial for evaluating whether study patients are representative of the reader's

Treatment

All treatments, including the study intervention and any relevant adjunctive therapies, should be documented. Each treatment component should be described clearly enough to permit replication of the study by others.[2,27,30] Knowing the level of patient compliance with the study treatments also helps the reader. When compliance is poor, the authors should try to explain why, and offer suggestions for increasing compliance in clinical practice. Describing where the treatment was provided (e.g., physician's office, hospital ward, therapist's office) is also helpful in interpreting results, especially if the experimental and comparison groups were treated in different settings.

Complications

All important complications or side-effects during the period of treatment and subsequent follow-up should be reported.[18] Data should be tabulated to list each complication and its occurrence rate. The absence of potentially expected important complications (those requiring urgent treatment or prolonging hospitalization) should also be reported to inform readers that these were considered but did not occur.

Outcomes

Investigators should indicate which outcome measures were used, and when and where they were administered. All subjects entered into the study should be accounted for and all clinically relevant outcomes should be reported, including any repeat or additional back treatments. For these subsequent treatments, the specific intervention, indications, and timing should be detailed. For dichotomous outcomes (e.g., reoperated or not, returned to work or not), an effective way of presenting these data is by constructing a life-table that lists the number of patients evaluated during each post-treatment year, the number of unsuccessful outcomes, and the number of patients who were lost to follow-up. [24] Life-tables permit calculations of yearly and cumulative rates of success and failure, including occurrence of repeat treatments. These data can be used to compare outcomes across studies and to discuss prognosis with patients contemplating the treatment. [18]

CONCLUSIONS

We have discussed some principles of designing and reporting studies to improve the quality of back pain research. The generalizability of study results can be increased through careful attention to cohort assembly and data reporting. Randomized controlled trial designs with independent outcome raters can provide valid evidence of treatment effectiveness. Such trials, which can successfully be adapted for surgical interventions, do present logistic problems. An appropriate research team, including adequate biostatistical and data analysis support, must be assembled. Often these trials are lengthy and involve many patients.

Collaborative multicenter research groups, which could include community practices and academic centers, may provide access to large numbers of patients in a short period. These collaborations can increase generalizability because patients are being enrolled and followed in community clinical practices. Multicenter oncology groups and cardiovascular trials serve as models for such collaboration. Individual researchers or clinics can conduct case series or cohort studies. By adhering to sound methodologic principles, these observational studies can provide important information on technical feasibility and complications and can help identify predictors of successful outcomes.

The back pain research community can also take steps to improve the validity of individual studies. Establishing a standard minimum set of outcome measures, encompassing functional status and symptom relief, could increase the quality of back pain research. Furthermore, adopting a uniform back pain patient data format could facilitate comparisons among studies and enable the pooling of results, especially if a back surgery registry were established.

There are increasing economic pressures to contain health care costs and justify the effectiveness of treatments. The current back pain literature suffers from flawed research designs, leading to considerable uncertainty about which treatments are clinically effective and cost effective. The uncertainty can be resolved only by improving the quality of back pain research and publishing rigorous evaluations of back pain treatments.

References

1 Bergner M, Bobbitt RA, Carter WB, Gilson BS. The Sickness Impact Profile: Development and final revision of a health status measure. Med Care 1981;19:787-805.
2 Bloch R. Methodology in clinical back pain trials. Spine 1987;12:430-432.
3 Bonchek LI. The role of the randomized clinical trial in the evaluation of new operations. Surg Clin North Am 1982; 62:761-769.
4 Borenstein M, Cohen J. Statistical power analysis: A computer program. Hillsdale, NJ: Erlbaum, 1988.
5 Byar DP, Simon RM, Friedewald WT, et al. Randomized clinical trials: Perspectives on some recent ideas. N Engl J Med 1976;295:74-80.
6 Carette S, Marcoux S, Truchon R, Grondin C, Gagnon J, Allard Y, Latulippe M. A controlled trial of corticosteroid injections into facet joints for chronic low back pain. N Engl J Med 1991;325:1002-7.
7 Chalmers TC, Celano P, Sacks HS, Smith H. Bias in treatment assignment in controlled clinical trials. N Engl J Med 1983;309:1358-61.
8 Chang RW, Falconer J, Stulberg SD, Arnold WJ, Dyer AR. Prerandomization: An alternative to classic randomization. J Bone Joint Surg 1990;72-A:1451-5.
9 Cowell HR, Curtiss PH. Editorial. The randomized clinical trial. J Bone Joint Surg 1985;67-A:1151-1152.
10 Crawshaw C, Frazer AM, Merriam WF, Mulholland RC, Webb JK. A comparison of surgery and chemonucleolysis in the treatment of sciatica. A prospective randomized trial. Spine 1984;2:195-8.
11 Deyo RA. Clinical research methods in low back pain. Phys Med Rehab 1991;5:209-222.
12 Deyo RA, Ciol MA, Cherkin DC, Loeser JD, Bigos SJ. Lumbar spine fusion: A cohort study of complications, reoperations, and resource use in the Medicare population. Spine 1993;18:1463-1470.
13 Deyo RA, Walsh NE, Schoenfeld LS, Ramamurthy S. Can trials of physical treatments be blinded? The example of transcutaneous electrical nerve stimulation (TENS). Am J Phys Med Rehab 1990;69:6-10.
14 Donner A, Birkett N, Buck C. Randomization by cluster: Sample size requirements and analysis. Am J Epidemiol 1981;114:906-14.
15 Editorial. Blindness in surgical trials. Lancet 1980:1229-1230.
16 Ejeskär A, Nachemson A, Herberts P, Lysell E, Andersson G, Irstam L, Peterson L-E. Surgery versus chemonucleolysis for herniated lumbar discs: A prospective study with random assignment. Clin Orthop 1983;174:236-42.
17 Fairbank JCT, Davies JB, Mbaot JC, O'Brien JP. The Oswestry low back pain disability questionnaire. Physiotherapy 1980;66:271-3.
18 Gartland JJ. Orthopedic clinical research: Deficiencies in experimental design and determination of outcome. J Bone Joint Surg 1988;70-A:1357-1363.

[19] Gross M. A critique of the methodologies used in clinical studies of hip-joint arthroplasty published in the English-language orthopaedic literature. J Bone Joint Surg 1988;70A:1364-1371.

[20] Haines SJ. Randomized clinical trials in the evaluation of surgical innovation. J Neurosurg 1979;51:5-11.

[21] Haines SJ. Randomized clinical trials in neurosurgery. Neurosurgery 1983;12:259-264.

[22] Hoffman RM, Wheeler KJ, Deyo RA. Surgery for herniated lumbar discs: a literature synthesis. J Gen Intern Med IN PRESS.

[23] Javid MJ, Nordby EJ, Ford LT, Hejna WJ, Whisler WW, Burton C, Millett DK, Wiltse LL, Widell EH, Boyd RJ, Newton SE, Thisted R. Safety and efficacy of chymopapain in herniated nucleus pulposus with sciatica. JAMA 1983;249: 2489-2494.

[24] Kahn HA, Sempos CT. Statistical Methods in Epidemiology. New York: Oxford University Press, 1989;168-205.

[25] Lilius G, Laasonen EM, Myllynen P, Harilainen A, Gronlund G. Lumbar facet joint syndrome: A randomised clinical trial. J Bone Joint Surg [Br] 1989;71:681-4.

[26] Mathews JA, Hickling J. Lumbar traction: A double-blind controlled study for sciatica. Rheumatol Rehabil 1975;14:222-5.

[27] McPeek B, Mosteller F, McKneally M. Randomized clinical trials in surgery. Int J Technol Assess Health Care 1989;5:317-322.

[28] Miller JN, Colditz GA, Mosteller F. How study design affects outcomes in comparisons of therapy. II: Surgical Statistics in Medicine 1989;8:455-466.

[29] Muralikuttan KP, Hamilton A, Kernohan WG, Mollan RAB, Adair IV. A prospective randomized trial of chemonucleolysis and conventional disc surgery in single level lumbar disc herniation. Spine 1992;17:381-7.

[30] Nachemson AL, LaRocca H. Editorial: Spine 1987. Spine 1987;12:427-429.

[31] Pal B, Mangion P, Hossain MA, Diffey BL. A controlled trial of continuous lumbar traction in the treatment of back pain and sciatica. Br J Rheumatol 1986;25:181-3.

[32] Quebec Task Force on Spinal Disorders. Scientific approach to the assessment and management of activity-related spinal disorders: A monograph for clinicians. Spine 1987;12(Suppl 7):S16-21.

[33] Raskob GE, Lofthouse RN, Hull RD. Methodologic guidelines for clinical trials evaluating new therapeutic approaches in bone and joint surgery. J Bone Joint Surg 1985;67-A:1294-1297.

[34] Revel M, Payan C, Vallee C, et al. Automated percutaneous lumbar discectomy versus chemonucleolysis in the treatment of sciatica. A randomized multicenter trial. Spine 1993;18:1-7.

[35] Roland M, Morris R. Study of the natural history of back pain, part I: development of a reliable and sensitive measure of disability in low-back pain. Spine 1983;8:141-4.

[36] Rothman KJ. Modern Epidemiology. Boston: Little, Brown and Company, 1986;95-6.

[37] Rudicel S, Esdaile J. The randomized clinical trial in orthopaedics: Obligation or option? J Bone Joint Surg 1985;67A:1284-1293.

[38] Spodick D. The randomized controlled clinical trial: Scientific and ethical bases. Am J Med 1982;73:420-425.

[39] Salenius P, Laurent LE. Results of operative treatment of lumbar disc herniation. A survey of 886 patients. Acta Orthop Scand 1977;48:630-4.

[40] Taylor KM, Margolese RG, Soskolne CL. Physicians' reasons for not entering eligible patients in a randomized clinical trial of surgery for breast cancer. N Engl J Med 1984;310:1363-1367.

[41] Tullberg T, Isacson J, Weidenheilm L. Does microscopic removal of lumbar disc herniation lead to better results than the standard procedure? Results of a one-year randomized study. Spine 1992;18:24-27.

[42] Turner JA, Ersek M, Herron L, Deyo R. Surgery for lumbar spinal stenosis: Attempted meta-analysis of the literature. Spine 1992;17:1-8.

[43] Turner JA, Ersek M, Herron L, Haselkorri J, Kent D, Ciol MA, Deyo R. Patient outcomes after lumbar spinal fusions. JAMA 1992;268:907-911.

[44] van Alphen HAM, Braakman R, Bezemer PD, Broere G, Berfelo MW. Chemonucleolysis versus discectomy: A randomized multicenter trial. J Neurosurg 1989;70:869-75.

[45] Van der Linden W. On the generalization of surgical trial results. Acta Chir Scand 1980;146:229-234.

[46] Weber H. Lumbar disc herniation. A controlled, prospective study with ten years of observation. Spine 1983;8:131-40.

[47] Weber H. Traction therapy in sciatica due to disc prolapse (does traction treatment have any positive effect on patients suffering from sciatica caused by disc prolapse?): J Oslo City Hosp 1973;23:167-73.

[48] Weber H, Ljunggren AE, Walker L. Traction therapy in patients with herniated lumbar intervertebral discs. J Oslo City Hosp 1984;34:61-70.

University of Washington, Seattle, Washington
Judith Turner (Department of Psychiatry and Behavioral Sciences and Rehabilitation Centre)
Daniel Cherkin (Department of Health Services, Family Medicine)
Richard Deyo (Department of Medicine, Health Services)

Central Coast Spine Institute, San Luis Obispo, California
Larry Herron

Department of Medicine, University of Arizona, Tucson, Arizona
Richard Hoffman

Supported by grant no. HS-06344 (the Back Pain Outcome Assessment Team) from the Agency for Health Care Policy & Research and by the Northwest Health Services Research and Development Field Program, Seattle VA Medical Center.
Financial disclosure/device statement category: 3, 7.
Accepted for publication May 6, 1994.

This article was first published in the BMJ *and is reproduced by permission of the* BMJ

RANDOMISED CONTROLLED TRIAL OF EXERCISE FOR LOW BACK PAIN: CLINICAL OUTCOMES, COSTS, AND PREFERENCES

Jennifer Klaber Moffett, David Torgerson, Sally Bell-Syer, David Jackson, Hugh Llewlyn-Phillips, Amanda Farrin, Julie Barber

BMJ 1999;**319**:279–83

ABSTRACT

Objective To evaluate effectiveness of an exercise programme in a community setting for patients with low back pain to encourage a return to normal activities.
Design Randomised controlled trial of progressive exercise programme compared with usual primary care management. Patients' preferences for type of management were elicited independently of randomisation.
Participants 187 patients aged 18–60 years with mechanical low back pain of 4 weeks to 6 months' duration.
Interventions Exercise classes led by a physiotherapist that included strengthening exercises for all main muscle groups, stretching exercises, relaxation session, and brief education on back care. A cognitive-behavioural approach was used.
Main outcome measures Assessments of debilitating effects of back pain before and after intervention and at 6 months and 1 year later. Measures included Roland disability questionnaire, Aberdeen back pain scale, pain diaries, and use of healthcare services.
Results At 6 weeks after randomisation, the intervention group improved marginally more than the control group on the disability questionnaire and reported less distressing pain. At 6 months and 1 year, the intervention group showed significantly greater improvement in the disability questionnaire score (mean difference in changes 1.35, 95% confidence interval 0.13 to 2.57). At 1 year, the intervention group also showed significantly greater improvement in the Aberdeen back pain scale (4.44, 1.01 to 7.87) and reported only 378 days off work compared with 607 in the control group. The intervention group used fewer healthcare resources. Outcome was not influenced by patients' preferences.
Conclusions The exercise class was more clinically effective than traditional general practitioner management, regardless of patient preference, and was cost effective.

INTRODUCTION

Low back pain is common and, although it may settle quickly, recurrence rates are about 50% in the following 12 months.[1] Recent management guidelines recommend that an early return to physical activities should be encouraged,[2][3] but patients are often afraid of movement after an acute onset of back pain. Trials of specific exercise programmes for acute back pain have not shown them to be effective,[4][5] but a specific exercise programme may have to be tailored to suit the individual patient and so is less likely to be effective for a heterogeneous group of patients.

However, there is some evidence that a general exercise programme, which aims to increase individuals' confidence in the use of their spine and overcome the fear of physical activity, can be effective for patients with chronic back pain (of more than six months' duration). A recent randomised trial of a supervised exercise programme in a hospital setting reported significantly better outcomes at six months and two years for the exercise group compared with the control group.[6][7] Whether this approach would be effective and cost effective for patients with low back pain of less than six months' duration in a primary care setting is unknown.

An important methodological problem occurs when it is not possible to blind subjects to the treatment they receive, since outcome is probably directly influenced by their preconceived ideas regarding the effectiveness of intervention.[8] Thus, in trials where a double blind procedure is not feasible, participants who are not randomised to their treatment of choice may be disappointed and suffer from resentful demoralisation,[9] whereas those randomised to their preferred treatment may have a better outcome irrespective of the physiological efficacy of the intervention. However, this problem may be partly ameliorated if patients' treatment preferences are elicited before randomisation, so that they can be used to inform the analysis of costs and outcomes.[10][11]

In this paper, we report a fully randomised trial for the treatment of subacute low back pain in which the analysis was informed by patient preference.

SUBJECTS AND METHODS

Recruitment of subjects

Eighty seven general practitioners agreed to participate in the study, and the principal investigator (JKM) visited each practice to discuss participation. Selection of general practitioners was based in the York area and restricted by the need to provide easy access for patients to the classes. Only one invited practice declined to participate. Single handed practices were not invited. The general practitioners referred patients directly to the research team or sent a monthly list of patients who had consulted with back pain. Inclusion criteria were patients with mechanical low back pain of at least four weeks' duration but less than six months, aged between 18 and 60, declared medically fit by their general practitioner to undertake the exercise, and who had consulted one of the general practitioners participating in the study. Patients with any potentially serious pathology were excluded, as were any who would have been unable to attend or participate in the classes. The exclusion criteria were the same as described by Frost et al[7] except that concurrent physiotherapy rather than previous physiotherapy was an exclusion criterion in this trial.

Evaluation

Patients who seemed eligible were contacted by telephone and if they were interested in participating in the study were invited to an initial interview, at which the study and its implications for participants were explained. Patients who met all the eligibility criteria and consented to participate attended a first assessment a week later.

This included a physical examination (to exclude possible serious spinal pathology) and collection of baseline data by means of validated measures of health status. The main outcome measures were the Roland back pain disability questionnaire,[12] which measures functional limitations due to back pain, and the Aberdeen back pain scale,[13] which is more a measure of clinical status. The Roland disability questionnaire consists of a 24 point scale: a patient scoring three points on the scale means that he or she reports, for example, "Because of my back I am not doing any of the jobs that I usually do around the house, I use a handrail to get upstairs, and I lie down to rest more often:" We also administered the EuroQoL health index (EQ-5D)[14] and the fear and avoidance beliefs questionnaire (FABQ).[15]

The second assessment was carried out at the patients' general practice six weeks after randomisation to treatment. The brief physical examination was repeated, and the patients were asked to complete the same outcome questionnaires.

In addition, patients were asked to complete pain diaries in the week before their first assessment and in the week before their second assessment. The diaries were used to assess subjective pain reports and asked "How strong is the pain?" and "How distressing is the pain?"[6 16]

We also evaluated patients at six and 12 months' follow up by sending them outcome questionnaires to complete and return.

Randomisation and treatments

A pre-prepared randomisation list was generated from a random numbers table and participants were stratified by practice in blocks of six. The trial coordinator ensured concealment of allocation from the clinical researchers by providing the research physiotherapist with a sealed envelope for a named patient before

baseline assessment. A note inside the envelope invited the participant either to attend exercise classes or to continue with the current advice or treatment offered by his or her general practitioner. (One of the referring general practitioners used manipulation as usual treatment on most of his patients so that up to 37 patients in each arm of the study could also have received manipulation.) Each patient had an equal chance of being allocated to the intervention or the control group. Before patients were given their envelope they were asked whether they had any preference for the treatment assignment The participants opened the envelope after leaving the surgery.

Intervention group—The exercise programme consisted of eight sessions, each lasting an hour, spread out over four weeks, with up to 10 participants in each class. The programme was similar to the Oxford fitness programme[7] and included stretching exercises, low impact aerobic exercises, and strengthening exercises aimed at all the main muscle groups. The overall aim was to encourage normal movement of the spine. No special equipment was needed. Participants were discouraged from viewing themselves as invalids and from following the precept of "Let pain be your guide:" They were encouraged to improve their individual record and were selectively rewarded with attention and praise. Although partly based on a traditional physiotherapy approach, the programme used cognitive-behavioural principles. One simple educational message encouraging self reliance was delivered at each class. Participants were told that they should regard the classes as a stepping stone to increasing their own levels of activity.

Controls—Patients allocated to the control group continued under the care of their doctor and in some cases were referred to physiotherapy as usual. No attempt was made to regulate the treatment they received, but it was recorded.

Economic analysis

We recorded patients' use of healthcare services using a combination of retrospective questionnaires and prospective diary cards, which they returned at 6 and 12 months' follow up. From this information we estimated the cost of each patient's treatment. We compared the mean costs of treatment for the two groups by using Student's *t* tests and standard confidence intervals. However, as cost data were highly positively skewed, these results were checked with a nonparametric "bootstrap:"[17] The economic evaluation addressed both costs to the NHS and the costs to society. Participants were not charged for the classes, in line with any treatment currently available on the NHS.

Statistical analysis

Our original intention was to recruit 300 patients, which, given a standard deviation of 4, would have provided 90% power at the 5% significance level to detect a 1.5 point difference between the two groups in

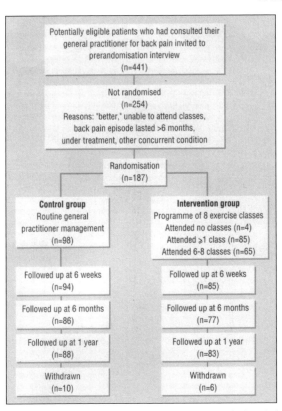

Flow chart describing patients' progress through the trial

the mean change on the Roland disability questionnaire. However, recruitment of patients to the study proved much slower than expected, and, because of the limitations of study resources, recruiting was stopped after 187 patients had been included into the study. This smaller sample reduced the power to detect such a difference to 72%, but there was still 90% power to detect a 2 point difference in outcome.

Our analysis was based on intention to treat. We estimated the effects of treatment on the outcome measures by means of analysis of covariance, with the change in scores as the dependent variable and adjustment being made for baseline score and patient preference. We used Student's *t* tests to analyse the data from the pain diaries as the baseline scores were quite similar.

RESULTS

Study population
Of the 187 patients included in the trial, 89 were randomised to the intervention and 98 to the control group. The figure shows their progress through the trial. In both groups those with the most severe back pain at randomisation were less likely to return follow up questionnaires: the mean Roland disability questionnaire score for responders at one year follow up was 5.80 (SD 3.48) compared with a mean score of 9.06 (4.58) for non responders respectively (P=0.002).

Baseline characteristics
The clinical and demographic characteristics of the patients in the two groups were fairly well balanced at randomisation (table 1), although those allocated to the

intervention group tended to report more disability on the Roland disability questionnaire than did the control group. Most patients (118, 63%), when asked, would have preferred to be allocated to the exercise programme. Attendance of the classes was considered quite good, with 73% of the intervention group attending between six and eight of the classes. Four people failed to attend any classes and were included in the intention to treat analysis. No patients allocated to the control group took part in the exercise programme.

Clinical outcomes
Table 2 shows the mean changes in outcome measures over time, from randomisation to final follow up at one year. After adjustment for baseline scores, the intervention group showed greater decreases in all measures of back pain and disability compared with the controls. At six weeks after randomisation, patients in the intervention group reported less distressing pain than the control group (P = 0.03) and a marginally significant difference on the Roland disability questionnaire scores. Other variables were not significantly different, but the differences in change were all in favour of the intervention group. At six months the difference of the mean change scores of the Roland disability questionnaire was significant, and at one year the differences in changes of both the Roland disability questionnaire and the Aberdeen back pain scale were significant (table 2). Most of the intervention group improved by at least three points on the Roland disability questionnaire: 53% (95% confidence interval

Table 1

Baseline characteristics of patients with mechanical low back pain included in study. Values are means (standard deviations) unless stated otherwise

Variable	Control group (n=98)	Intervention group (n=89)
Age (years)	42.6 (8.62)	41.1 (9.21)
No (%) of women	55 (56)	51 (57)
No (%) of non-smokers	69 (70)	64 (72)
No (%) who preferred to be allocated to exercise	65 (66)	53 (60)
No (%) who had physiotherapy in past 6 months	23 (24)	18 (20)
Number of visits to general practitioner in past 6 months	2.45 (2.36)	2.22 (3.32)
Roland disability questionnaire score (0–24 points)	5.56 (3.94)	6.65 (4.02)
Aberdeen back pain scale (0–100 points)	25.52 (10.85)	27.93 (11.07)
Fear-avoidance beliefs questionnaire:		
Work (0–42 points)	13.7 (9.83)	14.7 (10.10)
Physical activities (0–24 points)	12.7 (5.47)	13.8 (5.26)
EuroQoL health index (0–1 point)	0.73 (015)	0.71 (0.16)

Table 2

Changes in back pain scores from baseline values in intervention and control groups at 6 weeks, 6 months, and 1 year follow up

Outcome measure	Mean change in scores*		Difference (95% CI)	P value
	Control group	Intervention group		
At 6 weeks	**(n=94)**	**(n=85)**		
Roland disability questionnaire	−1.94	−2.86	0.92 (−0.02 to 1.87)	0.06
Aberdeen back pain scale	−8.99	−11.58	2.59 (−0.37 to 5.55)	0.09
Pain diary:	(n=89)	(n=82)		
Strength	−9.4	−12.2	2.8 (−1.67 to 7.30)	0.22
Distress	−5.0	−10.2	5.13 (0.41 to 9.85)	0.03
Fear and avoidance beliefs questionnaire:				
Work	−1.26	−2.98	1.72 (−0.34 to 3.78)	0.10
Physical activities	−2.02	−3.26	1.24 (−0.27 to 2.74)	0.11
EuroQoL health index	0.022	0.030	−0.01 (−0.09 to 0.07)	0.84
Mean (range) number of visits to general practitioner	0.41 (0–6)	0.20 (0–3)	NA	0.09
At 6 months	**(n=86)**	**(n=77)**		
Roland disability questionnaire	−1.64	−2.99	1.35 (0.13 to 2.57)	0.03
Aberdeen back pain scale	−8.11	−10.26	2.15 (−1.63 to 5.93)	0.26
EuroQoL health index	0.067	0.080	−0.01 (0.06 to 0.04)	0.60
Mean (range) number of visits to general practitioner	0.89 (0–8)	0.49 (0–4)	NA	
At 1 year	**(n=88)**	**(n=83)**		
Roland disability questionnaire	−1.77	−3.19	1.42 (0.29 to 2.56)	0.02
Aberdeen back pain scale	−8.48	−12.92	4.44 (1.01 to 7.87)	0.01
EuroQoL health index	0.089	0.111	−0.02 (−0.08 to 0.04)	0.47

*Adjusted for baseline scores. NA=Not applicable.

42% to 64%) had done so at six weeks, 60% (49% to 71%) at six months, and 64% (54% to 74%) at one year. A smaller proportion of the control group achieved this clinically important improvement: 31% (22% to 40%) at six weeks, 40% (29% to 50%) at six months, and 35% (25% to 45%) at one year.

Patients' preference

We examined the effect of patients' baseline preference for treatment on outcome after adjusting for baseline scores and main effects. Preference did not significantly affect response to treatment. The intervention had similar effects on both costs and outcomes regardless of baseline preference. For example, the change in the Roland disability questionnaire score at 12 months in the control group was −1.93 for patients who preferred intervention and −1.18 for those who were indifferent (95% confidence interval of difference −1.05 to 2.55), and in the intervention group the change in score was −3.10 for those who preferred intervention and −3.15 for those who were indifferent ((95% confidence interval of difference −1.47 to 3.08). As the interaction term (preference by random allocation) was non-

significant, the results shown in table 2 exclude the preference term.

Economic evaluation

Patients in the intervention group tended to use fewer healthcare and other resources compared with those in the control group (table 3). However, the mean difference, totalling £148 per patient, was not significant: the 95% confidence interval suggests there could have been a saving of as much as £442 per patient in the intervention group or an additional cost of up to £146. Patients in the control group took a total of 607 days off work during the 12 months after randomisation compared with 378 days taken off by the intervention group.

DISCUSSION

Our results support the hypothesis that a simple exercise class can lead to long term improvements for back pain sufferers. Studies have shown that a similar programme for patients with chronic back pain can be effective in the hospital setting.[6 7] In this study we show the clinical effectiveness for patients with subacute or recurrent low back pain who were referred by their general practitioner to a community programme.

Current management guidelines for low back pain recommend a return to physical activity and taking exercise. In particular, they recommend that patients who are not improving at six weeks after onset of back pain, which may be a higher proportion than previously realised,[1] should be referred to a reactivation programme. The programme we evaluated fits that requirement well. It shows participants how they can safely start moving again and increase their levels of physical activity. It is simple and less costly than individual treatment.

It seemed to have beneficial effects even one year later, as measured by functional disability (Roland disability questionnaire) and clinical status (Aberdeen back pain scale). The mean changes in scores on these instruments were small, with many patients reporting mild symptoms on the day of entry to the trial. However, a substantially larger proportion of participants in the exercise classes gained increases of over three points on the Roland disability questionnaire at six weeks, six months, and one year, which might be clinically important. At six weeks, participants in the exercise classes reported significantly less distressing pain compared with the control group, although the

Table 3

Use of services and their costs associated with back pain in the two study groups at 12 months follow up

Variable	Intervention group (n=70)*	Control group (n=74)*	Difference (95% CI) (Student's *t* test)
Health services			
No of exercise classes:	70	0	
Total cost (£25.20 per person per programme of 8 classes)	£1764	0	
No of visits to general practitioner:	139	266	
Total cost (£16 per visit)	£2224	£4256	
No of visits to a physiotherapist:	65	146	
Total cost (£18 per visit)	£1170	£2628	
No of visits to a chiropractor or osteopath:	27	25	
Total cost (£20 per visit)	£540	£500	
No of visits to orthopaedic surgeon:	0	1	
Total cost (£174 per visit)	0	£174	
No of MRI investigations:	1	1	
Total cost (£300 per visit)	£300	£300	
No of x ray investigations:	4	3	
Total cost (£20 per visit)	£80	£60	
No of nights in hospital:	0	2	
Total cost (£150 per night)	0	£300	
Total health service related costs	£6078	£8218	
Mean (SD) cost per patient	£86.83 (105.19)	£111.05 (205.11)	24.23 (−29.94 to 78.39) (P=0.38†)
Median (90 % range) cost per patient	£41.20 (25.20–353.20)	0 (0–532.00)	
Equipment (beds, stave modification, car seat)			
No of pieces of equipment:	4	4	
Total cost (item costs £10–800)	£2123	£2091	
Days off work			
Total No of days off work:	378	607	
Total cost (£45 per day)‡	£17 010	£27 315	
All costs (including equipment and days off work)			
Total costs	£25 211	£37 624	
Mean (SD) cost per patient	£360.15 (582.27)	£508.43 (1108.79)	148.28 (−145.92 to 442.48) (P=0.32§)
Median (90% range) cost per patient	£115.20 (25.20–1688.40)	£50.00 (0–2728.00)	

MRI=magnetic resonance imaging.

*Based on 144 subjects without missing data on resource use or costs.

†Bootstrap comparison of means P=0.38, accelerated 95% CI corrected for bias (−22.00 to 81.90).

‡Based on gross domestic product capita per head 1996.

§Bootstrap comparison of means P=0.33, accelerated 95% CI corrected for bias (−89.78 to 506.14).

intensity of pain was not significantly different. This is consistent with findings from a study of chronic back pain patients in Oxford, in which changes in distressing pain were much greater than were the changes in intensity of pain.[6]

People with back pain who use coping strategies that do not avoid movement and pain have less disability.[18-22] In our study the participants in the exercise classes were able to function better according to Roland disability questionnaire scores than the control group at six months and one year after randomisation to treatment, and at one year they also showed a significantly greater improvement in clinical status as measured by the Aberdeen back pain scale. This increase in differences in effect between the intervention and control groups over time is consistent with the results from long term follow up in comparable back pain trials.[23 24]

Study design

The design of this study was a conventional randomised controlled trial in that all eligible patients were randomised. However, the participants were asked to state their preferred treatment before they knew of their allocation. A study of antenatal services showed that preferences can be an important determinant of outcome,[10] but we did not find any strong effect of preference on the outcome, although a much larger sample size would be needed to confidently exclude any modest interaction between preference and outcome.[8] This information may be useful to clinicians in that it suggests that exercise classes are effective even in patients who are not highly motivated. Our trial design, of asking patients for their preferences at the outset, has substantial advantages over the usual patient preference design, in which costs and outcomes cannot be reliably controlled for confounding by preference.

Conclusions

Our exercise programme did not seem to influence the intensity of pain but did affect the participants' ability to cope with the pain in the short term and even more so in the longer term. It used a cognitive-behavioural model, shifting the emphasis away from a disease model to a model of normal human behaviour, and with minimal extra training a physiotherapist can run it. Patients' preferences did not seem to influence the outcome.

KEY MESSAGES

- Patients with back pain need to return to normal activities as soon as possible but are often afraid that movement or activity may be harmful

- An exercise programme led by a physiotherapist in the community and based on cognitive-behavioural principles helped patients to cope better with their pain and function better even one year later

- Patients' preferences for type of management did not affect outcome

- Patients in the intervention group tended to use fewer healthcare resources and took fewer days off work

- This type of exercise programme should be more widely available

Contributors: JKM conceived the study, developed the protocol, obtained funding, designed and directed the trial, recruited general practitioners, and drafted the paper. DT advised on the organisation and collection of economic data, carried out statistical analysis of the costs, and helped to write the paper. SB-S coordinated the study, assisted in its planning and data collection, and commented on early drafts of the paper. DJ and HL-P assisted in planning the trial and data collection, acted as exercise class leaders, and commented on early drafts of the paper. AF carried out the statistical analysis and helped to draft the paper. JB used the "bootstrapping" technique to help analysis of costs and commented on drafts of the paper. Trevor Sheldon and Alan Maynard (Centre for Health Economics, University of York) and Anthony Dowell (Centre for Primary Care Research, University of Leeds) helped develop the protocol and obtain funding. Trevor Sheldon provided further methodological support and advice. Ian Russell (Department of Health Sciences and Clinical Evaluation, University of York) advised on the statistical analysis. Of the 87 general practitioners who agreed to take part, most referred patients to the study and Drs Allan Harris, Trevor Julian, and John Bush facilitated recruitment of patients while Gillian Rodriguez and Michael White helped to set up exercise classes during the pilot phase. The patients participating in the trial responded to questionnaires at baseline and follow up. Vanessa Waby provided administrative support. JKM is guarantor for the study.

Funding: This research was funded by the Arthritis Research Campaign, the Northern and Yorkshire Regional Health Authority, and the National Back Pain Association.

Competing interests: None declared.

Centre for Health Economics, University of York, York
Jennifer Klaber Moffett, *research fellow*; David Torgerson, *research fellow*; Sally Bell-Syer, *research fellow*; David Jackson, *research fellow*; Hugh Llewlyn-Phillips, *research fellow*; Department of Health Sciences and Clinical Evaluation, University of York; Amanda Farrin, *trial statistician*; Department of Medical Statistics and Evaluation, Imperial College School of Medicine, University of London; Julie Barber, *research fellow in medical statistics*; Correspondence to: J Klaber Moffett, Institute of Rehabilitation, University of Hull, Hull HU3 2PG j.a.moffett@medschool.hull.ac.uk

References

1. Croft P, ed. *Low back pain*. Oxford: Radcliffe Medical Press, 1997.
2. Clinical Standards Advisory Group. *Back pain*. London: HMSO, 1994.
3. Waddell G, Feder G, McIntosh A, Lewis M, Hutchinson A. *Low back pain evidence review*. London: Royal College of General Practitioners, 1996.
4. Malmivaara A, Hakkinen U, Aro T, Heinrichs M, Koskenniemi L, Kuosma E, et al. The treatment of acute low back pain-bed rest, exercises or ordinary activity? *N Engl J Med* 1995;**332**:351–5.
5. Faas A, Chavannes A, van Eijk JTM, Gubbels J. A randomized, placebo-controlled trial of exercise therapy in patients with acute low back pain. *Spine* 1993;**18**:1388–95.
6. Frost H, Klaber Moffett J, Moser J, Fairbank J. Evaluation of a fitness programme for patients with chronic low back pain. *BMJ* 1995;**310**:151–4.

7   Frost H, Lamb S, Klaber Moffett J, Fairbank J, Moser J. A fitness programme for patients with chronic low back pain: 2 year follow-up of a randomised controlled trial. *Pain* 1998;**75**:273–9.

8   McPherson K, Britton A, Wennberg J. Are randomised controlled trials controlled? Patient preferences and unblind trials. *J R Soc Med* 1997;**90**:652–6.

9   Bradley C. Designing medical and educational studies. *Diabetes Care* 1993;**16**:509–18.

10   Clement S, Sikorski J, Wilson J, Candy B. Merits of alternative strategies for incorporating patient preferences into clinical trials must be considered carefully [letter]. *BMJ* 1998;**317**:78.

11   Torgerson D, Klaber Moffett J, Russell I. Patient preferences in randomised trials: threat or opportunity? *J Health Serv Res Policy* 1996;**1(4)**:194–7.

12   Roland M, Morris R. A study of the natural causes of back pain. Part 1: Development of a reliable and sensitive measure of disability in low-back pain. *Spine* 1983;**8**:141–4.

13   Ruta D, Garratt A, Wardlaw D, Russell I. Developing a valid and reliable measure of health outcome for patients with low back pain. *Spine* 1994;**19**:1887–96.

14   Brooks R with EuroQoL Group. EuroQoL: the current state of play. *Health Policy* 1996;**37**:53–72.

15   Waddell G, Newton M, Henderson I, Somerville D, Main C. A fear-avoidance beliefs questionnaire (FABQ) and the role of fear-avoidance beliefs in chronic low back pain and disability. *Pain* 1993;**52**:157–68.

16   Jensen M, McFarland G. Increasing the reliability and validity of pain intensity measurement in chronic pain patients. *Pain* 1993;**55**:195–203.

17   Efron B, Tibshirani R. *An introduction to bootstrap*. New York: Chapman and Hall, 1993.

18   Williams D, Keefe E. Pain beliefs and use of cognitive-behavioral coping strategies. *Pain* 1991;**46**:185–90.

19   Estlander A, Harkapaa K. Relationships between coping strategies, disability and pain levels in patients with chronic low back pain. *Scand J Behav Ther* 1989;**18**:56–69.

20   Holmes J, Stevenson C. Differential effects of avoidant and attentional coping strategies on adaption to chronic and recent-onset pain. *Health Psychology* 1990;**9**:577–84.

21   Rosenstiel A, Keefe F. The use of coping strategies in chronic low back pain patients: relationship to patient characteristics and current adjustments. *Pain* 1983;**17**:33–44.

22   Slade P, Troup J, Lethem J, Bentley G. The fear avoidance model of exaggerated pain perception II Preliminary studies of coping strategies for pain. *Behav Res Ther* 1983;**21**:409–16.

23   Meade T, Dyer S, Browne W, Frank A. Randomised comparison of chiropractic and hospital outpatient management for low back pain: results from extended follow up. *BMJ* 1995;**311**:349–51.

24   Cherkin D, Deyo R, Battle M, Street J, Barlow W. A comparison of physical therapy, chiropractic manipulation, and provision of an educational booklet for the treatment of patients with low back pain. *N Engl J Med* 1998;**339**:1021–9.

(*Accepted 20 May 1999*)

5

This article was first published in the BMJ *and is reproduced by permission of the* BMJ

Randomised clinical trial of manipulative therapy and physiotherapy for persistent back and neck complaints: results of one year follow up

BMJ 1992;**304**:601-5

Bart W Koes, Lex M Bouter, Henk van Mameren, Alex H M Essers, Gard M J R Verstegen,
Domien M Hofhuizen, Jo P Houben, Paul G Knipschild

Abstract

Objective — To compare the effectiveness of manipulative therapy, physiotherapy, treatment by the general practitioner, and placebo therapy in patients with persistent non-specific back and neck complaints.

Design — Randomised clinical trial.

Setting — Primary health care in the Netherlands.

Patients — 256 patients with non-specific back and neck complaints of at least six weeks' duration who had not received physiotherapy or manipulative therapy in the past two years.

Interventions — At the discretion of the manipulative therapists, physiotherapists, and general practitioners. Physiotherapy consisted of exercises, massage, and physical therapy (heat, electrotherapy, ultrasound, shortwave diathermy). Manipulative therapy consisted of manipulation and mobilisation of the spine. Treatment by general practitioners consisted of drugs (for example, analgesics), advice about posture, home exercises, and (bed)rest. Placebo treatment consisted of detuned shortwave diathermy (10 minutes) and detuned ultrasound (10 minutes).

Main outcome measures — Changes in severity of the main complaint and limitation of physical functioning measured on 10 point scales by a blinded research assistant and global perceived effect measured on a 6 point scale by the patients.

Results — Many patients in the general practitioner and placebo groups received other treatment during follow up. Improvement in the main complaint was larger with manipulative therapy (4.5) than with physiotherapy (3.8) after 12 months' follow up (difference 0.9; 95% confidence interval 0.1 to 1.7). Manipulative therapy also gave larger improvements in physical functioning (difference 0.6; -0.1 to 1.3). The global perceived effect after six and 12 months' follow up was similar for both treatments.

Conclusions — Manipulative therapy and physiotherapy are better than general practitioner and placebo treatment. Furthermore, manipulative therapy is slightly better than physiotherapy after 12 months.

Introduction

In most cases of back pain and neck pain no underlying disease can be established and the causes of the complaints remain unknown.[12] Fortunately, most patients with acute complaints recover within a few weeks, often with the help of (bed)rest, analgesics, and advice about posture and exercises.[3] The complaints disappear within a few months in about 90% of the cases [2,4,5] although the recurrence rate is high.[1] When the complaints persist there are several options for treatment. General practitioners in the Netherlands often refer patients with persisting complaints for physiotherapy or, less commonly, for manipulative therapy.

Physiotherapists usually give exercise therapy, alone or in combination with other treatments — for example, massage, heat, traction, ultrasound, or short wave diathermy.[6] We know of 16 randomised clinical trials investigating the efficacy of exercises given alone or in combination with additional physical treatments. Unfortunately, most of these studies had severe methodological flaws. Long term positive effects of exercises were reported in only one of the two studies that measured the effect after 12 months.[6] Despite its widespread use the efficacy of physiotherapy still remains questionable.[1,3-6] Most of 35 randomised controlled trials investigating the efficacy of manipulation and mobilisation for back and neck complaints also had severe methodological flaws and gave inconsistent results.[7] Only seven of the trials measured the effects at least 12 months after randomisation.[8-14] Long term positive effects favouring manipulation were reported in only one of these studies.[9]

We present the long term results of a randomised clinical trial comparing manipulative therapy, physiotherapy, treatment by the general practitioner, and a placebo treatment for patients with persistent back and neck complaints. The design of the study's and its short term results are reported in detail elsewhere.[16,17]

Subjects and methods
Selection of patients
Patients who had had back and neck pain for at least six weeks were selected by general practitioners and by advertisements in the local press over two years (January 1988-December 1989). Subsequently, all potential

participants were seen by the same research assistant (an experienced physiotherapist and manual therapist), who performed a physical examination and did the final check with respect to the admission criteria.[15] Patients had to meet the following criteria: the complaint was non-specific — that is, no underlying disease could be established (for example, malignity, osteoporosis, herniated disc); the duration of the complaint was six weeks or longer; no physiotherapy or manipulative therapy for back and neck complaints had been received in the past two years; and the complaint could be reproduced by active or passive physical examination.

The purpose of these criteria was to select a (relatively) homogeneous group of patients suitable for treatment with physiotherapy, manipulative therapy, and continued care by the general practitioner. Eligible patients gave informed consent by signing a letter. Subsequently, randomisation was carried out by a second research assistant using a list of random numbers.

Treatments

Four treatments were included in the trial. Firstly, physiotherapy, which consisted of exercises, massage and/or physical therapy modalities (heat, electrotherapy, ultrasound, shortwave diathermy). Secondly, manipulative therapy, which consisted of manipulative techniques (manipulation and mobilisation of the spine) included in the directives of the Dutch Society for Manual Therapy (NVMT). (The manual therapists were all physiotherapists with an additional three to four years' education in manipulation.) Thirdly, continued treatment by the general practitioner, which consisted of prescribed drugs (for example, analgesics, non-steroidal anti-inflammatory drugs), advice about posture, home exercises, participation in sports, (bed)rest, etc. Fourthly, placebo treatment, which in each session consisted of a physical examination and then detuned shortwave diathermy (10 minutes) and detuned ultrasound (10 minutes) carried out by the participating physiotherapists. The placebo treatment sessions were scheduled twice a week for six weeks.

All therapists (except for those giving placebo treatment) were free to choose from their usual therapeutic domain within some explicitly formulated limits (for example, no manipulative techniques could be performed by the physiotherapists). All treatments were given for a maximum of three months.

Outcome measures

Follow up measurements were carried out at six and 12 months after randomisation in order to study long term effects. Below, we focus on the three outcome measures which proved sensitive in measuring changes at the short term follow up (three, six, and 12 weeks after randomisation)[16,17]: severity of the main complaint, global perceived effect, and physical functioning.

The main complaint was determined as the complaint which the patient considered to be the most important at baseline. Its severity was assessed by the

research assistant on a 10 point scale (1 = minimal severity, 10 = maximal severity) based on history taking and physical examination. During all follow up measurements the research assistant was unaware of the treatment to which the patients were assigned. He also had no information about the previous scores. Global perceived effect was assessed by the patients on a 6 point scale (1=no benefit, 6=maximal benefit) after six and 12 months' follow up. Physical functioning was measured by the ability of patients to perform active spinal movements. Patients with neck complaints were asked to perform a standardised set of cervical movements (anteflexion, retroflexion, lateroflexion, and rotation); those with back complaints had to perform a similar set of trunk movements. At baseline the research assistant noted for each patient the movements (maximum of three) for which the patient reported the most severe pain or limitation of the range of motion. In addition, the severity of the pain (or of the limitation of range of motion) for these movements was scored on a 10 point scale (1 = minimal severity, 10 = maximal severity). At follow up the movements chosen at baseline were reassessed by the same (blinded) research assistant, who was unaware of the previous scores. The physical functioning score was calculated by adding the severity scores of all (maximum of three) movements at issue divided by the number of movements.[17]

Statistical analysis

The cumulative number of patients in each of the four treatment groups who had deviated from the allocated treatment after six and 12 months' follow up was calculated. The effects in the group receiving placebo therapy and the group receiving treatment by the general practitioner seemed to be seriously biased owing to contamination and cointerventions (see results). Therefore, we restricted the data analysis for the three outcome measures to the manipulative therapy and physiotherapy groups only.

For two outcome measures (severity of the main complaint and physical functioning) we calculated the differences between the follow up scores and the baseline score for individual patients. Subsequently, the two study groups were compared with each other for their improvement 12 months after randomisation. The global perceived effect at six and 12 months was also compared. In addition, we calculated the cumulative distributions of the improvement scores for the severity of the main complaint and for physical functioning and global perceived effect at 12 months' follow up. Group differences and 95% confidence intervals after six and 12 months' follow up were calculated for the three outcome measures with a linear regression model in order to estimate differences between groups after adjusting for small imbalances in important prognostic indicators at baseline. In the model we entered the following covariables: location and duration of the main complaint, the baseline score of the outcome measure at issue (except for global perceived effect in which case

6

Table I

Baseline characteristics of the study population

Characteristic	Manipulative therapy	Physiotherapy	Placebo therapy	General practitioner	All subjects
Total No of subjects	65	66	64	61	256
No (%) selected through advertisement	49 (75)	42 (64)	44 (69)	38 (62)	173 (68)
Mean age (years)	43	42	43	43	43
Sex (No (%) female)	35 (54)	32 (48)	33 (52)	23 (38)	123 (48)
Location of complaints (No(%)):					
Back	36 (55)	36 (54)	40 (62)	32 (53)	144 (56)
Neck	13 (20)	21 (32)	14 (22)	16 (26)	64 (25)
Back and neck	16 (25)	9 (14)	10 (16)	13 (21)	48 (19)
Median duration of present episode of complaints (weeks):					
Patients with back or neck complaints (n=208)	52	52	52	45	52
Patients with back and neck complaints (n=48):					
Back	78	26	92	78	79
Neck	91	26	65	52	52
No (%) who had had previous treatment:					
Physiotherapy	38 (58)	30 (45)	37 (58)	49 (48)	134 (52)
Manipulative therapy	8 (12)	12 (18)	3 (5)	6 (10)	29 (11)
Alternative medicine	9 (14)	12 (18)	6 (9)	12 (20)	39 (15)
Specialist	11 (17)	12 (18)	14 (22)	11 (18)	48 (19)
Mean severity of main complaint (10 point scale)	7.0	7.0	6.8	6.8	6.9
Mean physical functioning score (10 point scale)	5.9	5.8	5.7	5.7	5.8

severity of the main complaint at baseline was chosen), age, and recruitment status (general practitioner or advertisement). We also calculated the power of the study based on the results for severity of main complaint after 12 months' follow up (see appendix). The analyses were carried out with the biomedical programs data package, 1990 version.[18]

RESULTS

A total of 256 patients met the inclusion criteria and were randomly assigned to the four treatments. Table I shows the demographic and clinical characteristics of the participants. Comparability between the four groups for the main prognostic variables such as duration, severity, and location of the complaints and age was satisfactory. The median duration of the episode of back or neck pain for all patients was 52 weeks, indicating that most patients had very long periods of back or neck pain. About half the patients had previously received physiotherapy for their complaints (but not during the two years before entering the trial).

Table II shows the number of treatments, length of sessions, and duration of treatment for the four study groups. The manual therapy group had fewer treatments than the physiotherapy group (mean 5.4 v 14.7). Patients in the general practitioner group mostly paid only one visit to their general practitioner. Table III presents the cumulative number of the deviations from the allocated therapy at follow up after six and 12 months. Contamination and cointerventions mainly occurred among patients in the placebo and general practitioner groups.

In addition, there were three patients in the physiotherapy group and nine patients in the manipulative therapy group who continued their allocated treatment after the planned maximum of three months. Four patients in the physiotherapy group and three patients in the manipulative therapy group started a new period of the allocated treatment. Overall, the number of deviations from the study protocol among patients receiving manipulative therapy or physiotherapy seemed equally distributed.

After six month's follow up 11 (17%) patients in the physiotherapy group and seven (11%) patients in the manipulative therapy group did not fill out the written questionnaire. After 12 months' follow up 17 (26%) patients in the physiotherapy group and 10 (15%)

Table II

Mean (median) number of treatments, length of session, and duration of treatment during the intervention period

	No of treatments	Length of session (min)	Duration of treatment (weeks)
Manipulative therapy	5.4 (6)	41 (40)	8.9 (9)
Physiotherapy	14.7 (14)	35 (30)	7.8 (8)
Placebo therapy	11.1 (12)	29 (30)	5.8 (6)
General practitioner*			

*Treatment by the general practitioner consisted usually of a single visit by the patient at the general practice.

Table III

Cumulative number of deviations from the allocated therapy at follow up

Treatment group	6 Month follow up	12 Month follow up
Manipulative therapy	3 Physiotherapy 2 Specialist 1 Operation for herniated nucleus polposus 1 Injection 1 Alternative medicine	5 Physiotherapy 2 Specialist 1 Operation for herniated nucleus polposus 1 Injection 2 Alternative medicine
Physiotherapy	2 Manual therapy 1 Sport massage 1 Specialist 1 Alternative medicine	6 Manual therapy 1 Sport massage 7 Specialist 2 Alternative medicine
Placebo therapy	18 Physiotherapy 3 Manual therapy 1 Cesar therapy 2 Specialist 1 Operation for herniated nucleus polposus	19 Physiotherapy 3 Manual therapy 1 Cesar therapy 5 Specialist 1 Operation for herniated nucleus polposus
General practitioner	8 Physiotherapy 6 Manual therapy 2 Cesar therapy 1 Sport massage 2 Specialist 1 Operation for herniated nucleus polposus 1 Hospital admission 2 Alternative medicine	12 Physiotherapy 6 Manual therapy 2 Cesar therapy 1 Sport massage 2 Specialist 1 Operation for herniated nucleus polposus 1 Hospital admission 2 Alternative medicine

patients in the manipulative therapy group did not attend for the final assessment of effect (change in main complaint and physical functioning) by the research assistant. However, after 12 months' follow up most patients filled out the questionnaire: only six (9%) patients who received physiotherapy and five (8%) who received manipulative therapy could not be persuaded to do so. Table IV lists the results up to 12 months' follow up for the manipulative therapy and physiotherapy groups. With regard to the change of the main complaint, the manipulative therapy group showed the largest improvement (4.5 (SD 2.2)) after 12 months' follow up. The difference in improvement scores between both groups was 0.9 (95% confidence interval 0. 1 to 1.7). The manipulative therapy group showed consistently better results for physical functioning than the physiotherapy group at all follow up measurements. The difference between both groups after 12 months'

Table IV

Outcome of therapy at follow up

Outcome measure	3 Weeks	6 Weeks	12 Weeks	6 Months	12 Months	Difference (95% confidence interval) between manipulative therapy and physiotherapy groups*
Mean (SD) improvement in main complaint (10 point scale):						
Manipulative therapy	2.3 (2.1)	3.4 (2.1)	4.0 (2.6)		4.5 (2.2)	0.9 (0.1 to 1.7) at 12 months
Physiotherapy	2.0 (2.3)	3.4 (2.4)	3.8 (2.3)		3.8 (2.3)	
Mean (SD) global perceived effect (6 point scale):						
Manipulative therapy	2.5 (1.5)	3.4 (1.7)	3.4 (2.0)	3.5 (1.9)	3.5 (1.8)	0.3 (-0.4 to 1.0) at 6 months
Physiotherapy	2.6 (1.6)	3.3 (1.6)	3.7 (1.7)	3.5 (1.8)	3.2 (1.9)	0.4 (-0.3 to 1.4) at 12 months
Mean (SD) improvement in physical functioning (10 point scale):						
Manipulative therapy	2.3 (2.1)	3.5 (1.9)	4.0 (2.3)		4.2 (2.1)	0.6 (-0.1 to 1.3) at 12 months
Physiotherapy	1.6 (1.9)	3.1 (1.8)	3.2 (2.0)		3.7 (2.0)	

* The group differences (95% confidence intervals) were calculated with a linear regression model

follow up was 0.6 (-0.1 to 1.3). For global perceived effect, both groups showed similar results at all follow up measurements.

Even among patients assigned to manipulative therapy and physiotherapy there was a considerable number of missing values at 12 months' follow up. Therefore, we also conducted an alternative analysis, in which we substituted the last measurement available for missing values. The results of this analysis showed slightly smaller improvement scores for both groups. The mean (SD) improvement for the main complaint after 12 months in this alternative analysis was 4.1 (2.4) for manipulative therapy and 3.4 (2.7) for physiotherapy. The group difference was 0.9 (0.1 to 1.8). The mean (SD) improvement for the physical functioning was 3.8 (2.3) for manipulative therapy and 3.1 (2.2) for physiotherapy. The group difference was 0.8 (0.1 to 1.5). Both differences were significant at the 5% level.

Figure 1 shows the cumulative distribution of the improvement score for the main complaint in the groups that received manipulative therapy or physiotherapy. For any cut off point the proportion of patients in both study groups with at least that score can be read on the ordinate. For example, 75% in the manipulative therapy group and 65% in the physiotherapy group showed an improvement score of 3 points or more at 12 months' follow up. Manipulative

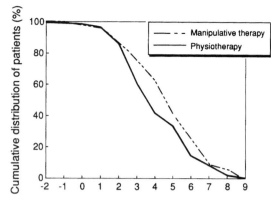

FIG 3 — *Cumulative distribution of improvement in score for physical functioning after 12 months' follow up in patients given manipulative therapy and physiotherapy*

therapy showed the best outcome for improvement scores of 7 points or less. Figure 2 gives the cumulative distribution of the global perceived effect at 12 months' follow up. The cumulative distributions of both groups were similar. Only for the benefit scores of 3 and 4 was the proportion of patients with at least that score higher among patients receiving manipulative therapy. Figure 3 gives the cumulative distribution of the improvement scores for physical functioning after 12 months' follow up. For any improvement score the proportion of patients with at least that score was higher among patients who received manipulative therapy than among those who received physiotherapy.

DISCUSSION

A large number of patients changed from the assigned treatment to another treatment during the one year follow up in the placebo and general practitioner groups. A change in treatment was not chosen as an outcome measure when the trial was designed, but this outcome clearly indicates the superiority of both manipulative therapy and physiotherapy over the two other treatments. The underlying assumption is that patients will in general turn to other treatments when the allocated treatment is not effective enough. Because of the large numbers of deviations from the allocated treatment in the placebo and general practitioner groups after six and 12 months' follow up we expected serious bias due to contamination and cointerventions. We therefore decided not to analyse the data on the outcome measures at these follow up measurements.

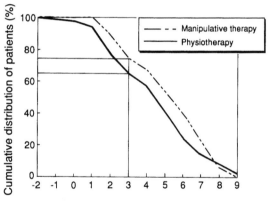

FIG 1 — *Cumulative distribution of improvement in score for main complaint after 12 months' follow up in patients given manipulative therapy and physiotherapy*

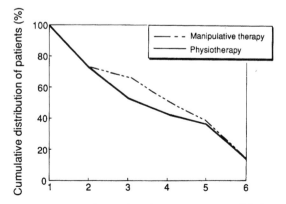

FIG 2 — *Cumulative distribution of score for global perceived effect after 12 months' follow up in patients given manipulative therapy and physiotherapy*

It might have been possible to perform a pragmatic analysis on the collected data. In retrospect, we would have classified the four study groups according to the treatment they actually received instead of the treatment they were originally assigned to. For methodological reasons, however, we decided not to perform such analysis because it would almost certainly bias outcomes. The main problem would be that the prognosis of patients who deviated from the assigned therapy would be different from that of those who did not. In fact, in a pragmatic analysis all the advantages of randomisation aiming at prognostic comparability of the study groups at baseline would be lost. Instead of an experimental design we would have been left with an observational study.

The comparison between manipulative therapy and physiotherapy at six and 12 months' follow up remained valid and relevant. The short term results had shown similar success rates in both these groups,[16,17] but long term effects are also important for patients with persistent back and neck complaints. After 12 months manipulative therapy had produced a larger mean improvement in the main complaint than physiotherapy. This pattern was also shown in the cumulative distributions of the improvement scores for the main complaint of both groups (fig 1). The difference between both groups was significant. Physical functioning also seemed to improve consistently more with manipulative therapy, but the difference was not significant after 12 months' follow up. For the global perceived effect we could not find any substantial difference between both therapies. At six months' follow up both groups showed equal scores (3.5 points). At 12 months' follow up the manipulative therapy group scored slightly higher than the physiotherapy group (3.5 v 3.2 points). The cumulative distributions showed some difference in favour of manipulative therapy only for benefit scores of 3 and 4 points. However, the 95% confidence interval for the group difference was -0.3 to 1.4.

It is remarkable that the patients in the manipulative therapy group showed better results compared with those in the physiotherapy group at 12 months' follow up. Long term benefits of manipulative therapy are seldomly reported.[7] The patients in the manipulative therapy group showed the highest improvement in scores at 12 months, while for most patients the time of greatest improvement was about nine months after the last treatment session. There are several explanations for this finding.

Firstly, it might be that the relatively large number of missing values after 12 months represent those who responded badly to treatment. The patients who did attend for the follow up assessment might therefore be a selected group of patients in whom the therapy was successful. In our alternative analysis, however, we substituted the last available measurement for missing values, and this did not change the results appreciably. Furthermore, the number of missing values was larger in the physiotherapy group (26%) than in the manipulative therapy group (15%). We therefore think that missing values cannot explain our findings.

Secondly, many patients might have received additional manipulative therapy or other cointerventions during the nine months after the intervention period. Table III shows that several patients did receive additional treatment, but the numbers were comparable with those in the physiotherapy group. Thirdly, it might be that the blinding of the research assistant was not fully successful. Although we did not measure the success of blinding explicitly, we have no reason to believe that it failed. Finally, manipulative therapy may help to restore the function of the spine better than physiotherapy. In the case of persistent conditions a relatively long period might be needed to achieve maximal reduction of the complaints. A physiological explanation for such a mechanism has not yet been shown. The few earlier studies which had included a long term follow up mostly did not report long term positive results of manipulation.[8,10-14] There is one study in which the authors report long term benefit of manipulation for chronic or severe pain, especially at longer term (two years) follow up. In this large multicentre trial chiropractic manipulation was compared with (physiotherapeutic) hospital outpatient treatment for low back pain.[9] An important extra finding was that the number of treatments was much lower for manipulative therapy than physiotherapy. This might be regarded as a considerable advantage.

We conclude that after 12 months' follow up both manipulative therapy and physiotherapy seem to be more effective than treatment by the general practitioner or placebo treatment in patients with persistent back and neck pain. Furthermore, the findings indicate a slightly better result from manipulative therapy compared with physiotherapy after 12 months' follow up. Further trials of manipulation are needed to determine its long term effects in patients with more specific conditions.

We thank Monique Latour for her help in conducting this study. This study was funded by the Dutch Ministry of Welfare, Health, and Cultural Affairs and by the Dutch National Health Insurance Council.

Department of Epidemiology and Biostatistics, University of Limburg, PO Box 616, 6200 MD Maastricht, Netherlands

Bart W Koes, MA, research fellow
Lex M Bouter, PHD, associate professor of epidemiology
Paul G Knipschild, MD, professor of epidemiology
Department of Anatomy and Embryology, University of Limburg
Henk van Mameren, MD, associate professor of anatomy
Department of Physiotherapy, University Hospital, Maastricht, Netherlands
Alex H M Essers, PT, research assistant
Department of Physiotherapy, Institute of Higher Education, Heerlen, Netherlands
Gard M J R Verstegen, PT, practitioner
Jo P Houben, PT, practitioner
Physiotherapy and Manual Therapy Practice, Maastricht, Netherlands
Domien M Hofhuizen, PT, practitioner
Correspondence to: Mr Koes.

References

1 Frymoyer JW. Back pain and sciatica. N Engl J Med 1988;**318**:291-300.
2 Waddell G. A new clinical model for the treatment of low-back pain. *Spine* 1987;**12**:632-44.
3 Nachemson A. A critical look at the treatment for low back pain. *Scand J Rehab Med* 1979;**11**:143-7.
4 Deyo RA. Conservative therapy for low back pain. *JAMA* 1983;**250**:1057-62.

6

5   Spitzer WO, Leblanc FE, Dupuis M. Scientific approach to the assessment and management of activity-related spinal disorders. *Spine* 1987;7 (suppl 1): 1-59.

6   Koes BW, Bouter LM, Beckerman H, van der Heijden GJMG, Knipschild PG. Physiotherapy exercises and back pain: a blinded review. *BMJ* 1991;**302**:1572-6.

7   Koes BW, Assendelft WJJ, van der Heiiden GJMG, Bouter LM, Knipschild PG. Spinal manipulation and mobilisation for back and neck complaints: a blinded review. BMJ 1991;303:1298-303.

8   Bergquist-Ullman M, Larsson M. Acute low back pain in industry: a controlled prospective study with special reference to therapy and confounding factors. *Acta Orthop Scand* 1977;**170** (suppl): 11-117.

9   Meade TW, Dyer S, Browne W, Townsend J, Frank AO. Low back pain of mechanical origin: randomised comparison of chiropractic and hospital outpatient treatment. *BMJ* 1990;**300**:1431-7.

10   Sims-Williams H, Jayson MIV, Young SMS, Baddeley H, Collins E. Controlled trial of mobilisation and manipulation for low back pain: hospital patients. *BMJ* 1979;ii:1318-20.

11   Doran DML, Newell DJ. Manipulation in treatment of low back pain: a multicentre study. BMJ 1975;ii: 161-4.

12   Coxhead CE, Inskip H, Meade TW, North WRS, Troup JDG. Multicentre trial of physiotherapy in the management of sciatic symptoms. *Lancet* 1981;i:1065-8.

13   Sims-Williams H, Jayson MIV, Young SMS, Baddeley H, Collins E. Controlled trial of mobilisation and manipulation for patients with low back pain in general practice. *BMJ* 1978;ii: 1338-40.

14   Siehl D, Olson DR, Ross HE, Rockwood EE. Manipulation of the lumbar spine with the patient under general anaesthesia: evaluation by electromyography and clinical-neurologic examination of its use for lumbar nerve root compression sydrome. *J Am Osteopath Assoc* 1971;**70**:433-50.

15   Koes BW, Bouter LM, Knipschild PG, van Mameren H, Essers AHM, Houben JP, et al. The effectiveness of manual therapy, physiotherapy and continued treatment by the general practitioner for non-specific back and neck complaints: design of a randomised clinical trial. *J Manipulative Physiol Ther* (in press.)

16   Koes BW, Bouter LM, van Mameren H, Essers AHM, Verstegen GMJR, Hofhuizen DM, *et al.* The effectiveness of manual therapy, physiotherapy and treatment by the general practitioner for non-specific back and neck complaints: a randomized clinical trial. *Spine* (in press).

17   Koes BW, Bouter LM, van Mameren H, Essers AHM, Verstegen GMJR, Hofhuizen DM, *et al.* A blinded randomized clinical trial of manual therapy and physiotherapy for chronic back and neck complaints: physical outcome measures. *J Manipulative Physiol Ther* (in press).

18   Dixon WJ, Brown MB, Engelman L, Jenrich RI. BMDP statistical software manual. Berkeley: University of California Press, 1990.

(Accepted 4 December 1991)

Appendix

We calculated the power of the study based on the primary outcome measure (severity of the main complaint measured on a 10 point scale) after 12 months' follow up. We used the following sample size equation:

$$n = \sqrt{\frac{2(Z\alpha + Z\beta)^2 \times 2\sigma_\Delta^2}{\Delta}}$$

n = The number of participants after correction for loss to follow up (50 participants in each study group after 12 months' follow up).

Δ = The minimal difference in improvement score between the two study groups that was considered to be of clinical relevance. This was set at 1 point ($\Delta = 1$).

$Z\alpha$ = The variable of the standard normal distribution corresponding with a significance level of 5%, two sided test.

σ_Δ = the variance of the difference scores (score at baseline minus score after 12 months' follow up) was estimated to be the square of 2.25 (derived from table IV).

$Z\beta$ = The parameter to be calculated.

The calculation shows that the power of the study to detect a difference in improvement scores of 1 point is 60%.

This information was first published in The Back Book *and is reproduced by permission of the HMSO*

The Back Book

Roland M, Waddell G, Moffett J, Burton K, Main C and Cantrell T

The New Approach to Back Pain

Back pain has always been very common and we have learned a great deal about it. There has been a revolution in thinking about back care, and we now approach it in a different way.

Most people can and do deal with back pain themselves most of the time. This booklet gives you the best and most up-to-date advice on how to deal with it, avoid disability and recover quickly. It is based on the latest research.

- Back pain or ache is usually not due to any serious disease.
- Most back pain settles quickly, at least enough to get on with your normal life.
- About half the people who get backache will have it again within a couple of years. But that still does not mean that it is serious. Between attacks most people return to normal activities with few if any symptoms.
- It can be very painful and you may need to reduce some activities for a time. But rest for more than a day or two usually does not help and may do more harm than good. So keep moving.
- Your back is designed for movement. The sooner you get back to normal activity the sooner your back will feel better.
- The people who cope best are those who stay active and get on with their life despite the pain.

Causes of Back Pain

Your spine is one of the strongest parts of your body. It is made of solid bony blocks joined by discs to give it strength and flexibility. It is reinforced by strong ligaments. It is surrounded by large and powerful muscles which protect it. It is surprisingly difficult to damage your spine.

People often have it wrong about back pain.

In fact:

- Most people with back pain or backache do not have any damage in their spine.
- Very few people with backache have a slipped disc or a trapped nerve. Even then a slipped disc usually gets better by itself.
- Most x-ray findings in your back are normal changes with age. That is not arthritis – it is normal, just like grey hair.

In most people we cannot pinpoint the exact source of the trouble. It can be frustrating not to know exactly what is wrong. But in another way it is good news – you do not have any serious disease or any serious damage in your back.

Most back pain comes from the muscles, ligaments and joints in your back. They are simply not moving and working as they should. You can think of your back as 'out of condition'. So what you need to do is get your back working properly again.

Stress can increase the amount of pain you feel. Tension can cause muscle spasm and the muscles themselves can become painful.

People who are physically fit generally get less back pain, and recover faster if they do get it.

So the answer to backache is to get your back moving and working properly again. Get back into condition and physically fit.

Rest or Active Exercise?

The old fashioned treatment for back pain was prolonged rest. But bed rest for more than a day or two is not good, because:

- Your bones get weaker.
- Your muscles get weaker.
- You get stiff.
- You lose physical fitness.
- You get depressed.
- The pain feels worse.
- It is harder and harder to get going again.

No wonder it didn't work! We no longer use bed rest to treat any other common condition. It is time to stop bed rest for backache. The message is clear: bed rest is bad for backs.

Of course, you might need to do a bit less when the pain is bad. You might be forced to have a day or two in bed at the start. But the most important thing is to get moving again as soon as you can.

Exercise is Good for You

Your body must stay active to stay healthy. It thrives on use.

Regular exercise:

- Gives you stronger bones.
- Develops fit active muscles.
- Keeps you supple.
- Makes you fit.
- Makes you feel good.
- Releases natural chemicals which reduce pain.

Even when your back is sore, you can make a start without putting too much stress on your back:

- Walking.
- Exercise bike.
- Swimming.

Walking, using an exercise bike, or swimming all use your muscles and get your joints moving. They make your heart and lungs work and are a start to physical fitness.

When you start to exercise you may need to build up gradually over a few days or weeks. You should then exercise regularly and keep it up – fitness takes time.

Different exercises suit different people. Find out what suits your back best. Rearrange your life to get some exercise every day. Try walking instead of going by car or bus. Some of the easiest activities to get back to are walking, swimming, cycling and smooth rhythmic exercises. The important thing is general exercise and physical fitness.

Athletes know that when they start training, their muscles can ache. That does not mean that they are doing any damage. The same applies to you and your back.

No-one pretends exercising is easy. Pain killers and other treatments can help to control the pain to let you get started. It often does hurt at first, but one thing is sure: the longer you put off exercise the harder and more painful it will be. There is no other way. You have a straight choice: rest, or work through your pain to recovery.

STAYING ACTIVE

Dealing with an acute attack

What you do depends on how bad your back feels. Remember, your back isn't badly damaged. You can usually:

- Use something to control the pain.
- Modify your activities.
- Stay active and at work.

If your pain is more severe you may have to rest for a few days. You might need stronger pain killers from your doctor, and you might even have to lie down for a day or two. But only for a day or two; don't think of rest as treatment. Too much rest is bad for your back. The faster you get going the sooner your back will feel better.

You should build up your activities and your exercise tolerance over several days or a few weeks. But the faster you get back to normal activities and back to work the better, even if you still have some pain and some restrictions. If you have a heavy job, you may need some help from your work mates. Simple changes can make your job easier. Talk to your foreman or boss if you need to.

Control of pain

There are many treatments which can help back pain. They may not remove the pain completely, but they should control it enough for you to get active. These treatments help to control the pain, but they do not cure your back. It is up to you to get going and get your back working again.

Pain killers

Paracetamol or soluble Aspirin are the simplest and safest pain killers. It may surprise you, but they are still often the most effective. Take two tablets every 4 – 6 hours. Or you can use anti-inflammatory tablets like Ibuprofen. You should usually take the pain killers for a day or two but you may need to take them for a few weeks. Take them regularly and do not wait till your pain is out of control. Do not take Aspirin or Ibuprofen if you have indigestion or an ulcer problem.

Heat or cold

In the first 48 hours you can try a cold pack on your back for 5 – 10 minutes at a time – a bag of frozen peas wrapped in a towel. Other people prefer heat – a hot water bottle, a bath or a shower.

Spinal manipulation

Most doctors now agree that manipulation can help. It is best within the first 6 weeks. Manipulation is carried out by osteopaths, chiropractors, some physiotherapists and a few doctors with special training. It is safe if it is done by a qualified professional.

Other treatments

Many other treatments are used and some people feel that they help. It is up to you to find out what helps you.

Stress and muscle tension

If stress is a problem you need to recognise it at an early stage and try to do something about it. It is not always possible to remove the cause of stress, but it is quite easy to learn to reduce its effects by breathing control, muscle relaxation and mental calming techniques.

HOW TO STAY ACTIVE

You can do most daily activities if you think about them first.

The basic idea is not to stay in one position or do any one thing for more than 20-30 minutes without a break. Then try to move a little further and faster every day.

☺ Some ways to help your pain

Lifting	Know your own strength: lift what you can handle. Always lift and carry close to your body. Bend your knees and make your legs do the work. Don't twist your back – turn with your feet.
Sitting	Use an upright chair. Try a folded towel in the small of your back. Get up and stretch every 20 – 30 minutes.
Standing	Try putting one foot on a low box or stool. Have your working surface at a comfortable height.
Driving	Adjust your seat from time to time. Try a folded towel in the small of your back.
Activity	20-30 minutes walking, cycling or swimming every day. Gradually increase physical activity.
Sleeping	Some people prefer a firm mattress or try boards beneath your mattress.
Relax	Learn how to reduce stress. Use relaxation techniques.

☹ Some things may make your pain worse

Lifting without thinking

A low, soft chair. Lack of back support. Sitting for a long time.

Long periods in one position.

Long drives without a break.

Sitting around all day. Not exercising: being unfit.

Staying in bed too long.

Worry: being tense.

What do you find helps you?

1 _____

2 _____

3 _____

4 _____

5 _____

What do you find makes your pain worse?

1 _____

2 _____

3 _____

4 _____

5 _____

You can deal with most back pain yourself, but there are times when you should see your doctor.

What doctors can and can't do

Doctors can diagnose and treat the few serious spinal diseases. But they have no quick fix for simple back pain. You must be realistic about what you can expect from your doctor and therapist.

- They can reassure you that you do not have any serious disease.
- They can try various treatments to help control your pain.
- They can advise you on how you can best deal with the pain and get on with your life.

It is natural to worry that back pain might be due to something serious. Usually it isn't. But you may still feel the need to check. That is one of the most important things that your doctor can do for you.

Warning signs

If you have severe pain which gets worse over several weeks instead of better, or if you are unwell with back pain, you should see your doctor.

Here are a few symptoms which are all very rare but if you do have back pain and suddenly develop any of these symptoms you should see a doctor straight away.

- Difficulty passing or controlling urine.
- Numbness around your back passage or genitals.
- Numbness, pins and needles or weakness in both legs.
- Unsteadiness on your feet.

Don't let that list worry you too much.

IT'S YOUR BACK

Backache is not a serious disease and it should not cripple you unless you let it. We have tried to show you the best way to deal with it. The important thing now is for you to get on with your life. How your backache affects you depends on how you react to the pain and what you do about it yourself.

There is no instant answer. You will have your ups and downs for a while – that is normal. But this is what you can do for yourself.

There are two types of sufferer

One who avoids activity, and one who copes.

☹ The *avoider* gets frightened by the pain and worries about the future.

- The *avoider* is afraid that hurting always means further damage – it doesn't.
- The *avoider* rests a lot, and waits for the pain to get better.

☺ The *coper* knows that the pain will get better and does not fear the future.

- The *coper* carries on as normally as possible.
- The *coper* deals with the pain by being positive, staying active or staying at work.

Who suffers most?

☹ *Avoiders* suffer the most. They have pain for longer, they have more time off work and they can become disabled.

☺ *Copers* suffer less at the time and they are healthier in the long run.

So how do I become a *Coper* and prevent unnecessary suffering?

Follow these guidelines – you really can help yourself.

☺ Live life as normally as possible. This is much better than staying in bed.

- Keep up daily activities – they will not cause damage. Just avoid really heavy things.
- Try to stay fit – walking, cycling or swimming will exercise your back and should make you feel better. And continue even after your back feels better.
- Start gradually and do a little more each day so you can see the progress you are making.
- Either stay at work or go back to work as soon as possible. If necessary, ask if you can get lighter duties for a week or two.

- Be patient. It is normal to get aches or twinges for a time.

☹ Don't just rely on pain killers. Stay positive and take control of the pain yourself.
- Don't stay at home or give up doing things you enjoy.
- Don't worry. It does not mean you are going to become an invalid.
- Don't listen to other people's horror stories – they're usually nonsense.
- Don't get gloomy on the down days.

Remember:
- Back pain is common but it is rarely due to any serious disease.
- Even when it is very painful that usually does not mean there is any serious damage to your back. Hurt does not mean harm.
- Mostly it gets better with little or no medical treatment.
- Bed rest for more than a day or two is usually bad for your back.
- Staying active will help you get better faster and prevent more back trouble.
- The sooner you get going, the sooner you will get better.
- Regular exercise and staying fit helps your general health and your back.
- You have to run your own life and do the things you want to do. Don't let your back take over.

This leaflet was first published by the Royal College of General Practitioners and is reproduced with the permission of the RCGP

Clinical Guidelines for the Management of

ACUTE LOW BACK PAIN

Contributing Organisations
Royal College of General Practitioners
Chartered Society of Physiotherapy
British Osteopathic Association
British Chiropractic Association
National Back Pain Association

Review Date: December 2001

**Further information and copies of
the full evidence base for these
guidelines are available from:**

Paula-Jayne McDowell,
Royal College of General Practitioners,
14 Princes Gate, Hyde Park, London,
SW7 1PU

or at website –
http://www.rcgp.org.uk

We are grateful to:
Professor Gordon Waddell
NHS Executive,
Clinical Standards Advisory Group,

U.S. Agency for Health Care
Policy & Research,

Swedish SBU,
NZ National Health Committee

This document may be photocopied freely

DIAGNOSTIC TRIAGE

Diagnostic triage is the differential diagnosis between:
- Simple backache (non specific low back pain)
- Nerve root pain
- Possible serious spinal pathology

Simple backache: *specialist referral not required*
- Presentation 20-55 years
- Lumbosacral, buttocks & thighs
- "Mechanical" pain
- Patient well

Nerve root pain: *specialist referral not generally required within first 4 weeks, provided resolving*
- Unilateral leg pain worse than low back pain
- Radiates to foot or toes
- Numbness & paraesthesia in same distribution
- SLR reproduces leg pain
- Localised neurological signs

Red flags for *possible* **serious spinal pathology:** *consider prompt investigation or referral (less than 4 weeks)*
- Presentation under age 20 or onset over 55
- Non-mechanical pain
- Thoracic pain
- Past history – carcinoma, steroids, HIV
- Unwell, weight loss
- Widespread neurological symptoms or signs
- Structural deformity

Cauda equina syndrome: *emergency referral*
- Sphincter disturbance
- Gait disturbance
- Saddle anaesthesia

The evidence is weighted as follows:
★★★ Generally consistent finding in a majority of acceptable studies.
★★ Either based on a single acceptable study, or a weak or inconsistent finding in some of multiple acceptable studies.
★ Limited scientific evidence, which does not meet all the criteria of 'acceptable' studies.

PRINCIPAL RECOMMENDATIONS

EVIDENCE

Assessment

- Carry out diagnostic triage (see left).
- X-Rays are not routinely indicated in simple backache.
- Consider psychosocial 'yellow flags' (see over).

★ Diagnostic triage forms the basis for referral, investigation and management.
★ Royal College of Radiologists Guidelines.
★★★ Psychosocial factors play an important role in low back pain and disability and influence the patient's response to treatment and rehabilitation.

SIMPLE BACKACHE

Drug Therapy

- Prescribe analgesics at regular intervals, not p.r.n.
- Start with paracetamol. If inadequate, substitute NSAIDs (eg ibuprofen or diclofenac) and then paracetamol-weak opioid compound (eg codydramol or coproxamol). Finally, consider adding a short course of muscle relaxant (eg diazepam or baclofen).
- Avoid strong opioids if possible.

★★ Paracetamol effectively reduces low back pain.
★★★ NSAIDs effectively reduce pain. Ibuprofen and diclofenac have lower risks of GI complications.
★★ Paracetamol-weak opioid compounds may be effective when NSAIDs or paracetamol alone are inadequate.
★★★ Muscle relaxants effectively reduce low back pain.

Bed Rest

- Do not recommend or use bed rest as a treatment.
- Some patients may be confined to bed for a few days as a consequence of their pain but this should not be considered a treatment.

★★★ Bed rest for 2-7 days is worse than placebo or ordinary activity and is not as effective as alternative treatments for relief of pain, rate of recovery, return to daily activities and work.

Advice on Staying Active

- Advise patients to stay as active as possible and to continue normal daily activities.
- Advise patients to increase their physical activities progressively over a few days or weeks.
- If a patient is working, then advice to stay at work or return to work as soon as possible is probably beneficial.

★★★ Advice to continue ordinary activity can give equivalent or faster symptomatic recovery from the acute attack and lead to less chronic disability and less time off work.

Manipulation

- Consider manipulative treatment for patients who need additional help with pain relief or who are failing to return to normal activities.

★★★ Manipulation can provide short-term improvement in pain and activity levels and higher patient satisfaction.
★★ The optimum timing for this intervention is unclear.
★★ The risks of manipulation are very low in skilled hands.

Back Exercises

- Referral for reactivation / rehabilitation should be considered for patients who have not returned to ordinary activities and work by 6 weeks.

★★★ It is doubtful that specific back exercises produce clinically significant improvement in acute low back pain.
★★ There is some evidence that exercise programmes and physical reconditioning can improve pain and functional levels in patients with chronic low back pain. There are theoretical arguments for starting this at around 6 weeks.

These brief clinical guidelines and their supporting base of research evidence are intended to assist in the management of acute low back pain. It presents a synthesis of up-to-date international evidence and makes recommendations on case management.

Recommendations and evidence relate primarily to the first six weeks of an episode, when management decisions may be required in a changing clinical picture. However, the guidelines may also be useful in the sub-acute period.

These guidelines have been constructed by a multi-professional group and subjected to extensive professional review.

They are intended to be used as a guide by the whole range of health professionals who advise people with acute low back pain, particularly simple backache, in the NHS and in private practice.

PSYCHOSOCIAL 'YELLOW FLAGS'

When conducting assessment, it may be useful to consider psychosocial 'yellow flags' (beliefs or behaviours on the part of the patient which may predict poor outcomes).
The following factors are important and consistently predict poor outcomes:

- a belief that back pain is harmful or potentially severely disabling
- fear-avoidance behaviour and reduced activity levels
- tendency to low mood and withdrawal from social interaction
- expectation of passive treatment(s) rather than a belief that active participation will help

KEY PATIENT INFORMATION POINTS

SIMPLE BACKACHE
- *give positive messages*

- There is nothing to worry about.
  Backache is very common.

- No sign of any serious damage or disease.
  Full recovery in days or weeks – but may vary.

- No permanent weakness.
  Recurrence possible – but does not mean re-injury.

- Activity is helpful, too much rest is not.
  Hurting does not mean harm.

NERVE ROOT PAIN
- *give guarded positive messages*

- No cause for alarm. No sign of disease.

- Conservative treatment should suffice – but may take a month or two.

- Full recovery expected – but recurrence possible.

POSSIBLE SERIOUS SPINAL PATHOLOGY
- *avoid negative messages*

- Some tests are needed to make the diagnosis.

- Often these tests are negative.

- The specialist will advise on the best treatment.

- Rest or activity avoidance until appointment to see specialist.

PATIENT BOOKLET

The above messages can be enhanced by an educational booklet given at consultation. *The Back Book* is an evidence-based booklet developed for use with these guidelines, and is published by The Stationery Office (ISBN 011 702 0788).

Additional Resource Material

Altman D (1996). Better reporting of randomised controlled trials: the CONSORT statement *British Medical Journal* **313**, 570-1.

Archibald CP, Lee HP (1995). Sample size estimation for clinicians. *Annals of Academic Medicine* Singapore **24**, 328-32.

Black N (1996). Why we need observational studies to evaluate the effectiveness of health care. *British Medical Journal* **312**, 1215-18.

Department of Health NHS Indemnity (1997). *Arrangements for clinical negligence claims in the NHS*. London, HMSO.

Edwards SJL, Lilford RJ, Hewison J (1998). The ethics of randomised controlled trials from the perspectives of patients, the public, and healthcare professionals. *British Medical Journal* **317**, 1209-12.

Hannaford P, 1999. The RCGP Centre for Primary Care Research and Epidemiology. In: Carter Y Thomas C (eds) *Research Methods in Primary Care*. Abingdon, Radcliffe Medical Press.

Hannaford P, Kay C (1998). The risk of serious illness among oral contraceptive users: evidence from the RCGP's oral contraceptive study. *British Journal of General Practice* **48**, 1657-62.

ICH Harmonised Tripartite Guideline for good clinical practice (1997). Richmond, Brookwood Medical Publications Ltd.

Jones B, Jarvis P, Lewis JA et al. (1999). Trials to assess equivalence: the importance of rigorous methods. *British Medical Journal* **313**, 36-39.

Kerry SM, Bland JM (1998). Sample size in cluster randomisation. *British Medical Journal* **316**, 549.

Kliejnen J, Gotzsche P, Kunz RH et al. (1997). So what's so special about randomisation? In: Maynard A, Chalmers I (eds). *Non-random reflections on health services research: on the 25th anniversary of Archie Cochrane's Effectiveness and Efficiency*. 93-106. London, BMJ Publishing Group.

Medical Research Council (1998). MRC Guidelines for good practice in clinical trials. London, MRC.

Multi-Centre Research Ethics Committees (1999). MREC Application form and General Guidance for Researchers. Plymouth, NHS Executive South and East Research and Development Directorate.

Silverman WA, Altman DG (1996). Patients' preferences and randomised trials. *Lancet* **347**, 171-174.

South and East Research and Development Directorate (1999). Patient Information Sheet Checklist. Plymouth, NHS Executive South and East Research and Development Directorate.

The standards of reporting trials group (1994). A proposal for structuring reporting of randomized controlled trials. *JAMA* **272**, 1926-31.

Torgerson D, Roland M (1998). Understanding controlled trials: what is Zelen's design? *British Medical Journal* **316**, 606.

Torgerson D, Sibbald B (1998). Understanding controlled trial: what is a patient preference trial? *British Medical Journal* **316**, 360.

Underwood MR, Barnett AG, Hajioff S (1998). Cluster randomization; A trap for the unwary. *British Journal of General Practice* **48**, 1089-90.

Ward E, King M, Lloyd M et al. (1999). Conducting randomized trials in general practice: methodological and practical issues. *British Journal of General Practice* **49**, 919.

This article was first published by the BMJ *and is reproduced with permission of the* BMJ

Editorials

BETTER REPORTING OF RANDOMISED CONTROLLED TRIALS: THE CONSORT STATEMENT

Authors must provide enough information for readers to know how the trial was performed

Randomised controlled trials are the best way to compare the effectiveness of different interventions. Only randomised trials allow valid inferences of cause and effect. Only randomised trials have the potential directly to affect patient care—occasionally as single trials but more often as the body of evidence from several trials, whether or not combined formally by meta-analysis. It is thus entirely reasonable to require higher standards for papers reporting randomised trials than those describing other types of study.

Like all studies, randomised trials are open to bias if done badly.[1] It is thus essential that randomised trials are done well and reported adequately. Readers should not have to infer what was probably done, they should be told explicitly. Proper methodology should be used and be seen to have been used. Yet reviews of published trials have consistently found major deficiencies in reporting,[2] [3] [4] making the task for those carrying out systematic reviews much harder. Almost 50 years after the first publication of a randomised trial,[5] the guarantee of adequate reporting of these important studies is surely long overdue.

In 1994 two groups independently published proposals for requirements for the reporting of randomised trials.[6] [7] In an editorial in JAMA Drummond Rennie suggested that the two groups should combine to produce a unified statement,[8] and the outcome of this process was published last week.[9] The new CONSORT statement lists 21 items that should be included in a report (see table 1) as well as a flow chart describing patient progress through the trial (fig 1). In addition, a few specific subheadings are suggested within the methods and results sections of the paper. In the spirit of the times, the recommendations are evidence based where possible, with common sense dictating the remainder.

In essence the requirement is that authors should provide enough information for readers to know how the trial was performed so that they can judge whether the findings are likely to be reliable. The CONSORT statement means that authors will no longer be able to hide inadequacies in their study by omitting important information. For example, at present authors can, and often do, hide their procedures behind the single word "randomised." Authors will now be required to give details of the randomisation procedure. If authors have used an inferior approach, such as alternate allocation, they will have to say so. The *BMJ* has in fact refused to publish trials that were not truly randomised since 1991,[10] a position justified by subsequent empirical findings.[1]

As the authors of the CONSORT statement note,[9] the checklist applies to the most common design of randomised trial—trials with two parallel groups. Some modification is needed for special types of trial such as crossover trials and those with more than two treatment groups. Also, the list should be taken in conjunction with existing general requirements—for example, the requirement to specify all statistical methods used in the analysis. This and other items appear on the checklist for controlled trials that has been used by the *BMJ*'s statistical referees for over 10 years.[11]

Some of the items on the checklist would benefit from greater explanation than is possible in the CONSORT statement. In time a fuller accompanying explanatory paper could be valuable. For example, while the advantages of randomisation have been apparent for several decades, understanding the rationale for it remains poor and so its importance is not fully appreciated by researchers.[12]

The *BMJ* supports the CONSORT statement and is adopting its recommendations. So too are *JAMA*, *Lancet*, and some other journals. Trialists are encouraged to follow the statement right away, but from 1 January 1997 they will be required to do so. Authors should submit with their papers a copy of the completed checklist indicating on which page of the manuscript each item is addressed. The checklist will be used by the editors and supplied to referees. In the published papers

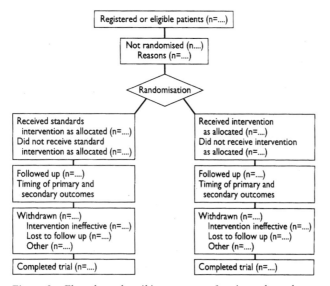

Figure 1 – Flow chart describing progress of patients through randomised trial (reproduced from JAMA*)*[9]

Table 1

Items that should be included in reports of randomised trials (reproduced from *JAMA*)[9]

Heading	Subheading	Descriptor
Title		Identify the study as a randomised trial
Abstract		Use a structured format
Introduction		State prospectively defined hypothesis, clinical objectives, and planned subgroup or covariate analyses
Methods	Protocol	Describe Planned study population, together with inclusion or exclusion criteria Planned interventions and their timing Primary and secondary outcome measure(s) and the minimum important difference(s), and indicate how the target sample size was projected Rationale and methods for statistical analyses, detailing main comparative analyses and whether they were completed on an intention to treat basis Prospectively defined stopping rules (if warranted)
	Assignment	Describe Unit of randomisation (for example, individual, cluster, geographic) Method used to generate the allocation schedule Method of allocation concealment and timing of assignment Method to separate the generator from the executor of assignment
	Masking (blinding)	Describe Mechanism (for example, capsules, tablets) Similarity of treatment characteristics (for example, appearance, taste) Allocation schedule control (location of code during trial and when broken) Evidence for successful blinding among participants, person doing intervention, outcome assessors, and data analysts
Results	Participant flow and follow up	Provide a trial profile (fig 1) summarising participant flow, numbers and timing of randomisation assignment, interventions, and measurements for each randomised group
	Analysis	State estimated effect of intervention on primary and secondary outcome measures, including a point estimate and measure of precision (confidence interval) State results in absolute numbers when feasible (for example, 10/20, not 50%) Present summary data and appropriate descriptive and interferential statistics in sufficient detail to permit alternative analyses and replication Describe prognostic variables by treatment group and any attempt to adjust for them Describe protocol deviations from the study as planned, together with the reasons
Discussion		State specific interpretation of study findings, including sources of bias and imprecision (internal validity) and discussion of external validity, including appropriate quantitative measures when possible State general interpretation of the data in light of the totality of the available evidence

the *BMJ* will use the additional subheadings suggested by CONSORT.

It seems reasonable to hope that, in addition to improved reporting, the wide adoption of this new publication standard will improve the conduct of future research by increasing awareness of the requirements for a good trial. Such success might lead to similar initiatives for other types of research.

DOUGLAS G ALTMAN
Head

ICRF Medical Statistics Group,
Centre for Statistics in Medicine,
Institute of Health Sciences,
Oxford OX3 7LF

References

1   Schulz KF, Chalmers I, Hayes R, Altman DG. Empirical evidence of bias. Dimensions of methodological quality associated with estimates of treatment effects in controlled trials. *JAMA* 1995;**273**:408-12.

2   Mosteller F, Gilbert JP, McPeek B. Reporting standards and research strategies for controlled trials. Agenda for the editor. *Controlled Clin Trials* 1980;**1**:37-58.

3   Pocock SJ, Hughes MD, Lee RJ. Statistical problems in the reporting of clinical trials. *N Engl J Med* 1987;**317**:426-32.

4   Schulz KF, Chalmers I, Grimes DA, Altman DG. Assessing the quality of randomization from reports of controlled trials published in obstetrics and gynecology journals. *JAMA* 1994;**272**:125-8.

5   Medical Research Council. Streptomycin treatment of pulmonary tuberculosis. *BMJ* 1948;ii:769-82.

6   Standards of Reporting Trials Group. A proposal for structured reporting of randomized controlled trials. *JAMA* 1994;**272**:1926-31.

7   Working Group on Recommendations for Reporting of Clinical Trials in the Biomedical Literature. Call for comments on a proposal to improve reporting of clinical trials in the biomedical literature: a position paper. *Ann Intern Med* 1994;**121**:894-5.

8   Rennie D. Reporting randomised controlled trials: an experiment and a call for responses from readers. *JAMA* 1995;**273**:1054-5.

9   Begg C, Cho M, Eastwood S, Horton R, Moher D, Olkin I, et al. Improving the quality of reporting of randomized controlled trials: the CONSORT statement. *JAMA* 1996;**276**:637-9.

10 Altman DG. Randomisation. *BMJ* 1991;**302**:1481-2.

11 Gardner MJ, Machin D, Campbell MJ. *The use of checklists in assessing the statistical content of medical studies BMJ* 1986;**292**:810-2.

12 Schulz KF. Subverting randomization in controlled trials. *JAMA* 1996;**274**:1456-8.

9

This article was first published in the Annals Academy of Medicine *and is reproduced by permission of Annals, Academy of Medicine, Singapore*

SAMPLE SIZE ESTIMATION FOR CLINICIANS

CP Archibald, (*Teaching Fellow*) MDCM, FRCPC (Can), HP Lee, (*Professor and Head*) FAMS, MBBS, FFPHM(UK)
Department of Community, Occupational and Family Medicine, National University of Singapore

ABSTRACT

The purpose of this paper is to describe the importance of an adequate sample size in clinical research and to enable clinicians to estimate their own sample size requirements for the more common types of studies (comparison of two means or two proportions). Four pieces of information are required to determine sample size: the desired level of statistical power, the level of statistical significance, the variability of the data, and the smallest difference between the study groups that is considered to be of clinical significance. Worked examples from the literature are used to illustrate how clinicians may easily do their own sample size calculations using published tables or available computer software, or both. The consideration of sample size and power during the planning stages of clinical research is crucial to the subsequent interpretation of study results, especially if the study is negative, and yet this point is often neglected in the medical literature. Attention to these simple guidelines will help ensure that research results lead to valid conclusions.

Ann Acad Med Singapore 1995; **24**:328-32

Keywords:
Clinical significance, Clinical trial, Statistical power

INTRODUCTION

One of the most common questions asked by clinicians starting research projects pertains to the sample size required for their purposes. Whether the investigator is an oncologist comparing two treatment modalities for nasopharyngeal carcinoma or a family physician comparing antibiotics for otitis media, the question of how many patients to allocate to each treatment group must be considered. The determination of sample size is an important part of any clinical trial and it is crucial to consider it in the planning stages prior to study implementation. Although it is widely appreciated that sample size consideration is important, the reasons for this importance and the implications of an inadequate sample size are not so well-known.

In this paper, the significance of an adequate sample size is described and the four pieces of information needed to calculate sample size are explained. Worked examples are provided to illustrate how clinicians may do their own calculations using published tables or available computer software, or both.

The Importance of an Adequate Sample Size in Clinical Research

An adequate sample size confers a number of benefits. Firstly, it allows for more precision (a narrower confidence interval) in the estimation of sample parameters such as the mean. Secondly, it makes it more likely that the assumptions are met for certain statistical tests that one may wish to carry out.[1] Thirdly, and most importantly, an adequate sample size gives a study more statistical power.

And what is power? It is the ability to detect a difference between the study groups if one truly exists. A study such as a clinical trial may find a difference between the treatment and control groups (a positive study) or it may find no difference (a negative study). In each case, one needs to be concerned with whether the result is true or false (Table I). For positive studies, this concern is answered by the use of conventional statistical tests and the associated consideration of the probability (p) value familiar to most clinicians. For example, if the p value is below a predetermined level (often set at 0.05), then the difference is said to be "statistically significant" which means that it is unlikely to be due to chance. The difference is then accepted as a "true positive", although there is still a small possibility (equal to the p value) that the result is in fact a "false positive" (due to chance alone). If one is satisfied that the difference is real, then one goes on to consider whether it is also clinically important. That is, whether a difference of that magnitude is important for prognosis or patient management.

For negative studies, on the other hand, no statistically significant difference is found between the study groups (p >0.05). The main concern in such cases is whether the result is a "true negative" (no clinically important difference exists between the study groups) or

Table I

The four possible results from a study examining the difference between two groups

		Does a difference truly exist?	
		Yes (+)	No (-)
Did the study find a statistically significant difference?	Yes (+)	True positive result	False positive result
	No (-)	False negative result	True negative result

a "false negative" (a clinically important difference exists but the study did not detect it). The answer depends on the power of the study: the more power a study has, the more likely it is to detect a statistically significant difference in situations where a genuine clinically important difference exists between the study groups. This is the most important benefit of an adequate sample size: it ensures that the study has sufficient power to detect differences that are clinically important.

Clinicians may find it helpful to compare the interpretation of the results of clinical studies with the interpretation of diagnostic tests. Using p values to assess the likelihood of a positive result being true is similar to using the specificity of a diagnostic test to assess whether a positive test result is correct (the higher the specificity the more likely a positive test result is a "true positive"). Conversely, using power to assess a negative study is similar to using sensitivity to assess a negative test result (the higher the sensitivity the more likely it is a true negative"). Therefore, just as clinicians realize the importance of considering both specificity and sensitivity in the interpretation of diagnostic tests, so they should realize the importance of both statistical significance and power for the proper interpretation of research results.

Let us illustrate the concept of power using a clinical example from the literature. Walt et al [2] carried out a clinical trial to compare the duodenal ulcer healing rates of two medications, cimetidine (43 patients out of 51 or 84% healed after one month of treatment) and ranitidine (40/52 or 77% healed). This difference was not statistically significant (p >0.05). How sure can the authors be that there is really no clinically important difference in the healing rates between these two treatments? One may calculate the power of this study (see later) and it turns out there is only a 37% chance of detecting an absolute difference of 15% or more between the two cure rates. Thus an important difference (such as one of 15%) could easily be missed and the negative finding of this study is difficult to interpret because one cannot be very sure that it is a "true negative".

This example is not an isolated case. In general, the medical literature has focused on assessing the statistical significance of any observed difference to estimate the probability that a positive result is "true" or "false". On the other side of the coin – assessing whether negative results are likely to be true or false – has been virtually ignored. Freiman et al [3] conducted a review of 71 negative clinical trials published in 20 different medical journals during the period 1968-1977. The sample size was found to be so small in 50 (70%) of the studies that the authors would have failed to detect a 50% improvement in therapeutic results. Similarly, in 1982 DerSimonian et al [4] reviewed 67 clinical trials published in four leading British and American journals and found that only 8 (12%) addressed the issues of power and sample size. While a number of journals now actively encourage sample size discussions for papers on clinical trials, many journals still publish papers that have negative findings and yet do not discuss sample size or

power. Clinical researchers can dramatically improve the quality of their work by the simple measure of taking into account power and sample size, and the best news is that it is not difficult to do, as will now be shown.

Information Required for a Sample Size Calculation

To calculate sample size, four pieces of information are required: (1) the level of power desired for the study; (2) the variability of the data; (3) the level of significance for statistical tests; and (4) the smallest difference that is considered to be of clinical importance. These four factors will now be discussed in more detail.

The Level of Power

This is the researcher's decision and a power of 0.8 (or 80%) is commonly chosen. Obviously if one wants to be more sure of not missing a specified difference, then one will choose a higher level (say 0.9). However, more power comes at a price and the price is a larger required sample size. This is a key relationship: sample size is directly related to power and increasing the sample size is one of the most useful ways to increase power, since it is usually under the control of the investigator.

Variability of Data

The variability of the data is measured by the variance and the related statistic, standard deviation. Often this is not known in advance of doing the study, but an estimate may be obtained by doing a pilot study or by searching the literature for work done in similar populations. The more variable the data, the higher the standard deviation, and the greater the sample size required to produce a given level of power (or the lower the power for a given sample size). Note, however, that the variability of the data does not enter into the calculation of sample size when the outcome of interest is a proportion because the variance of a proportion depends only on the value of the proportion and the sample size on which it is based. The key point to remember is that for continuous outcomes like blood pressure or serum cholesterol, the variability of the data must be known or estimated to calculate sample size; for dichotomous outcomes where a proportion may be calculated, such as dead/alive or cured/not cured, the variability of the data may be ignored.

The Level of Significance

The level of significance for a statistical test that may be performed on the data is termed the alpha level. By convention, it is usually set at 0.05, but the investigator may choose a different value for a specific purpose. For example, if one is particularly concerned about avoiding a false negative conclusion, then an alpha of 0.1 would be more appropriate (or 0.01 to avoid a false positive conclusion). Note that increasing the alpha level increases power, however, this is generally not very useful because it also increases the chances of making a false positive conclusion.

The Smallest Clinically Important Difference

The question of how large a difference must be to have clinical importance is a difficult one and yet no one is in a better position to answer it than the investigator. This difference may be estimated before the study is carried out by considering what is known about the condition under study both from the literature and the investigator's own clinical experience. For example, McDonald and coauthors[5] planned to compare oxytocin alone versus oxytocin and ergometrine for the active management of the third stage of labour. They used a "best guess" to estimate that the frequency of post-partum haemorrhage in the oxytocin group would be about 7.5%, and decided that if the use of oxytocin-ergometrine reduced it to 5%, then this would be sufficient to influence the choice of drug for clinical management. Since small differences are harder to detect than large ones, this small absolute difference of 2.5% required over 1700 women in each study group to achieve a power of 0.8. The smaller the difference you want to detect, the larger the required sample size. In situations where it is difficult to decide on a specific clinically important difference, one may calculate a number of sample sizes for a range of possible differences as a guide in planning the study.

In summary, the required sample size increases as the desired level of power increases, as the standard deviation increases, as the alpha level decreases, and as the size of the difference of interest decreases. It is important to remember that sample size calculations and the consideration of power are done during the planning stages of a study when alterations are relatively easy to make. The actual sample size required for a good study may sometimes be a shock to the investigator, but it is preferable to be shocked before doing the study than after all the work has been done. Choosing a sample size is always a tradeoff between what one would like and what one can realistically achieve, and calculating the sample size beforehand enables the investigator to know what compromises need to be made. On occasion, the best course of action may be to plan a different study rather than to carry out one which is unlikely to produce meaningful results.

Worked Examples of Sample Size Calculations

Sample size calculations vary with the exact comparison of interest in a particular study and the associated statistical test. Examples will be shown here for the two most common situations: comparing two independent proportions and two independent means.

Comparing Two Independent Proportions

Example A: Hammermeister et al[6] recently compared 11-year survival rates in men who received either a mechanical valve or a bioprosthetic valve during aortic valve replacement surgery. There were 198 patients in the mechanical valve group with 47% survival and 196 in the bioprosthetic valve group with 41% survival (p = 0.26). The authors do not discuss sample size

calculation or power and so the reader does not know the validity of the authors' conclusion that there is no difference in survival rate between these two valve types. To interpret these results, one may calculate the sample size required for a standard power of 0.8 and an alpha level of 0.05. Since we are dealing with a proportion (percentage surviving after 11 years), we do not need to consider data variability. Regarding the minimum clinically significant difference, from the paper we know that 50% is the approximate 11-year survival rate after such surgery. Let us assume (since it is not discussed in the paper) that an increase in the survival rate to 65% or more would be clinically important.

We are now ready to calculate the sample size required to have an 80% chance of detecting an absolute difference of 15% or more in survival rates at alpha = 0.05. Referring to Table II, we look up 50% along the left-hand column (the smaller of the two percentages) and move across to the column corresponding to 65%. The number there is 182 which is the required sample size per group, or 364 in total. Thus, the sample size in this paper was in fact adequate. However, the authors could have made their conclusion much stronger by discussing power and explicitly stating that the study had enough power to detect clinically important differences.

Example B: Gimson and colleagues[7] compared two methods of treating bleeding oesophageal varices, banding ligation and sclerotherapy. The complication rate for oesophageal ulcers was 36/54 (67%) in patients treated with ligation and 28/49 (57%) in those treated with sclerotherapy. The authors concluded there was no difference in the frequency of this complication between the two treatment methods (p = 0.43). Neither sample size nor power are discussed in the paper and so the reader is left to decide whether this conclusion is valid. Given a baseline complication rate of about 60%, one may assume a clinically important change would be one of 20%. So if we want to detect a complication rate of 80% or more (absolute difference = 80-60 = 20%) at alpha = 0.05 and power = 0.8, the required sample size is 91 per group or 182 in total (Table II. Thus this paper had only about half the sample size required to detect with 80% certainty an absolute difference of 20% and this seriously weakens the authors' conclusion that the complication rates for the two methods are equal.

Comparing Two Independent Means

An example of sample size calculations in this setting is provided by Boone et al [8] who studied the effect of electrotherapy on the urodynamic characteristics of neurogenic bladders in children. One of their outcome measures was bladder capacity and they found no differences between treatment (mean 203 ml, n = 18) and control groups (mean = 206 ml, n = 13) (p >0.05). Power is not discussed, so we need to calculate sample size ourselves to be able to interpret these negative findings. Regarding data variability, the paper gives the standard deviation of the bladder capacity measurements

Table II

Sample sizes per study group for the comparison of two independent proportions with a power of 0.8 and a significance level of 0.05 (two-tailed test). P1 is the smaller of the two proportions and P2 the larger.

P1 \ P2	0.1	0.15	0.2	0.25	0.3	0.35	0.4	0.45	0.5	0.55	0.6	0.65	0.7	0.75	0.8	0.85	0.9	0.95
0.05	474	160	88	58	43	33	27	22	18	16	14	12	10	9	8	7	6	5
0.1		725	219	113	71	50	38	30	24	20	17	14	12	11	9	8	7	6
0.15			945	270	134	82	57	42	32	26	21	18	15	13	11	9	8	7
0.2				1134	313	151	91	62	45	34	27	22	18	15	13	11	9	8
0.25					1291	348	165	98	65	47	36	28	22	8	15	13	11	9
0.3						1416	376	175	103	68	48	36	28	22	18	15	12	10
0.35							1511	395	182	106	69	49	36	28	22	18	14	12
0.4								1573	407	186	107	69	48	36	27	21	17	14
0.45									1605	411	186	106	68	47	34	26	20	16
0.5										1605	407	182	103	65	45	32	24	18
0.55											1573	365	175	98	62	42	30	22
0.6												1511	376	165	91	57	38	27
0.65													1416	348	151	82	50	33
0.7														1291	313	134	71	43
0.75															1134	270	113	58
0.8																945	219	88
0.85																	725	160
0.9																		474

as 92 and 104 for the two groups under study: we will use a value of 98. For an estimate of a clinically important difference, let us use a difference of 100 ml which would represent a 50% increase in bladder capacity. The sample size is dependent on the ratio of the minimum difference of interest to the standard deviation which in our case is 100/98 or about 1.0. Referring to Table III (for power of 0.8 and alpha of 0.05), we look up the sample size corresponding to this ratio and it is 16 per group or 32 in total. The authors had sample sizes of 13 and 18 per group which would not quite be enough to have an 80% chance of detecting an increase of 100 m or more in bladder capacity. Note that 100 ml is a large relative increase and this study would be seriously deficient in sample size if smaller differences were of interest.

Published Tables and/or Computer Programs

The tables presented in this article assume a power of 0.8 and a level of significance of 0.05. They also assume the total sample size is equally divided between the two study groups which maximizes power for a given total sample size. For situations involving the comparison of two proportions or means where the investigator wishes to use different levels of power and/or alpha, the reader is referred to Fleiss[9] (Table A.3), Machin and Campbell[10] (Tables 3.1 and 7.2), and Cohen[11] (Tables 8.3.1, 8.3.12 and 8.3.23). For comparisons other than of two proportions or means, refer to Machin and Campbell,[10]

Lachin,[12] or Cohen.[11] Dupont and Plummer[13] have developed a computer program to do sample size calculations under a wide variety of situations and the program is available from the authors of the present paper. Additional discussions of the importance of sample size and power for clinical research are provided by Sackett et al,[14] Dawson-Saunders and Trapp,[1] and Young et al.[15]

In this article, we have focused on the calculation of sample size for a desired level of power, but the same equations may be used to calculate power for a given sample size. The latter calculation is especially useful for interpreting published studies where one would like to know the power the study had to detect a certain difference. Tables II and III may be used as rough guides to judge whether the power was greater or less than 0.8 by checking whether the sample size was greater or less than the number required for a power of 0.8. For calculation of the exact power, refer to the computer program by Dupont and Plummer.[13]

Conclusion

The most important message is that clinical investigators should consider power and sample size in the planning stages of their research. This will help ensure that the study results, whether positive or negative, are meaningful and contribute to medical knowledge. The tables presented here allow for sample size estimation in common clinical research settings. For other situations,

Table III

Sample sizes per study group (n) for the comparison of two independent means with a power of 0.8 and a significance level of 0.05 (two-tailed test). R is the ratio of the difference between the two means to the standard deviation.

R	0.1	0.15	0.2	0.25	0.3	0.35	0.4	0.45	0.5
n	1571	699	393	252	175	129	99	79	64

R	0.6	0.7	0.8	0.9	1.0	1.1	1.3	1.5	2.0
n	45	33	26	20	16	14	10	8	5

the reader may refer to the cited references or consult a biostatistician. And if the latter route is chosen, you will greatly impress your consultant by already knowing the answers to the four questions you will be asked.

Acknowledgements

The authors are indebted to Professor James Lee for helpful advice and to Dr Goh Lee Gan for constructive comments on the manuscript.

Address for Reprints: Dr H P Lee, Department of Community, Occupational and Family Medicine, National University of Singapore, Lower Kent Ridge Road, Singapore 0511.

References

1   Dawson-Saunders B, Trapp R G. Basic and clinical biostatistics. East Norwalk: Appleton & Lange, 1990.
2   Walt RP, Trotman I F, Frost R, Colding P L, Sheperd T H, Rawlings J, et al. Comparison of twice-daily ranitidine with standard cimetidine treatment of duodenal ulcer. Gut 1981; 22:319-22.
3   Freiman J A, Chalmers T C, Smith H, Kuebler R R. The importance of beta, the Type II error and sample size in the design and interpretation of the randomized control trial. Survey of 71 negative trials. N Engl J Med 1978; 299:690-4.
4   DerSimonian R, Charette L J, McPeek B, Mosteller F. Reporting on methods in clinical trials. N Engl J Med 1982; 306:1332-8.
5   McDonald S J, Prendiville W J, Blair E. Randomised controlled trial of oxytocin alone versus oxytocin and ergometrine in active management of third stage of labour. *BMJ* 1993; 307:1167-71.
6   Hammermeister K E, Sethick G K, Henerson W G, Oprian C, Kim T, Rahimtoola S. A comparison of outcomes in men 11 years after heart-valve replacement with a mechanical valve or bioprosthesis. N Engl J Med 1993; 328: 1289-96.
7   Gimson A E, Ramage J K, Panos M Z, Hayllar K, Harrison P M, Williams R, et al. Randomised trial of variceal banding ligation versus injection sclerotherapy for bleeding oesophageal varices. Lancet 1993; 342:391-4.
8   Boone T B, Roehrborn C G, Hurt G. Transurethral intravesical electrotherapy for neurogenic bladder dysfunction in children with myelodysplasia: a prospective randomized clinical trial. J Urol 1992; 148:550-4.
9   Fleiss J L. Statistical methods for rates and proportions. 2nd ed. New York: John Wiley and Sons, 1981.
10 Machin D, Campbell M J. Statistical tables for the design of clinical trials. London: Blackwell Scientific Publications, 1987.
11 Cohen J. Statistical power analysis for the behavioural sciences. 2nd ed. Hillsdale: Lawrence Erlbaum Associates, 1988.
12 Lachin J M. Introduction to sample size determination and power analysis for clinical trials. Controlled Clin Trials 1981; 2: 93-113.
13 Dupont W D, Plummer W D Jr. Power and sample size calculations. Controlled Clin Trials 1990; 11:116-8.
14 Sackett D L, Haynes R B, Guyatt C H, Tugwell P. Clinical epidemiology. A basic science for clinicians. 2nd ed. Boston: Little, Brown and Company, 1991.
15 Young M J, Bresnitz E A, Strom B L. Sample size nomograms for interpreting negative clinical studies. Ann Intern Med 1983; 99:248-51.

10

This article was first published in the BMJ *and is reproduced with permission of the* BMJ

WHY WE NEED OBSERVATIONAL STUDIES TO EVALUATE THE EFFECTIVENESS OF HEALTH CARE

Nick Black

Health Services Research Unit, Department of Public Health and Policy, London School of Hygiene and Tropical Medicine, Keppel Street, London WC1E 7HT
Nick Black, *professor of health services research*

BMJ 1996;**312**:1215–8

The view is widely held that experimental methods (randomised controlled trials) are the "gold standard" for evaluation and that observational methods (cohort and case control studies) have little or no value. This ignores the limitations of randomised trials, which may prove unnecessary, inappropriate, impossible, or inadequate. Many of the problems of conducting randomised trials could often, in theory, be overcome, but the practical implications for researchers and funding bodies mean that this is often not possible. The false conflict between those who advocate randomised trials in all situations and those who believe observational data provide sufficient evidence needs to be replaced with mutual recognition of the complementary roles of the two approaches. Researchers should be united in their quest for scientific rigour in evaluation, regardless of the method used.

Despite the essential role of observational methods in shedding light on the effectiveness of many aspects of health care, some scientists believe such methods have little or even nothing to contribute. In his summing up at a major conference held in 1993, the eminent medical epidemiologist Richard Doll concluded that observational methods "provide no useful means of assessing the value of a therapy."[1] The widely held view that experimental methods (randomised controlled trials) are the "gold standard" for evaluation has led to the denigration of non-experimental methods, to the extent that research funding bodies and journal editors automatically reject them. I suggest that such attitudes limit our potential to evaluate health care and hence to improve the scientific basis of how to treat individuals and how to organise services.

My main contention is that those who are opposed to the use of observational methods have assumed that they represent an alternative to experimentation rather than a set of complementary approaches. This in turn stems from a misguided notion that everything can be investigated using a randomised controlled trial. In response I want to outline the limitations of randomised trials and show that observational methods are needed both to evaluate the parts randomised trials cannot

reach and to help design and interpret correctly the results obtained from these trials.

Before doing so I must clarify what I mean by "observational" in this context. I am referring exclusively to quantitative, epidemiological methods and not qualitative, sociological methods in which data are collected through observation. The principal observational epidemiological methods are non-randomised trials, cohort studies (prospective and retrospective), and case-control methods, though relatively little use has been made of the latter beyond evaluating preventive measures.

The limitations of randomised trials can be seen as deriving from either the inherent nature of the method (a limitation in principle) or from the way trials are conducted (a limitation in procedure). The importance of this distinction is that while little can be done about the former, improvements in the conduct of randomised trials could, in theory, overcome some or all of the latter. I will return to this distinction later, but first it is necessary to document the reasons why observational methods are needed. There are four main reasons: experimentation may be unnecessary, inappropriate, impossible, or inadequate.

EXPERIMENTATION MAY BE UNNECESSARY

When the effect of an intervention is dramatic, the likelihood of unknown confounding factors being important is so small that they can be ignored. There are many well known examples of such interventions: penicillin for bacterial infections; smallpox vaccination; thyroxine in hypothyroidism; vitamin B12 replacement; insulin in insulin dependent diabetes; anaesthesia for surgical operations; immobilisation of fractured bones. In all these examples observational studies were adequate to demonstrate effectiveness.

EXPERIMENTATION MAYBE INAPPROPRIATE

There are four situations in which randomised trials may be inappropriate. The first is that they are rarely large enough to measure accurately infrequent adverse outcomes. This limitation has been addressed by the establishment, in many countries, of postmarketing surveillance schemes to detect rare adverse effects of drugs. The use of such observational data can be illustrated by the case of benoxaprofen (Opren), a drug launched in 1980. Despite preceding clinical trials on over 3000 patients, the drug had to be withdrawn two years after its launch because of reports of serious side effects, including 61 deaths.[2] Similar surveillance schemes are needed for non-pharmaceutical interventions. The lack of such schemes means that there is still uncertainty as to whether or not laparoscopic techniques are associated with an increased risk of injuries, such as bile duct damage during cholecystectomy.[3] Huge observational datasets are the only practical means of acquiring such vital information.

A second limitation, also arising from study size, is the difficulty of evaluating interventions designed to prevent rare events. Examples include accident prevention schemes and placing infants supine or on their side to sleep to prevent sudden infant death syndrome. A randomised trial would have needed a few hundred thousand babies.

A third limitation of trials is when the outcomes of interest are far in the future. Three well known examples are the long term consequences of oral contraceptives, which may not be manifest for decades; the use of hormone replacement therapy to prevent femoral fractures; and the loosening of artificial hip joints, for which a 10 to 15 year follow up is needed. The practical difficulties in maintaining such prolonged prospective studies (whether experimental or observational) are considerable, as are their costs. With luck, there will occasionally be times when a randomised trial addressing the question of current interest has already been established decades before and patients from it can then be followed up. Unfortunately such serendipity is all too rare. As a practical alternative to doing nothing, retrospective observational studies can be used to obtain some information on long term outcomes.[4]

What works well in pharmacological research may not work in the messier world of clinical care

MIKE WINDHAM PICTURE COLLECTION

Self Defeating

Finally, a randomised trial may be inappropriate because the very act of random allocation may reduce the effectiveness of the intervention. This arises when the effectiveness of the intervention depends on the subject's active participation, which, in turn, depends on the subject's beliefs and preferences. As a consequence, the lack of any subsequent difference in outcome between comparison groups may underestimate the benefits of the intervention. For example, it is well recognised that clinical audit is successful in improving the quality of health care only if the clinicians participating have a sense of ownership of the process.[5] Such a "bottom up" approach is in stark contrast to experimentation, in which the investigator seeks to impose as much control on the subjects in the study as possible—that is, a "top down" approach. As a consequence, randomised trials of audit might find less benefit than observational studies. The same may be true for many interventions for which clinicians, or patients, or both, have a preference (despite agreeing to random allocation), and where patients need to participate in the intervention—psychotherapy, for example.[6] Many interventions to promote health or prevent disease fall into this category, particularly those based on community development. It is at least as plausible to assume that experimentation reduces the effectiveness of such interventions as to assume, as most researchers have done, that the results of observational studies are wrong.

EXPERIMENTATION MAY BE IMPOSSIBLE

There are some people who believe that any and every intervention can be subjected to a randomised trial, and that those who challenge this have simply not made sufficient effort and are methodologically incompetent. Such a view minimises the impact of seven serious obstacles that researchers have to face all too often. The exact nature of the obstacles will depend on the cultural, political, and social characteristics of the situation and, clearly, therefore, will vary over time.

The first, and most familiar, is the reluctance and refusal of clinicians and other key people to participate. Just because clinical uncertainty, manifest by variation in practice, may exist, this does not mean that each individual clinician is uncertain about how to practise. In 1991 most gynaecologists and urologists in the North Thames region agreed that a randomised trial was needed to investigate the effectiveness of surgery for stress incontinence, but none was prepared to participate as each believed in the correctness of their own practice style. In other words, although "collective equipoise" existed, "individual equipoise" was absent.[7] Even when clinicians purport to participate, randomisation may be subverted by clinicians deciphering the assignment sequence.[8]

Ethical objections are a second potential obstacle. It is most unlikely that any ethics committee in an

11

industrialised country would sanction the random allocation of patients to intensive care versus ward care, or cardiac transplantation versus medical management. Observational studies provide an alternative to leaving the question of the effectiveness of these expensive services unevaluated. Furthermore, the results of such studies may generate sufficient uncertainty as to make an experimental study acceptable. This happened in the case of surgery for benign prostatic hyperplasia.[9] [10]

Political And Legal Obstacles

Thirdly, there may be political obstacles if those who fund and manage health services do not want their policies studied. In the United Kingdom this was true for general practitioner fundholding and the introduction of an internal market. As a result, researchers have been able to perform only a few observational studies, mostly with retrospective controls.[11] [12]

Researchers may also meet legal obstacles to performing a randomised trial. The classic example is the attempt to subject radial keratotomy (an operation to correct short sightedness) to a randomised trial in the United States.[13] The researchers were blocked by private sector ophthalmologists who faced a major loss of income if the procedure was declared "experimental" because this would have meant that health insurance companies would no longer reimburse them. As a result of legal action, the academic ophthalmologists were forced to declare the operation safe and effective and abandon any attempt at evaluation.

Fortunately, legal obstacles are rare, but a common problem is that some interventions simply cannot be allocated on a random basis. These tend to be questions of how best to organise and deliver an intervention. For example, a current consensus is that clinicians and hospitals treating a high volume of patients achieve better results than those treating a low volume.[14] If true, the policy implications for the way health services are organised are immense. While experimental methods could, in theory, help resolve this, randomisation is unlikely to be acceptable to patients, clinicians, or managers. The spectre of transporting patients to more distant facilities on a randomly allocated basis would find little support from any of the interested parties. Careful observational methods provide a means of investigating the value of regionalising services.[15]

Contamination And Scale

The sixth problem is that of contamination. This can take several forms. If in a trial a clinician is expected to provide care in more than one way, it is possible that each approach will influence the way they provide care to patients in the other arms of the study. Consider, for example, a randomised trial to see if explaining treatments fully to patients, rather than telling them the bare minimum, would achieve better outcomes. This would rely on clinicians being able to change character repeatedly and convincingly. Fortunately there are few

Dr Jekylls in clinical practice. Randomisation of clinicians (rather than patients) may sometimes help, though contamination between colleagues may occur, and randomisation of centres requires a much larger study at far greater cost. The seventh and final reason why it will not always be possible to conduct randomised trials is simply the scale of the task confronting the research community. There are an immense number of health care interventions in use, added to which, most interventions have many components. Consider a simple surgical operation: this entails preoperative tests, anaesthesia, the surgical approach, wound management, postoperative nursing, and discharge practice. And these are just the principal components. It will only ever be practical to subject a limited number of items to experimental evaluation.[16] We therefore need to take advantage of other methods to try and fill in the huge gaps that are always likely to exist in the experimental published findings.

EXPERIMENTATION MAY BE INADEQUATE

The external validity, or "generalisability," of the results of randomised trials is often low.[17] The extent to which the results of a trial are generalisable depends on the extent to which the outcome of the intervention is determined by the particular person providing the care. At one extreme the outcome of pharmaceutical treatment is, to a large extent, not affected by the characteristics of the prescribing doctor. The results of drug trials can, in the main, be generalised to other doctors and settings. In contrast, the outcome of activities such as surgery, physiotherapy, psychotherapy, and community nursing may be highly dependent on the characteristics of the provider, setting, and patients. As a consequence, unless care is taken in the design and conduct of a randomised trial, the results may not be generalisable.

There are three reasons why randomised trials in many areas of health care may have low external validity. The first is that the health care professionals who participate may be unrepresentative. They may have a particular interest in the topic or be enthusiasts and innovators. The setting may also be atypical, a teaching hospital for example. In one of the few randomised trials of surgery for glue ear undertaken in the United Kingdom, all the outpatient and surgical care was performed by a highly experienced consultant surgeon; in real life most such work is performed by relatively inexperienced junior surgeons.[18]

Secondly, the patients who participate may be atypical. All trials exclude certain categories of patients. Often the exclusion criteria are so restrictive that the patients who are eligible for inclusion represent only a small proportion of the patients being treated in normal practice. Only 4% of patients currently undergoing coronary revascularisation in the United States would have been eligible for inclusion in the trials that were conducted in the 1970s.[19] It has been suggested that the same problem will limit the usefulness of the current randomised controlled trials comparing coronary artery surgery and angioplasty.[20] Similar problems occur in trials of cancer treatment.[21] Another facet of this problem is the absence of privately funded patients from almost all randomised trials in the United Kingdom. The problem of eligibility may be exacerbated by a poor recruitment rate. Although most trials fail to report their recruitment rate,[4] those that do suggest rates are often very low. As little is yet known about the sort of people who are prepared to have their treatment allocated on a random basis, it seems wise to assume that they may differ in important ways from those who decline to take part.

And the third and final problem in generalising the results of randomised trials is that treatment may be atypical. Patients who participate may receive better care, regardless of which arm of the trial they are in.[22]

As a result of these problems, randomised trials generally offer an indication of the efficacy of an intervention rather than its effectiveness in everyday practice. While the latter can be achieved through "pragmatic" trials which evaluate normal clinical practice, these are rarely undertaken.[23] Most randomised trials are "explanatory"—that is, they provide evidence of what can be achieved in the most favourable circumstances.

The question of external validity has received little attention from those who promote randomised trials as the gold standard. None of the 25 instruments that have been developed to judge the methodological quality of trials includes any consideration of this aspect.[24] The same is true for the guidance provided by the Cochrane Collaboration.[25]

DISCUSSION

Randomised controlled trials occupy a special place in the pantheon of methods for assessing the effectiveness of health care interventions. When appropriate, practical, and ethical, a randomised trial design should be used. I have tried to show that, for all their well known methodological strengths, trials cannot meet all our needs as patients, practitioners, managers, and policy makers. There are situations in which the use of randomised trials is limited either because of problems that derive from their inherent nature or from practical obstacles. While nothing can be done to remedy the former, improvement in the design and execution of trials could, in theory at least, overcome the latter.

Principles Versus Practice

The problems that could in theory be overcome (and how that could be achieved) include:

- Failure to assess rare outcomes (by mounting large trials with thousands of patients)

- Failure to assess long term outcomes (by continuing to follow up patients for many years)

- Elimination of clinicians' and patients' preferences (by introducing preference arms[26])

- Refusal by clinicians to participate (by using more acceptable methods of randomisation[27])

- Ethical objections to randomisation (by exploring alternative less demanding methods of obtaining informed consent[28])

- Political and legal obstacles (by persuasion)

- The daunting size of the task (by vastly expanding the available funds for experimental studies)

- Overrestrictive patient eligibility criteria (by undertaking pragmatic rather than explanatory trials[23])

While all the proposed solutions could work in theory, few of them are realistic in practice, presenting as they do enormous problems for researchers and, more importantly, for research funding bodies. For example, it is feasible to randomise tens of thousands of people in a drug trial in which death is the only outcome of interest, but it is unrealistic if more complex and sophisticated outcomes are the relevant endpoints. In many ways the problems that randomised trials encounter arise from a largely uncritical transfer of a well developed scientific method in pharmacological research to the evaluation of other health technologies and to health services. Several of the other limitations cannot be polarised between principle and practice but are a complex mix of the two. These include:

- Contamination between treatment groups

- The unrepresentativeness of clinicians who volunteer to participate

- Poor patient recruitment rates

- The better care that trial participants receive

In theory all of these could be overcome, although in practice it is hard to see how without the cost of the study becoming astronomical.

Assuming procedural problems could be overcome, two problems of principle inherent in the method would remain. Firstly, the artificiality of a randomised trial probably reduces the placebo element of any intervention. Given that the placebo effect accounts for a large proportion of the effect of many interventions, the results of a trial will inevitably reflect the minimum level of benefit that can be expected. This may be one reason (along with confounding) why experimental studies often yield smaller estimates of treatment effects than studies using observational methods.[29]

Secondly, a randomised trial provides information on the value of an intervention shorn of all context, such as patients' beliefs and wishes and clinicians' attitudes and beliefs, despite the fact that such aspects may be crucial to determining the success of the intervention.[30] In contrast, observational methods maintain the integrity of the context in which care is provided. For these two reasons, the notion that information from randomised trials represents a gold standard, while that derived from observational studies is viewed as wrong, may be too simplistic. An alternative perspective is that randomised trials provide an indication of the minimum effect of an intervention whereas observational studies offer an estimate of the maximum effect. If this is so then policymakers need data from both approaches when making decisions about health services, and neither should reign supreme.

Redressing The Balance

My intention in focusing on the limitations of trials is not to suggest that observational methods are unproblematic but to redress the balance. The shortcomings of non-experimental approaches have been widely and frequently aired. The principal problem is that their internal validity may be undermined by previously unrecognised confounding factors which may not be evenly distributed between intervention groups. It is currently unclear how serious and how insurmountable a methodological problem this is in practice. While some investigations of this issue have been undertaken,[19] more studies comparing experimental and observational designs are urgently needed.

For too long a false conflict has been created between those who advocate randomised trials in all situations and those who believe observational data provide sufficient evidence. Neither position is helpful. There is no such thing as a perfect method; each method has its strengths and weaknesses. The two approaches should be seen as complementary. After all, experimental methods depend on observational ones to generate clinical uncertainty; generate hypotheses; identify the structures, processes, and outcomes that should be measured in a trial; and help to establish the appropriate sample size for a randomised trial. When trials cannot be conducted, well designed observational methods offer an alternative to doing nothing. They also offer the opportunity to establish high external validity, something that is difficult to achieve in randomised trials.

Instead of advocates of each approach criticising the other method, everyone should be striving for greater rigour in the execution of research, regardless of the method used.

"Every research strategy within a discipline contributes importantly relevant and complementary information to a totality of evidence upon which rational clinical decision-making and public policy can be reliably based. In this context, observational evidence has provided and will continue to make unique and important contributions to this totality of evidence upon which to support a judgment of proof beyond a reasonable doubt in the evaluation of interventions."[31]

I thank Nicholas Mays, Martin McKee, Colin Sanderson, and the reviewer for their comments, but I take full responsibility for the views expressed in this article.
Funding: None.
Conflict of interest: None.

References

1 Doll R. Summation of conference. Doing more good than harm: the evaluation of health care interventions. *Ann NY Acad Sci* 1994;**703**:313.
2 Opren scandal. *Lancet* 1983;**i**:219–20.
3 Downs SH, Black NA, Devlin HB, Royston C, Russell C. A systematic review of the safety and effectiveness of laparoscopic cholecystectomy. *Ann R Coll Surg Engl* 1996;**78**:211–23.
4 Stauffer RN. Ten-year follow-up study of total hip replacement. *J Bone Joint Surg Am* 1982;**64**:983–90.
5 Black NA. The relationship between evaluative research and audit. *J Public Health Med* 1992;**14**:361–6.
6 Brewin CR, Bradley C. Patient preferences and randomised clinical trials. *BMJ* 1989;**299**:313–15.
7 Lilford R, Jackson J. Equipoise and the ethics of randomization. *J R Soc Med* 1995;**88**:552–9.
8 Schulz KF. Subverting randomization in controlled trials. *JAMA* 1995;**274**: 1456–8.
9 Fowler FJ, Wennberg JE, Timothy RP, Barry MJ, Malley AG, Hanley D. Symptom status and quality of life following prostatectomy. *JAMA* 1988;**259**:3018–22.
10 Wasson JH, Reda DJ, Bruskewitz RC, Elinson J, Kelley AM, Henderson WG. A comparison of transurethral surgery with watchful waiting for moderate symptoms of benign prostatic hyperplasia. *N Engl J Med* 1995;**332**:75–9.
11 Dixon J, Glennerster H. What do we know about fundholding in general practice? *BMJ* 1995;**311**:727–30.
12 Clinical Standards Advisory Group. *Access to and availability of coronary artery bypass grafting and coronary angioplasty*. London: HMSO, 1993.
13 Chalmers I. Minimizing harm and maximizing benefit during innovation in health care: controlled or uncontrolled experimentation? *Birth* 1986;**13**:155–64.
14 Black NA, Johnston A. Volume and outcome in hospital care: evidence, explanations and implications. *Health Service Management Research* 1990;**3**:108–14.
15 Sowden AJ, Decks JJ, Sheldon TA. Volume and outcome in coronary artery bypass graft surgery: true association or artefact? *BMJ* 1995;**311**:115–18.
16 Dorey F, Grigoris P, Amstutz H. Making do without randomised trials. *J Bone Joint Surg Br* 1994;**76-B**:1–3.
17 Cross design synthesis: a new strategy for studying medical outcomes? *Lancet* 1992;**340**:944–6.
18 Maw R, Bawden R. Spontaneous resolution of severe chronic glue ear in children and the effect of adenoidectomy, tonsillectomy, and insertion of ventilation rubes (grommets). *BMJ* 1993;**306**:756–60.
19 Hlatky MA, Califf RM, Harrell FE, Lee KL, Mark DB, Pryor D. Comparison of predictions based on observational data with the results of randomised controlled trials of coronary artery bypass surgery. *J Am Coll Cardiol* 1988;**11**:237–45.
20 White HD. Angioplasty versus bypass surgery. *Lancet* 1995;**346**:1174–5.
21 Ward LC, Fielding JWL, Dunn JA, Kelly KA. The selection of cases for randomised trials: a registry of concurrent trial and non-trial participants. *Br J Cancer* 1992;**66**:943–50.
22 Stiller CA. Centralised treatment, entry to trials, and survival. *Br J Cancer* 1994;**70**:352–62.

23 Schwartz D, Lellouch J. Explanatory and pragmatic attitudes in clinical trials. *J Chron Dis* 1967;**20**:637–48.

24 Moher D, Jadad AR, Nichol G, Penman M, Tugwell P, Walsh S. Assessing the quality of randomized controlled trials: an annotated bibliography of scales and checklists. *Controlled Clin Trials* 1995;**16**:62–73.

25 Oxman AD, ed. Section VI: Preparing and maintaining systematic reviews. *Cochrane Collaboration handbook*. Oxford: Cochrane Collaboration, 1994.

26 Wennberg JE, Barry MJ, Fowler FJ, Mulley A. Outcomes research, PORTs, and health care reform. Doing more good than harm: the evaluation of health care interventions. *Ann NY Acad Sci* 1994;**703**:56.

27 Korn EL, Baumrind S. Randomised clinical trials with clinician-preferred treatment. *Lancet* 1991;**337**:149–52.

28 Zelen M. A new design for randomised clinical trials. *N Engl J Med* 1979;**300**:1242–5.

29 Schulz KF, Charmers I, Hayes RJ, Altman DG. Empirical evidence of bias. Dimensions of methodological quality associated with estimates of treatment effects in controlled trials. *JAMA* 1995;**273**:408–12.

30 Beecher HK. Surgery as placebo. *JAMA* 1961;**176**:1102–7.

31 Hennekens CH, Buying JE. Observational evidence. Doing more good than harm: the evaluation of health care interventions. *Ann NY Acad Sci* 1994;**703**:22.

(Accepted 7 March 1996)

11

This document was first published by the Department of Health and is crown copyright material. It is reproduced by permission of the Controller of Her Majesty's Stationery Office

NHS INDEMNITY:
ARRANGEMENTS FOR CLINICAL NEGLIGENCE CLAIMS IN THE NHS

EXECUTIVE SUMMARY
Introduction
This is a summary of the main points contained within *NHS Indemnity: Arrangements for clinical negligence claims in the NHS*, issued under cover of HSG 96/48. The booklet includes a Q&A section covering the applicability of NHS indemnity to common situations and an annex on sponsored trials. It covers NHS indemnity for clinical negligence but not for any other liability such as product liability, employers liability or liability for NHS trust board members.

Clinical Negligence
Clinical negligence is defined as "a breach of duty of care by members of the health care professions employed by NHS bodies or by others consequent on decisions or judgements made by members of those professions acting in their professional capacity in the course of their employment, and which are admitted as negligent by the employer or are determined as such through the legal process".

The term health care professional includes hospital doctors, dentists, nurses, midwives, health visitors, pharmacy practitioners, registered ophthalmic or dispensing opticians (working in a hospital setting), members of professions allied to medicine and dentistry, ambulance personnel, laboratory staff and relevant technicians.

Main Principles
NHS bodies are vicariously liable for the negligent acts and omissions of their employees and should have arrangements for meeting this liability.

NHS Indemnity applies where

(a) the negligent health care professional was:

(i) working under a contract of employment and the negligence occurred in the course of that employment;

(ii) not working under a contract of employment but was contracted to an NHS body to provide services to persons to whom that NHS body owed a duty of care.

(iii) neither of the above but otherwise owed a duty of care to the persons injured.

(b) persons, not employed under a contract of employment and who may or may not be a health care professional, who owe a duty of care to the persons injured. These include locums; medical academic staff with honorary contracts; students; those conducting clinical trials; charitable volunteers; persons undergoing further professional education, training and examinations; students and staff working on income generation projects.

Where these principles apply, NHS bodies should accept full financial liability where negligent harm has occurred, and not seek to recover their costs from the health care professional involved.

Who Is Not Covered
NHS Indemnity does not apply to family health service practitioners working under contracts for services, eg GPs (including fundholders), general dental practitioners family dentists, pharmacists or optometrists; other self employed health care professionals, eg independent midwives; employees of FHS practices; employees of private hospitals; local education authorities; voluntary agencies. Exceptions to the normal cover arrangements are set out in the main document.

Circumstances Covered
NHS Indemnity covers negligent harm caused to patients or healthy volunteers in the following circumstances: whenever they are receiving an established treatment, whether or not in accordance with an agreed guideline or protocol; whenever they are receiving a novel or unusual treatment which, in the judgement of the health care professional, is appropriate for that particular patient; whenever they are subjects as patients or healthy volunteers of clinical research aimed at benefitting patients now or in the future.

Expenses Met
Where negligence is alleged, NHS bodies are responsible for meeting: the legal and administrative costs of defending the claim or, if appropriate, of reaching a settlement; the plaintiffs costs, as agreed by the two parties or as awarded by the court; the damages awarded either as a one-off payment or as a structured settlement.

NHS INDEMNITY
Clinical Negligence – Definition

1. Clinical negligence is defined as:

"A breach of duty of care by members of the health care professions employed by NHS bodies or by others consequent on decisions or judgements made by members of those professions acting in their professional capacity in the course of employment, and which are admitted as negligent by the employer or are determined as such through the legal process."*

2. In this definition "breach of duty of care" has its legal meaning. NHS bodies will need to take legal advice in individual cases, but the general position will be that the following must all apply before liability for negligence exists:

2.1 There must have been a duty of care owed to the person treated by the relevant professional(s);

2.2 The standard of care appropriate to such duty must not have been attained and therefore the duty breached, whether by action or inaction, advice given or failure to advise;

2.3 Such a breach must be demonstrated to have caused the injury and therefore the resulting loss complained about by the patient;

2.4 Any loss sustained as a result of the injury and complained about by the person treated must be of a kind that the courts recognize and for which they allow compensation; and

2.5 The injury and resulting loss complained about by the person treated must have been reasonably foreseeable as a possible consequence of the breach.

3. This booklet is concerned with NHS indemnity for clinical negligence and does not cover indemnity for any other liability such as product liability, employers liability or liability for NHS trust board members.

Other Terms

4. Throughout this guidance:

4.1 The terms "an NHS body" and "NHS bodies" include Health Authorities, Special Health Authorities and NHS Trusts but excludes all GP practices whether fundholding or not, general dental practices, pharmacies and opticians' practices

4.2 The term "health care professional" includes:

Doctors, dentists, nurses, midwives, health visitors, hospital pharmacy practitioners, registered ophthalmic or registered dispensing opticians working in a hospital setting, members of professions supplementary to medicine and dentistry, ambulance personnel, laboratory staff and relevant technicians.

Principles

5. NHS bodies are legally liable for the negligent acts and omissions of their employees (the principle of vicarious liability), and should have arrangements for meeting this liability. NHS Indemnity applies where:

5.1 the negligent health care professional was working under a contract of employment (as opposed to a contract for services) and the negligence occurred in the course of that employment; or

5.2 the negligent health care professional, although not working under a contract of employment, was contracted to an NHS body to provide services to persons to whom that NHS body owed a duty of care.

6. Where the principles outlined in paragraph 5 apply, NHS bodies should accept full financial liability where negligent harm has occurred. They should not seek to recover their costs either in part or in full from the health care professional concerned or from any indemnities they may have. NHS bodies may carry this risk entirely or spread it through membership of the Clinical Negligence Scheme for Trusts (CNST – see EL(95)40).

Who is Covered

7. NHS Indemnity covers the actions of staff in the course of their NHS employment. It also covers people in certain other categories whenever the NHS body owes a duty of care to the person harmed, including, for example, locums, medical academic staff with honorary contracts, students, those conducting clinical trials, charitable volunteers and people undergoing further professional education, training and examinations. This includes staff working on income generation projects. GPs or dentists who are directly employed by Health Authorities, eg as Public Health doctors (including port medical officers and medical inspectors of immigrants at UK air/sea ports), are covered.

8. Examples of the applicability of NHS Indemnity to common situations are set out in question and answer format in Annex A.

Who is not Covered

9. NHS Indemnity does not apply to general medical and dental practitioners working under contracts for services. General practitioners, including GP fundholders, are responsible for making their own indemnity arrangements, as are other self-employed health care professionals such as independent midwives. Neither does NHS Indemnity apply to employees of general practices, whether fundholding or not, or to employees of private hospitals (even when treating NHS patients) local education authorities or voluntary agencies.

---

* The NHS (clinical Negligence Scheme) Regulations 1996, which established the Clinical Negligence Scheme for Trusts, defines clinical negligence in terms of '...a liability in tort owed by a member to a third party in respect of or consequent upon personal injury or loss arising out of or in connection with any breach of a duty of care owed by that body to any person in connection with the diagnosis of any illness, or the care or treatment of any patient, in consequence of any act or omission to act on the part of a person employed or engaged by a member in connection with any relevant function of that member'.

10. Examples of circumstances in which independent practitioners or staff who normally work for private employers are covered by NHS Indemnity are given in Annex A. The NHS Executive advises independent practitioners to check their own indemnity position.

11. Examples of circumstances in which NHS employees are not covered by NHS Indemnity are also given in Annex A.

Circumstances Covered

12. NHS bodies owe a duty of care to healthy volunteers or patients treated or undergoing tests which they administer. NHS Indemnity covers negligent harm caused to these people in the following circumstances:

12.1 whenever they are receiving an established treatment, whether or not in accordance with an agreed guideline or protocol;

12.2 whenever they are receiving a novel or unusual treatment which in the clinical judgement of the health care professional is appropriate for the particular patient;

12.3 whenever they are subjects of clinical research aimed at benefitting patients now or in the future, whether as patients or as healthy volunteers. (Special arrangements, including the availability of no-fault indemnity apply where research is sponsored by pharmaceutical companies. See Annex B.)

Expenses Met

13. Where negligence is alleged NHS bodies are responsible for meeting:

13.1 the legal and administrative costs of defending the claim and, if appropriate, of reaching a settlement, including the cost of any mediation;

13.2 where appropriate, plaintiffs costs, either as agreed between the parties or as awarded by a court of law;

13.3 the damages agreed or awarded, whether as a one-off payment or a structured settlement.

Claims Management Principles

14. NHS bodies should take the essential decisions on the handling of claims of clinical negligence against their staff, using professional defence organizations or others as their agents and advisers as appropriate.

Financial Support Arrangements

15. Details of the Clinical Negligence Scheme for Trusts (CNST) were announced in EL(95)40 on 29 March 1995.

16. All financial arrangements in respect of clinical negligence costs for NHS bodies have been reviewed and guidance on transitional arrangements (for funding clinical accidents which happened before 1 April 1995), was issued on 27 November 1995 under cover of FDL(95)56. FDL(96)36 provided further guidance on a number of detailed questions.

ANNEX A
Questions and Answers on NHS Indemnity
Below are replies to some of the questions most commonly asked about NHS Indemnity.

1. Who is covered by NHS Indemnity?

NHS bodies are liable at law for the negligent acts and omissions of their staff in the course of their NHS employment. Under NHS Indemnity, NHS bodies take direct responsibility for costs and damages arising from clinical negligence where they (as employers) are vicariously liable for the acts and omissions of their health care professional staff.

2. Would health care professionals opting to work under contracts for services rather than as employees of the NHS be covered?

Where an NHS body is responsible for providing care to patients NHS Indemnity will apply whether the health care professional involved is an employee or not. For example a doctor working under a contract for services with an NHS Trust would be covered because the Trust has responsibility for the care of its patients. A consultant undertaking contracted NHS work in a private hospital would also be covered.

3. Does this include clinical academics and research workers?

NHS bodies are vicariously liable for the work done by university medical staff and other research workers (eg employees of the MRC) under their honorary contracts, but not for pre-clinical or other work in the university.

4. Are GP practices covered?

GPs, whether fundholders or not [and who are not employed by Health Authorities as public health doctors], are independent practitioners and therefore they and their employed staff are not covered by NHS indemnity.

5. is a hospital doctor doing a GP locum covered?

This would not be the responsibility of the NHS body since it would be outside the contract of employment. The hospital doctor and the general practitioners concerned should ensure that there is appropriate professional liability cover.

6. Is a GP seeing a patient in hospital covered?

A GP providing medical care to patients in hospital under a contractual arrangement, eg where the GP was employed as a clinical assistant, will be covered by NHS Indemnity, as will a GP who provides services in NHS hospitals under staff fund contracts (known as "bed funds"). Where there is no such contractual arrangement, and the NHS body provides facilities for patient(s) who continue to be the clinical responsibility of the GP, the GP would be responsible and professional liability cover would be appropriate. However, junior medical staff, nurses or members of the professions supplementary to medicine involved in the care of a GP's patients in NHS hospitals under their contract of employment would be covered.

7. Are GP trainees working in general practice covered?

In general practice the responsibility for training and for paying the salary of a GP trainee rests with the trainer. While the trainee is receiving a salary in general practice it is advisable that both the trainee and the trainer, and indeed other members of the practice, should have appropriate professional liability cover as NHS indemnity will not apply.

8. Are NHS employees working under contracts with GP fundholders covered?

If their employing NHS body has agreed a contract to provide services to a GP fundholding practice's patients, NHS employees will be working under the terms of their contracts of employment and NHS Indemnity will cover them. If NHS employees themselves contract with GP fundholders (or any other independent body) to do work outside their NHS contract of employment they should ensure that they have separate indemnity cover.

9. Is academic General Practice covered?

The Department has no plans to extend NHS Indemnity to academic departments of general practice. In respect of general medical services, Health Authorities' payments of fees and allowances include an element for expenses, of which medical defence subscriptions are a part.

10. Is private work in NHS hospitals covered by NHS Indemnity?

NHS bodies will not be responsible for a health care professional's private practice, even in an NHS hospital. However, where junior medical staff, nurses or members of professions supplementary to medicine are involved in the care of private patients in NHS hospitals, they would normally be doing so as part of their NHS contract, and would therefore be covered. It remains advisable that health professionals who might be involved in work outside the scope of his or her NHS employment should have professional liability cover.

11. Is Category 2 work covered?

Category 2 work (eg reports for insurance companies) is by definition not undertaken for the employing NHS body and is therefore not covered by NHS Indemnity. Unless the work is carried out on behalf of the employing NHS body, professional liability cover would be needed.

12. Are disciplinary proceedings of statutory bodies covered?

NHS bodies are not financially responsible for the defence of staff involved in disciplinary proceedings conducted by statutory bodies such as the GMC (doctors), UKCC (nurses and midwives), GDC (dentists) CPSM (professions supplementary to medicine) and RPSGB (pharmacists). it is the responsibility of the practitioner concerned to take out professional liability cover against such an eventuality.

13. Are clinical trials covered?

In the case of negligent harm, health care professionals undertaking clinical trials or studies on volunteers, whether healthy or patients, in the course of their NHS employment are covered by NHS Indemnity. Similarly, for a trial not involving medicines, the NHS body would take financial responsibility unless the trial were covered by such other indemnity as may have been agreed between the NHS body and those responsible for the trial. In any case, NHS bodies should ensure that they are informed of clinical trials in which their staff are taking part in their NHS employment and that these trials have the required Research Ethics Committee approval. For non-negligent harm, see question 16 below.

14. Is harm resulting from a fault in the drug/equipment covered?

Where harm is caused due to a fault in the manufacture of a drug or piece of equipment then, under the terms of the Consumer Protection Act 1987, it is no defence for the producer to show that he exercised reasonable care. Under normal circumstances, therefore, NHS indemnity would not apply unless there was a question whether the health care professional either knew or should reasonably have known that the drug/equipment was faulty but continued to use it. Strict liability could apply if the drug/equipment had been manufactured by an NHS body itself, for example a prototype as part of a research programme.

15. Are Local Research Ethics Committees (LRECs) covered?

Under the Department's guidelines an LREC is appointed by the Health Authority to provide independent advice to NHS bodies within its area on the ethics of research proposals. The Health Authority should take financial responsibility for members' acts and omissions in the course of performance of their duties as LREC members.

16. Is there liability for non-negligent harm?

Apart from liability for defective products, legal liability does not arise where a person is harmed but no one has acted negligently. An example of this would be unexpected side-effects of drugs during clinical trials. In exceptional circumstances (and within the delegated limit of £50,000) NHS bodies may consider whether an ex-gratia payment could be offered. NHS bodies may not offer advance indemnities or take out commercial insurance for non-negligent harm.

17. What arrangements can non-NHS bodies make for non-negligent harm?

Arrangements will depend on the status of the non-NHS body. Arrangements for clinical trials sponsored by the pharmaceutical industry are set out in Annex B.

12

Other independent sector sponsors of clinical research involving NHS patients (eg universities and medical research charities) may also make arrangements to indemnify research subjects for non-negligent harm. Public sector research funding bodies such as the Medical Research Council (MRC) may not offer advance indemnities nor take out commercial insurance for non-negligent harm. The MRC offers the assurance that it will give sympathetic consideration to claims in respect of non-negligent harm arising from an MRC funded trial. NHS bodies should not make ex-gratia payments for non-negligent harm where research is sponsored by a non-NHS body.

18. Would health care professionals be covered if they were working other than in accordance with the duties of their post?

Health care professionals would be covered by NHS Indemnity for actions in the course of NHS employment, and this should be interpreted liberally. For work not covered in this way health care professionals may have a civil, or even, in extreme circumstances, criminal liability for their actions.

19. Are health care professionals attending accident victims ("Good Samaritan" acts) covered?

"Good Samaritan" acts are not part of the health care professional's work for the employing body. Medical defence organizations are willing to provide low-cost cover against the (unusual) event of anyone performing such an act being sued for negligence. Ambulance services can, with the agreement of staff, include an additional term in the individual employee contracts to the effect that the member of staff is expected to provide assistance in any emergency outside of duty hours where it is appropriate to do so.

20. Are NHS staff in public health medicine or in community health services doing work for local authorities covered? Are occupational physicians covered?

Staff working in public health medicine, clinical medical officers or therapists carrying out local authority functions under their NHS contract would be acting in the course of their NHS employment. They will therefore be covered by NHS Indemnity. The same principle applies to occupational physicians employed by NHS bodies.

21. Are NHS staff working for other agencies, eg the Prison Service, covered?

In general, NHS bodies are not financially responsible for the acts of NHS staff when they are working on an individual contractual basis for other agencies. (Conversely, they are responsible where, for example, a Ministry of Defence doctor works in an NHS hospital.) Either the non-NHS body commissioning the work would be responsible, or the health care professional should have separate indemnity cover. However, NHS Indemnity should cover work for which the NHS body pays the health care professional a fee, such as domiciliary visits, and family planning services.

22. Are former NHS staff covered?

NHS Indemnity will cover staff who have subsequently left the Service (eg on retirement) provided the liability arose in respect of acts or omissions in the course of their NHS employment, regardless of when the claim was notified. NHS bodies may seek the co-operation of former staff in providing statements in the defence of a case.

23. Are NHS staff offering services to voluntary bodies such as the Red Cross or hospices covered?

The NHS body would be responsible for the actions of its staff only if it were contractually responsible for the clinical staffing of the voluntary body. If not, the staff concerned may wish to ensure that they have separate indemnity cover.

24. Do NHS bodies provide cover for locums?

NHS bodies take financial responsibility for the acts and omissions of a locum health care professional, whether "internal" or provided by an external agency, doing the work of a colleague who would be covered.

25. What are the arrangements for staff employed by one trust working in another?

This depends on the contractual arrangements. If the work is being done as part of a formal agreement between the trusts, then the staff involved will be acting within their normal NHS duties and, unless the agreement states otherwise, the employing trust will be liable. The NHS Executive does not recommend the use of ad hoc arrangements, eg a doctor in one trust asking a doctor in another to provide an informal second opinion, unless there is an agreement between the trusts as to which of them will accept liability for the "visiting" doctor in such circumstances.

26. Are private sector rotations for hospital staff covered?

The medical staff of independent hospitals are responsible for their own professional liability cover, subject to the requirements of the hospital managers. If NHS staff in the training grades work in independent hospitals as part of their NHS training, they would be covered by NHS Indemnity, provided that such work was covered by an NHS contract of employment.

27. Are voluntary workers covered?

Where volunteers work in NHS bodies, they are covered by NHS Indemnity. NHS managers should be aware of all voluntary activity going on in their organizations and should wherever possible confirm volunteers' indemnity position in writing.

28. Are students covered?

NHS Indemnity applies where students are working under the supervision of NHS employees. This should be made clear in the agreement between the NHS body and the student's educational body. This will apply to students of all the health care professions and to school students on, for example, work experience placements. Students working in NHS premises, under supervision of medical academic staff employed by universities holding honorary contracts, are also covered. Students who spend time in a primary care setting will only be covered if this is part of an NHS contract. Potential students making preliminary visits and school placements should be adequately supervised and should not become involved in any clinical work. Therefore, no clinical negligence should arise on their part.

In the unlikely event of a school making a negligent choice of work placement for a pupil to work in the NHS, then the school, and not NHS indemnity, should pick up the legal responsibility for the actions of that pupil. The contractual arrangement between the NHS and the school should make this clear.

29. Are health care professionals undergoing on-the-job training covered?

Where an NHS body's staff are providing on-the-job training (eg refresher or skills updating courses) for health care professionals, the trainees are covered by NHS Indemnity whether they are normally employed by the NHS or not.

30. Are independent midwives covered?

Independent midwives are self-employed practitioners. In common with all other health care professionals working outside the NHS, they are responsible for making their own indemnity arrangements.

31. Are overseas doctors who have come to the UK temporarily, perhaps to demonstrate a new technique, covered?

The NHS body which has invited the overseas doctor will owe a duty of care to the patients on whom the technique is demonstrated and so NHS indemnity will apply. NHS bodies, therefore, need to make sure that they are kept informed of any such demonstration visits which are proposed and of the nature of the technique to be demonstrated. Where visiting clinicians are not formally registered as students, or are not employees, an honorary contract should be arranged.

32. Are staff who are qualified in another member state of the European Union covered?

Staff qualified in another member state of the European Union, and who are undertaking an adaptation period in accordance with EEC directive 89/4/ EEC and the European Communities (Recognition of Professional Qualifications) Regulations 1991 which implements EEC Directive 89/48/EEC) and EEC Directive 92/51/EEC, must be treated in a manner consistent with their qualified status in another member state, and should be covered.

ANNEX B
Indemnity for Clinical Studies Sponsored by Pharmaceutical companies

Section One

1. Clinical research involving the administration of drugs to patients or non-patient human volunteers is frequently undertaken under the auspices of Health Authorities or NHS Trusts.

2. When the study is sponsored by a pharmaceutical company, issues of liability and indemnity may arise in case of injury associated with administration of the drug or other aspects of the conduct of the trial.

3. When the study is not sponsored by a company but has been independently organised by clinicians, the NHS body will carry full legal liability for claims in negligence arising from harm to subjects in the study.

4. The guidance in Section 2 and the Appendix has three purposes:

• to ensure that NHS bodies enter into appropriate agreements which will provide indemnity against claims and proceedings arising from company-sponsored clinical studies;

• to ensure that NHS bodies, where appropriate, use a standard form of agreement (Appendix) which has been drawn up in consultation with the Association of the British Pharmaceutical industry (ABPI);

• to advise Local Research Ethics Committees (LRECs) of the standard form of agreement.

Section Two

1. A wide variety of clinical studies involving experimental or investigational use of drugs is carried out within NHS bodies. This includes studies in patients (clinical trials) and studies in healthy human volunteers. They may involve administration of a totally new (unlicensed) drug (active substance or 'NAS') or the administration of an established (licensed) drug by a novel route, for a new therapeutic indication, or in a novel formulation or combination.

2. Detailed guidance on the design, conduct, and ethical implications of clinical studies is given in:

HSG(91)5: Local Research Ethics Committees (with accompanying booklet). NHS Executive: 1991;

Guidelines for Medical Experiments in non-Patient Human Volunteers ABPI:1988, amended 1990;

Research Involving Patients, Royal College of Physicians of London: 1990;

Guidelines in the Practice of Ethics Committees in Medical Research, 2nd edition; Royal College of Physicians of London:1990;

Clinical Trial Compensation Guidelines ABPI: 1991

12

3. The Medicines Act 1968 provides the regulatory framework for clinical studies involving administration of drugs to patients. Drugs which are used in a sponsored* clinical study in patients will be the subject of either a product licence (PL), a clinical trial certificate (CTC), or clinical trial exemption (CTX) which is held by the company as appropriate. A non-sponsored study conducted independently by a practitioner must be notified to the Licensing Authority under the Doctors and Dentists Exemption (DDX) scheme. Studies in healthy volunteers are not subject to regulation under the Medicines Act and do not require a CTC, CTX, or DDX. Further particulars of these arrangements are provided in Medicines Act leaflet *MAL 30: A guide to the provisions affecting doctors and dentists (DHSS: 1985).*

4. Participants in a clinical study may suffer adverse effects due to the drug or clinical procedures. The appendix to this annex is a model form of agreement between the company sponsoring a study and the NHS body involved, which indemnifies the authority or trust against claims and proceedings arising from the study. The model agreement has been drawn up in consultation with the Association of the British Pharmaceutical Industry (ABPI).

5. This form of indemnity will not normally apply to clinical studies which are not directly sponsored by the company providing the product for research, but have been independently organised by clinicians. In this case, the NHS body will normally carry full legal liability for any claims in negligence arising from harm to subjects in the study.

6. The NHS body will also carry full legal liability for any claims in negligence (or compensation under the indemnity will be abated) where there has been significant non-adherence to the agreed protocol or there has been negligence on the part of an NHS employee, for example, by failing to deal adequately with an adverse drug reaction.

7. The form of indemnity may not be readily accepted by sponsoring companies outside the UK or who are not members of the ABPI. NHS bodies should, as part of their risk management, consider the value of indemnities which are offered and consider whether companies should have alternative arrangements in place.

8. Several health authorities and trusts have independently developed forms of indemnity agreement. However, difficulties have arisen when different authorities have required varying terms of indemnity and this has, on occasion, impeded the progress of clinical research within the NHS. Particular difficulties may arise in large multi-centre trials involving many NHS bodies when it is clearly desirable to have standardised terms of indemnity to provide equal protection to all participants in the study.

9. Responsibility for deciding whether a particular company-sponsored research proposal should proceed within the NHS rests with the Health Authority or Trust within which the research would take place, after consideration of ethical, clinical, managerial, financial, resource, and legal liability issues. The NHS body is responsible for securing an appropriate indemnity agreement and should maintain a register of all clinical studies undertaken under its auspices with an indication whether it is a company-sponsored study and, if so, with confirmation that an indemnity agreement is in place. If for any reason it is considered that the model form of indemnity is not appropriate or that amendments are required, the NHS body involved should seek legal advice on the form or amendments proposed.

10. Even when the model form of indemnity is agreed, the NHS body should satisfy itself that the company sponsoring the study is substantial and reputable and has appropriate arrangements in place (for example insurance cover) to support the indemnity. The NHS body will carry full liability for any claims in negligence if the indemnity is not honoured and there is not supporting insurance.

11. Where a clinical study includes patients or subjects within several NHS bodies, for example in a multi-centre clinical trial, it is necessary for each Authority or Trust to complete an appropriate indemnity agreement with the sponsoring company.

12. Where independent practitioners, such as general medical practitioners, are engaged in clinical studies, Health Authorities should seek to ensure that such studies are the subject of an appropriate indemnity agreement. It is good practice for the GP to notify the Health Authority of his participation in any clinical study.

13. Clinical investigators should ensure that details of any proposed research study are lodged with the appropriate NHS body and should not commence company-sponsored research unless an indemnity agreement is in place.

14. Local Research Ethics Committees (LRECs) provide independent advice to NHS and other bodies and to clinical researchers on the ethics of proposed research projects that involve human subjects [HSG(91)5]. Clinical investigators should not commence any research project involving patients or human volunteers without LREC agreement. Acceptance of the ABM guidelines and the terms of the model indemnity agreement should normally be a condition of LREC approval of any pharmaceutical company sponsored project.

---

* A sponsored study may be defined as one carried out under arrangements made by or on behalf of the company who manufactured the product, the company responsible for its composition, or the company selling or supplying the product.

ANNEX B: APPENDIX
Form of indemnity for Clinical Studies

TO: [Name and address of sponsoring company] ("the Sponsor")

From: [Name and address of Health Authority/Health Board/NHS Trust] ("the Authority")

Re: Clinical Study No [ ] with [name of product]

1. It is proposed that the Authority should agree to participate in the above sponsored study ("the Study") involving [patients of the Authority] [non-patient volunteers] ("the Subjects") to be conducted by [name of investigator(s)] ("the Investigator") in accordance with the protocol annexed, as amended from time to time with the agreement of the Sponsor and the Investigator ("the Protocol"). The Sponsor confirms that it is a term of its agreement with the Investigator that the Investigator shall obtain all necessary approvals of the applicable Local Research Ethics Committee and shall resolve with the Authority any issues of a revenue nature.

2. The Authority agrees to participate by allowing the Study to be undertaken on its premises utilising such facilities, personnel and equipment as the Investigator may reasonably need for the purpose of the Study.

3. In consideration of such participation by the Authority, and subject to paragraph 4 below, the Sponsor indemnifies and holds harmless the Authority and its employees and agents against all claims and proceedings (to include any settlements or ex-gratia payments made with the consent of the parties hereto and reasonable legal and expert costs and expenses) made or brought (whether successfully or otherwise):

(a) by or on behalf of Subjects taking part in the Study (or their dependants) against the Authority or any of its employees or agents for personal injury (including death) to Subjects arising out of or relating to the administration of the product(s) under investigation or any clinical intervention or procedure provided for or required by the Protocol to which the Subjects would not have been exposed but for their participation in the Study.

(b) by the Authority, its employees or agents or by or on behalf of a Subject for a declaration concerning the treatment of a Subject who has suffered such personal injury.

4. The above indemnity by the Sponsor shall not apply to any such claim or proceeding:

4.1 to the extent that such personal injury (including death) is caused by the negligent or wrongful acts or omissions or breach of statutory duty of the Authority, its employees or agents;

4.2 to the extent that such personal injury (including death) is caused by the failure of the Authority, its employees, or agents to conduct the Study in accordance with the Protocol;

4.3 unless as soon as reasonably practicable following receipt of notice of such claim or proceeding, the Authority shall have notified the Sponsor in writing of it and shall, upon the Sponsor's request, and at the Sponsor's cost, have permitted the Sponsor to have full care and control of the claim or proceeding using legal representation of its own choosing;

4.4 if the Authority, its employees, or agents shall have made any admission in respect of such claim or proceeding or taken any action relating to such claim or proceeding prejudicial to the defence of it without the written consent of the Sponsor such consent not to be unreasonably withheld provided that this condition shall not be treated as breached by any statement properly made by the Authority, its employees or agents in connection with the operation of the Authority's internal complaint procedures, accident reporting procedures or disciplinary procedures or where such statement is required by law.

5. The Sponsor shall keep the Authority and its legal advisers fully informed of the progress of any such claim or proceeding, will consult fully with the Authority on the nature of any defence to be advanced and will not settle any such claim or proceeding without the written approval of the Authority (such approval not to be unreasonably withheld).

6. Without prejudice to the provisions of paragraph 4.3 above, the Authority will use its reasonable endeavours to inform the Sponsor promptly of any circumstances reasonably thought likely to give rise to any such claim or proceeding of which it is directly aware and shall keep the Sponsor reasonably informed of developments in relation to any such claim or proceeding even where the Authority decides not to make a claim under this indemnity. Likewise, the Sponsor shall use its reasonable endeavours to inform the Authority of any such circumstances and shall keep the Authority reasonably informed of developments in relation to any such claim or proceeding made or brought against the Sponsor alone.

12

7. The Authority and the Sponsor will each give to the other such help as may reasonably be required for the efficient conduct and prompt handling of any claim or proceeding by or on behalf of Subjects (or their dependants) or concerning such a declaration as is referred to in paragraph 3(b) above.

8. Without prejudice to the foregoing if injury is suffered by a Subject while participating in the Study, the Sponsor agrees to operate in good faith the Guidelines published in 1991 by The Association of the British Pharmaceutical Industry and entitled "Clinical Trial Compensation Guidelines" (where the Subject is a patient) and the Guidelines published in 1988 by the same Association and entitled "Guidelines for Medical Experiments in non-patient Human Volunteers" (where the Subject is not a patient) and shall request the Investigator to make clear to the Subjects that the Study is being conducted subject to the applicable Association Guidelines.

9. For the purpose of this indemnity, the expression "agents" shall be deemed to include without limitation any nurse or other health professional providing services to the Authority under a contract for services or otherwise and any person carrying out work for the Authority under such a contract connected with such of the Authority's facilities and equipment as are made available for the Study under paragraph 2 above.

10. This indemnity shall be governed by and construed in accordance with English/Scottish* law.

SIGNED on behalf of the Health Authority/Health Board/NHS Trust ....

Chief Executive/
District General Manager

SIGNED on behalf of the Company ....

Dated ....

12

* Delete as appropriate

This article was first published in the BMJ *and is reproduced with permission of the* BMJ

CLINICAL REVIEW

The ethics of randomised controlled trials from the perspectives of patients, the public, and healthcare professionals

Sarah J L, Edwards, R J Lilford, J Hewison
Correspondence to: Ms Edwards S.J.Edwards@bham.ac.uk
BMJ 1998;**317**:1209–12

Since the introduction of randomised controlled trials, professionals and lay people alike have worried over whether doing this sort of experiment in humans is ethical. It has been argued that participants may be called to sacrifice their own best interests for the benefit of future patients.[1] The scientific rationale for conducting a trial rests in collective equipoise, which means that the medical community as a whole is genuinely uncertain over which treatment is best. The key point, however, is that future patients benefit at no cost to participants, provided that participants are in personal equipoise and give informed consent on this basis. In these circumstances, the trial arms are an equally good bet prospectively.[2]

METHODS

To find out what patients, the general public, and healthcare professionals thought about trials, we undertook a review of the ethics of randomised controlled trials from these perspectives as part of a broader review relating to the ethics of designing and conducting clinical trials.[1] We searched BIDS, Medline, and Psychlit (for strategy see the *BMJ* website). There were 61 studies on attitudes to trials, 54 based on quantitative methods and eight based on qualitative ones (one study used both). Twenty studies made use of hypothetical trial scenarios. Seven studies focused on early trials (phases I and II). Our search also identified three reviews that included views on clinical trials,[3–5] but only one was a systematic review and even this study gave only limited information about the quality of the composite studies.[4] In all three reviews, the number of studies cited was much lower than the number we found.

Abstraction of results and quality assessment for all studies were carried out independently by SE and JH. We have chosen to focus here on the issues of informed consent, doctor-patient relationship, what motivates participants, equipoise, and restricting new treatments to trials. Other issues are summarised elsewhere.[1] Quality assessment was difficult in many cases because insufficient information was given by the authors—perhaps itself an indicator of poor quality. The dimensions of methodological rigour used are listed in table 1. Our detailed findings are available in the form of a *Health Technology Assessment* monograph.[1] Here,

Summary points

Doctors do not seem to take informed consent from competent patients as seriously as they should; ways in which practice might be improved need to be tested empirically

Most doctors expressed willingness to enter their patients in trials even when the treatments offered were widely available but were not an equal bet prospectively; the fact that members of the public suspect this might undermine their confidence in trials

Willingness to undergo randomisation drops as prospective participants are given more preliminary data and as they are made aware of any accumulating evidence of effectiveness

A large number of participants, even in phase III trials, emerge from consultations expecting to benefit personally; self interest, rather than altruism, seems to be their motive for participating

we discuss the salient findings in narrative style. The results were often surprising and sometimes even shocking.

INFORMED CONSENT

The concept that informed consent should always be obtained from competent patients was widely, though not universally, accepted.[6–13] Two of these studies (one as recent as 1994) found that up to one in five doctors regularly entered competent patients in trials without even obtaining informed consent.[12 13]

In three studies, trialists were asked how confident they were that participants had grasped the key issues. An astonishing 47% of responding doctors in a multinational study thought that few patients knew they were taking part in a controlled experiment, even though they had given written consent.[13] Even more extreme results were obtained in the two remaining studies, in which more than three quarters of responding doctors thought their patients rarely understood all the information given to them.[14 15] These three studies were all carried out in the 1980s and involved clinicians from North America and Europe.

Table 1

Quality of evidence checklist

Code	Dimension of methodology
A	External validity of study-that is, how clearly defined was the target population which the sample results may in theory be generalised? (+ acceptable, – flawed)
B	Sampling: how representative is the sample of the target population?
	1 Entire population (consenters and refusers) approached or random selection of eligible patients
	2 "Quota" sampling (deliberate selection from specific groups)
	3 Grab sampling
	4 Not reported
C	Response rate must be given and acceptable at 70% or above (+ acceptable, – flawed)
D	Interobserver reliability should be assessed where appropriate for questionnaires or interviews (particularly where open ended questionnaires are used) (+ acceptable, – flawed)
E	Questionnaire should be supplied in study or available from author (+ acceptable, – flawed)
F	The statistical method used to analyse data must be appropriate (+ acceptable, – flawed)

Despite this, patients generally seemed content with the information they received. The experiences of patients who had actually taken part in clinical trials were audited in four studies, which reported that at least 80% of responding participants were satisfied that they had made an autonomous decision to take part.[16–19] Of course, there is no way of knowing whether they really had received or understood all that they would have wished.

Views of healthcare professionals on the amount of information required to make consent valid were sought in a further six studies. In three Spanish studies, over 90% of trialists agreed on a minimum dataset for all patients,[7–9] and, in another study, a substantial proportion (58%) of doctors from the United Kingdom and eastern Europe said that they tried to give all information that might be pertinent.[12] However, 83% of respondents thought that patients may be overloaded with information,[6] and about half the trialists doubted their capacity to judge what information to give patients.[13] These results may reflect a widespread concern that fully informed consent may cause anxiety[20] and may even be needlessly cruel.[21]

Expectations with respect to informed consent varied according to the type of experiment in question. Some responding doctors believed that informed consent was obtained more rigorously in phase I trials than in phases II or III studies,[22] and in trials of supportive care, than in trials testing curative or palliative therapies.[12]

EFFECT ON DOCTOR-PATIENT RELATIONSHIP

Since the time of Hippocrates, the doctor-patient relationship has been the cornerstone of medical practice. Five studies reported the views of doctors on the effect of offering trial entry on the doctor-patient relationship.[6 13–15 23] Of these, all but one small study[15] showed that there was considerable concern among doctors about the effect of discussing trial entry on the trust and wellbeing of patients.

MOTIVATION

Self interest was more commonly given than altruism as a reason for participating in trials (table 2). This was so whether the study was based on real (n=13) or hypothetical (n=9) scenarios. Fourteen studies explicitly involved phase III trials, and half of these recorded self interest as strongly influential. This is strange as patients have nothing to gain prospectively, save a putative non-specific trial effect, given personal equipoise and freely available treatments. Few of those asked were likely to have been aware of the extra medical attention that may go hand in hand with participating in a trial.[1] The way in which this information was elicited varied strikingly across the studies; some researchers recorded both motivations, others recorded only one. Of these, some had forced a choice, others had not, and, in some cases it was not even clear what exactly the researchers had done. As a result, the studies are not strictly comparable, but our main criticism is that they gave only a weak clue

Table 2

Frequency with which self interested motivations and altruism were expressed by respondents

Motivation	Frequency
Self interest	
Real scenarios:	Over 70 % in four studies[18 34 35 36]
	Between 30% and 55% in eight studies[17 19 37 38 39 40 41 42]
	Under 20% in one study[43]
Hypothetical scenarios:	Over 50% in two studies[26 44]
	Between 25% and 50% in five studies[10 26 38 45 46]
Altruism	
Real scenarios:	Over 60% in 3 studies[35 36 38]
	Between 40% and 60% in four studies[17 18 39 40]
	Under 40% in three studies[41 42 43]
Hypothetical scenarios:	Over 65% in four studies[10 27 44 46]
	Between 20% and 60% in three studies[26 38 45]
	Under 15% in one study[47]

as to what patients had understood of the questions and hence what they meant by their responses. The majority of studies were (post-licensing) phase III trials comparing treatments which would normally be available in routine practice. Did the respondents realise this? They may not even have appreciated that they could be allocated to a control arm, and there is some literature to suggest that they might not.[33]

PERSONAL EQUIPOISE

In regard to personal equipoise, there are two issues: firstly, are decisions ever so finely balanced that a situation of personal equipoise may exist, and, secondly, what does and should happen when trial treatments are freely available but when personal equipoise does not apply? Regarding the first, Alderson and colleagues reported, on the basis of a standardised questionnaire, that only 25% of doctors could envisage themselves being in personal equipoise and still fewer (18%) thought their patients could ever reach this state.[10] By contrast, it is possible to elicit Bayesian prior probabilities from clinicians[24] and these may interact, at least in theory, with a particular patient's values to produce equal expected utifities—that is, equipoise.

Clinicians were frequently prepared to enter their patients in trials of freely available treatments even though they preferred one arm to another. This issue would not be important if patients could be "fully" informed. Over half (53%) of doctors who preferred tamoxifen for early breast cancer were prepared to enter their patients in a placebo controlled trial of this potentially lifesaving treatment.[10] Nearly three quarters (73%) of the responding surgeons thought a trial of hormone replacement therapy in patients with treated breast cancer would be ethical, even though only 28% were "uncertain" whether this treatment could provoke a recurrence of this hormone sensitive tumour (J Marsden et al, unpublished data). It is possible, however, that they thought equipoise could exist nevertheless, as some patients might be prepared to trade off some survival advantage against the relief of symptoms. Taylor and Kelner explored this issue in more detail and found that 36% of clinicians thought that it was appropriate to enter patients in trials despite thinking that the treatments were an unequal bet prospectively. Eighty seven per cent went so far as to say that they would enter more patients if they could dispense with informed consent altogether, which could mean that they put greater store by scientific knowledge than the participants' welfare in phase III trials.[25] But would these doctors subject one of their children to randomisation in such circumstances—and if not, would they at least disclose their prior opinion on the effects of the treatments in question? Otherwise doctors may have been allowing scientific affiliations to affect their behaviour.

And patients suspected as much—the proportion of patients or members of the public who thought it likely that doctors put people in trials even if equipoise was not present ranged from 26% to 70% across two studies, both of which used hypothetical trial scenarios.[26 27] Such

variation might be explained in part by the populations sampled: an exclusively African-American population and the general public respectively.

Two studies examined the effect of preliminary information on willingness to participate in a hypothetical trial and found that fewer people were willing to enter a hypothetical trial when preliminary data indicated either an increasing difference in the effectiveness of the two treatments or an increasing statistical significance of that difference.[28] Consistent with these findings is the further observation that people given explicit data concerning the effects of hormone replacement therapy, along with the problems inherent in the interpretation of the data, were less willing to be randomised than those given less detail and told simply that the effects on the various outcomes were "uncertain" (JA Wragg et al, unpublished data). This is in keeping with the finding, based on comparative studies of different methods for obtaining consent to randomised controlled trials, that more information was associated with lower consent rates.[1]

RESTRICTIONS ON ACCESS

What did patients think about restricting potentially lifesaving treatments, where no "proved" treatment exists already, to trials for the sake of assessment? A large proportion (79%) of responding AIDS patients across two studies,[29 30] and parents of very ill children in a further study,[31] thought that such drugs should be available to patients outside the trial. Another study, brought people together by focus groups to discuss the scenario where the new treatment was available only within a trial. Even when the patients were not desperate, they preferred a three way choice—that is, treatment A, treatment B, or trial of A versus B (J Marsden et al, unpublished data). The preference for wide availability even before licensing has been taken up by Minogue, who argued that by offering potentially lifesaving treatments only within the confines of a trial, patient autonomy is infringed and it is desperation that compels them to "consent."[32] Logue, on the other hand, argued that although there are fewer options (either enter a trial or not), patient autonomy is not infringed, for limited choice is an inevitable part of everyday life.[33]

CONCLUSION

The finding that so many people participate out of self interest needs exploring. Although the studies were of poor quality, especially regarding what exactly the respondents understood of the questions and hence what they meant by their answers, it is important to find out what well informed members of the public really think about trials and why they expect to benefit, if indeed they do. The finding that self interest features so strongly, even in phase III trials, is consistent with our other findings that patients do not always understand that they have been randomised to a control group,[31] which was just what the doctors had anticipated.[15] Given equipoise and freely available treatments, gain is not a realistic aim prospectively in late phase trials. Even if a trial effect is real,[1] this can hardly be used as an inducement to participate because to do so would violate the Declaration of Helsinki. Because patients are required to make informed choices, it is important that they both understand and accept that they stand neither to lose nor to gain in such cases. Rationally, the reason for such participation must be an altruistic one or else a way of resolving an otherwise difficult (or finely balanced) decision—this latter reason was picked up by respondents in Snowdon et al's study.[31] If patients expect to be personally worse off by being in a trial but nevertheless give their consent, they would be altruistic in a strong sense, meaning that they expect to sacrifice clinical benefit for the psychological satisfaction of helping others.

The other main theme is that a surprising number of doctors "owned up" to entering their patients when the treatments in the trial were probably otherwise freely available but when patients harboured a personal preference for one of the treatments. Worse, doctors seemed to have been aware that patients may not have fully understood what was going on. For many,

informed consent seemed little more than a ritual. More research needs to be carried out to see precisely what factors motivate doctors to offer randomised controlled trials as an option in health care. It is interesting to speculate, though. Doctors may feel torn by their obligations to individual patients and to society at large, and they may even have got the impression, perhaps hyped up by advocates of evidence based medicine, that they are obliged to participate in research for the common good, even when they have a slight or moderate treatment preference. As, a result, there may be a stark difference of opinion between ethicists and practitioners over what is ethically acceptable. This brings us back to the need for clear public discussion of ethics and the conduct of medical research.

Funding: Health Technology Assessment Methodology Programme. Competing interests: None declared.

Department of Public Health and Epidemiology, University of Birmingham, Birmingham B15 2TT
Sarah J L Edwards *research fellow*
R J Lilford *professor of health services research*

Department of Psychology, University of Leeds, Leeds LS2 9JT
J Hewison *senior lecturer*

References

1. Edwards SJL, Lilford RJ, Jackson JC, Hewison J, Thornton J. Ethical issues in the design and conduct of randomised controlled trials. *Health Technology Assessment* (in press).

2. Lilford RJ, Jackson JC. Equipoise and the ethics of randomisation. *J R Soc Med* 1995;**88**:552–9.

3. King J. Informed consent. A review of the empirical evidence. *Institute of Medical Ethics Bulletin* 1986 December.

4. Meisel A, Roth L. Toward a informed discussion of informed consent a review and critique of the empirical studies. *Arizona Law Review* 1983;**25**:246–65.

5. Schain WS. Barriers to clinical trials. Part II: knowledge and attitudes of potential participants. *Cancer* 1994;**74(suppl)**:2666–76.

6. Benson AB, Pregler JP, Bean JA, Rademaker AG, Fritter B, et al. Oncologists reluctance to accrue patients onto clinical trials: an Illinois Center study. *J Clin Oncol* 1991;**9**:2067–75.

7. Dal-Re R. Informed consent in clinical research with drugs in Spain: Perspectives of clinical trials committee members. *Eur J Clin Pharmacol* 1990;**38**:319–24.

8. Dal-Re R. Elements of informed consent in clinical research with drugs: a survey of Spanish clinical investigators. *J Intern Med* 1992;**231**:375–9.

9. Dal-Re R. Good clinical practice in clinical trials: the responsibilities of the investigator. A survey of 827 hospital physicians (and II). Patient consent. *Medicina Clinica* 1993;**100**:423–7.

10. Alderson P, Madden M, Oakley A, Wilkins R. *Women's knowledge and experience of breast cancer treatment and research.* London: Social Science Research Unit, 1994.

11. Taylor KM. Integrating conflicting professional roles: physician participation in randomized clinical trials. *Soc Sci Med* 1992;**35**:217–24.

12. Williams CJ, Zwitter M. Informed consent in European multicentre randomized clinical trials—are patients really informed? *Eur J Cancer* 1994;**30**:907–10.

13. Taylor KM, Kelner M. Interpreting physician participation in randomized clinical trials: the physician orientation profile. *J Health Soc Behaviour* 1987;**28**:389–400.

14. Blum AL, Chalmers TC, Deutch E, Koch-Weser J, Rosen A, Tygstrup N, et al. The Lugano statement on controlled clinical trials. *J Int Med Res* 1987;**15**:2–22.

15. Spaight SJ, Nash S, Finison LJ, Patterson WB. Medical oncologists' participation in cancer clinical trials. *Progress Clin Biol Res* 1984;**156**:4961.

16. Harth SC, Thong YH. Parental perceptions and attitudes about informed consent in clinical research involving children. *Soc Sci Med* 1995;**40**:1573–7.

17. Lynoe N, Sandlund M, Dahlqvist G, Jacobsson L. Informed consent: study of the quality of information given to participants in a clinical trial. *BMJ* 1991;**303**:610–3.

18. Penman D, Holland JC, Bahna GE, Morrow G, Schmale AH, Derogatis LR, et al. Informed consent for investigational chemotherapy: patients' and physicians' perceptions. *J Clin Oncol* 1984;**2**:849–55.

19. Rodenhuis S, vanden Heuvel WS, Annyas AA, Koops HS, Sleiffer DT, Mulder NH. Patient motivation and informed consent in a phase I study of anticancer agent. *Eur J Cancer Clin Oncol* 1984;**20**:457–62.

20. Simes RJ, Tattersall MHN, Coates AS, Raghaven D, Solomon HJ, Smartt H. Randomised comparison of procedures for obtaining informed consent in clinical trials of treatment of cancer. *BMJ* 1986;**293**:1065–8.

21. Tobias JS, Souhami RL. Fully informed consent can be needlessly cruel. *BMJ* 1993;**307**:1199–201.

22. Kodish E, Stocking C, Ratain MJ, Kohrman A, Siegler M. Ethical issues in phase I oncology research: a comparison of investigators and institutional review board chairpersons. *J Clin Oncol* 1992;**10**:1810–6.

23. Taylor KM, Margolese RG, Soskolne CL. Physicians reasons for not entering patients in a randomized control clinical trial of surgery for breast cancer. *N Engl J Med* 1984;**310**:1363–7.

24 Lilford RJ for the Fetal Compromise Group. Formal measurement of clinical uncertainty: prelude to a trial in perinatal medicine. *BMJ* 1994;**308**:111–2.

25 Taylor KM, Kelner M. Informed consent: the physicians' perspective. *Soc Sci Med* 1987;**24**:135–43.

26 Millon-Underwood Determinants of participation in state-of-the-art cancer prevention, early detection? screening, and treatment trials. *Cancer Nurs* 1993;**16**:25–33.

27 Cassileth BR, Lusk EJ, Miller DS, Hurtwitz S. Attitudes toward clinical trials among patients and the public. *JAMA* 1982;**248**:968–970.

28 Ubel PA, Metz JF, Shea J, Asch DA. How preliminary data affect people's stated willingness to enter a hypothetical randomized controlled trial. *J Invest Med* 1997;**45**:561–6.

29 Tindall B, et al. Effects of two formats of informed consent on knowledge amongst persons with advanced HIV disease in a clinical trial of didanosine. *Patient Educ Counselling* 1994;**24**:261–6.

30 Twomey JG. Investigating pedantic HIV research ethics in the field. *Weston J Nurs Res* 1994;**16**:404–13.

31 Snowdon C, Garcia J, Elbourne D. Making sense of randomisation: responses of parents of critically ill babies to random allocation of treatment in a clinical trial. *Soc Sci Med* 1997;**45**:1337–55.

32 Minogue BP, Palmer-Ferandez G, Udell L, Waller BN. Individual autonomy and the double-blind controlled experiment: the case of the desperate volunteer. *J Med Philosophy* 1995;**20**:43–55.

33 Logue G, Wear S. A desperate solution: individual autonomy and the double-blind controlled experiment. *J Med Philosophy* 1995;**20**:57–64.

34 Daugherty C, Ratain MJ, Grochowski E, Stocking C, Kodish E, Mick R, et al. Perceptions of ancer patients and their physicians involved in phase I trials. *J Clin Oncol* 1995;**13**:1062–72.

35 Harth SC, Thong YH. Socio-demographic and motivational characteristics of parents who volunteer their children for clinical research: a controlled study. *BMJ* 1990;**300**:1372.

36 Mattson ME, Curb D, McArdle R and AMIS and BHAT Research Groups. Participation in a clinical trial: the patients' point of view. *Control Clin Trials* 1985;**6**:156–67.

37 Barofsky I, Sugarbaker PH. Determinants of nonparticipation in randomized clinical trials for the treatment of sarcomas. *Cancer Clin Trials* 1979;**2**:237–46.

38 Bevan EG, Chee LC, McGhee SM, and McInnes GI. Patients' attitudes to participation in clinical trials. *Br J Clin Pharmacol* 1993;**35**:204–7.

39 Hassar M, Weintraub M. "Uninformed" consent and the wealthy volunteer: an analysis of patient volunteers in a clinical trial of a new antiflammatory drug. *Clin Pharmacol Therapeutics* 1976;**20**:379–86.

40 Jensen AB, Madsen B, Anderson P, Rose C. Information for cancer patients entering a clinical trial: evaluation of an information strategy. *Eur J Cancer* 1993;**29**:2235–8.

41 Vogt TM, Ireland CC, Black D, Camel G, Hughes G. Recruitment of elderly volunteers for a multicentre clinical trial. *Control Clin Trials* 1986;**7**:118–33.

42 Wilcox M, Schroer S. The perspectives of patients with vascular disease on participation in clinical trials. *J Med Ethics* 1994;**12**:112–6.

43 Henzlova MJ, Blackburn GH, Bradley EJ, Rogers WJ. Patient perception of a long-term clinical trial: experience using a close-out questionnaire in the studies of left ventricular dysfunction (SOLVD) trial. *Control Clin Trials* 1994;**15**:284–93.

44 Flattery M, Gravdal J, Hendrix P, Hoffman W, King P, May D, et al. Just sign here…. *S Dakota J Med* 1978;**31**:33.

45 Slevin M, Mossman J, Bowling A, Leonard R, Steward W, Harper P, et al. Volunteers or victims: patients' views of randomised clinical trials. *Br J Cancer* 1995;**71**:1270–4.

46 Autret E, Dutertre JP, Barbier P, Jonville AP, Pierre F, Berger C. Parental opinions about biomedical research in children in Tours, France. *Devel Pharmacol Therapeutics* 1993;**20**:64–71.

47 Kemp N, Skinner E, Toms J. Randomized clinical trials of cancer treatment—a public opinion survey. *Clin Oncol* 1974;**10**:155–161.

13

(*Accepted 2 October 1998*)

This chapter was first published in Research Opportunities in Primary Care *and is reproduced by permission of Radcliffe Medical Press*

THE RCGP CENTRE FOR PRIMARY CARE RESEARCH AND EPIDEMIOLOGY

Philip Hannaford (In: Carter Y and Thomas C (eds).
Research Opportunities in Primary Care. Abingdon: Radcliffe Medical Press, 1999.)

THE OPPORTUNITY FOR EPIDEMIOLOGICAL RESEARCH

The central position of the primary care team within the NHS provides an important opportunity to undertake long-term epidemiological research. Almost everyone living in the UK is registered with a named general practitioner who contracts to provide primary care services. Each practice, therefore, cares for a defined population from which individuals with particular characteristics can be identified and recruited for research purposes. These characteristics might include the existence of a medical condition such as diabetes or hypertension, use of a particular service or receipt of a specified treatment. The practice list also facilitates the identification of individuals without the chosen characteristic, so that a suitable comparison group can be assembled. The effort needed to identify potential subjects for a study has been reduced in recent years by the widespread computerisation of general practices.

The gatekeeper role of the GP means that few patients are seen by colleagues in the secondary or tertiary care sector without referral from a GP. This is especially so in the era of fundholding and locality-based commissioning of services. The usual feedback of information about the outcome of the hospital visit enables practices to compile comprehensive records of a person's use of medical services. The transfer of these records from the old practice to the new one when a patient moves helps ensure that the records contain details of the main medical events occurring during a person's life.

The quality and comprehensiveness of the medical records held by the primary care team is constantly being improved. This is partly because of a growing awareness of the medicolegal importance of having complete and accurate medical records. It also reflects recent trends towards giving the primary care team a central role in the coordination of preventive services, such as childhood immunisation programmes, the detection of hypertension and screening for cervical and breast cancer. A further impetus has been the increasing use of computers in the consultation room to record information about presenting symptoms, examination findings, diagnoses, information likely to be useful in future consultations (such as smoking and drinking habits), medical procedures provided and prescriptions issued.

THE SUCCESSFUL EXPLOITATION OF THIS OPPORTUNITY

For nearly 30 years, the Royal College of General Practitioners (RCGP) Centre for Primary Care Research and Epidemiology (formerly RCGP Manchester Research Unit) has successfully exploited the opportunity provided by general practice to undertake epidemiological research. A particular strength of the Centre is its ability to recruit hundreds of GPs willing to provide, often on an unpaid basis, comprehensive patient-specific data for extended periods of time. By asking a large number of practitioners (or their staff) to each supply information about a comparatively small number of patients, the workload of the individual practitioner is kept small. The use of simple data collection forms, with the minimum of rules for their completion, also reduces the workload. By successfully coordinating this collective effort, the Centre manages to accumulate the vast quantities of data required for its research.

All of the Centre's senior scientific staff has experience of general practice. Indeed, the Manchester Research Unit's first director, Dr Clifford Kay, combined an internationally recognised research career with that of a busy GP for more than 25 years. This involvement with general practice helps to ensure that the Centre's work is relevant to the primary care team. It also means that there is a strong understanding of the strengths and weaknesses of data collected from general practice, thereby avoiding the erroneous interpretation of such information.

ORAL CONTRACEPTION STUDY

The Centre was established in 1968 to conduct the Oral Contraception Study, an investigation which illustrates many of the principles employed in the subsequent studies.

By the mid-1960s, a rapidly increasing number of women were using oral contraceptives. It was recognized, however, that little was known about the health effects of these preparations especially in the long term. New studies were needed, not only to confirm or refute problems already thought to be associated with the use of oral contraception, but also to detect effects not previously suspected. A cohort study which collected information about a variety of health outcomes represented the most efficient way of determining the overall risks and benefits associated with the use of oral contraception. Furthermore, since this type of study involves the calculation of disease incidence rates, information would become available about the absolute risks (or benefits) associated with the use of oral contraception, enabling women and their advisors to put any effects into perspective. Basing a new cohort study in general practice offered two distinct advantages. First, the opportunity to collect information about the wide range of medical problems presented to the GP, including those that rarely result in referral to hospital. Second, the possibility of making the study large enough to permit detailed examination of the relationship between uncommon disease and the use of the Pill.

During a 14-month period starting in May 1968, 1400 GPs throughout the UK recruited 23 000 women who were using oral contraceptives and a similar number who had never done so.[1] All of the women were married or living as married, their average age was 29 years and most were Caucasian. Information collected at recruitment included details of any previous use of oral contraception, the occupation of the woman's husband (to determine her social class), the woman's smoking habits, parity and significant past medical history. Patient confidentiality was maintained by allocating each woman a unique study number, the key to which only the GP held; all correspondence between the Centre and the doctor has used this study number.

At 6-monthly intervals since recruitment, participating doctors have supplied details of any hormonal preparations prescribed (initially oral contraceptives but more recently hormone replacement therapies), pregnancies and their outcome, surgery and the reason for it, all new episodes of illness reported to the GP and, when appropriate, date and cause of death. Diagnostic criteria have not been provided for the GPs. In some cases, the reported diagnoses have been those made by the participating GP or another member of the primary care team. In others, the participating doctors will have simply reported the opinion of hospital colleagues who may have had access to the results of investigations, operation notes or post-mortem findings. Serious conditions which are more likely to result in referral to hospital, such as cancers or cardiovascular events, have a higher proportion of reports based on this supplementary information than less serious conditions which are managed more frequently in the community. As well as having access to the opinion of hospital colleagues, the GPs in the study benefit from observing their patients over a prolonged period of time. Diagnoses which are initially uncertain may become clearer later. Indeed, the study often needs to revise its recorded diagnoses as additional information becomes available. In general, the study's findings have been consistent with those from other studies, including those which used specific diagnostic criteria.

Nearly three-quarters of the cohort has now been lost to GP follow-up, mainly because of the women leaving the recruiting practice. During the early years of the study attempts were made to trace women to their new practice to seek its help with the follow-up. Unfortunately, the procedure met with only limited success and so had to be abandoned. No data collected for the study, however, is wasted, since all women contribute to the database up to the date they leave the study. In addition, during the late 1970s, 75% of the cohort was flagged at the NHS Central Registries in Southport and Edinburgh. This means that the Centre is notified of any deaths or cancer registrations occurring in these women, even among those no longer under GP observation. (The remaining 25% of women could not be flagged because they, or their GP, had already left the study when the flagging procedure took place.)

So far, the study has accumulated more than 550000 woman-years of observation making it one of the largest detailed studies of oral contraception in the world. It was among the first to show that the risk of cardiovascular disease among Pill users who smoke is much higher than that among users who do not smoke, especially in older women.[2,3] These findings continue to influence clinical practice. The study was the first to demonstrate that the risk of hypertension[4] and arterial disease[5] is related to the progestogen content of the Pill. Evidence from the study that users of combined oral contraceptives may have a lower risk of rheumatoid arthritis[6] led to a flurry of new studies around the world investigating this unexpected finding. A recent analysis of the database to examine the long-term cardiovascular sequelae of toxaemia of pregnancy (now generally referred to as pre-eclampsia) indicated that women with a history of this condition have higher risks of hypertension, invocardial infarction, other forms of ischaemic heart disease, venous thromboembolic disease and possibly stroke than women without such a history.[7] This finding has led to the launch of a new study, the Aberdeen Study of Cardiovascular Health in Women, which will investigate further this intriguing relationship.

ATTITUDES TO PREGNANCY STUDY

The rising number of women having an induced abortion during the early 1970s led to questions being raised in Parliament regarding the safety of this procedure. Aware of the success of the Oral Contraception Study, the Department of Health approached the RCGP to see whether it could undertake a similar observational study of the health effects of induced abortion. This led to the euphemistically titled Attitudes to Pregnancy Study, a collaborative effort between the RCGP and the Royal College of Obstetricians and Gynaecologists. The study was coordinated by the Manchester Research Unit under the supervision of its former deputy director, Dr Peter Frank.

Between 1976 and 1978, 1509 GPs in England, Scotland and Wales recruited about 7000 women who had an induced abortion and 7000 women who presented with an unplanned pregnancy who did not

14

request a termination of pregnancy.[8] Baseline information collected included the woman's age, marital status, smoking habits, age at completion of full-time education (used to measure social status), and previous medical, psychiatric and obstetric history. Nearly 800 gynaecologists working in both the NHS and the private sector provided details of the consultation during which the abortion request was considered, and if performed, gave details of the operation and its early complications. The GPs subsequently supplied, for up to ten years, information about any new pregnancies and their outcome, reported morbidities and, when appropriate, cause of death.

The study was able to assess the effects of induced abortion on short-term health,[9] future fertility,[10] subsequent pregnancies[11] and psychiatric health.[12] In general, the results were reassuring, with few associations observed either in the short or long term. Given the sensitive nature of the operation, a major strength of the study was its ability to maintain patient confidentiality by using the system of allocating a special study number developed for the Oral Contraception Study. Indeed, in a pilot survey, nearly half the women who had an induced abortion said they would refuse to participate in a study if they could not remain anonymous.

OTHER WORK

The Centre's expertise in providing the logistic support needed to undertake large-scale studies has been used successfully in a number of other studies. The RCGP Myocardial Infarction Study was an 18-month investigation of the safety and feasibility of the domiciliary use of anistreplase by GPs.[13] The Evaluation of Take Care project assessed whether the introduction of a commercially sponsored education programme improved the ability of GPs to recognise psychological illness.[14] The Wythenshawe Community Asthma Project is a continuing longitudinal study of the natural history of respiratory symptoms affecting patients from two practices in South Manchester, UK.[15] The project will also examine the costs associated with treating asthma.

Less successful was the Centre's involvement in the early 1990s in the European Investigation of Cancer (EPIC), a European-wide prospective study of the relationship between diet and cancer. In conjunction with the Imperial Cancer Research Fund's (ICRF) Cancer Epidemiology Unit in Oxford, UK, the Centre agreed to be responsible for recruiting 50 000 men and women via GPs working throughout the UK. Participation in EPIC also appeared to provide a useful opportunity to investigate the long-term effects of hormone replacement therapy. The study was launched in Scotland with subsequent extensions into northern England. To ease administration of the study, women were to be recruited first; participating practices being asked to recruit two users and two non-users of hormone replacement therapy each month. The recruitment procedure, however, was far from simple.

The doctors needed to identify suitable patients during routine consultations, obtain written informed consent, complete a complicated recruitment form and take a blood sample for dispatch to a central laboratory in Cambridge. The women also had to complete a detailed food frequency questionnaire and a food diary. Not surprisingly, few doctors felt able to commit time to the study even though many felt that the research questions were important. The poor recruitment rates meant that recruitment via the GP had to be abandoned. More successful, alternative methods of recruitment have now been established; these are now being coordinated by the ICRF Unit in Oxford.

Several hard but important lessons were learnt during the Centre's involvement in EPIC. First, it is vital to remember the realities of life in a busy general practice; wherever possible simplify, simplify and simplify again the recruitment procedures. In particular, do not overcomplicate matters by trying to too many research questions at the same time. Second, if we intend to ask members of the primary care team to help us in our research, we must actively seek (and obtain) some way of compensating them for their work. Alternatively, we must put research personnel into practices to undertake the work. Third, although we piloted the recruitment procedures for EPIC, these pilot studies were clearly not extensive enough to give us a reliable picture of likely recruitment in the main study.

FUTURE DEVELOPMENTS

In September 1997, the RCGP Manchester Research Unit was relocated to RCGP Centre of Primary Care Research and Epidemiology within the Department of General Practice and Primary Care at the University of Aberdeen. The Centre is the new home for the valuable datasets accumulated in Manchester. These databases offer the opportunity to gain new insights into the aetiology of many diseases, particularly those affecting women.

Over the years, the Centre's research interests have broadened from the effects of specific medical interventions to more general issues that come under the heading of primary care epidemiology. Thus, the Centre is now interested in issues such as the measurement of the frequency of disease and symptoms recorded by the primary care team or reported by patients in the community; the factors likely to influence the onset of these diseases or symptoms; the long-term impact of these problems on subsequent health; and the appropriate role of screening for disease in the primary care setting. The relocation of the Centre to Aberdeen provides easier access to colleagues with recognized expertise in the measurement of symptoms and health outcomes, health economics and molecular science; skills which complement those within the Centre and which are likely to be needed in future research projects. The development of new multidisciplinary, collaborative studies will ensure that the Centre continues to provide the primary care team with some of the information that it needs to practise evidence-based medicine.

References

1. Royal College of General Practitioners (1974) *Oral Contraceptives and Health*. Pitman Medical Publishing, Tunbridge Wells.

2. Royal College of General Practitioners' Oral Contraception Study (1977) Mortality among oral contraceptive users. *Lancet*. ii: 727-31.

3. Royal College of General Practitioners' Oral Contraception Study (1983) Incidence of arterial disease among oral contraceptive users. *Journal of the Royal College of General Practitioners*. 33: 75-82.

4. Royal College of General Practitioners' Oral Contraception Study (1977) Effect on hypertension and benign breast disease of progestogen component in combined oral contraceptives. *Lancet*. i: 624.

5. Kay CR (1982) Progestogens and arterial disease – evidence from the Royal College of General Practitioners' study. *American Journal of Obstetrics and Gynaecology*. 142: 762-5.

6. Royal College of General Practitioners' Oral Contraception Study (1978) Reduction in the incidence of rheumatoid arthritis associated with oral contraceptives. *Lancet*. i: 569-71.

7. Hannaford P, Ferry S and Hirsch S (1997) Cardiovascular sequelae of toxaemia of pregnancy. *Heart*. 77: 154-8.

8. Kay CR and Frank PI (1981) Characteristics of women recruited to a long-term study of the sequelae of induced abortion. *Journal of the Royal College of General Practitioners*. 31: 473-7.

9. Joint Study of the Royal College of General Practitioners and the Royal College of Obstetricians and Gynaecologists (1985) Induced abortion operations and their early sequelae. *Journal of the Royal College of General Practitioners*. 35: 175-80.

10. Frank P, McNamee R, Hannaford PC et al. (1993) The effect of induced abortion on subsequent fertility. *British Journal of Obstetrics and Gynaecology*. 100: 575-80.

11. Frank PI, McNamee R, Hannaford PC et al. (1991) The effect of induced abortion on subsequent pregnancy outcome. *British Journal of Obstetrics and Gynaecology*. 98: 1015-24.

12. Gilchrist AC, Hannaford PC, Frank P et al. (1995) Termination of pregnancy and psychiatric morbidity. *British Journal of Psychiatry*. 167: 243-8.

13. Hannaford P, Vincent R, Ferry S et al. (1995) Assessment of the practicality and safety of thrombolysis with anistreplase given by general practitioners. *British Journal of General Practice*. 45: 175-9.

14. Hannaford PC, Thompson C and Simpson M (1996) Evaluation of an educational programme to improve the recognition of psychological illness by general practitioners. *British Journal of General Practice*. 46: 333-7.

15. Frank P, Ferry S, Moorhead T et al. (1996) Use of a postal questionnaire to estimate the likely under-diagnosis of asthma-like illness in adults. *British Journal of General Practice*. 46: 295-7.

14

This article was first published in the British Journal of General Practice *and is reproduced with permission of the* BJGP

The risk of serious illness among oral contraceptive users: evidence from the RCGP's oral contraceptive study

Philip C Hannaford, Clifford R Kay

BJGP, 1998, **48**, 1657-1662

SUMMARY

Background. So far, no-one has attempted to evaluate the overall balance of serious, but not necessarily fatal, disease among a cohort of oral contraceptive users.

Aim. To empirically assess the balance of risk of serious illness among a cohort of oral contraceptive users followed up for up to 28 years.

Methods. Oral contraceptive-associated serious disease was defined as that which is often life-threatening and/or associated with long-term disability, and which has been found, or postulated, to be associated with use of combined oral contraceptives. Data from the Royal College of General Practitioners' (RCGP) Oral Contraception Study were examined to determine the rate of such conditions during 335 181 woman-years of observation in 'ever users' and 228 727 woman-years in 'never users'. The rates were standardized for age, parity, social class, and smoking.

Results. Compared with never users, ever users had a small increased risk of any serious disease (relative risk = 1.17; 95% confidence interval = 1.09–1.25). Ever users had an excess risk of cerebrovascular disease, pulmonary embolism, and venous thromboembolism, and reduced risk of ovarian and endometrial cancer. The increased risk was seen only in younger women; by the age of 50, ever users had the same risk as never users. The risk appeared to be confined to women using older oral contraceptives containing 50 micrograms or more of oestrogen.

Conclusions. Past users of older, higher dose oral contraceptives can be reassured that the small increased risk of serious disease seen during current use does not persist after stopping, and that latent effects do not appear later in life. Currently available oral contraceptives, containing less than 50 micrograms of oestrogen accompanied by the progestogen, levonorgestrel, or norethisterone acetate, do not appear to be associated with an increased net risk of serious disease.

Keywords: oral contraceptives; risk-benefits; cohort study; serious disease.

INTRODUCTION

Since their introduction more than 35 years ago, combined oral contraceptives have been implicated with an increased risk of a number of illnesses, particularly vascular conditions such as stroke, ischaemic heart disease, venous thrombosis, and peripheral vascular disease.[1] They have also been found to be associated with important benefits, most notably protection against ovarian and endometrial cancer, which is sustained for many years after stopping oral contraception.[1] It is important, therefore, to consider the overall balance of risks and benefits when assessing the safety of this method of birth control.

Most overall assessments so far have considered the risk of dying among women using oral contraceptives. Two approaches have been adopted. The first involves constructing a computer model in which summary risk estimates for various oral contraceptive-associated clinical events are applied to hypothetical populations of women using different methods of contraception.[1-6] The second method empirically compares the risk of death among women who have used oral contraceptives with another group of similarly aged women who have not.[7-9] Intuitively, the second approach is more attractive, since it avoids many of the assumptions made when using computer modelling, especially the assumption that all of the risks and benefits have been determined with reasonable precision.

Mortality data, however, only provide one aspect of the contraceptive pill's safety. Since, even though the long-term, all-cause mortality among ever users appears to be similar to that of never users,[7-9] oral contraceptive use might still be associated with an elevated risk of serious but non-fatal illness. This is particularly so when considering vascular events such as stroke or heart disease, many of which are non-fatal but produce long-term disability. This paper presents the first attempt to empirically assess the balance of risk of serious illness among a cohort of oral contraceptive users followed for up to 28 years.

METHOD

The RCGP Oral Contraception Study was established during 1968 and 1969, when 1400 general practitioners throughout the United Kingdom recruited 23 000 women who were using the pill and a similar number who had never used this method of contraception.[10] The average age of the two groups at recruitment was 29 years, most were white, and all were married or living as married. Information collected at recruitment included smoking habits, parity, husband's occupation (for social class), and important past medical history. At regular intervals, the doctors have supplied comprehensive information about any hormonal preparations prescribed; all reported new episodes of illness, surgery, pregnancy, and, when appropriate, cause of death.

Any evaluation using morbidity as the outcome must compare events of approximately equal severity. It would be inappropriate to compare a reduced risk of common but usually relatively mild conditions, such as anaemia or menstrual problems, with an increased risk of rare but more serious problems, such as stroke or heart disease. For this paper, therefore, an oral contraceptive-associated serious condition was defined as one that is often life-threatening and/or associated with long-term disability, and which has been found, or postulated, to be associated with use of combined oral contraceptives. Using these criteria, the following conditions were included in the analysis: ischaemic heart disease (International Classification of Diseases, 8th revision (ICD-8) code 410-413); cerebrovascular disease (ICD-8 code 430-438); peripheral vascular disease (ICD-8 code 440-442, 4439, 444); pulmonary embolus (ICD-8 code 450); venous thromboembolism (ICD-8 code 452, 4531, 4539); ill-defined heart disease (ICD-8 code 427-429); cancer of the large bowel and rectum (ICD-8 code 153, 154), liver and gallbladder (ICD-8 code 155, 156), melanoma (ICD-8 code 172), breast (ICD-8 code 174), cervix (ICD-8 code 180), endometrium (ICD-8 code 182), ovary (ICD-8 code 183), pituitary and central nervous system (ICD-8 code 191, 1943), and unknown origin (ICD-8 code 199); liver disease (ICD-8 code 070, 570-573); diabetes mellitus (ICD-8 code 250); multiple sclerosis (ICD-8 code 340); inflammatory bowel disease (ICD-8 code 563); and rheumatoid arthritis (ICD-8 code 712).

Using data available at November 1996, the rate of first ever diagnosis of these serious illnesses among ever and never users was calculated. For each calendar month in which a subject used an oral contraceptive, one month was added to the period of exposure (denominator) of ever users. When a woman stopped using the pill, her subsequent periods of observation were still included in the ever user group. Never users were those women who had never used oral contraceptives. If a woman was recruited as a never user but started to use oral contraception at a later date, her subsequent experience was included in the ever user group. Events occurring in women known to have had the same condition before recruitment were excluded from the analysis, as were events and periods of observation related to pregnancy. Only the first event in each diagnostic category was counted in the numerator, although the women continued to contribute to the appropriate denominator as they remained at risk of experiencing another type of serious event. This procedure will tend to reduce the estimated rates of disease, although the effects are likely to be small because of the large accumulated periods of observation in the study. Indeed, in an unpublished analysis of hypertension data from the study, there was very little difference between incidence rates calculated using all accumulated periods of observation and those that only used periods of observation up to the date of diagnosis (P Hannaford, personal communication, 1993). All women recruited to the study contributed data to the appropriate numerator and denominator up to the point that they left the study or to November 1996.

A total of 335 181 woman-years of experience for ever users and 228 727 woman-years for never users was available for analysis. The rates were directly standardized for age and parity at time of event, and for smoking and social class at recruitment. The 95% confidence intervals for the risk ratios were derived from the assumption that the standard deviation of the log relative risk is equal to the sum of the reciprocals of the observed number of cases in the two groups being compared.

RESULTS

Compared with never users, women who had ever used oral contraceptives had a small increased risk of experiencing one of the selected serious conditions (adjusted relative risk (RR) = 1.17; 95% confidence interval (CI) = 1.09–1.25: Table 1). Oral contraceptive users had a significantly elevated risk of cerebrovascular disease, pulmonary embolism, and venous thromboembolism, and a reduced risk of endometrial and ovarian cancer. The age-specific relative risks for ever versus never users tended to be highest among women aged less than 35 years (Table 2). By the age of 50 years, women who had ever used oral contraceptives had the same risk of serious disease as never users.

The incidence of disease in women who smoked, however, was higher than that in non-smokers, irrespective of their contraceptive use (Table 3). For each category of cigarette consumption, the incidence of serious illness was significantly greater in ever users than never users. The absolute (attributable) risk of serious illness among non-smoking oral contraceptive users was 80.2 per 100 000 woman-years, compared with 98.9 per 100 000 woman-years in ever users who smoked one to 14 cigarettes per day at recruitment and 186.8 per 100 000 woman-years in ever users who smoked 15 or more cigarettes daily at recruitment.

There was a suggestion that the risk of serious illness was higher among parous ever users than nulliparous ever users (Table 4). The adjusted relative risk for serious illness between ever users of non-manual social class and non-manual never users was 1.31 (95% CI = 1.16–1.48). In comparison, the adjusted relative risk between manual ever and never users was 1.13 (95% CI 1.04–1.23).

There was no evidence that women who had used oral contraceptives for a long time had a greater risk of serious disease than those who used them for short periods (Table 5). Neither was there a consistent relationship between serious disease and time since stopping oral contraception (Table 6). In particular, there was no evidence of important risks becoming apparent many years after stopping.

In current users, the risk of experiencing a serious illness appeared to be confined to women who were using older oral contraceptives containing 50 μg or more of oestrogen (Table 7). In our study, virtually all of the lower dose oral contraceptives containing less than 50 μg of oestrogen had levonorgestrel or norethisterone acetate as the accompanying progestogen. The data relating to progestogen-only preparations were too sparse to reliably determine the risk of serious illness associated with these particular products.

DISCUSSION

In our study, ever users of oral contraceptives had a small overall elevated risk of serious disease, mainly because of an increased risk of cardiovascular disease. This risk occurred at a young age when the background incidence of disease is low. There was no evidence of a persisting risk among ever

15

Table 1

Risk of OC-associated serious illness in the RCGP Oral Contraception Study between 1968-1995: standardized rate per 100 000 woman-years (number of events in brackets).

Condition	ICD code	Standardized rate[a]		Relative risk	
		Ever users	Never users	Ever : never	95% CI
Ischaemic heart disease	410-413	146.2 (469)	143.0 (338)	1.02	(0.89–1.17)
Cerebrovascular disease	430-438	84.0 (272)	61.3 (154)	1.37	(1.12–1.67)
Peripheral vascular disease	440-442, 4439, 444	45.0 (151)	36.8 (85)	1.22	(0.94–1.59)
Pulmonary embolus	450	36.1 (124)	23.2 (56)	1.56	(1.14–2.14)
Venous thromboembolism	452, 4531, 4539	62.2 (215)	38.9 (92)	1.60	(1.25–2.04)
Ill-defined heart disease	427–429	123.2(406)	131.4 (311)	0.94	(0.81–1.09)
Malignancies:					
Large bowel and rectum	153–154	16.8 (52)	18.4 (43)	0.91	(0.61–1.36)
Gallbladder/liver	155–156	2.1 (5)	2.2 (6)	0.95	(0.29–3.11)
Melanoma	172	12.6 (40)	12.0 (29)	1.05	(0.65–1.69)
Breast	174	96.0 (297)	86.4 (212)	1.11	(0.93–1.32)
Invasive cervix	180	17.4 (60)	11.0 (22)	1.58	(0.97–2.58)
Endometrium	182	3.7 (12)	11.0 (30)	0.34	(0.17–0.66)
Ovary	183	8.2 (26)	16.7 (42)	0.49	(0.30–0.80)
CNS/pituitary	191, 1943	3.1 (11)	1.3 (3)	2.38	(0.66–8.53)
Site unknown	199	4.2 (13)	7.1 (18)	0.59	(0.29–1.20)
Liver disease	070, 570, 571–573	51.8 (180)	48.2 (105)	1.07	(0.84–1.36)
Diabetes mellitus	250	48.0 (158)	56.7 (142)	0.85	(0.68–1.07)
Multiple sclerosis	340	21.5 (75)	16.9 (39)	1.27	(0.86–1.87)
Inflammatory bowel disease	563	33.4 (113)	26.4 (59)	1.27	(0.93–1.74)
Rheumatoid arthritis	712	73.6 (245)	68.2 (157)	1.08	(0.88–1.32)
Any serious illness[b]	All above	683.9 (2261)	582.2 (1378)	1.17	(1.09–1.25)

[a]Standardized for age (<29, 30–34, 35–39, 40–44, 45–49, 50+), parity (0, 1, 2, 3+) at diagnosis, social class (manual, non-manual) and smoking habits (0, 1–14, 15+ daily) at recruitment. CI = confidence interval. [b]Only the first illness is counted; the total number of events is, therefore, less than the sum of each condition taken separately.

Table 2

Risk of OC-associated serious illness by age: standardized rates per 100 000 woman-years (number of events in brackets).

Age at diagnosis	Standardized rate[a]		Relative risk	
	Ever users	Never users	Ever : never	(95% CI)
<29	441.8 (238)	318.4 (96)	1.39	(1.10–1.76)
30–34	506.9 (270)	337.1 (112)	1.50	(1.20–1.87)
35–39	485.1 (302)	395.2 (151)	1.23	(1.01–1.50)
40–44	674.9 (411)	527.3 (206)	1.28	(1.08–1.51)
45–49	820.1 (406)	659.5 (232)	1.24	(1.06–1.46)
50+	1130.8 (634)	1181.5 (581)	0.96	(0.86–1.07)

[a]Standardized for parity (0, 1, 2, 3+) at diagnosis, for social class (manual, non-manual), and smoking habits (0, 1–14, 15+ daily) at recruitment. CI = confidence interval.

Table 3

Risk of OC-associated serious illness by smoking: standardized rates per 100 000 woman-years (number of events in brackets).

Daily cigarette consumption at recruitment	Standardized rate[a]		Relative risk	
	Ever users	Never users	Ever : never	(95% CI)
Nil	619.8 (1055)	539.6 (769)	1.15	(1.05–1.26)
1–14	699.8 (641)	600.9 (352)	1.16	(1.02–1.32)
15 +	862.5 (565)	675.7 (257)	1.28	(1.10–1.48)

[a]Standardized for age (<29, 30–34, 35–39, 40–44, 45–49, 50+), parity (0, 1, 2, 3+) at diagnosis, and social class (manual, non-manual) at recruitment. CI = confidence interval.

Table 4

Risk of OC-associated serious illness by parity: standardized rates per 100 000 woman-years (number of events in brackets).

Parity at event	Standardized rate[a]		Relative risk	
	Ever users	Never users	Ever : never	(95% CI)
0	712.6 (89)	696.2 (147)	1.02	(0.78 - 1.33)
1	710.0 (257)	525.8 (212)	1.35	(1.13 - 1.62)
2	669.7 (852)	578.2 (518)	1.16	(1.04 - 1.29)
3+	689.3 (1063)	595.7 (501)	1.16	(1.04 - 1.29)

[a]Standardized for age (<29, 30–34, 35–39, 40–44, 45–49, 50+) at diagnosis, smoking habits (0, 1–14, 15+ daily) and social class (manual, non-manual) at recruitment. CI = confidence interval.

Table 5

Risk of OC-associated serious illness by duration of use: standardized rates per 100 000 woman-years (number of events in brackets).

Months of use	Standardized rate[a]	Relative risk	(95% CI)
0	582.2 (1378)	1.0	
1-	742.5 (370)	1.28	(1.14–1.44)
13-	666.3 (264)	1.14	(1.00–1.30)
25-	775.8 (447)	1.33	(1.20–1.48)
49-	686.8 (373)	1.18	(1.05–1.32)
73-	718.3 (286)	1.23	(1.08–1.40)
97+	625.8 (521)	1.08	(0.98–1.19)

[a]Standardized for age (<29, 30–34, 35–39, 40–44, 45–49, 50+), parity (0, 1, 2, 3+) at diagnosis, smoking habits (0, 1–14, 15+ daily) and social class (manual, non-manual) at recruitment. CI = confidence interval.

Table 6

Risk of OC-associated serious illness by time since stopping oral contraception: Standardized rates per 100 000 women-years (number of events in brackets).

Years since last use	Standardized rate[a]	Relative risk	(95% CI)
0 (Never user at time of event)	582.2 (1378)	1.0	
0 (Current user at time of event)	840.6 (642)	1.44	(1.31–1.58)
Past			
<1 year	731.5 (145)	1.26	(1.06–1.50)
1–2 years	519.6 (91)	0.89	(0.72–1.10)
3–4 years	544.1 (177)	0.93	(0.80–1.09)
5–6 years	702.4 (194)	1.21	(1.04–1.41)
7–8 years	575.5 (143)	0.99	(0.83–1.18)
8+ years	542.2 (869)	0.93	(0.85–1.01)

[a]Standardized for age (<29, 30–34, 35–39, 40–44, 45–49, 50+, parity (0, 1, 2, 3+) at diagnosis, smoking habits (0, 1–14, 15+ daily) and social class (manual, non-manual) at recruitment. CI = confidence interval.

Table 7

Risk of OC-associated serious illness by oestrogen content of oral contraceptive used at time of event: standardized rates per 100 000 woman-years (number of events in brackets).

	Standardized rate[a]	Relative risk	(95% CI)	Periods of observation (woman-years)
Never users	582.2 (1378)	1.0		228 727
Current users: Oestrogen[b] content				
>50μg	988.2 (92)	1.70	(1.38 - 2.10)	14 152
50μg	974.0 (479)	1.67	(1.51 - 1.85)	79 213
<50μg	448.1 (51)	0.77	(0.58 - 1.02)	9858
Current users: Progestogen only	881.2 (20)	1.51	(0.97 - 2.35)	3220

[a]Standardized for age (<29, 30–34, 35–39, 40–44, 45–49, 50+), parity (0, 1, 2, 3+) at diagnosis, smoking habits (0, 1–14, 15+ daily) and social class (manual, non-manual) at recruitment. CI = confidence interval. [b]Either mestranol or ethinyloestradiol.

15

users older than 50 years. Furthermore, the risk in current users appeared to be confined to women using oral contraceptives containing 50 mg of oestrogen or more.

The largest group of conditions contributing to the overall risk was the cardiovascular events. Current consensus is that the cardiovascular risks are limited to current users, with no persisting risk in past users.[11] In fact, there is little in the literature to suggest that any of the reported adverse effects of oral contraception persist for prolonged periods after stopping. Even the small increased risk of breast cancer seen in current users seems to disappear within 10 years of stopping.[12] Our findings confirm an absence of persisting serious illness in past users. Furthermore, they show that latent illnesses do not appear many years after stopping.

Our observations cannot be due to oral contraceptives accelerating the presentation of disease in women at risk of developing disease. If this were the case, we would expect to see reduced relative risks in older ever users and with greater time since stopping oral contraception, neither of which were observed. Small, statistically significant, increased relative risks were observed in ever users during the first year after stopping oral contraception and at 5–6 years (Table 6). The first year elevation may have been a reporting artefact due to women developing symptoms of disease while using oral contraception and stopping before the diagnosis is confirmed. There is no obvious explanation for the elevated risk in the 5–6 year grouping, and this may have been due to chance.

The risk of serious disease in women using oral contraceptives containing less than 50 mg of oestrogen at the time of the event was substantially lower than that observed among users of higher dose preparations. Standardization of the results for age, smoking, social class, and parity should have removed any effects of these potential, confounding variables. Furthermore, the first event type of analysis, which involved the exclusion of events occurring in women with a past history of any of the selected morbidities, means that the finding cannot be due to the differential use of higher dose formulations by women with an adverse past history. Alternative explanations for the findings include real reductions in the risk potential of the newer low dose oral contraceptives, a more thorough assessment and monitoring of users of these products (especially with regard to blood pressure), or a combination of both factors.

Study limitations

Our analysis had a number of limitations. By including all conditions that have been found, or postulated, to be associated with oral contraceptive use, we sought to avoid making judgements about whether a causal relationship has been established. This approach would exclude unknown relationships that have yet to emerge. After more than three decades of intensive research, however, the chances of fresh associations appearing seem small, except possibly in relation to new health problems such as HIV infection and AIDS (problems that have occurred very rarely in our cohort). On the other hand, if a suspected condition was wrongly attributed to oral contraceptive use, its inclusion in the analysis would bias the results towards the null hypothesis; common conditions having a greater effect than rare ones. As a check, we performed an analysis that included all cancers, together with the other serious conditions mentioned in the methodology section. There were 2459 events in the ever users and 1530 in never users, with a standardized relative risk of 1.15 (95% CI = 1.08–1.23).

Several potentially important conditions were excluded from the analysis. The incidence of pelvic inflammatory disease is affected by several methods of birth control. For instance, oral contraceptive users appear to have a lower risk of pelvic inflammatory disease,[13] and male condoms reduce the risk of sexually transmitted diseases that can cause pelvic infections.[14] Life-long comprehensive contraceptive histories other than for oral contraceptives have not been collected from women in the RCGP study. It is possible, therefore, that observed reductions in the incidence of pelvic inflammatory disease among contraceptive users[10] were due to differences in the proportion of women in the contraceptive groups using alternative methods of birth control that affect the risk, rather than a direct biological effect of oral contraception. Given the uncertainty, we felt that we should exclude this condition from the analysis. In addition, we omitted ovarian cysts and benign breast disease because they are rarely life-threatening or are frequently associated with long-erm sequelae. Both conditions have been found to be reduced in oral contraceptive users[10]. The likely effect of these decisions will have been to overstate the harmful effects of oral contraception.

Carcinoma-in-situ of the cervix was excluded because, with appropriate treatment, there should be few long-term complications. Hypertension was excluded because of the difficulty of differentiating between raised blood pressure in current oral contraceptive users and idiopathic essential hypertension. However, the main sequelae of hypertension, vascular disease, were included.

With proper use, oral contraceptives are highly effective at protecting against pregnancy and pregnancy-related serious disease. Ideally, the analysis should have included pregnancy-related events resulting from contraceptive failure in the two comparison groups. In the RCGP study, comprehensive data were collected about events occurring during all pregnancies reported since 1968. Information was not collected, however, about whether the pregnancy was the result of failed contraception. It was impossible, therefore, to determine whether pregnancy-related serious events reported during the study occurred in a planned or unplanned pregnancy. We chose, therefore, to exclude serious events occurring during pregnancy and the puerperium from the main analysis. The effect of this exclusion will have been to exaggerate the harmful effect of oral contraceptives because, in our study, pregnancy occurred more frequently in never users.[10] Given the rarity of pregnancy-related events, however, the effect will have been small. Indeed, in a separate analysis, which included serious conditions occurring during pregnancy as well as ectopic pregnancy and eclampsia, the relative risk between ever and never users was 1.16 (95% CI = 1.09–1.24).

We tried to include, in the main analyses, conditions of reasonably similar severity. The decision about whether an illness is life-threatening and/or associated with long-term disability was based on our clinical experience. We are unaware of a recognized, readily available system for ranking diseases into groups of similar seriousness. Most serious illnesses were included, however, with the exception of some respiratory conditions, such as asthma, chronic obstructive pulmonary disease, and bronchial carcinoma. None of these conditions have been postulated to be associated with oral contraceptive use, so their inclusion would tend to bias the overall results towards the null hypothesis.

Diagnoses recorded in the RCGP study are those reported by the participating general practitioners; diagnostic criteria are not specified. For some events, the diagnosis will have been that made in general practice; for others, the family doctor will simply have reported the opinion and findings of hospital colleagues who may have had access to the results of appropriate investigations, operation notes, or necropsy findings. As well as having access to specialist opinion, the general practitioners are usually able to observe their patients for a prolonged period of time. Diagnoses that are initially uncertain may become clearer later. Indeed, study data are often revised as extra information becomes available. In general, the findings of the RCGP study have been remarkably consistent with those of other studies. Referral and diagnostic bias, however, could still have affected its results. For instance, it is possible that a doctor's knowledge of a woman's use of oral contraception influenced the diagnosis, particularly of some cardiovascular events. Thus, women who used oral contraception and who complained of leg or chest pain may have been more likely to have a thorough assessment, including hospital investigations, than never users with the same symptoms, thereby increasing the detection of disease among oral contraception users. Such biases are most likely to occur in current users and would tend to overestimate the risks associated with the pill. Episodes of deep venous thrombosis might be more prone to diagnostic and other selection biases than other conditions. Excluding these events from the analysis, the overall relative risk between ever and never users became 1.15 (95% CI = 1.07–1.23).

The RCGP study has been subject to large losses to follow-up. By November 1996, approximately 75% of the original cohort was no longer under general practitioner observation. Most of the loss has been a result of women leaving the practice area of the recruiting doctors. In order to affect our results, one has to argue that, among women of similar risk, those who had ever used the pill and who were going to develop serious disease were more, or less, likely to leave the study than never users who were going to develop serious disease. There is no reason to suppose that this has occurred. Indeed, examination of mortality data

from the study (which are available for 75% of the original cohort) has not found any evidence of material biases being introduced by the large attrition rates.[9]

Although we found that ever users of oral contraceptives had a small increased risk of serious disease, the absolute (attributable) risk was small: 101.7 per 100 000 woman-years. Much of the risk was experienced by users of older oral contraceptives containing 50 mg or more of oestrogen. The risk did not persist after stopping oral contraception and there was no evidence of latent disease appearing in later years when many conditions become more common. We believe that many women will be reassured by these findings. The apparent absence of risk of serious disease among users of newer oral contraceptives represented in our database (formulations containing less than 50 mg of oestrogen mostly accompanied by levonorgestrel or norethisterone acetate) was also reassuring. This said, there remain major deficiencies in our understanding of the overall balance of the health risks and benefits of other lower-dose oral contraceptives containing gestodene, desogestrel, or norgestimate. Recent studies have emphasized the importance of not assuming that all oral contraceptives have the same safety profile,[15-18] and have highlighted the need for continued research into this popular method of contraception.

References

1. Vessey MP. The Jephcott Lecture, 1989: An overview of the benefits and risks of combined oral contraceptives. In: Mann RD (ed.). *Oral Contraceptives and Breast Cancer.* Carnforth, Lancs: Parthenon Publishing Group 1990.
2. Tietze C, Bongaarts J, Schearer B. Mortality associated with the control of fertility. *Fam Planning Perspect* 1976; **8**: 6-14.
3. Tietze C, Lewit S. Life risks associated with reversible methods of fertility regulation. *Int J Gynaecol Obstet* 1979; **16**: 456-459.
4. Kost K, Forrest JD, Harlap S. Comparing the health risks and benefits of contraceptive choices. *Fam Planning Perspect* 1991; **23**: 54-61.
5. Vessey M, Milne R. Modelling the impact on mortality of the use of combined oral contraceptives. *Br J Fam Planning* 1991; **17**: 34-38.
6. Kawachi I, Colditz GA, Hankinson S. Long-term benefits and risks of alternative methods of fertility control in the United States. *Contraception* 1994; **50**: 1-16.
7. Vessey MP, Villard-Mackintosh L, McPherson K, Yeates D. Mortality among oral contraceptive users: 20 year follow-up of women in a cohort study. *BMJ* 1989; **299**: 1487-1491.
8. Colditz GA for The Nurses' Health Study Research Group. Oral contraceptive use and mortality during 12 years of follow-up: The Nurses' Health Study. *Ann Intern Med* 1994; **120**: 821-826.
9. Beral V, Hermon C, Kay C, *et al.* Mortality in relation to method of follow-up in the Royal College of General Practitioners' Oral Contraception Study. In: Hannaford PC, Webb AMC (eds). *Evidence-Guided Prescribing of the Pill.* Carnforth, Lancs: Parthenon Publishing Group 1996.
10. Royal College of General Practitioners. *Oral Contraceptives and Health.* London: Pitman Medical, 1974.
11. WHO Scientific Group on Cardiovascular Disease and Steroid Hormone Contraception. *Cardiovascular Disease and Steroid Hormone Contraception: Report of a Scientific Group.* WHO Technical report Series; 877. Geneva: Switzerland, 1998.
12. Collaborative Group on Hormonal Factors in Breast Cancer. Breast cancer and hormonal contraceptives: collaborative re-analysis of individual data on 53 297 women with breast cancer and 100 239 women without breast cancer from 54 epidemiological studies. *Lancet* 1996; **347**: 1713-1727.
13. Wølner-Hanssen P. Relationship between oral contraceptives and pelvic inflammatory disease and associated sexually transmitted diseases. In: Hannaford PC, Webb AM (eds). *Evidence-Guided Prescribing of the Pill.* Carnforth, Lancs: Parthenon Publishing Group 1996.
14. Hicks D. Sexually transmitted diseases and contraceptive methods. *Fertil Control Rev* 1994; **3**: 3-8.
15. World Health Organization Collaborative Study of Cardiovascular Disease and Steroid Hormone Contraception. Effect of different progestogens in low oestrogen oral contraceptives on venous thromboembolic disease. *Lancet* 1995; **346**: 1582-1588.
16. Jick H, Jick SS, Gurewich V, *et al.* Risk of idiopathic cardiovascular death and non-fatal venous thromboembolism in women using oral contraceptives with differing progestogen components. *Lancet* 1995; **346**: 1589-1593.
17. Bloemenkamp KWM, Rosendaal FR, Helmerhorst FM, *et al.* Enhancement by factor V Leiden mutation of risk of deep-vein thrombosis associated with oral contraceptives containing third-generation progestogen. *Lancet* 1995; **346**: 1593-1596.
18. Spitzer WO, Lewis MA, Heinemann LAJ, Thorogood M, MacRae KD, on behalf of Transnational Research Group on Oral Contraceptives and Health of Young Women. Third generation of oral contraceptives and risk of venous thromboembolic disorders: an international case-control study. *BMJ* 1996; **312**: 83-88.

15

Acknowledgements

We thank the many practitioners and their staff who have contributed data to the study. The RCGP Manchester Research Unit has received unconditional financial support from the Royal College of General Practitioners, Schering AG, Schering Health Care, and Wyeth-Ayerst International. The Manchester Research Unit has now moved to the RCGP Centre for Primary Care Research and Epidemiology in the Department of General Practice and Primary Care.

Address for correspondence

Professor Philip C Hannaford, Director, Department of General Practice & Primary Care, University of Aberdeen, Foresterhill Health Centre, Westburn Road, Aberdeen AB25 2AY.

This article was first published by Brookwood Medical Publications and is reproduced by permission of Brookwood Medical Publications

ICH Harmonised Tripartite Guideline for Good Medical Practice

Introduction

Good Clinical Practice (GCP) is an international ethical and scientific quality standard for designing, conducting, recording and reporting trials that involve the participation of human subjects. Compliance with this standard provides public assurance that the rights, safety and well being of trial subjects are protected, consistent with the principles that have their origin in the Declaration of Helsinki, and that the clinical trial data are credible.

The objective of this ICH GCP Guideline is to provide a unified standard for the European Union (EU), Japan and the United States to facilitate the mutual acceptance of clinical data by the regulatory authorities in these jurisdictions.

The guideline was developed with consideration of the current good clinical practices of the European Union, Japan, and the United States, as well as those of Australia, Canada, the Nordic countries and the World Health Organization (WHO).

This guideline should be followed when generating clinical trial data that are intended to be submitted to regulatory authorities.

The principles established in this guideline may also be applied to other clinical investigations that may have an impact on the safety and well-being of human subjects.

1. Glossary

1.1 Adverse Drug Reaction (ADR)

In the pre-approval clinical experience with a new medicinal product or its new usages, particularly as the therapeutic dose(s) may not be established: all noxious and unintended responses to a medicinal product related to any dose should be considered adverse drug reactions. The phrase responses to a medicinal product means that a causal relationship between a medicinal product and an adverse event is at least a reasonable possibility, ie. the relationship cannot be ruled out.

Regarding marketed medicinal products: a response to a drug which is noxious and unintended and which occurs at doses normally used in man for prophylaxis, diagnosis, or therapy of diseases or for modification of physiological function (see the ICH Guideline for Clinical Safety Data Management: Definitions and Standards for Expedited Reporting).

1.2 Adverse Event (AE)

Any untoward medical occurrence in a patient or clinical investigation subject administered a pharmaceutical product and which does not necessarily have a causal relationship with this treatment. An adverse event (AE) can therefore be any unfavourable and unintended sign (including an abnormal laboratory finding), symptom, or disease temporarily associated with the use of a medicinal (investigational) product, whether or not related to the medicinal (investigational) product (see the ICH Guideline for Clinical Safety Data Management: Definitions and Standards for Expedited Reporting).

1.3 Amendment (to the protocol)

See Protocol Amendment.

1.4 Applicable Regulatory Requirement(s)

Any law(s) and regulation(s) addressing the conduct of clinical trials of investigational products.

1.5 Approval (in relation to Institutional Review Boards)

The affirmative decision of the IRB that the clinical trial has been reviewed and may be conducted at the institution site within constraints set forth by the IRB, the institution, Good Clinical Practice (GCP), and the applicable regulatory requirements.

1.6 Audit

A systematic and independent examination of trial related activities and documents to determine whether the evaluated trial related activities were conducted, and the data were recorded, analyzed and accurately reported according to the protocol, sponsor's standard operating procedures (SOPs), Good Clinical Practice (GCP), and the applicable regulatory requirements.

1.7 Audit Certificate

A declaration of confirmation by the auditor that an audit has taken place.

1.8 Audit Report

A written evaluation by the sponsor's auditor of the results of the audit.

1.9 Audit Trail

Documentation that allows reconstruction of the course of events.

1.10 Blinding/Masking

A procedure in which one or more parties to the trial are kept unaware of the treatment assignment(s). Single-blinding usually refers to the subject(s) being unaware, and double-blinding usually refers to the subject(s), investigator(s), monitor, and, in some cases, data analyst(s) being unaware of the treatment assignment(s).

1.11 Case Report Form (CRF)
A printed, optical, or electronic document designed to record all of the protocol required information to be reported to the sponsor on each trial subject.

1.12 Clinical Trial/Study
Any investigation in human subjects intended to discover or verify the clinical, pharmacological and/or other pharmacodynamic effects of an investigational product(s), and/or to identify any adverse reactions to an investigational product(s), and/or to study absorption, distribution, metabolism, and excretion of an investigational product(s)with the object of ascertaining is safety and/or efficacy. The terms clinical trial and clinical study are synonymous.

1.13 Clinical Trial/Study Report
A written description of a trial/study of any therapeutic, prophylactic, or diagnostic agent conducted in human subjects, in which the clinical and statistical description, presentations, and analyses are fully integrated into a single report (see the ICH Guideline for Structure and Content of Clinical Study Reports).

1.14 Comparator (Product)
An investigational or marketed product (ie. active control), or placebo, used as a reference in a clinical trial.

1.15 Compliance (in relation to trials)
Adherence to all the trial-related requirements, Good Clinical Practice (GCP) requirements, and the applicable regulatory requirements.

1.16 Confidentiality
Prevention of disclosure, to other than authorized individuals, of a sponsor's proprietary information of a subject's identity.

1.17 Contract
A written, dated, and signed agreement between two or more involved parties that sets out any arrangements on delegation and distribution of tasks and obligations and, if appropriate, on financial matters. The protocol may serve as the basis of a contract.

1.18 Coordinating Committee
A committee that a sponsor may organize to coordinate the conduct of a multicentre trial.

1.19 Coordinating Investigator
An investigator assigned the responsibility for the coordination of investigators at different centres participating in a multicentre trial.

1.20 Contract Research Organization (CRO)
A person or an organization (commercial, academic, or other) contracted by the sponsor to perform one or more of a sponsor's trial-related duties and functions.

1.21 Direct Access
Permission to examine, analyze, verify, and reproduce any records and reports that are important to evaluation of a clinical trial. Any party (e.g., domestic and foreign regulatory authorities, sponsor's monitors and auditors) with direct access should take all reasonable precautions within the constraints of the applicable regulatory requirement(s) to maintain the confidentiality of subjects' identities and sponsor's proprietary information.

1.22 Documentation
All records, in any form (including, but not limited to, written, electronic, magnetic, and optical records, and scans, x-rays, and electrocardiograms) that describe or record the methods, conduct, and/or results of a trial, the factors affecting a trial, and the actions taken.

1.23 Essential Documents
Documents which individually and collectively permit evaluation of the conduct of a study and the quality of the data produced (see 8. Essential Documents for the Conduct of a Clinical Trial).

1.24 Good Clinical Practice (GCP)
A standard for the design, conduct, performance, monitoring, auditing, recording, analyses, and reporting of clinical trials that provides assurance that the data and reported results are credible and accurate, and that the rights, integrity, and confidentiality of trial subjects are protected.

1.25 Independent Data Monitoring Committee (IDMC) (Data and Safety Monitoring Board, Monitoring Committee, Data Monitoring Committee)
An independent data-monitoring committee that may be established by the sponsor to assess at intervals the progress of a clinical trial, the safety data, and the critical efficacy endpoints, and to recommend to the sponsor whether to continue, modify, or stop a trial.

1.26 Impartial Witness
A person, who is independent of the trial, who cannot be unfairly influenced by people involved with the trial, who attends the informed consent process if the subject or the subject's legally acceptable representative cannot read, and who reads the informed consent form and any other written information supplied to the subject.

1.27 Independent Ethics Committee (IEC)
An independent body (a review board or a committee, institutional, regional, national, or supranational), constituted of medical/scientific professionals and non-

16

medical/non-scientific members, whose responsibility it is to ensure the protection of the rights, safety and well-being of human subjects involved in a trial and to provide public assurance of that protection, by, among other things, reviewing and approving/providing favourable opinion on, the trial protocol, the suitability of the investigator(s), facilities, and the methods and material to be used in obtaining and documenting informed consent of the trial subjects.

The legal status composition, function, operations and regulatory requirements pertaining to Independent Ethics Committees may differ among countries, but should allow the Independent Ethics Committee to act in agreement with GCP as described in this guideline.

1.28 Informed Consent

A process by which a subject voluntarily confirms his or her willingness to participate in a particular trial, after having been informed of all aspects of the trial that are relevant to the subject's decision to participate. Informed consent is documented by means of a written, signed and dated informed consent form.

1.29 Inspection

The act by a regulatory authority(ies) of conducting an official review of documents, facilities, records, and any other resources that are deemed by the authority(ies) to be related to the clinical trial and that may be located at the site of the trial, at the sponsor's and/or contract research organization's (CRO's) facilities, or at other establishments deemed appropriate by the regulatory authority(ies).

1.30 Institution (medical)

Any public or private entity or agency or medical or dental facility where clinical trials are conducted.

1.31 Institutional Review Board (IRB)

An independent body constituted of medical, scientific, and non-scientific members, whose responsibility is to ensure the protection of the rights, safety and well-being of human subjects involved in a trial by, among other things, reviewing, approving, and providing continuing review of trial protocol and amendments and of the methods and material to be used in obtaining and documenting informed consent of the trial subjects.

1.32 Interim Clinical Trial/Study Report

A report of intermediate results and their evaluation based on analyses performed during the course of a trial.

1.33 Investigational Product

A pharmaceutical form of an active ingredient or placebo being tested or used as a reference in a clinical trial, including a product with a marketing authorization when used or assembled (formulated or packaged) in a way different from the approved form, or when used for an unapproved indication, or when used to gain further information about an approved use.

1.34 Investigator

A person responsible for the conduct of the clinical trial at a trial site. If a trial is conducted by a team of individuals at a trial site, the investigator is the responsible leader of the team and may be called the principal investigator. See also *Subinvestigator*.

1.35 Investigator / Institution

An expression meaning "the investigator and/or institution, where required by the applicable regulatory requirements".

1.36 Investigator's Brochure

A compilation of the clinical and nonclinical data on the investigational product(s) which is relevant to the study of the investigational product(s) in human subjects (see 7. *Investigator's Brochure*).

1.37 Legally Acceptable Representative

An individual or juridical or other body authorized under applicable law to consent, on behalf of a prospective subject, to the subject's participation in the clinical trial.

1.38 Monitoring

The act of overseeing the progress of a clinical trial, and of ensuring that it is conducted, recorded, and reported in accordance with the protocol, Standard Operating Procedures (SOPs), Good Clinical Practice (GCP), and the applicable regulatory requirement(s).

1.39 Monitoring Report

A written report from the monitor to the sponsor after each site visit and/or other trial-related communication according to the sponsor's SOPs.

1.40 Multicentre Trial

A clinical trial conducted according to a single protocol but at more than one site, and, therefore, carried out by more than one investigator.

1.41 Nonclinical Study

Biomedical studies not performed on human subjects.

1.42 Opinion (in relation to Independent Ethics Committee)

The judgement and/or the advice provided by an Independent Ethics Committee (IEC).

1.43 Original Medical Record

See Source Documents.

1.44 Protocol

A document that describes the objective(s), design, methodology, statistical considerations, and organization of a trial. The protocol usually also gives the background and rationale for the trial, but these could be provided in other protocol referenced documents. Throughout the ICH GCP Guideline the term protocol refers to protocol and protocol amendments.

1.45 Protocol Amendment

A written description of a change(s) to or formal clarification of a protocol.

1.46 Quality Assurance (QA)

All those planned and systematic actions that are established to ensure that the trial is performed and the data are generated, documented (recorded), and reported in compliance with Good Clinical Practice (GCP) and the applicable regulatory requirement(s).

1.47 Quality Control (QC)

The operational techniques and activities undertaken within the quality assurance system to verify that the requirements for quality of the trial-related activities have been fulfilled.

1.48 Randomization

The process of assigning trial subjects to treatment or control groups using an element of chance to determine the assignments in order to reduce bias.

1.49 Regulatory Authorities

Bodies having the power to regulate. In the ICH GCP guideline the expression Regulatory Authorities includes the authorities that review submitted clinical data and those that conduct inspections (see 1.29). These bodies are sometimes referred to as competent authorities.

1.50 Serious Adverse Event (SAE) or Serious Adverse Drug Reaction (Serious ADR)

Any untoward medical occurrence that at any dose:

– results in death,
– is life-threatening,
– requires inpatient hospitalization or prolongation of existing hospitalization,
– results in persistent or significant disability/incapacity, or
– is a congenital anomaly/birth defect (see the ICH Guideline for Clinical Safety Data Management: Definitions and Standards for Expedited Reporting).

1.51 Source Data

All information in original records and certified copies of original records of clinical findings, observations, or other activities in a clinical trial necessary for the reconstruction and evaluation of the trial. Source data are contained in source documents (original records or certified copies).

1.52 Source Documents

Original documents, data, and records (eg. hospital records, clinical and office charts, laboratory notes, memoranda, subjects' diaries or evaluation checklists, pharmacy dispensing records, recorded data from automated instruments, copies or transcriptions certified after verification as being accurate copies, microfiches, photographic negatives, microfilm or magnetic media, x-rays, subject files, and records kept at the pharmacy, at the laboratories and at medico-technical departments involved in the clinical trial).

1.53 Sponsor

An individual, company, institution, or organization which takes responsibility for the initiation, management, and/or financing of a clinical trial.

1.54 Sponsor-Investigator

An individual who both initiates and conducts, alone or with others, a clinical trial, and under whose immediate direction the investigational product is administered to, dispensed to, or used by a subject. The term does not include any person other than an individual (eg. it does not include a corporation or an agency). The obligations of a sponsor-investigator include both those of a sponsor and those of an investigator.

1.55 Standard Operating Procedures (SOPs)

Detailed, written instructions to achieve uniformity of the performance of a specific function.

1.56 Subinvestigator

Any individual member of the clinical trial team designated and supervised by the investigator at a trial site to perform critical trial-related procedures and/or to make important trial-related decisions (eg. associates, residents, research fellows). See also *Investigator*.

1.57 Subject/Trial Subject

An individual who participates in a clinical trial, either as a recipient of the investigational product(s) or as a control.

1.58 Subject Identification Code

A unique identifier assigned by the investigator to each trial subject to protect the subject's identity and used in lieu of the subject's name when the investigator reports adverse events and/or other trial related data.

16

1.59 Trial Site

The location(s) where trial-related activities are actually conducted.

1.60 Unexpected Adverse Drug Reaction

An adverse reaction, the nature or severity of which is not consistent with the applicable product information (eg. Investigator's Brochure for an unapproved investigational product or package insert/summary of product characteristics for an approved product) (see the ICH Guideline for Clinical Safety Data Management: Definitions and Standards for Expedited Reporting).

1.61 Vulnerable Subjects

Individuals whose willingness to volunteer in a clinical trial may be unduly influenced by the expectation, whether justified or not, of benefits associated with participation, or of a retaliatory response from senior members of a hierarchy in case of refusal to participate.

Examples are members of a group with a hierarchical structure, such as medical, pharmacy, dental, and nursing students, subordinate hospital and laboratory personnel, employees of the pharmaceutical industry, members of the armed forces, and persons kept in detention. Other vulnerable subjects include patients with incurable diseases, persons in nursing homes, unemployed or impoverished persons, patients in emergency situations, ethnic minority groups, homeless persons, nomads, refugees, minors, and those incapable of giving consent.

1.62 Well-being (of the trial subjects)

The physical and mental integrity of the subjects participating in a clinical trial.

2. The Principles of ICH GCP

2.1 Clinical trials should be conducted in accordance with the ethical principles that have their origin in the Declaration of Helsinki, and that are consistent with GCP and the applicable regulatory requirement(s).

2.2 Before a trial is initiated, foreseeable risks and inconveniences should be weighed against the anticipated benefit for the individual trial subject and society. A trial should be initiated and continued only if the anticipated benefits justify the risks.

2.3 The rights, safety, and well-being of the trial subjects are the most important considerations and should prevail over interests of science and society.

2.4 The available nonclinical and clinical information on an investigational product should be adequate to support the proposed clinical trial.

2.5 Clinical trials should be scientifically sound, and described in a clear, detailed protocol.

2.6 A trial should be conducted in compliance with the protocol that has received prior institutional review board (IRB)/independent ethics committee (IEC) approval/ favourable opinion.

2.7 The medical care given to, and medical decisions made on behalf of, subjects should always be the responsibility of a qualified physician or, when appropriate, of a qualified dentist.

2.8 Each individual involved in conducting a trial should be qualified by education, training, and experience to perform his or her respective task(s).

2.9 Freely given informed consent should be obtained from every subject prior to clinical trial participation.

2.10 All clinical trial information should be recorded, handled, and stored in a way that allows its accurate reporting, interpretation and verification.

2.11 The confidentiality of records that could identify subjects should be protected, respecting the privacy and confidentiality rules in accordance with the applicable regulatory requirement(s).

2.12 Investigational products should be manufactured, handled, and stored in accordance with applicable good manufacturing practice (GMP). They should be used in accordance with the approved protocol.

2.13 Systems with procedures that assure the quality of every aspect of the trial should be implemented.

3. Institutional Review Board/ Independent Ethics Committee (IRB/IEC)
3.1 Responsibilities

3.1.1 An IRB/IEC should safeguard the rights, safety, and well-being of all trial subjects. Special attention should be paid to trials that may include vulnerable subjects.

3.1.2 The IRB/IEC should obtain the following documents: trial protocol(s)/amendment(s), written informed consent form(s) and consent form updates that the investigator proposes for use in the trial, subject recruitment procedures (eg. advertisements), written information to be provided to subjects, Investigator's Brochure (IB), available safety information, information about payments and compensation available to subjects, the investigator's current curriculum vitae and/or other documentation evidencing qualifications, and any other documents that the IRB/IEC may need to fulfil its responsibilities.

The IRB/IEC should review a proposed clinical trial within a reasonable time and document its views in writing, clearly identifying the trial, the documents reviewed and the dates for the following:

– approval/favourable opinion;
– modifications required prior to its approval/favourable opinion;
– disapproval/negative opinion; and
– termination/suspension of any prior approval/favourable opinion.

3.1.3 The IRB/IEC should consider the qualifications of the investigator for the proposed trial, as documented by a current curriculum vitae and/or by any other relevant documentation the IRB/IEC requests.

3.1.4 The IRB/IEC should conduct continuing review of each ongoing trial at intervals appropriate to the degree of risk to human subjects, but at least once per year.

3.1.5 The IRB/IEC may request more information than is outlined in paragraph 4.8. 10 be given to subjects when, in the judgement of the IRB/IEC, the additional information would add meaningfully to the protection of the rights, safety and/or well-being of the subjects.

3.1.6 When a non-therapeutic trial is to be carried out with the consent of the subject's legally acceptable representative (see 4.8.12, 4.8.14), the IRB/IEC should determine that the proposed protocol and/or other document(s) adequately addresses relevant ethical concerns and meets applicable regulatory requirements for such trials.

3.1.7 Where the protocol indicates that prior consent of the trial subject or the subject's legally acceptable representative is not possible (see 4.8.15), the IRB/IEC should determine that the proposed protocol and/or other document(s) adequately addresses relevant ethical concerns and meets applicable regulatory requirements for such trials (ie. in emergency situations).

3.1.8 The IRB/IEC should review both the amount and method of payment to subjects to assure that neither presents problems of coercion or undue influence on the trial subjects. Payments to a subject should be prorated and not wholly contingent on completion of the trial by the subject.

3.1.9 The IRB/IEC should ensure that information regarding payment to subjects, including the methods, amounts, and schedule of payment to trial subjects, is set forth in the written informed consent form and any other written information to be provided to subjects. The way payment will be prorated should be specified.

3.2 Composition, Functions and Operations

3.2.1 The IRB/IEC should consist of a reasonable number of members, who collectively have the qualifications and experience to review and evaluate the science, medical aspects, and ethics of the proposed trial. It is recommended that the IRB/IEC should include:

(a) At least five members.
(b) At least one member whose primary area of interest is in a nonscientific area.
(c) At least one member who is independent of the institution/trial site.

Only those IRB/IEC members who are independent of the investigator and the sponsor of the trial should vote/provide opinion on a trial-related matter.

A list of IRB/IEC members and their qualifications should be maintained.

3.2.2 The IRB/IEC should perform its functions according to written operating procedures, should maintain written records of its activities and minutes of its meetings, and should comply with GCP and with the applicable regulatory requirement(s).

3.2.3 An IRB/IEC should make its decisions at announced meetings at which at least a quorum, as stipulated in its written operating procedures, is present.

3.2.4 Only members who participate in the IRB/IEC review and discussion should vote/provide their opinion and/or advise.

3.2.5 The investigator may provide information on any aspect of the trial, but should not participate in the deliberations of the IRB/IEC or in the vote/opinion of the IRB/IEC.

3.2.6 An IRB/IEC may invite nonmembers with expertise in special areas for assistance.

3.3 Procedures

The IRB/IEC should establish, document in writing, and follow its procedures, which should include:

3.3.1 Determining its composition (names and qualifications of the members) and the authority under which it is established.

3.3.2 Scheduling, notifying its members of, and conducting its meetings.

3.3.3 Conducting initial and continuing review of trials.

3.3.4 Determining the frequency of continuing review, as appropriate.

3.3.5 Providing, according to the applicable regulatory requirements, expedited review and approval/favourable opinion of minor change(s) in ongoing trials that have the approval/favourable opinion of the IRB/IEC.

3.3.6 Specifying that no subject should be admitted to a trial before the IRB/IEC issues its written approval/favourable opinion of the trial.

3.3.7 Specifying that no deviations from, or changes of, the protocol should be initiated without prior written IRB/IEC approval/favourable opinion of an appropriate amendment, except when necessary to eliminate immediate hazards to the subjects or when the change(s) involves only logistical or administrative aspects of the trial (eg. change of monitor(s), telephone number(s)) (see 4.5.2).

3.3.8 Specifying that the investigator should promptly report to the IRB/IEC:

(a) Deviations from, or changes of, the protocol to eliminate immediate hazards to the trial subjects (see 3.3.7, 4.5.2, 4.5.4).
(b) Changes increasing the risk to subjects and/or affecting significantly the conduct of the trial (see 4.10.2).
(c) All adverse drug reactions (ADRs) that are both serious and unexpected.
(d) New information that may affect adversely the safety of the subjects or the conduct of the trial.

3.3.9 Ensuring that the IRB/IEC promptly notify in writing the investigator/institution concerning:

(a) Its trial-related decisions/opinions.
(b) The reasons for its decisions/opinions.
(c) Procedures for appeal of its decisions/opinions.

3.4 Records

The IRB/IEC should retain all relevant records (eg. written procedures, membership lists, lists of occupations/affiliations of members, submitted documents, minutes of meetings, and correspondence) for a period of at least 3 years after completion of the trial and make them available upon request from the regulatory authority(ies).

The IRB/IEC may be asked by investigators, sponsors or regulatory authorities to provide its written procedures and membership lists.

16

4. INVESTIGATOR

4.1 Investigator's Qualifications and Agreements

4.1.1 The investigator(s) should be qualified by education, training, and experience to assume responsibility for the proper conduct of the trial, should meet all the qualifications specified by the applicable regulatory requirement(s), and should provide evidence of such qualifications through up-to-date curriculum vitae and/or other relevant documentation requested by the sponsor, the IRB/IEC, and/or the regulatory authority(ies).

4.1.2 The investigator should be thoroughly familiar with the appropriate use of the investigational product(s), as described in the protocol, in the current Investigator's Brochure, in the product information and in other information sources provided by the sponsor.

4.1.3 The investigator should be aware of, and should comply with, GCP and the applicable regulatory requirements.

4.1.4 The investigator/institution should permit monitoring and auditing by the sponsor, and inspection by the appropriate regulatory authority(ies).

4.1.5 The investigator should maintain a list of appropriately qualified persons to whom the investigator has delegated significant trial-related duties.

4.2 Adequate Resources

4.2.1 The investigator should be able to demonstrate (eg. based on retrospective data) a potential for recruiting the required number of suitable subjects within the agreed recruitment period.

4.2.2 The investigator should have sufficient time to properly conduct and complete the trial within the agreed trial period.

4.2.3 The investigator should have available an adequate number of qualified staff and adequate facilities for the foreseen duration of the trial to conduct the trial properly and safely.

4.2.4 The investigator should ensure that all persons assisting with the trial are adequately informed about the protocol, the investigational product(s), and their trial-related duties and functions.

4.3 Medical Care of Trial Subjects

4.3.1 A qualified physician (or dentist, when appropriate), who is an investigator or a sub-investigator for the trial, should be responsible for all trial-related medical (or dental) decisions.

4.3.2 During and following a subject's participation in a trial, the investigator/institution should ensure that adequate medical care is provided to a subject for any adverse events, including clinically significant laboratory values, related to the trial. The investigator/institution should inform a subject when medical care is needed for intercurrent illness(es) of which the investigator becomes aware.

4.3.3 It is recommended that the investigator inform the subject's primary physician about the subject's participation in the trial if the subject has a primary physician and if the subject agrees to the primary physician being informed.

4.3.4 Although a subject is not obliged to give his/her reason(s) for withdrawing prematurely from a trial, the investigator should make a reasonable effort to ascertain the reason(s), while fully respecting the subject's rights.

4.4 Communication with IRB/IEC

4.4.1 Before initiating a trial, the investigator/institution should have written and dated approval/favourable opinion from the IRB/IEC for the trial protocol, written informed consent form, consent form updates, subject recruitment procedures (eg. advertisements), and any other written information to be provided to subjects.

4.4.2 As part of the investigator's/institution's written application to the IRB/IEC, the IRB/IEC should provide the IRB/IEC with a current copy of the Investigator's Brochure. If the Investigator's Brochure is updated during the trial, the investigator/institution should supply a copy of the updated Investigator's Brochure to the IRB/IEC.

4.4.3 During the trial the investigator/ institution should provide to the IRB/IEC all documents subject to review.

4.5 Compliance with Protocol

4.5.1 The investigator/institution should conduct the trial in compliance with the protocol agreed to by the sponsor and, if required, by the regulatory authority(ies) and which was given approval/favourable opinion by the IRB/IEC. The investigator/ institution and the sponsor should sign the protocol, or an alternative contract, to confirm agreement.

4.5.2 The investigator should not implement any deviation from, or changes of the protocol without agreement by the sponsor and prior review and documented approval/favourable opinion from the IRB/IEC of an amendment, except where necessary to eliminate an immediate hazard(s) to trial subjects, or when the change(s) involves only logistical or administrative aspects of the trial (eg. change in monitor(s), change of telephone number(s)).

4.5.3 The investigator, or person designated by the investigator, should document and explain any deviation from the approved protocol.

4.5.4 The investigator may implement a deviation from, or a change of, the protocol to eliminate an immediate hazard(s) to trial subjects without prior IRB/IEC approval/favourable opinion. As soon as possible, the implemented deviation or change, the reasons for it, and, if appropriate, the proposed protocol amendment(s) should be submitted:

(a) to the IRB/IEC for review and approval/favourable opinion,

(b) to the sponsor for agreement and, if required,

(c) to the regulatory authority(ies).

4.6 Investigational Product(s)

4.6.1 Responsibility for investigational product(s) accountability at the trial site(s) rests with the investigator/institution.

4.6.2 Where allowed/required, the investigator/institution may/should assign some or all of the investigator's/institution's duties for investigational product(s) accountability at the trial site(s) to an appropriate pharmacist or another appropriate individual who is under the supervision of the investigator/institution.

4.6.3 The investigator/institution and/or a pharmacist or other appropriate individual, who is designated by the investigator/institution, should maintain records of the product's delivery to the trial site, the inventory at the site, the use by each subject, and the return to the sponsor or alternative disposition of unused product(s). These records should include dates, quantities, batch/serial numbers, expiration dates (if applicable), and the unique code numbers assigned to the investigational product(s) and trial subjects. Investigators should maintain records that document adequately that the subjects were provided the doses specified by the protocol and reconcile all investigational product(s) received from the sponsor.

4.6.4 The investigational product(s) should be stored as specified by the sponsor (see 5.13.2 and 5.14.3) and in accordance with applicable regulatory requirement(s).

4.6.5 The investigator should ensure that the investigational product(s) are used only in accordance with the approved protocol.

4.6.6 The investigator, or a person designated by the investigator/institution, should explain the correct use of the investigational product(s) to each subject and should check, at intervals appropriate for the trial, that each subject is following the instructions properly.

4.7 Randomization Procedures and Unblinding

The investigator should follow the trial's randomization procedures, if any, and should ensure that the code is broken only in accordance with the protocol. If the trial is blinded, the investigator should promptly document and explain to the sponsor any premature unblinding (eg. accidental unblinding, unblinding due to a serious adverse event) of the investigational product(s).

4.8 Informed Consent of Trial Subjects

4.8.1 In obtaining and documenting informed consent, the investigator should comply with the applicable regulatory requirement(s), and should adhere to GCP and to the ethical principles that have their origin in the Declaration of Helsinki. Prior to the beginning of the trial, the investigator should have the IRB/IEC's written approval/favourable opinion of the written informed consent form and any other written information to be provided to subjects.

4.8.2 The written informed consent form and any other written information to be provided to subjects should be revised whenever important new information becomes available that may be relevant to the subject's consent. Any revised written informed consent form, and written information should receive the IRB/IEC's approval/favourable opinion in advance of use. The subject or the subject's legally acceptable representative should be informed in a timely manner if new information becomes available that may be relevant to the subject's willingness to continue participation in the trial. The communication of this information should be documented.

4.8.3 Neither the investigator, nor the trial staff, should coerce or unduly influence a subject to participate or to continue to participate in a trial.

4.8.4 None of the oral and written information concerning the trial, including the written informed consent form, should contain any language that causes the subject or the subject's legally acceptable representative to waive or to appear to waive any legal rights, or that releases or appears to release the investigator, the institution, the sponsor, or their agents from liability for negligence.

4.8.5 The investigator, or a person designated by the investigator, should fully inform the subject or, if the subject is unable to provide informed consent, the subject's legally acceptable representative, of all pertinent aspects of the trial including the written information given approval/favourable opinion by the IRB/IEC.

4.8.6 The language used in the oral and written information about the trial, including the written informed consent form, should be as nontechnical as practical and should be understandable to the subject or the subject's legally acceptable representative and the impartial witness, where applicable.

4.8.7 Before informed consent may be obtained, the investigator, or a person designated by the investigator, should provide the subject or the subject's legally acceptable representative ample time and opportunity to inquire about details of the trial and to decide whether or not to participate in the trial. All questions about the trial should be answered to the satisfaction of the subject or the subject's legally acceptable representative.

4.8.8 Prior to a subject's participation in the trial, the written informed consent form should be signed and personally dated by the subject or by the subject's legally acceptable representative, and by the person who conducted the informed consent discussion.

4.8.9 If a subject is unable to read or if a legally acceptable representative is unable to read, an impartial witness should be present during the entire informed consent discussion. After the written informed consent form and any other written information to be provided to subjects, is read and explained to the subject or the subject's legally

16

acceptable representative, and after the subject or the subject's legally acceptable representative has orally consented to the subject's participation in the trial and, if capable of doing so, has signed and personally dated the informed consent form, the witness should sign and personally date the consent form. By signing the consent form, the witness attests that the information in the consent form and any other written information was accurately explained to, and apparently understood by, the subject or the subject's legally acceptable representative, and that informed consent was freely given by the subject or the subject's legally acceptable representative.

4.8.10 Both the informed consent discussion and the written informed consent form and any other written information to be provided to subjects should include explanations of the following:

(a) That the trial involves research.
(b) The purpose of the trial.
(c) The trial treatment(s) and the probability for random assignment to each treatment.
(d) The trial procedures to be followed, including all invasive procedures.
(e) The subject's responsibilities.
(f) Those aspects of the trial that are experimental.
(g) The reasonably foreseeable risks or inconveniences to the subject and, when applicable, to an embryo, fetus, or nursing infant.
(h) The reasonably expected benefits. When there is no intended clinical benefit to the subject, the subject should be made aware of this.
(i) The alternative procedure(s) or course(s) of treatment that may be available to the subject, and their important potential benefits and risks.
(j) The compensation and/or treatment available to the subject in the event of trial-related injury.
(k) The anticipated prorated payment, if any, to the subject for participating in the trial.
(l) The anticipated expenses, if any, to the subject for participating in the trial.
(m) That the subject's participation in the trial is voluntary and that the subject may refuse to participate or withdraw from the trial, at any time, without penalty or loss of benefits to which the subject is otherwise entitled.
(n) That the monitor(s), the auditor(s), the IRB/IEC, and the regulatory authority(ies) will be granted direct access to the subject's original medical records for verification of clinical trial procedures and/or data, without violating the confidentiality of the subject, to the extent permitted by the applicable laws and regulations and that, by signing a written informed consent form, the subject or the subject's legally acceptable representative is authorizing such access.
(o) That records identifying the subject will be kept confidential and, to the extent permitted by the applicable laws and/or regulations, will not be made publicly available. If the results of the trial are published, the subject's identity will remain confidential.
(p) That the subject or the subject's legally acceptable representative will be informed in a timely manner if information becomes available that may be relevant to the subject's willingness to continue participation in the trial.
(q) The person(s) to contact for further information regarding the trial and the rights of trial subjects, and whom to contact in the event of trial-related injury.
(r) The foreseeable circumstances and/or reasons under which the subject's participation in the trial may be terminated.
(s) The expected duration of the subject's participation in the trial.
(t) The approximate number of subjects involved in the trial.

4.8.11 Prior to participation in the trial, the subject or the subject's legally acceptable representative should receive a copy of the signed and dated written informed consent form and any other written information provided to the subjects. During a subject's participation in the trial, the subject or the subject's legally acceptable representative should receive a copy of the signed and dated consent form updates and a copy of any amendments to the written information provided to subjects.

4.8.12 When a clinical trial (therapeutic or non-therapeutic) includes subjects who can only be enrolled in the trial with the consent of the subject's legally acceptable representative (eg. minors, or patients with severe dementia), the subject should be informed about the trial to the extent compatible with the subject's understanding and, if capable, the subject should sign and personally date the written informed consent.

4.8.13 Except as described in 4.8.14, a non-therapeutic trial (ie. a trial in which there is no anticipated direct clinical benefit to the subject), should be conducted in subjects who personally give consent and who sign and date the written informed consent form.

4.8.14 Non-therapeutic trials may be conducted in subjects with consent of a legally acceptable representative provided the following conditions are fulfilled:

(a) The objectives of the trial can not be met by means of a trial in subjects who can give informed consent personally.
(b) The foreseeable risks to the subjects are low.
(c) The negative impact on the subject's well-being is minimized and low.
(d) The trial is not prohibited by law.
(e) The approval/favourable opinion of the IRB/IEC is expressly sought on the inclusion of such subjects, and the written approval/favourable opinion covers this aspect.

Such trials, unless an exception is justified, should be conducted in patients having a disease or condition for which the investigational product is intended. Subjects in these trials should be particularly closely monitored and should be withdrawn if they appear to be unduly distressed.

4.8.15 In emergency situations, when prior consent of the subject is not possible, the consent of the subject's legally acceptable representative, if present, should be requested. When prior consent of the subject is not possible, and the subject's legally acceptable representative is not available, enrolment of the subject should require measures described in the protocol and/or elsewhere, with documented approval/favourable opinion by the IRB/IEC, to protect the rights, safety and well-being of the subject and to ensure compliance with applicable regulatory requirements. The subject or the subject's legally acceptable representative should be informed about the trial as soon as possible and consent to continue and other consent as appropriate (see 4.8.10) should be requested.

4.9 Records and Reports

4.9.1 The investigator should ensure the accuracy, completeness, legibility, and timeliness of the data reported to the sponsor in the CRFs and in all required reports.

4.9.2 Data reported on the CRF, that are derived from source documents, should be consistent with the source documents or the discrepancies should be explained.

4.9.3 Any change or correction to a CRF should be dated, initialled, and explained (if necessary) and should not obscure the original entry (ie. an audit trail should be maintained); this applies to both written and electronic changes or corrections (see 5.18.4 (n)). Sponsors should provide guidance to investigators and/or the investigators' designated representatives on making such corrections, Sponsors should have written procedures to assure that changes or corrections in CRFs made by sponsor's designated representatives are documented, are necessary, and are endorsed by the investigator. The investigator should retain records of the changes and corrections.

4.9.4 The investigator/institution should maintain the trial documents as specified in Essential Documents for the Conduct of a Clinical Trial (see 8,) and as required by the applicable regulatory requirement(s). The investigator/institution should take measures to prevent accidental or premature destruction of these documents.

4.9.5 Essential documents should be retained until at least 2 years after the last approval of a marketing application in an ICH region and until there are no pending or contemplated marketing applications in an ICH region or at least 2 years have elapsed since the formal discontinuation of clinical development of the investigational product. These documents should be retained for a longer period however if required by the applicable regulatory requirements or by an agreement with the sponsor. It is the responsibility of

the sponsor to inform the investigator/institution as to when these documents no longer need to be retained (see 5.5.12).

4.9.6 The financial aspects of the trial should be documented in an agreement between the sponsor and the investigator/institution.

4.9.7 Upon request of the monitor, auditor, IRB/IEC, or regulatory authority, the investigator/institution should make available for direct access all requested trial-related records.

4.10 Progress Reports

4.10.1 The investigator should submit written summaries of the trial status to the IRB/IEC annually, or more frequently, if requested by the IRB/IEC.

4.10.2 The investigator should promptly provide written reports to the sponsor, the IRB/IEC (see 3.3.8) and, where applicable, the institution on any changes significantly affecting the conduct of the trial, and/or increasing the risk to subjects.

4.11 Safety Reporting

4.11.1 All serious adverse events (SAEs) should be reported immediately to the sponsor except for those SAEs that the protocol or other document (eg. Investigator's Brochure) identifies as not needing immediate reporting. The immediate reports should be followed promptly by detailed, written reports. The immediate and follow-up reports should identify subjects by unique code numbers assigned to the trial subjects rather than by the subjects' names, personal identification numbers, and/or addresses. The investigator should also comply with the applicable regulatory requirement(s) related to the reporting of unexpected serious adverse drug reactions to the regulatory authority(ies) and the IRB/IEC.

4.11.2 Adverse events and/or laboratory abnormalities identified in the protocol as critical to safety evaluations should be reported to the sponsor according to the reporting requirements and within the time periods specified by the sponsor in the protocol.

4.11.3 For reported deaths, the investigator should supply the sponsor and the IRB/IEC with any additional requested information (eg. autopsy reports and terminal medical reports).

4.12 Premature Termination or Suspension of a Trial

If the trial is prematurely terminated or suspended for any reason, the investigator/institution should promptly inform the trial subjects, should assure appropriate therapy and follow-up for the subjects, and, where required by the applicable regulatory requirement(s), should inform the regulatory authority(ies). In addition:

4.12.1 If the investigator terminates or suspends a trial without prior agreement of the sponsor, the investigator

16

should inform the institution where applicable, and the investigator/institution should promptly inform the sponsor and the IRB/IEC, and should provide the sponsor and the IRB/IEC a detailed written explanation of the termination or suspension.

4.12.2 If the sponsor terminates or suspends a trial (see 5.21), the investigator should promptly inform the institution where applicable and the investigator/institution should promptly inform the IRB/IEC and provide the IRB/IEC a detailed written explanation of the termination or suspension.

4.12.3 If the IRB/IEC terminates or suspends its approval/favourable opinion of a trial (see 3.1.2 and 3.3.9), the investigator should inform the institution where applicable and the investigator/institution should promptly notify the sponsor and provide the sponsor with a detailed written explanation of the termination or suspension.

4.13 Final Report(s) by Investigator

Upon completion of the trial, the investigator, where applicable, should inform the institution; the investigator/institution should provide the IRB/IEC with a summary of the trial's outcome, and the regulatory authority(ies) with any reports required.

5. SPONSOR

5.1 Quality Assurance and Quality Control

5.1.1 The sponsor is responsible for implementing and maintaining quality assurance and quality control systems with written SOPs to ensure that trials are conducted and data are generated, documented (recorded), and reported in compliance with the protocol, GCP, and the applicable regulatory requirement(s).

5.1.2 The sponsor is responsible for securing agreement from all involved parties to ensure direct access (see 1.21) to all trial related sites, source data/documents, and reports for the purpose of monitoring and auditing by the sponsor, and inspection by domestic and foreign regulatory authorities.

5.1.3 Quality control should be applied to each stage of data handling to ensure that all data are reliable and have been processed correctly.

5.1.4 Agreements, made by the sponsor with the investigator/institution and any other parties involved with the clinical trial, should be in writing, as part of the protocol or in a separate agreement.

5.2 Contract Research Organization (CRO)

5.2.1 A sponsor may transfer any or all of the sponsor's trial-related duties and functions to a CRO, but the ultimate responsibility for the quality and integrity of the trial data always resides with the sponsor. The CRO should implement quality assurance and quality control.

5.2.2 Any trial-related duty and function that is transferred to and assumed by a CRO should be specified in writing.

5.2.3 Any trial-related duties and functions not specifically transferred to and assumed by a CRO are retained by the sponsor.

5.2.4 All references to a sponsor in this guideline also apply to a CRO to the extent that a CRO has assumed the trial related duties and functions of a sponsor.

5.3 Medical Expertise

The sponsor should designate appropriately qualified medical personnel who will be readily available to advise on trial related medical questions or problems. If necessary, outside consultant(s) may be appointed for this purpose.

5.4 Trial Design

5.4.1 The sponsor should utilize qualified individuals (eg. biostatisticians, clinical pharmacologists, and physicians) as appropriate, throughout all stages of the trial process, from designing the protocol and CRFs and planning the analyses to analyzing and preparing interim and final clinical trial reports.

5.4.2 For further guidance: Clinical Trial Protocol and Protocol Amendment(s) (see 6.), the ICH Guideline for Structure and Content of Clinical Study Reports, and other appropriate ICH guidance on trial design, protocol and conduct.

5.5 Trial Management, Data Handling, and Record Keeping

5.5.1 The sponsor should utilize appropriately qualified individuals to supervise the overall conduct of the trial, to handle the data, to verify the data, to conduct the statistical analyses, and to prepare the trial reports.

5.5.2 The sponsor may consider establishing an independent data-monitoring committee (IDMC) to assess the progress of a clinical trial, including the safety data and the critical efficacy endpoints at intervals, and to recommend to the sponsor whether to continue, modify, or stop a trial. The IDMC should have written operating procedures and maintain written records of all its meetings.

5.5.3 When using electronic trial data handling and/or remote electronic trial data systems, the sponsor should:

(a) Ensure and document that the electronic data processing system(s) conforms to the sponsor's established requirements for completeness, accuracy, reliability, and consistent intended performance (ie. validation).
(b) Maintains SOPs for using these systems.
(c) Ensure that the systems are designed to permit data changes in such a way that the data changes are documented and that there is no deletion of entered data (ie. maintain an audit trail, data trail, edit trail).
(d) Maintain a security system that prevents unauthorized access to the data.
(e) Maintain a list of the individuals who are authorized to make data changes (see 4.1.5 and 4.9.3).

(f) Maintain adequate backup of the data.

(g) Safeguard the blinding, if any (eg. maintain the blinding during data entry and processing).

5.5.4 If data are transformed during processing, it should always be possible to compare the original data and observations with the processed data.

5.5.5 The sponsor should use an unambiguous subject identification code (see 1.58) that allows identification of all the data reported for each subject.

5.5.6 The sponsor, or other owners of the data, should retain all of the sponsor-specific essential documents pertaining to the trial (see 8. Essential Documents for the Conduct of a Clinical Trial).

5.5.7 The sponsor should retain all sponsor-specific essential documents in conformance with the applicable regulatory requirement(s) of the country(ies) where the product is approved, and/or where the sponsor intends to apply for approval(s).

5.5.8 If the sponsor discontinues the clinical development of an investigational product (ie. for any or all indications, routes of administration, or dosage forms), the sponsor should maintain all sponsor-specific essential documents for at least 2 years after formal discontinuation or in conformance with the applicable regulatory requirement(s).

5.5.9 If the sponsor discontinues the clinical development of an investigational product, the sponsor should notify all the trial investigators/institutions and all the regulatory authorities.

5.5.10 Any transfer of ownership of the data should be reported to the appropriate authority(ies), as required by the applicable regulatory requirement(s).

5.5.11 The sponsor specific essential documents should be retained until at least 2 years after the last approval of a marketing application in an ICH region and until there are no pending or contemplated marketing applications in an ICH region or at least 2 years have elapsed since the formal discontinuation of clinical development of the investigational product. These documents should be retained for a longer period however if required by the applicable regulatory requirement(s) or if needed by the sponsor.

5.5.12 The sponsor should inform the investigator(s)/institution(s) in writing of the need for record retention and should notify the investigator(s)/institution(s) in writing when the trial related records are no longer needed.

5.6 Investigator Selection

5.6.1 The sponsor is responsible for selecting the investigator(s)/institution(s). Each investigator should be qualified by training and experience and should have adequate resources (see 4.1, 4.2) to properly conduct the trial for which the investigator is selected. If organization of a coordinating committee and/or selection of coordinating investigator(s) are to be utilized in multicentre trials, their organization and/or selection are the sponsor's responsibility.

5.6.2 Before entering an agreement with an investigator/institution to conduct a trial, the sponsor should provide the investigator(s)/institution(s) with the protocol and an up-to-date Investigator's Brochure, and should provide sufficient time for the investigator/institution to review the protocol and the information provided.

5.6.3 The sponsor should obtain the investigator's/institution's agreement:

(a) to conduct the trial in compliance with GCP, with the applicable regulatory requirement(s) (see 4.1.3), and with the protocol agreed to by the sponsor and given approval/favourable opinion by the IRB/IEC (see 4.5.1);

(b) to comply with procedures for data recording/reporting;

(c) to permit monitoring, auditing and inspection (see 4.1.4) and

(d) to retain the trial related essential documents until the sponsor informs the investigator/institution these documents are no longer needed (see 4.9.4 and 5.5.12).

The sponsor and the investigator/institution should sign the protocol, or an alternative document, to confirm this agreement.

5.7 Allocation of Duties and Functions

Prior to initiating a trial, the sponsor should define, establish, and allocate all trial-related duties and functions.

5.8 Compensation to Subjects and Investigators

5.8.1 If required by the applicable regulatory requirement(s), the sponsor should provide insurance or should indemnify (legal and financial coverage) the investigator/the institution against claims arising from the trial, except for claims that arise from malpractice and/or negligence.

5.8.2 The sponsor's policies and procedures should address the costs of treatment of trial subjects in the event of trial-related injuries in accordance with applicable regulatory requirement(s).

5.8.3 When trial subjects receive compensation, the method and manner of compensation should comply with applicable regulatory requirement(s).

5.9 Financing

The financial aspects of the trial should be documented in an agreement between the sponsor and the investigator/institution.

5.10 Notification/Submission to Regulatory Authority(ies)

Before initiating the clinical trial(s), the sponsor (or the sponsor and the investigator, 'if required by the applicable regulatory requirement(s)) should submit any required application(s) to the appropriate authority(ies) for review,

16

acceptance, and/or permission (as required by the applicable regulatory requirement(s) to begin the trial(s). Any notification/submission should be dated and contain sufficient information to identify the protocol.

5.11 Confirmation of Review by IRB/IEC

5.11.1 The sponsor should obtain from the investigator/institution:

(a) The name and address of the investigator's/institution's IRB/IEC.
(b) A statement obtained from the IRB/IEC that it is organized and operates according to GCP and the applicable laws and regulations.
(c) Documented IRB/IEC approval/favourable opinion and, if requested by the sponsor, a current copy of protocol, written informed consent form(s) and any other written information to be provided to subjects, subject recruiting procedures, and documents related to payments and compensation available to the subjects, and any other documents that the IRB/IEC may have requested.

5.11.2 If the IRB/IEC conditions its approval/favourable opinion upon change(s) in any aspect of the trial, such as modification(s) of the protocol, written informed consent form and any other written information to be provided to subjects, and/or other procedures, the sponsor should obtain from the investigator/ institution a copy of the modification(s) made and the date approval/favourable opinion was given by the IRB/IEC.

5.11.3 The sponsor should obtain from the investigator/institution documentation and dates of any IRB/IEC reapprovals/re-evaluations with favourable opinion, and of any withdrawals or suspensions of approval/favourable opinion.

5.12 Information on Investigational Product(s)

5.12.1 When planning trials, the sponsor should ensure that sufficient safety and efficacy data from nonclinical studies and/or clinical trials are available to support human exposure by the route, at the dosages, for the duration, and in the trial population to be studied.

5.12.2 The sponsor should update the Investigator's Brochure as significant new information becomes available (see 7. *Investigator's Brochure*).

5.13 Manufacturing, Packaging, Labelling, and Coding Investigational Product(s)

5.13.1 The sponsor should ensure that the investigational product(s) (including active comparator(s) and placebo, if applicable) is characterized as appropriate to the stage of development of the product(s), is manufactured in accordance with any applicable GMP, and is coded and labelled in a manner that protects the blinding, if applicable. In addition, the labelling should comply with applicable regulatory requirement(s).

5.13.2 The sponsor should determine, for the investigational product(s), acceptable storage temperatures, storage conditions (eg. protection from light), storage times, reconstitution fluids and procedures, and devices for product infusion, if any. The sponsor should inform all involved parties (eg. monitors, investigators, pharmacists, storage managers) of these determinations.

5.13.3 The investigational product(s) should be packaged to prevent contamination and unacceptable deterioration during transport and storage.

5.13.4 In blinded trials, the coding system for the investigational product(s) should include a mechanism that permits rapid identification of the product(s) in case of a medical emergency, but does not permit undetectable breaks of the blinding.

5.13.5 If significant formulation changes are made in the investigational or comparator product(s) during the course of clinical development, the results of any additional studies of the formulated product(s) (eg. stability, dissolution rate, bioavailability) needed to assess whether these changes would significantly alter the pharmacokinetic profile of the product should be available prior to the use of the new formulation in clinical trials.

5.14 Supplying and Handling Investigational Product(s)

5.14.1 The sponsor is responsible for supplying the investigator(s)/institution(s) with the investigational product(s).

5.14.2 The sponsor should not supply an investigator/institution with the investigational product(s) until the sponsor obtains all required documentation (eg. approval/favourable opinion from IRB/IEC and regulatory authority(ies)).

5.14.3 The sponsor should ensure that written procedures include instructions that the investigator/institution should follow for the handling and storage of investigational product(s) for the trial and documentation thereof. The procedures should address adequate and safe receipt, handling, storage, dispensing, retrieval of unused product from subjects, and return of unused investigational product(s) to the sponsor (or alternative disposition if authorized by the sponsor and in compliance with the applicable regulatory requirement(s)).

5.14.4 The sponsor should:

(a) Ensure timely delivery of investigational product(s) to the investigator(s).
(b) Maintain records that document shipment, receipt, disposition, return, and destruction of the investigational product(s) (see 8. Essential Documents for the Conduct of a Clinical Trial).
(c) Maintain a system for retrieving investigational products and documenting this retrieval (eg. for deficient product recall, reclaim after trial completion, expired product reclaim).

(d) Maintain a system for the disposition of unused investigational product(s) and for the documentation of this disposition.

5.14.5 The sponsor should:

(a) Take steps to ensure that the investigational product(s) are stable over the period of use.
(b) Maintain sufficient quantities of the investigational product(s) used in the trials to reconfirm specifications, should this become necessary, and maintain records of batch sample analyses and characteristics. To the extent stability permits, samples should be retained either until the analyses of the trial data are complete or as required by the applicable regulatory requirement(s), whichever represents the longer retention period.

5.15 Record Access

5.15.1 The sponsor should ensure that it is specified in the protocol or other written agreement that the investigator(s)/institution(s) provide direct access to source data/documents for trial-related monitoring, audits, IRB/IEC review, and regulatory inspection.

5.15.2 The sponsor should verify that each subject has consented, in writing, to direct access to his/her original medical records for trial-related monitoring, audit, IRB/IEC review, and regulatory inspection.

5.16 Safety Information

5.16.1 The sponsor is responsible for the ongoing safety evaluation of the investigational product(s).

5.16.2 The sponsor should promptly notify all concerned investigator(s)l institution(s) and the regulatory authority(ies) of findings that could affect adversely the safety of subjects, impact the conduct of the trial, or alter the IRB/IEC's approval/favourable opinion to continue the trial.

5.17 Adverse Drug Reaction Reporting

5.17.1 The sponsor should expedite the reporting to all concerned investigator(s)/institutions(s), to the IRB(s)/IEC(s), where required, and to the regulatory authority(ies) of all adverse drug reactions (ADRs) that are both serious and unexpected.

5.17.2 Such expedited reports should comply with the applicable regulatory requirement(s) and with the ICH Guideline for Clinical Safety Data Management: Definitions and Standards for Expedited Reporting.

5.17.3 The sponsor should submit to the regulatory authority(ies) all safety updates and periodic reports as required by applicable regulator requirement(s).

5.18 Monitoring

5.18.1 *Purpose*

The purposes of trial monitoring are to verify that:

(a) The rights and well-being of human subjects are protected.

(b) The reported trial data are accurate, complete, and verifiable from source documents.
(c) The conduct of the trial is in compliance with the currently approved protocol/amendment(s), with GCP, and with the applicable regulatory requirement(s).

5.18.2 *Selection and Qualifications of Monitors*

(a) Monitors should be appointed by the sponsor.
(b) Monitors should be appropriately trained, and should have the scientific and/or clinical knowledge needed to monitor the trial adequately. A monitor's qualifications should be documented.
(c) Monitors should be thoroughly familiar with the investigational product(s), the protocol, written informed consent form and any other written information to be provided to subjects, the sponsor's SOPs, GCP, and the applicable regulatory requirement(s).

5.18.3 *Extent and Nature of Monitoring*

The sponsor should ensure that the trials are adequately monitored. The sponsor should determine the appropriate extent and nature of monitoring. The determination of the extent and nature of monitoring should be based on considerations such as the objective, purpose, design, complexity, blinding, size, and endpoints of the trial. In general there is a need for on-site monitoring, before, during, and after the trial; however in exceptional circumstances the sponsor may determine that central monitoring in conjunction with procedures such as investigators' training and meetings, an extensive written guidance can assure appropriate conduct of the trial in accordance with GCP. Statistically controlled sampling may be an acceptable method for selecting the data to be verified.

15.18.4 *Monitor's Responsibilities*

The monitor(s) in accordance with the sponsor's requirements should ensure that the trial is conducted and documented properly by carrying out the following activities when relevant and necessary to the trial and the trial site:

(a) Acting as the main line of communication between the sponsor and the investigator.
(b) Verifying that the investigator has adequate qualifications and resources (see 4.1, 4.2, 5.6) and remain adequate throughout the trial period, that facilities, including laboratories, equipment, arid staff, are adequate to safely and properly conduct the trial and remain adequate throughout the trial period.
(c) Verifying, for the investigational product(s):
   (i) That storage times and conditions are acceptable, and that supplies are sufficient throughout the trial.
   (ii) That the investigational product(s) are supplied only to subjects who are eligible to receive it and at the protocol specified dose(s).

16

(iii) That subjects are provided with necessary instruction on properly using, handling, storing, and returning the investigational product(s).

(iv) That the receipt, use, and return of the investigational product(s) at the trial sites are controlled and documented adequately.

(v) That the disposition of unused investigational product(s) at the trial sites complies with applicable regulatory requirement(s) and is in accordance with the sponsor.

(d) Verifying that the investigator follows the approved protocol and all approved amendment(s), if any.

(e) Verifying that written informed consent was obtained before each subject's participation in the trial.

(f) Ensuring that the investigator receives the current Investigator's Brochure, all documents, and all trial supplies needed to conduct the trial properly and to comply with the applicable regulatory requirement(s).

(g) Ensuring that the investigator and the investigator's trial staff are adequately informed about the trial.

(h) Verifying that the investigator and the investigator's trial staff are performing the specified trial functions, in accordance with the protocol and any other written agreement between the sponsor and the investigator/institution, and have not delegated these functions to unauthorized individuals.

(i) Verifying that the investigator is enroling only eligible subjects.

(j) Reporting the subject recruitment rate.

(k) Verifying that source documents and other trial records are accurate, complete, kept up-to-date and maintained.

(l) Verifying that the investigator provides all the required reports, notifications, applications, and submissions, and that these documents are accurate, complete, timely, legible, dated, and identify the trial.

(m) Checking the accuracy and completeness of the CRF entries, source documents and other trial-related records against each other. The monitor specifically should verify that:

(i) The data required by the protocol are reported accurately on the CRFs and are consistent with the source documents.

(ii) Any dose and/or therapy modifications are well documented for each of the trial subjects.

(iii) Adverse events, concomitant medications and intercurrent illnesses are reported in accordance with the protocol on the CRFs.

(iv) Visits that the subjects fail to make, tests that are not conducted, and examinations that are not performed are clearly reported as such on the CRFs.

(v) All withdrawals and dropouts of enrolled subjects from the trial are reported and explained on the CRFs.

(n) Informing the investigator of any CRF entry error, omission, or illegibility. The monitor should ensure that appropriate corrections, additions, or deletions are made, dated, explained (if necessary), and initialled by the investigator or by a member of the investigator's trial staff who is authorized to initial CRF changes for the investigator. This authorization should be documented.

(o) Determining whether all adverse events (AEs) are appropriately reported within the time periods required by GCP, the protocol, the IRB/IEC, the sponsor, and the applicable regulatory requirement(s).

(p) Determining whether the investigator is maintaining the essential documents (see 8. Essential Documents for the Conduct of a Clinical Trial).

(q) Communicating deviations from the protocol, SOPs, GCP, and the applicable regulatory requirements to the investigator and taking appropriate action designed to prevent recurrence of the detected deviations.

5.18.5 *Monitoring Procedures*

The monitor(s) should follow the sponsor's established written SOPs as well as those procedures that are specified by the sponsor for monitoring a specific trial.

5.18.6 Monitoring Report

(a) The monitor should submit a written report to the sponsor after each trial-site visit or trial-related communication.

(b) Reports should include the date, site, name of the monitor, and name of the investigator or other individual(s) contacted.

(c) Reports should include a summary of what the monitor reviewed and the monitor's statements concerning the significant findings/facts, deviations and deficiencies, conclusions, actions taken or to be taken and/or actions recommended to secure compliance.

(d) The review and follow-up of the monitoring report with the sponsor should be documented by the sponsor's designated representative.

5.19 Audit

If or when sponsors perform audits, as part of implementing quality assurance, they should consider:

5.19.1 *Purpose*

The purpose of a sponsor's audit, which is independent of and separate from routine monitoring or quality control functions, should be to evaluate trial conduct and compliance with the protocol, SOPs, GCP, and the applicable regulatory requirements.

5.19.2 *Selection and Qualification of Auditors*

(a) The sponsor should appoint individuals, who are independent of the clinical trials/systems, to conduct audits.

(b) The sponsor should ensure that the auditors are qualified by training and experience to conduct audits properly. An auditor's qualifications should be documented.

5.19.3 *Auditing Procedures*

(a) The sponsor should ensure that the auditing of clinical trials/systems is conducted in accordance with the sponsor's written procedures on what to audit, how to audit, the frequency of audits, and the form and content of audit reports.

(b) The sponsor's audit plan and procedures for a trial audit should be guided by the importance of the trial to submissions to regulatory authorities, the number of subjects in the trial, the type and complexity of the trial, the level of risks to the trial subjects, and any identified problem(s).

(c) The observations and findings of the auditor(s) should be documented.

(d) To preserve the independence and value of the audit function, the regulatory authority(ies) should not routinely request the audit reports. Regulatory Authority(ies) may seek access to an audit report on a case by case basis when evidence of serious GCP non-compliance exists, or in the course of legal proceedings.

(e) When required by applicable law or regulation, the sponsor should provide an audit certificate.

5.20 Noncompliance

5.20.1 Noncompliance with the protocol, SOPs, GCP, and/or applicable regulatory requirement(s) by an investigator/institution, or by member(s) of the sponsor's staff should lead to prompt action by the sponsor to secure compliance.

5.20.2 If the monitoring and/or auditing identifies serious and/or persistent noncompliance on the part of an investigator/institution, the sponsor should terminate the investigator's/institution's participation in the trial. When an investigator's/institution's participation is terminated because of noncompliance, the sponsor should notify promptly the regulatory authority(ies).

5.21 Premature Termination or Suspension of a Trial

If a trial is prematurely terminated or suspended, the sponsor should promptly inform the investigators/institutions, and the regulatory authority(ies) of the termination or suspension and the reason(s) for the termination or suspension. The IRB/IEC should also be informed promptly and provided the reason(s) for the termination or suspension by the sponsor or by the investigator/ institution, as specified by the applicable regulatory requirement(s).

5.22 Clinical Trial/Study Reports

Whether the trial is completed or prematurely terminated, the sponsor should ensure that the clinical trial reports are prepared and provided to the regulatory agency(ies) as required by the applicable regulatory requirement(s). The sponsor should also ensure that the clinical trial reports in marketing applications meet the standards of the ICH Guideline for Structure and Content of Clinical Study Reports. (NOTE: The ICH Guideline for Structure and Content of Clinical Study Reports specifies that abbreviated study reports may be acceptable in certain cases.)

5.23 Multicentre Trials

For multicentre trials, the sponsor should ensure that:

5.23.1 All investigators conduct the trial in strict compliance with the protocol agreed to by the sponsor and, if required, by the regulatory authority(ies), and given approval/ favourable opinion by the IRB/IEC.

5.23.2 The CRFs are designed to capture the required data at all multicentre trial sites. For those investigators who are collecting additional data, supplemental CRFs should also be provided that are designed to capture the additional data.

5.23.3 The responsibilities of coordinating investigator(s) and the other participating investigators are documented prior to the start of the trial.

5.23.4 All investigators are given instructions on following the protocol, on complying with a uniform set of standards for the assessment of clinical and laboratory findings, and on completing the CRFs.

5.23.5 Communication between investigators is facilitated.

6. CLINICAL TRIAL PROTOCOL AND PROTOCOL AMENDMENT(S)

The contents of a trial protocol should generally include the following topics. However, site specific information may be provided on separate protocol page(s), or addressed in a separate agreement, and some of the information listed below may be contained in other protocol referenced documents, such as an Investigator's Brochure.

6.1 General Information

6.1.1 Protocol title, protocol identifying number, and date. Any amendment(s) should also bear the amendment number(s) and date(s).

6.1.2 Name and address of the sponsor and monitor (if other than the sponsor).

6.1.3 Name and title of the person(s) authorized to sign the protocol and the protocol amendment(s) for the sponsor.

6.1.4 Name, title, address, and telephone number(s) of the sponsor's medical expert (or dentist when appropriate) for the trial.

6.1.5 Name and title of the investigator(s) who is (are) responsible for conducting the trial, and the address and telephone number(s) of the trial site(s).

16

6.1.6 Name, title, address, and telephone number(s) of the qualified physician (or dentist, if applicable), who is responsible for all trial-site related medical (or dental) decisions (if other than investigator).

6.1.7 Name(s) and address(es) of the clinical laboratory(ies) and other medical and/or technical department(s) and/or institutions involved in the trial.

6.2 Background Information

6.2.1 Name and description of the investigational product(s).

6.2.2 A summary of findings from nonclinical studies that potentially have clinical significance and from clinical trials that are relevant to the trial.

6.2.3 Summary of the known arid potential risks and benefits, if any, to human subjects.

6.2.4 Description of and justification for the route of administration, dosage, dosage regimen, and treatment period(s).

6.2.5 A statement that the trial will be conducted in compliance with the protocol, GCP and the applicable regulatory requirement(s).

6.2.6 Description of the population to be studied.

6.2.7 References to literature and data that are relevant to the trial, and that provide background for the trial.

6.3 Trial Objectives and Purpose

A detailed description of the objectives and the purpose of the trial.

6.4 Trial Design

The scientific integrity of the trial and the credibility of the data from the trial depend substantially on the trial design. A description of the trial design, should include:

6.4.1 A specific statement of the primary endpoints and the secondary endpoints, if any, to be measured during the trial.

6.4.2 A description of the type/design of trial to be conducted (eg. double-blind, placebo-controlled, parallel design) and a schematic diagram of trial design, procedures and stages.

6.4.3 A description of the measures taken to minimize/avoid bias, including:

(a) Randomization.
(b) Blinding.

6.4.4 A description of the trial treatment(s) and the dosage and dosage regimen of the investigational product(s). Also include a description of the dosage form, packaging, and labelling of the investigational product(s).

6.4.5 The expected duration of subject participation, and a description of the sequence and duration of all trial periods, including follow-up, if any.

6.4.6 A description of the "stopping rules" or "discontinuation criteria" for individual subjects, parts of trial and entire trial.

6.4.7 Accountability procedures for the investigational product(s), including the placebo(s) and comparator(s), if any.

6.4.8 Maintenance of trial treatment randomization codes and procedures for breaking codes.

6.4.9 The identification of any data to be recorded directly on the CRFs (ie. no prior written or electronic record of data), and to be considered to be source data.

6.5 Selection and Withdrawal of Subjects

6.5.1 Subject inclusion criteria.

6.5.2 Subject exclusion criteria.

6.5.3 Subject withdrawal criteria (ie. terminating investigational product treatment/trial treatment) and procedures specifying:

(a) When and how to withdraw subjects from the trial/investigational product treatment.
(b) The type and timing of the data to be collected for withdrawn subjects.
(c) Whether and how subjects are to be replaced.
(d) The follow-up for subjects withdrawn from investigational product treatment/trial treatment.

6.6 Treatment of Subjects

6.6.1 The treatment(s) to be administered, including the name(s) of all the product(s), the dose(s), the dosing schedule(s), the route/mode(s) of administration, and the treatment period(s), including the follow-up period(s) for subjects for each investigational product treatment/trial treatment group/arm of the trial.

6.6.2 Medication(s)/treatment(s) permitted (including rescue medication) and not permitted before and/or during the trial.

6.6.3 Procedures for monitoring subject compliance.

6.7 Assessment of Efficacy

6.7.1 Specification of the efficacy parameters.

6.7.2 Methods and timing for assessing, recording and analysing of efficiency parameters.

6.8 Assessment of Safety

6.8.1 Specification of safety parameters.

6.8.2 The methods and timing for assessing, recording, and analysing safety parameters.

6.8.3 Procedures for eliciting reports of and for recording and reporting adverse event and intercurrent illnesses.

6.8.4 The type and duration of the follow-up of subjects after adverse events.

16

6.9 Statistics

6.9.1 A description of the statistical methods to be employed, including timing of any planned interim analysis(ses).

6.9.2 The number of subjects planned to be enrolled. In multicentre trials, the numbers of enrolled subjects projected for each trial site should be specified. Reason for choice of sample size, including reflections on (or calculations of) the power of the trial and clinical justification.

6.9.3 The level of significance to be used.

6.9.4 Criteria for the termination of the trial.

6.9.5 Procedure for accounting for missing, unused, and spurious data.

6.9.6 Procedures for reporting any deviation(s) from the original statistical plan (any deviation(s) from the original statistical plan should be described and justified in protocol and/or in the final report, as appropriate).

6.9.7 The selection of subjects to be included in the analyses (eg. all randomized subjects, all dosed subjects, all eligible subjects, evaluable subjects).

6.10 Direct Access to Source Data/Documents

The sponsor should ensure that it is specified in the protocol or other written agreement that the investigator(s)/ institution(s) will permit trial-related monitoring, audits, IRB/IEC review, and regulatory inspection(s), providing direct access to source data/documents.

6.11 Quality Control and Quality Assurance

6.12 Ethics

Description of ethical considerations relating to the trial.

6.13 Data Handling and Record Keeping

6.14 Financing and Insurance

Financing and insurance if not addressed in a separate agreement.

6.15 Publication Policy

Publication policy, if not addressed in a separate agreement.

6.16 Supplements

(NOTE: Since the protocol and the clinical trial/study report are closely related, further relevant information can be found in the ICH Guideline for Structure and Content of Clinical Study Reports.)

7. INVESTIGATOR'S BROCHURE
7.1 Introduction

The Investigator's Brochure (IB) is a compilation of the clinical and nonclinical data on the investigational product(s) that are relevant to the study of the product(s) in human subjects. Its purpose is to provide the investigators and others involved in the trial with the information to facilitate their understanding of the rationale for, and their compliance with, many key features of the protocol, such as the dose, dose frequency/interval, methods of administration: and safety monitoring procedures. The IB also provides insight to support the clinical management of the study subjects during the course of the clinical trial. The information should be presented in a concise, simple, objective, balanced, and non-promotional form that enables a clinician, or potential investigator, to understand it and make his/her own unbiased risk-benefit assessment of the appropriateness of the proposed trial. For this reason, a medically qualified person should generally participate in the editing of an IB, but the contents of the IB should be approved by the disciplines that generated the described data.

This guideline delineates the minimum information that should be included in an IB and provides suggestions for its layout. It is expected that the type and extent of information available will vary with the stage of development of the investigational product. If the investigational product is marketed and its pharmacology is widely understood by medical practitioners, an extensive IB may not be necessary. Where permitted by regulatory authorities, a basic product information brochure, package leaflet, or labelling may be an appropriate alternative, provided that it includes current, comprehensive, and detailed information on all aspects of the investigational product that might be of importance to the investigator. If a marketed product is being studied for a new use (ie., a new indication), an IB specific to that new use should be prepared. The IB should be reviewed at least annually and revised as necessary in compliance with a sponsor's written procedures. More frequent revision may be appropriate depending on the stage of development and the generation of relevant new information. However, in accordance with Good Clinical Practice, relevant new information may be so important that it should be communicated to the investigators, and possibly to the Institutional Review Boards (IRBs)/Independent Ethics Committees (IECs) and/or regulatory authorities before it is included in a revised IB.

Generally, the sponsor is responsible for ensuring that an up-to-date IB is made available to the investigator(s) and the investigators are responsible for providing the up-to-date IB to the responsible IRBs/IECs. In the case of an investigator sponsored trial, the sponsor-investigator should determine whether a brochure is available from the commercial manufacturer. If the investigational product is provided by the sponsor-investigator, then he or she should provide the necessary information to the trial personnel. In cases where preparation of a formal IB is impractical, the sponsor-investigator should provide, as a substitute, an expanded background information section in the trial protocol that contains the minimum current information described in this guideline.

16

7.2 General Considerations

The IB should include:

7.2.1 *Title Page*

This should provide the sponsor's name, the identity of each investigational product (ie. research number, chemical or approved generic name, and trade name(s) where legally permissible and desired by the sponsor), and the release date. It is also suggested that an edition number, and a reference to the number and date of the edition it supersedes, be provided. An example is given in Appendix 1.

7.2.2 *Confidentiality Statement*

The sponsor may wish to include a statement instructing the investigator/recipients to treat the IB as a confidential document for the sole information and use of the investigator's team and the IRB/IEC.

7.3 Contents of the Investigator's Brochure

The IB should contain the following sections, each with literature references where appropriate:

7.3.1 *Table of Contents*

An example of the Table of Contents is given in Appendix 2

7.3.2 *Summary*

A brief summary (preferably not exceeding two pages) should be given, highlighting the significant physical, chemical, pharmaceutical, pharmacological, toxicological, pharmacokinetic. metabolic, and clinical information available that is relevant to the stage of clinical development of the investigational product.

7.3.3 *Introduction*

A brief introductory statement should be provided that contains the chemical name (and generic and trade name(s) when approved) of the investigational product(s), all active ingredients, the investigational product(s) pharmacological class and its expected position within this class (eg. advantages), the rationale for performing research with the investigational product(s), and the anticipated prophylactic, therapeutic, or diagnostic indication(s). Finally, the introductory statement should provide the general approach to be followed in evaluating the investigational product.

7.3.4 *Physical, Chemical, and Pharmaceutical Properties and Formulation*

A description should be provided of the investigational product substance(s) (including the chemical and/or structural formula(e)), and a brief summary should be given of the relevant physical, chemical, and pharmaceutical properties.

To permit appropriate safety measures to be taken in the course of the trial, a description of the formulation(s) to be used, including excipients, should be provided and justified if clinically relevant. Instructions for the storage and handling of the dosage form(s) should also be given.

Any structural similarities to other known compounds should be mentioned.

7.3.5 *Nonclinical Studies*

Introduction:

The results of all relevant nonclinical pharmacology, toxicology, pharmacokinetic, and investigational product metabolism studies should be provided in summary form. This summary should address the methodology used, the results, and a discussion of the relevance of the findings to the investigated therapeutic and the possible unfavourable and unintended effects in humans.

The information provided may include the following, as appropriate, if known/available:

- Species tested
- Number and sex of animals in each group
- Unit dose (eg. milligram/kilogram (mg/kg))
- Dose interval
- Route of administration
- Duration of dosing
- Information on systemic distribution
- Duration of post-exposure follow-up
- Results, including the following aspects:
  - Nature and frequency of pharmacological or toxic effects
  - Severity or intensity of pharmacological or toxic effects
  - Time to onset of effects
  - Reversibility of effects
  - Duration of effects
  - Dose response

Tabular format/listings should be used whenever possible to enhance the clarity of the presentation.

The following sections should discuss the most important findings from the studies, including the dose response of observed effects, the relevance to humans, and any aspects to be studied in humans. If applicable, the effective and nontoxic dose findings in the same animal species should be compared (ie. the therapeutic index should be discussed). The relevance of this information to the proposed human dosing should be addressed. Whenever possible, comparisons should be made in terms of blood/tissue levels rather than on a mg/kg basis.

(a) *Nonclinical Pharmacology*

A summary of the pharmacological aspects of the investigational product and, where appropriate, its significant metabolites studied in animals, should be included. Such a summary should incorporate studies that assess potential therapeutic activity (eg. efficacy models, receptor binding, and specificity) as well as those that assess safety (eg. special studies to assess pharmacological actions other than the intended therapeutic effect(s)).

16

(b) *Pharmacokinetics and Product Metabolism in Animals*

A summary of the pharmacokinetics and biological transformation and disposition of the investigational product in all species studied should be given. The discussion of the findings should address the absorption and the local and systemic bioavailability of the investigational product and its metabolites, and their relationship to the pharmacological and toxicological findings in animal species.

(c) *Toxicology*

A summary of the toxicological effects found in relevant studies conducted in different animal species should be described under the following headings where appropriate:

– Single dose
– Repeated dose
– Carcinogenicity
– Special studies (eg. irritancy and sensitisation)
– Reproductive toxicity
– Genotoxicity (mutagenicity)

7.3.6 *Effects in Humans*

Introduction:

A thorough discussion of the known effects of the investigational product(s) in humans should be provided, including information on pharmacokinetics, metabolism, pharmacodynamics, dose response, safety, efficacy, and other pharmacological activities. Where possible, a summary of each completed clinical trial should be provided. Information should also be provided regarding results of any use of the investigational product(s) other than from in clinical trials, such as from experience during marketing.

(a) *Pharmacokinetics and Product Metabolism in Humans*

– A summary of information on the pharmacokinetics of the investigational product(s) should be presented, including the following, if available:
– Pharmacokinetics (including metabolism, as appropriate, and absorption, plasma protein binding, distribution, and elimination).
– Bioavailability of the investigational product (absolute, where possible, and/or relative) using a reference dosage form.
– Population subgroups (eg. gender, age, and impaired organ function).
– Interactions (eg. product-product interactions and effects of food).
– Other pharmacokinetic data (eg. results of population studies performed within clinical trial(s).

(b) *Safety and Efficacy*

A summary of information should be provided about the investigational product's/products' (including metabolites, where appropriate) safety, pharmacodynamics, efficacy, and dose response that were obtained from preceding trials in humans (healthy volunteers and/or patients). The implications of this information should be discussed. In cases where a number of clinical trials have been completed, the use of summaries of safety and efficacy across multiple trials by indications in subgroups may provide a clear presentation of the data. Tabular summaries of adverse drug reactions for all the clinical trials (including those for all the studied indications) would be useful. Important differences in adverse drug reaction patterns/incidences across indications or subgroups should be discussed.

The IB should provide a description of the possible risks and adverse drug reactions to be anticipated on the basis of prior experiences with the product under investigation and with related products. A description should also be provided of the precautions or special monitoring to be done as part of the investigational use of the product(s).

(c) *Marketing Experience*

The IB should identify countries where the investigational product has been marketed or approved. Any significant information arising from the marketed use should be summarised (eg. formulations, dosages, routes of administration, and adverse product reactions). The IB should also identify all the countries where the investigational product did not receive approval/registration for marketing or was withdrawn from marketing/registration.

7.3.7 *Summary of Data and Guidance for the Investigator*

This section should provide an overall discussion of the nonclinical and clinical data, and should summarise the information from various sources on different aspects of the investigational product(s), wherever possible. In this way, the investigator can be provided with the most informative interpretation of the available data and with an assessment of the implications of the information for future clinical trials.

Where appropriate, the published reports on related products should be discussed. This could help the investigator to anticipate adverse drug reactions or other problems in clinical trials.

The overall aim of this section is to provide the investigator with a clear understanding of the possible risks and adverse reactions, and of the specific tests, observations, and precautions that may be needed for a clinical trial. This understanding should be based on the available physical, chemical, pharmaceutical, pharmacological, toxicological, and clinical information on the investigational product(s). Guidance should also be provided to the clinical investigator on the recognition and treatment of possible overdose and adverse drug reactions that is based on previous human experience and on the pharmacology of the investigational product.

7.4 Appendix 1:

Title page (*Example*)

Sponsor's name

Product:

Research Number:

Name(s): Chemical, Generic (if approved)

        Trade Name(s) (if legally permissible and desired by the sponsor)

Investigator's brochure

Edition Number:

Release Date:

Replaces Previous Edition Number:

Date:

7.5 Appendix 2:

Table of contents of investigator's brochure (*Example*)

– Confidentiality Statement (optional)

– Signature Page (optional)

1 Table of Contents

2 Summary

3 Introduction

4 Physical, Chemical, and Pharmaceutical Properties and Formulation

5 Nonclinical Studies

    5.1 Nonclinical Pharmacology

    5.2 Pharmacokinetics and Product Metabolism in Animals

    5.3 Toxicology

6 Effects in Humans

    6.1 Pharmacokinetics and Product Metabolism in Humans

    6.2 Safety and Efficacy

    6.3 Marketing Experience

7 Summary of Data and Guidance

for the Investigator

NB: References on 1. Publications 2. Reports

These references should be found at the end of each chapter

Appendices (if any)

8. ESSENTIAL DOCUMENTS FOR THE CONDUCT OF A CLINICAL TRIAL

8.1 Introduction

Essential Documents are those documents which individually and collectively permit evaluation of the conduct of a trial and the quality of the data produced. These documents serve to demonstrate the compliance of the investigator, sponsor and monitor with the standards of Good Clinical Practice and with all applicable regulatory requirements.

Essential Documents also serve a number of other important purposes. Filing essential documents at the investigator/institution and sponsor sites in a timely manner can greatly assist in the successful management of a trial by the investigator, sponsor and monitor. These documents are also the ones which are usually audited by the sponsor's independent audit function and inspected by the regulatory authority(ies) as part of the process to confirm the validity of the trial conduct and the integrity of data collected.

The minimum list of essential documents which has been developed follows. The various documents are grouped in three sections according to the stage of the trial during which they will normally be generated:

1) before the clinical phase of the trial commences, 2) during the clinical conduct of the trial, and 3) after completion or termination of the trial. A description is given of the purpose of each document, and whether it should be filed in either the investigator/institution or sponsor files, or both. It is acceptable to combine some of the documents, provided the individual elements are readily identifiable.

Trial master files should be established at the beginning of the trial, both at the investigator/institution's site and at the sponsor's office. A final close-out of a trial can only be done when the monitor has reviewed both investigator/institution and sponsor files and confirmed that all necessary documents are in the appropriate files.

Any or all of the documents addressed in this guideline may be subject to, and should be available for, audit by the sponsor's auditor and inspection by the regulatory authority(ies).

16

Title of Document	Purpose	Located in Files of	
		Investigator/ Institution	Sponsor

8.2 Before the Clinical Phase of the Trial Commences

During this planning stage the following documents should be generated and should be on file before the trial formally starts

Title of Document	Purpose	Investigator/ Institution	Sponsor
8.2.1 Investigators brochure	To document that relevant and current scientific information about the investigational product has been provided to the investigator	X	X
8.2.2 signed protocol and amendments, if any, and sample case report form (CRF)	To document investigator and sponsor agreement to the protocol/amendment(s) and CRF	X	X
8.2.3 Information Given To Trial Subject			
- informed consent form (including all applicable translations)	To document the informed consent	X	X
- Any Other Written Information	To document that subjects will be given appropriate written information (content and wording) to support their ability to give fully informed consent	X	X
- Advertisement For Subject Recruitment (If Used)	To document that recruitment measures are appropriate and not coercive	X	
8.2.4 Financial Aspects Of The Trial	To document the financial agreement between the investigator/institution and the sponsor for the trial	X	X
8.2.5 Insurance Statement (where required)	To document that compensation to subject(s) for trial-related injury will be available	X	X
8.2.6 Signed Agreement Between Involved Parties, eg.:	To document agreements		
- investigator/institution and sponsor		X	X
- investigator/institution and CRO		X	X (where required)
- sponsor and CRO			X
- investigator/institution and authority(ies) (where required)		X	X
8.2.7 Dated, Documented Approval/Favourable Opinion Of Institutional Review Board (IRB)/ Independent Ethics Committee (IEC) Of The Following:	To document that the trial has been subject to IRB/IEC review and given approval/favourable opinion. To identify the version number and date of the document(s)	X	X
- protocol and any amendments			
- CRF (if applicable)			
- informed consent form(s)			

16

Title of Document	Purpose	Located in Files of Investigator/ Institution	Sponsor
- any other written information to be provided to the subject(s)			
- advertisement for subject recruitment (if used)			
- subject compensation (if any)			
- any other documents given approval/ favourable opinion			
8.2.8 Institutional Review Board/Independent Ethics Committee Composition	To document that the IRB/IEC is constituted in agreement with GCP	X	X (where required)
8.2.9 Regulatory Authority(ies) Authorisation/Approval/ Notification Of Protocol (where required)	To document appropriate authorisation/approval/ notification by the regulatory authority(ies) has been obtained prior to initiation of the trial in compliance with the applicable regulatory requirement(s)	X (where required)	X (where required)
8.2.10 Curriculum Vitae And/ Or Other Relevant Documents Evidencing Qualifications Of Investigator(s) And Subinvestigator(s)	To document qualifications and eligibility to conduct trial and/or provide medical supervision of subjects	X	X
8.2.11 Normal Value(s)/Range(s) For Medical/Laboratory/ Technical Procedure(s) And/Or Test(s) Included In The Protocol	To document normal values and/or ranges of the tests	X	X
8.3.2 Any Revision To: - protocol/amendment(s) and CRF - informed consent form - any other written information provided to subjects - advertisement for subject recruitment (if used)	To document revisions of these trial related documents that take effect during trial	X	X
8.3.3 Dated, Documented Approval/Favourable Opinion Of Institutional Review Board (IRB)/Independent Ethics Committee (IEC) Of The Following: - protocol amendment(s) - revision(s) of: - informed consent form - any other written information to be provided to the subject - advertisement for subject recruitment (if used) - any other documents - given approval/favourable opinion - continuing review of trial (where required)	To document that the amendment(s) and/or revision(s) have been subject to IRB/IEC review and were given approval/favourable opinion. To identify the version number and date of the document(s).	X	X

16

Title of Document	Purpose	Located in Files of	
		Investigator/ Institution	Sponsor
8.3.4 **Regulatory Authority(ies) Authorisations/Approvals/ Notifications Where Required For**: - protocol amendment(s) and other documents	To document compliance with applicable regulatory requirements	X (where required)	X
8.3.5 **Curriculum Vitae For New Investigator(s) And/Or Subinvestigator(s)**	(see 8.2.10)	X	X
8.3.6 **Updates To Normal Value(s)/Range(s) For Medical/Laboratory/Technical Procedure(s)/Test(s) Included In The Protocol**	To document normal values and ranges that are revised during the trial (see 8.2.11)	X	X
8.3.7 **Updates Of Medical/ Laboratory/Technical Procedures/Tests** - certification or - accreditation or - established quality control and/ or external quality assessment or - other validation (where required)	To document that tests remain adequate throughout the trial period (see 8.2.12)	X (where required)	X
8.3.8 **Documentation Of Investigational Product(S) And Trial-Related Materials Shipment**	(see 8.2.15)	X	X
8.3.9 **Certificate(s) Of Analysis For New Batches Of Investigational Products**	(see 8.2.16)		X
8.3.10 **Monitoring Visit Reports**	To document site visits by, and findings of, the monitor		X
8.3.11 **Relevant Communications Other Than Site Visits** - letters - meeting notes - notes of telephone calls	To document any agreements or significant discussions regarding trial administration, protocol violations, trial conduct, adverse event (AE) reporting	X	X
8.3.12 **Signed Informed Consent Forms**	To document that consent is obtained in accordance with GCP and protocol and dated prior to participation of each subject in trial. Also to document direct access permission (see 8.2.3)	X	

16

Title of Document	Purpose	Located in Files of	
		Investigator/ Institution	Sponsor
8.3.13 **Source Documents**	To document the existence of the subject and substantiate integrity of trial data collected. To include original documents related to the trial, to medical treatment, and history of subject	X	
8.3.14 **Signed, Dated And Completed Case Report Forms (CRF)**	To document that the investigator or authorised member of the investigator's stag confirms the observations recorded	X (copy)	X (original)
8.3.15 **Documentation Of CRF Corrections**	To document all changes/additions or corrections made to CRF after initial data were recorded	X (copy)	X (original)
8.3.16 **Notification By Originating Investigator To Sponsor Of Serious Adverse Events And Related Reports**	Notification by originating investigator to sponsor of serious adverse events and related reports in accordance with 4.11	X	X
8.3.17 **Notification By Sponsor And/Or Investigator, Where Applicable, To Regulatory Authority(IES) And IRB(s)/ IEC(s) Of Unexpected Serious Adverse Drug Reactions And Of Other Safety Information**	Notification by sponsor and/or investigator, where applicable, to regulatory authorities and IRB(s)/ IEC(s) of unexpected serious adverse drug reactions in accordance with 5.17 and 4.11.1 and of other safety information in accordance with 5.16.2	X (where required)	X
8.3.18 **Notification By Sponsor To Investigators Of Safety Information**	Notification by sponsor to investigators of safety information in accordance with 5.16.2	X	X
8.3.19 **Interim Or Annual Reports To IRB/IEC And Authority(ies)**	Interim or annual reports provided to IRB/IEC in accordance with 4.10 and to authority(ies) in accordance with 5.17.3	X	X (where required)
8.3.20 **Subject Screening Log**	To document identification of subjects who entered pre-trial screening	X	X (where required)
8.3.21 **Subject Identification Code List**	To document that investigator/institution keeps a confidential list of names of all subjects allocated to trial numbers on enrolling in the trial. Allows investigator/institution to reveal identity of any subject	X	
8.3.22 **Subject Enrolment Log**	To document chronological enrolment of subjects by trial number	X	
8.3.23 **Investigational Products Accountability At The Site**	To document that investigational product(s) have been used according to the protocol	X	X
8.3.24 **Signature Sheet**	To document signatures and initials of all persons authorised to make entries and/or corrections on CRF's	X	X

16

Title of Document	Purpose	Located in Files of Investigator/ Institution	Sponsor
8.3.25 **Record Of Retained Body Fluids/Tissue Samples (If Any)**	To document location and identification of retained samples if assays need to be repeated	X	X

8.4 After Completion or Termination of the Trial

After completion or termination of the trial, all of the documents identified in sections 8.2 and 8.3 should be in the file together with the following

Title of Document	Purpose	Located in Files of Investigator/ Institution	Sponsor
8.4.1 **Investigational Product(S) Accountability At Site**	To document that the investigational product(s) have been used according to the protocol. To documents the final accounting of investigational product(s) received at the site, dispensed to subjects, returned by the subjects, and returned to sponsor	X	X
8.4.2 **Documentation Of Investigational Product Destruction**	To document destruction of unused investigational products by sponsor or at site	X (if destroyed at site)	X
8.4.3 **Completed Subject Identification Code List**	To permit identification of all subjects enrolled in the trial in case follow-up is required. List should be kept in a confidential manner and for agreed upon time	X	
8.4.4 **Audit Certificate** (if available)	To document that audit was performed		X
8.4.5 **Final Trial Close-Out Monitoring Report**	To document that all activities required for trial close-out are completed, and copies of essential documents are held in the appropriate files		X
8.4.6 **Treatment Allocation And Decoding Documentation**	Returned to sponsor to document any decoding that may have occurred		X
8.4.7 **Final Report By Investigator To IRB/IEC Where Required, And Where Applicable, To The Regulatory Authority(IES)**	To document completion of the trial	X	
8.4.8 **Clinical Study Report**	To document results and interpretation of trial	X	X (if applicable)

16

This article was published in the BMJ *and is reproduced by permission of the* BMJ

TRIALS TO ASSESS EQUIVALENCE:
THE IMPORTANCE OF RIGOROUS METHODS

B Jones, P Jarvis, J A Lewis, A F Ebbutt

BMJ 1996;**313**:36–9

The aim of an equivalence trial is to show the therapeutic equivalence of two treatments, usually a new drug under development and an existing drug for the same disease used as a standard active comparator. Unfortunately the principles that govern the design, conduct, and analysis of equivalence trials are not as well understood as they should be. Consequently such trials often include too few patients or have intrinsic design biases which tend towards the conclusion of no difference. In addition the application of hypothesis testing in analysing and interpreting data from such trials sometimes compounds the drawing of inappropriate conclusions, and the inclusion and exclusion of patients from analysis may be poorly managed.

The design of equivalence trials should mirror that of earlier successful trials of the active comparator as closely as possible. Patient losses and other deviations from the protocol should be minimised; analysis strategies to deal with unavoidable problems should not centre on an "intention to treat" analysis but should seek to show the similarity of results from a range of approaches. Analysis should be based on confidence intervals, and this also carries implications for the estimation of the required numbers of patients at the design stage.

The gold standard in clinical research is the randomised placebo controlled double blind clinical trial. This design is favoured for confirmatory trials carried out as part of the phase III development of new medicines. Because of the number and range of medicines already available, however, new medicines are increasingly being developed for indications in which a placebo control group would be unethical. In such situations one obvious solution is to use as an active comparator an existing drug already licensed and regularly used for the indications in question. Some authors have questioned whether placebo controlled trials are used excessively and unethically,[1–3] and such views would reinforce the trend towards using active comparators. Others have proposed that, once licensed, new drugs should be compared with existing treatments for the same indication in order to examine their relative cost effectiveness and that large randomised trials are the appropriate tool.[4]

When an active comparator is used the expectation may sometimes be that the new treatment will be better than the standard, and the objective is to demonstrate this fact unequivocally. This situation is similar to using a placebo control and poses no special methodological problems. More probably, however, the new treatment is simply expected to match the efficacy of the standard treatment but have advantages in safety, convenience, or cost; in some cases the new treatment may have no immediate advantage but may present an alternative or second line therapy. Under these circumstances the objective of the trial is to show equivalent efficacy—the so called "equivalence" trial. Such trials have been referred to as "active control equivalence studies"[5] or "positive control studies."[6]

This paper describes the methodological issues that surround equivalence trials and explains their implications. We explain why equivalence trials generally need to be larger than their placebo controlled counterparts; why their standard of conduct needs to be especially high; why the handling of withdrawals, losses, and protocol deviations needs more care than usual; and why different approaches to analysis and interpretation are appropriate. A proper appreciation of these issues ensures that when equivalence trials are conducted they reach the scientific standards necessary for reliable conclusions to be drawn.

There are two fundamental methodological features of equivalence trials which underlie the general approach to their design and analysis, and these will be addressed first. These features distinguish equivalence trials from trials whose aim is to detect a difference between two treatments and which are referred to here as "comparative" trials.

CONFIDENCE INTERVALS AND SAMPLE SIZE

The first feature relates to the statistical methods used for analysis and the consequences for determining the required number of patients. In a comparative trial the standard analysis uses statistical significance tests to determine whether the null hypothesis of "no difference" may be rejected, together with confidence limits to place bounds on the possible size of the difference between the treatments. In an equivalence trial the conventional significance test has little relevance: failure to detect a difference does not imply equivalence;[7] a difference which is detected may not have any clinical relevance and may correspond to practical equivalence. The relevance of the confidence interval, however, is easier to see. This defines a range for the possible true difference between the treatments, any point of which is reasonably compatible with the observed data. If every point within this range corresponds to a difference of no clinical importance then the treatments may be considered to be equivalent.

It is important to emphasise that absolute equivalence can never be demonstrated: it is possible only to assert that the true difference is unlikely to be outside a range which depends on the size of the trial, the results of the trial, and the specified probabilities of error. If we have predefined a range of equivalence as an interval from $-\Delta$ to $+\Delta$ we can then simply check whether the confidence interval centred on the observed difference lies entirely between $-\Delta$ and $+\Delta$. If it does, equivalence is demonstrated; if it does not, there is still room for doubt.

Possible results of the comparison of a confidence interval with a predefined range of equivalence are shown in figure 1, and the importance of not basing conclusions on statistical significance can also be seen in this figure. Any confidence interval which does not overlap zero corresponds to a statistically significant difference.

This intuitive procedure of checking whether a confidence interval lies within a range of equivalence does in fact correspond to a significance testing procedure, but one in which the roles of the usual null and alternative hypotheses are reversed. In comparative trials the null hypothesis is that there is no difference between the treatments. The alternative hypothesis is that a difference exists. In equivalence testing the relevant null hypothesis is that a difference of at least Δ exists, and the trial is targeted at disproving this in favour of the alternative that no difference exists. This formulation is important in validating the intuitive confidence interval procedure, and it also helps in calculating sample sizes. The formulas for calculating sample sizes for normally distributed and binary data are provided in the appendix. Values need to be specified for the range of equivalence (Δ) and the probabilities of type I and II errors (α and β, respectively). An

Example of sample size calculation

Two inhalers used for the relief of asthma attacks are to be assessed for equivalence. They will be considered equivalent if the 95% two sided confidence interval for the treatment difference, measured using morning peak expiratory flow rate (1/min), falls wholly within the interval ±15 1/min — that is, $\Delta = 15$ and $\alpha = (1-0.95)/2$. From a previous trial the prior estimate of δ^2, the between subject variance of morning peak expiratory flow rate, is 1600 (1/min)². The sample size of each group is to be such that there is a power of 0.80 that the inhalers will be deemed equivalent if they are, in fact, identical. To use the formula for normally distributed data given in the appendix, we note that

$$z_{(1-\alpha)} = z_{(0.975)} = 1.96$$

$$\text{and } z_{(1-\beta/2)} = z_{(0.90)} > = 1.28$$

from tables of the normal distribution, so

$$n = \frac{2 \times 40^2 [1.96 + 1.28]^2}{15^2} = 149.3 \approx 150.$$

Each group should contain 150 patients.

important point to note is that if a $100(1-2\alpha)$% confidence interval is used to decide on equivalence then the significance level is α—that is, the probability of the type I error is α. So, for example, if a 95% interval is used then $\alpha = 0.025$. The choice of Δ is difficult and requires extensive debate with knowledgable clinical experts, and the chosen Δ should generally be smaller than in a comparative trial. In comparative trials against placebo, Δ is often set equal to a difference of undisputed clinical importance, and hence may be above the minimum difference of clinical interest by a factor of perhaps two or more; there may be scientific reasons to expect a treatment to have more than a minimal effect. However, when comparing a new agent with a standard comparator it is necessary to show that the new agent is sufficiently similar to the standard to be clinically indistinguishable. This entails using smaller values of Δ than were used to detect the effect of the standard relative to placebo. A factor of two does not seem inappropriate, leading to sample sizes roughly four times as large as those in similar comparative trials. The selection of α and β follows similar lines as for

17

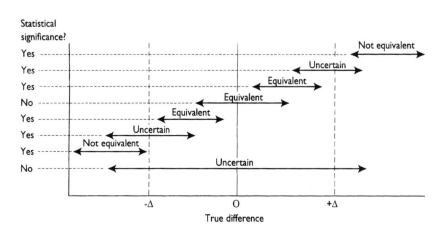

Statistical significance?

Fig 1—*Examples of possible results of using the confidence interval approach: $-\Delta$ to $+\Delta$ is the prespecified range of equivalence; the horizontal lines correspond to possible trial outcomes expressed as confidence intervals, with the associated significance test result shown on the left; above each line is the decision concerning equivalence*

comparative trials. The use of a 95% confidence interval in an equivalence trial, as recommended by the European Committee for Proprietary Medicinal Products in its note for guidance on biostatistics,[8 9] corresponds to a value for a of 0.025. However, β is treated identically, and is generally set to 0.1 (to give a power of 0.90) or 0.2 (to give a power of 0.8). The distinction between one sided and two sided tests of statistical significance also carries over into the confidence interval approach. For a one sided test equivalence is declared if the lower one sided confidence limit exceeds −Δ. This approach is indicated when the objective is to ensure that the new agent is not inferior to the standard. Equivalence or superiority are both regarded as positive outcomes.

INTERNAL VALIDITY OF TRIALS

The second special feature affecting the equivalence trial is the lack of any natural internal check on its validity.[6] In a comparative trial there is a strong incentive to remove any sloppiness in design, conduct, and analysis because such sloppiness is likely to obscure any differences between the treatments. As a consequence, the detection of a treatment difference not only implies that a difference exists but also that the trial was of sufficient quality to detect it. Such an incentive and natural check on quality are lacking in an equivalence trial, where the finding of equivalence may arise either from true equivalence or from a trial with poor discriminatory power—a trial which was too small, for example, or one in which most patients were likely to improve spontaneously without medical intervention. The finding in a trial that two treatments are equivalent does not require that both treatments were effective; it is equally compatible with the alternative that neither was. In any equivalence trial, therefore, it is vitally important to have some means of confirming that both treatments were indeed effective. We need to be certain that if a third placebo arm had been included both active treatments would have been shown to be superior to placebo.

The degree of certainty can be increased only by paying careful attention to the design of the equivalence trial, by being strict about matters of conduct, and by making additional checks during analysis. The active comparator is usually a licensed medicine which has been evaluated in controlled trials against placebo, perhaps during the phase III studies used to support its marketing application. If the equivalence trial mirrors as closely as possible the methods used in these earlier placebo controlled trials then confidence in its results will be increased, since the methods have been positively validated in a similar context.

Important design features to follow as closely as possible are the inclusion and exclusion criteria (defining the patient population), the dosing schedule of the standard treatment, the use of concomitant medication and other interventions, and the primary response variable and its schedule of measurements. During

analysis it is valuable to show similarities between the equivalence trial and the earlier comparative trials in terms of patient compliance, the response during any run in period, and the scale of patient losses and the reasons for them.

The two major features covered so far provide the background for some brief comments on other considerations in the design, conduct, and analysis of equivalence trials.

DESIGN AND CONDUCT

The amount of information available to plan an equivalence trial will generally exceed the amount available at the time of planning earlier trials of the active comparator. There should be little excuse, therefore, for poor design. Double blinding of medication may pose extra difficulties but is no less important than in comparative trials, and randomisation is equally important. Inclusion and exclusion criteria must be carefully chosen on the basis of prior experience of the active comparator to ensure that the trial contains patients likely to respond to the active comparator and hence avoid a conclusion of equivalence through non-response. Care in this choice should be mirrored in the response observed to the trial treatments. The level of success for success/failure outcomes should be similar to that seen in previous trials of the active comparator. For more quantitative endpoints, improvements from baseline in the course of the trial provide some assurance that the trial treatments have both been effective.

The dosing regimen and period of dosing of the active comparator should reflect the standard manner of use known to be effective on the basis of earlier clinical trials; and there should be a sound rationale for the choice of the potentially equivalent dosing regimen of the new medication. If the doses chosen for both agents

---

Example: Assessment of equivalence

Two inhalers, R and T, used for the relief of asthma attacks were compared in an equivalence trial using morning peak expiratory flow rate (1/min) as the primary measurement. The range of equivalence was set at ±15 1/min—that is, Δ = 15. The results of the trial were as follows:

Mean morning peak expiratory flow rate on treatment

R = 420 1/min (150 patients)

T = 417 1/min (150 patients)

Mean difference between R and T, $\bar{d}$ = 3

Estimated standard error of the mean difference, SE($\bar{d}$), = 4

The 95% confidence interval for the true difference ranges from −1.96 SE$\bar{d}$ to +1.96 SE$\bar{d}$, where 1.96 is the appropriate value from tables of the normal distribution (that is, $z_{(0.975)}$). This interval is −4.8 to 10.8 and lies entirely within the range of equivalence of −15 1/min to +15 1/min and so equivalence is confirmed.

are too high then patients may reach an upper threshold in response, leading to a conclusion of equivalence which may not carry over to the doses more likely to be used in practice. Unreasonably low doses may lead to similar false conclusions, through lack of response. It is sometimes necessary to check that all patients can tolerate one or both treatments in order to maintain patient numbers and hence power, and this should be done during a run in period before randomisation.

The use in all patients of a standard dose of concomitant medication with known beneficial effects can also result in patients reaching their upper threshold of response and hence lead to the masking of treatment differences. Alternatively, if the use of concomitant medication is flexible, greater use in one arm of the trial may produce a bias towards equivalence. Similar biases towards equivalence can arise from the use of "rescue" medication in patients in whom treatment fails—that is, from patients who withdraw from randomised treatment because of lack of efficacy. These issues are closely connected with the means adopted for dealing with such patients in the analysis.

ANALYSIS

The most difficult issue relating to the analysis of an equivalence trial concerns which patients and which data from these patients to include. The most common approaches to the analysis of randomised trials are "intention to treat" and "per protocol" analyses. A fuller discussion of intention to treat can be found in Lewis and Machin,[10] and a severe criticism in Salsburg.[11]

In an intention to treat analysis patients are analysed according to their randomised treatment, irrespective of whether they actually received the treatment. Patients may fail to take a treatment altogether, may be given the wrong treatment, or may violate the protocol in some other way, but under an intention to treat analysis this does not affect matters. The strength claimed for such an analysis is that it is pragmatic—that is, that it mirrors what will happen when the treatment is used in practice. In a comparative trial, where the aim is to decide if two treatments are different, an intention to treat analysis is generally conservative: the inclusion of protocol violators and withdrawals will usually tend to make the results from the two treatment groups more similar. However, for an equivalence trial this effect is no longer conservative: any blurring of the difference between the treatment groups will increase the chance of declaring equivalence.

A per protocol analysis compares patients according to the treatment actually received and includes only those patients who satisfied the entry criteria and properly followed the protocol. This approach might be expected to enhance any difference between the treatments rather than diminishing it, because of the removal of uninformative "noise." Unfortunately it is possible to envisage circumstances under which the exclusion of patients in a per protocol analysis might bias the results towards a conclusion of no difference—for example, if patients not responding to one of the two treatments dropped out early. For this reason the subgroup of patients excluded from a per protocol analysis should be examined carefully to explore whether any biases of this nature might have occurred. Indeed, if the two treatments produce a different pattern of withdrawal for adverse events or lack of effect then this in itself is evidence that they are not entirely equivalent.

In an equivalence trial it is probably best to carry out both types of analysis and hope to show equivalence in either case. In preparation for this policy it is important to collect complete follow up data on all randomised patients as per protocol, irrespective of whether they are subsequently found to have failed entry criteria, withdraw from trial medication prematurely, or violate the protocol in some other way. Such a rigid approach to data collection allows maximum flexibility during later analysis and hence provides a more robust basis for decisions.

With respect to other aspects of analysis, equivalence trials are similar in nature to comparative trials.

The result of the analysis of the primary endpoint should be one of the following:
• that the confidence interval for the difference between the two treatments lies entirely within the equivalence range so that equivalence may be concluded with only a small probability of error;
• that the confidence interval covers at least some points which lie outside the equivalence range, so that differences of potential clinical importance remain a real possibility and equivalence cannot safely be concluded; and
• that the confidence interval is wholly outside the equivalence range (though this is likely to be rare).

DISCUSSION

The most common failing of reported equivalence studies is that they are planned and analysed as if they were comparative studies, and the lack of a statistically significant difference is then taken as proof of equivalence. The material covered in this paper should make it clear that such an approach is likely to lead to wrong conclusions.

Improvements to the standards of this type of research could be encouraged if journal editors and referees adopted a more critical attitude. The following is a suggested minimal set of criteria against which to judge reports of clinical trials in which the equivalence of two treatments is claimed.
• The size of the trial should be based on a null hypothesis of non-equivalence and an alternative hypothesis of equivalence.
• Conclusions should be drawn on the basis of an appropriate confidence interval using the prespecified criteria of equivalence used in the sample size calculation.
• The results of both intention to treat and per protocol analyses should be presented.
• There should be adequate evidence on the rigour of the trial and of the similarity of important features of

17

design to those of earlier comparative trials which showed useful clinical effects.

• The trial data should provide some evidence of the efficacy of the treatments; this might be success rates similar to those of previous trials, or clinically important changes from baseline treatments.

• Some of these aspects could most easily be covered by insisting that papers submitted to journals referred to published trials of the standard comparator against placebo with similar methods. Referees should also be familiar with the special difficulties surrounding equivalence trials in the relevant clinical area.

• Improving the standards of equivalence trials has consequences for the resources required. Such trials will become larger and their monitoring will become more labour intensive in order to ensure they are conducted in close accordance with the protocol, so minimising the occurrence of biases towards a conclusion of no difference.

Funding: BJ and PJ thank Glaxo Wellcome Ltd for providing a research grant.
Conflict of interest: None.

APPENDIX: SAMPLE SIZE AND POWER FORMULAS

Normally distributed data (comparison of means)

We assume that subjects are randomised into two treatment groups of equal size n, the groups being denoted by R (reference treatment) and T (test treatment). Let μ_R and μ_T denote the expected mean values of the normally distributed observations in groups R and T, respectively, and let s^2 be an estimate of σ^2 the variance of the observations, assumed to be the same in the two groups.

In the confidence interval approach equivalence is concluded if the interval falls entirely within two prespecified tolerance limits, $-\Delta$ and $+\Delta$. If $\bar{x}_R$ and $\bar{x}_T$ denote the observed means of the reference and treatment groups respectively, then, provided n is reasonably large, the two sided $100(1-2\alpha)$% confidence interval for $\mu_R - \mu_T$ is

$$\bar{x}_R - \bar{x}_T \pm z_{(1-\alpha)}\sqrt{2s^2/n}$$

where $z_{(1-\alpha)}$ is the $100(1-\alpha)$% point of the normal distribution. That is, if X has the standard normal distribution with mean 0 and variance 1 then,

$$Pr(X \le z_{(1-\alpha)}) = 1 - \alpha.$$

When the confidence interval (or significance testing) approach is used to assess equivalence, two sorts of mistake can occur: we can decide that the treatments are equivalent when they are not (the type I error with probability α) or we can decide the treatments are not equivalent when they are (the type II error with probability β). These definitions are an exact switch of those applying to conventional significance testing.[12] The values of α and β depend on the size of the true

difference between the treatment means $\delta = \mu_R - \mu_T$. The value of a reaches a maximum on the boundary of the range of equivalence (that is, when $|\delta| = \Delta$) and this is the value of a used in calculations. The value of β is usually calculated at the point of equivalence (that is, at $\delta = 0$). The corresponding power of the trial, $1-\beta$, is the probability of correctly declaring equivalence when $\delta = 0$.

The sample size and the power formulas for a $100(1-2\alpha)$% two sided interval are as follows.
The null hypothesis is $H_0 : |\mu_R - \mu_T| \ge \Delta$ (inequivalence)
The alternative hypothesis is $H_1 : -\Delta < \mu_R - \mu_T < \Delta$ (equivalence)

$$n = \frac{2s^2}{\Delta^2}[z_{(1-\alpha)} + z_{(1-\beta/2)}]^2$$

$$Power = 2\Phi\left(\frac{\Delta}{\sqrt{s^2(\frac{2}{n})}}\right) - z_{(1-\alpha)} - 1$$

where $\Phi(x)$ denotes $Pr(X \ge x)$ and X has the standard normal distribution with mean 0 and variance 1.
For a $100(1-\alpha)$% one sided interval the corresponding formulas are:
$H_0 : \mu_R - \mu_T \Delta\ \Delta$ (inequivalence)
$H_1 : \mu_R - \mu_T < \Delta$ (equivalence)

$$n = \frac{2s^2}{\Delta^2}[z_{(1-\alpha)} + z_{(1-\beta)}]^2$$

$$Power = \Phi\left(\frac{\Delta}{\sqrt{s^2(\frac{2}{n})}}\right) - z_{(1-\alpha)} - 1$$

Binary data (comparison of percentages)

Using notation found in Pocock,[13] we define p to be the overall percentage of successes to be expected if the treatments are equivalent and use Δ to define the range of equivalence for the difference in percentage success rates. Other notation is unchanged.
The required size of each treatment group and the power can be calculated as follows[14]:

• Two sided case:

$$n = \frac{2p(100-p)}{\Delta^2}\left[z_{(1-\alpha)} + z_{(1-\frac{\beta}{2})}\right]^2$$

$$Power = 2\Phi\left(\frac{\Delta}{\sqrt{p(100-p)(\frac{2}{n})}} - z_{(1-\alpha)}\right) - 1$$

• One sided case:

$$n = \frac{2p(100-p)}{\Delta^2}\left[z_{(1-\alpha)} + z_{(1-\beta)}\right]^2$$

$$Power = \Phi\left(\frac{\Delta}{\sqrt{p(100-p)(\frac{2}{n})}} - z_{(1-\alpha)}\right) - 1$$

Department of Medical Statistics, School of Computing Sciences, De Montfort University, Leicester LE1 9BH
B Jones, *professor of medical statistics*
P Jarvis, *senior lecturer in medical statistics*
J A Lewis, *visiting professor in medical statistics*
Glaxo Wellcome Ltd, Greenford, Middlesex UB6 0HE
A F Ebbutt, *director of European clinical statistics*
Correspondence to: Professor J A Lewis, Medicines Control Agency, London SW8 5NQ.

References

1   Rothman KJ, Michels KB. The continuing unethical use of placebo controls. *N Engl J Med* 1994;**331**:394–8.
2   Taubes G. Use of placebo controls in clinical trials disputed. *Science* 1995;**267**:25–6.
3   The use of placebo controls. *N Engl J Med* 1995;**332**:60–2.
4   Henry D, Hill S. Comparing treatments: comparison should be against active treatments rather than placebo. *BMJ* 1995;**310**:1279.
5   Makuch RW, Pledger G, Hall DB, Johnson MF, Herson J, Hsu J-P. Active control equivalence studies. In: Peace K, ed. *Statistical issues in drug research and development.* New York: Marcel Dekker, 1990:225–62.
6   Temple R. Government viewpoint of clinical trials. *Drug Information Journal* 1982;**16**:10–7.
7   Altman DG, Bland JM. Absence of evidence is not evidence of absence. *BMJ* 1995;**311**:485.
8   Lewis JA, Jones DR, Röhmel J. Biostatistical methodology in clinical trials—a European guideline. *Statistics in Medicine* 1995;**14**:1655–7.
9   CPMP Working Party on Efficacy of Medicinal Products. Biostatistical methodology in clinical trials in applications for marketing authorizations for medicinal products. Note for guidance III/3630/92-EN. *Statistics in Medicine* 1995;**14**:1658–82.
10 Lewis JA, Machin D. Intention to treat—who should use ITT. *Br J Cancer* 1992;**68**:647–50.
11 Salsburg D. Intent to treat: the reductio ad absurdum that became gospel. *Pharmacoepidemiology and Drug Safety* 1994;**3**:329–35.
12 Campbell MJ, Julious SA, Altman DG. Estimating sample sizes for binary, ordered categorical and continuous outcomes in two group comparisons. *BMJ* 1995;**311**:1145–8.
13 Pocock SJ. *Clinical trick: a practical approach.* Chichester: Wiley, 1983.
14 Makuch R, Simon R. Sample size requirements for evaluating a conservative therapy. *Cancer Treatment Reports* 1978;**62**:1037–40.

17

This article was first published in the BMJ *and is reproduced with permission of the* BMJ

EDUCATION AND DEBATE

Statistics notes: Sample size in cluster randomisation

Sally M Kerry, statistician

Division of General Practice and Primary Care, St George's Hospital Medical School, London SW17 0RE

J Martin Bland, professor of medical statistics

Department of Public Health Sciences
Correspondence to: Mrs Kerry

BMJ 1998;316:549 (14 February)

Techniques for estimating sample size for randomised trials are well established,[1,2] but most texts do not discuss sample size for trials which randomise groups (clusters) of people rather than individuals. For example, in a study of different preparations to control head lice all children in the same class were allocated to receive the same preparation. This was done to avoid contaminating the treatment groups through contact with control children in the same class.[3] The children in the class cannot be considered independent of one another and the analysis should take this into account.[4][5] There will be some loss of power due to randomising by cluster rather than individual and this should be reflected in the sample size calculations. Here we describe sample size calculations for a cluster randomised trial.

For a conventional randomised trial assessing the difference between two sample means the number of subjects required in each group, n, to detect a difference of d using a significance level of 5% and a power of 90% is given by $n = 21s^2 / d^2$ where s is the standard deviation of the outcome measure. Other values of power and significance can be used.[1]

For a trial using cluster randomisation we need to take the design into account. For a continuous outcome measurement such as serum cholesterol values, a simple method of analysis is based on the mean of the observations for all subjects in the cluster and compares these means between the treatment groups. We will denote the variance of observations within one cluster by s_w^2 and assume that this variance is the same for all clusters. If there are m subjects in each cluster then the variance of a single sample mean is s_w^2 / m. The true cluster mean (unknown) will vary from cluster to cluster, with variance s_c^2. The observed variance of the cluster means will be the sum of the variance between clusters and the variance within clusters—that is, variance of outcome $= s_c^2 + s_w^2 / m$. Hence we can replace s^2 by $s_c^2 + s_w^2 / m$ in the formula for sample size above to obtain the number of clusters required in each intervention group. To do this we need estimates of s_c^2 and s_w^2.

For example, in a proposed study of a behavioural intervention in general practice to lower cholesterol concentrations practices were to be randomised into two groups, one to offer intensive dietary intervention by practice nurses using a behavioural approach and the other to offer usual general practice care. The outcome measure would be mean cholesterol values in patients attending each practice one year later. Estimates of between practice variance and within practice variance were obtained from the Medical Research Council thrombosis prevention trial[6] and were $s_c^2 = 0.0046$ and $s_w^2 = 1.28$ respectively. The minimum difference considered to be clinically relevant was 0.1 mmol/l. If we recruit 50 patients per practice, we would have $s^2 = s_c^2 + s_w^2 / m = 0.0046 + 1.28 / 50 = 0.0302$. The number of practices is given by $n = 21 \times 0.0302 / 0.1^2 = 63$ in each group. We would require 63 practices in each group to detect a difference of 0.1 mmol/l with a power of 90% using a 5% significance level—a total of 3150 patients in each group.

It can be seen from the formula for the variance of the outcome that when the number of patients within a practice, m, is very large, s_w^2 / m will be very small and so the overall variance is roughly the same as the variance between practices. In this situation, increasing the number of patients per practice will not increase the power of the study. The table shows the number of practices required for different values of m, the number of subjects per practice. In all situations the total number of subjects required is greater than if simple random allocation had been used.

The ratio of the total number of subjects required using cluster randomisation to the number required using simple randomisation is called the design effect. Thus a cluster randomised trial which has a large design effect will require many more subjects than a trial of the same intervention which randomises individuals. As the number of patients per practice increases so does the design effect. In the table, the design effect is very small when m is less than 10. This would involve recruiting a total of 558 practices, and the nature of the intervention

Table 1

Total number of practices required to detect a difference of 0.1 mmol/l cholesterol with 90% power at 5% significance level

No of patients per practice (m)	Standard deviation	No of practices	No of patients	Design effect
10	0.364	558	5 580	1.04
25	0.236	234	5 850	1.09
50	0.173	126	6 300	1.17
100	0.132	74	7 400	1.38
500	0.085	32	16 000	2.98
No needed with individual randomisation			5 364	1.00

and difficulties in recruiting practices made this impractical. Thus it was decided to recruit fewer practices. The design effect of using 126 practices with 50 patients from each practice was 1.17. This design requires the total sample size to be inflated by 17%. If the study involves training practice based staff it may be cost effective to reduce the number of practices even further. If we chose to use 32 practices then we would need 500 patients from each practice and the design effect would be 2.98. Thus the cluster design with 32 practices would require the total sample size to be trebled to maintain the same level of power.

We shall discuss the use of the intracluster correlation coefficient in these calculations in a future statistics note.

References

1   Florey C du V. Sample size for beginners. *BMJ* 1993;306:1181-4.
2   Machin D, Campbell MJ. *Statistical tables for the design of clinical trials.* Oxford: Blackwell, 1987.
3   Chosidow O, Chastang C, Brue C, Bouvet E, Izri M, Monteny N, et al. Controlled study of malathion and d-phenothrin lotions for *Pediculus humanus* var *capitis*-infested schoolchildren. *Lancet* 1994;344:1724-7.
4   Bland JM, Kerry SM. Trials randomised in clusters. *BMJ* 1997;315:600.
5   Kerry SM, Bland JM. Analysis of a trial randomised in clusters. *BMJ* 1998;316:54.
6   Meade TW, Roderick PJ, Brennan PJ, Wilkes HC, Kelleher CC. Extracranial bleeding and other symptoms due to low dose aspirin and low intensity oral anticoagulation. *Thromb Haemostasis* 1992:68:1-6.

18

This chapter was first published in Non-random Reflections on Health Services Research *and is reproduced by permission of the* BMJ Publishing Group

SO WHAT'S SO SPECIAL ABOUT RANDOMISATION?

(Maynard A and Chalmers I (Eds) (1997).
Non-random Reflections on Health Services Research. London, BMJ Publishing.)

Jos Kleijnen, Peter Gotzsche, Regina A Kunz, Andy D Oxman, Iain Chalmers.

Why bother to assess the effects of health and social care?

Human beings have a substantial natural capacity to overcome "dis-ease" in many of its various physical, psychological, and social manifestations, and this is often achieved without any assistance from professionals. This "self healing", restorative tendency can be enhanced by social and psychological factors, such as optimism in the affected person; attention, kindness, and encouragement from others; and physical environments which are conducive to recovery.

In helping people to overcome their "dis-ease", effective professionals exploit the restorative effects of these social, psychological, and environmental aspects of care. This is true for professionals from both conventional and complementary medicine. In addition, professionals usually draw on a range of more specific strategies which are supposed to have or are known to have beneficial effects on the natural histories of the various forms of "dis-ease" which lead people to seek professional help. Although these interventions are offered in good faith, most if not all of them have the capacity for causing inadvertent harm as well as intended benefit. With the best of intentions, professionals offering health and social care have often inadvertently harmed those who have turned to them for help.[1-4] At its most extreme, the harm done has been lethal—by social workers[5] as well as by health professionals.[6] Short of death, the adverse effects of well meant professional prescriptions and proscriptions for care have resulted in much non-lethal morbidity and a good deal of misery.

We believe that people seeking help from professionals have a right to expect that formal measures will be taken to assess the relative merits of the various alternative forms of health and social care on offer, be these radical surgery for prostate cancer or custodial sentences for young offenders.

When is formal assessment of care necessary?

There is increasingly wide support for the principle of reliable assessment of the effects of health and social interventions on outcomes that matter to the people to whom they are offered. Debate continues, however, about the methods of assessment that should be used in implementing this principle in practice.[7] Any attempt to evaluate the effects of professional care must necessarily entail some kind of comparison, even if the comparison is an informal one. Occasionally, the effects of professional interventions are so obvious and dramatic that informal comparisons are an adequate basis for strong causal inferences about the effects of care. When the prognosis of the condition in question is known with great confidence, identifying the effects of professional interventions can be straightforward. Examples include identifying the effects of haemostasis in preventing death from exsanguination, the effects of a sensitive social worker who helps an illiterate person to obtain their entitlements through the social security system, the effect of defibrillation in cardiac arrest, and the effect of hip replacement in osteoarthrosis with severe pain and immobility.

In the more common circumstances when the effects of care are less dramatic, steps must be taken to reduce the likelihood that systematic errors (biases) or random errors (the play of chance) in the comparisons made will lead people to conclude either that a form of care is helpful when it is not, or that it is useless or harmful when the reverse is true. It is because these errors may be dangerously misleading that most countries have national drug assessment procedures intended to help protect the public, and it is becoming increasingly accepted that formal assessment should be extended to other interventions in health and social care to try to ensure that they do more good than harm.

How should groups be assembled for formal treatment comparisons?

One of the most important biases that may distort treatment comparisons is that which can result from the way that comparison groups are assembled.[8,9] Comparison groups can be assembled prospectively or retrospectively, concurrently or at different points in time, and consideration has been given to the extent to which each of these methods is likely to be susceptible to bias. Over 30 years ago, two psychologists outlined a hierarchy of methods for assembling comparison groups, based on the assumed reliability of each for making causal inferences.[10] They placed controlled trials with random assignment to experimental groups at the top of the hierarchy. Below these randomised controlled trials came pretest-post-test comparisons and interrupted time series designs (studies using historical controls). Single group pretest-post-test or post-test only designs (case series or single cases) were judged to provide the least reliable basis for causal inferences. Variations of this basic hierarchy are still being proposed by social and health scientists and drug regulatory authorities.[11–15] Why is it that those who have proposed these hierarchies seem to agree that randomised trials should be regarded as the best way to assemble comparison groups upon which to base causal inferences about the effects of care?

What is special about randomised controlled trials?

The main challenge facing those wishing to assess the relative merits of alternative forms of care is to ensure as far as possible that, on average, the people who make up the comparison groups are comparable in respect of prognosis and responsiveness to treatment. Unless this can be achieved, there is clearly a danger that any observed differences in "outcome" may simply reflect prior differences in the prognoses and therapeutic sensitivity of the people in the comparison groups.

The only special claim that can be made for random allocation is that allocation to the comparison groups is unbiased in respect of prognosis and responsiveness to treatment. No other way of creating comparison groups has these properties because it can never be assumed that all factors relevant to prognosis and responsiveness to treatment have been distributed in an unbiased way between the comparison groups. Due solely to chance, there will always be smaller or larger differences of prognosis and responsiveness to treatment; but the larger the size of the trial, the more likely is it that such differences will be trivial.

When random allocation is not used it may be possible to control for differences between comparison groups in other ways—for example, by adjusting for known differences in the analysis. However, this is only possible for factors that are known and measured. Randomisation is the only means of allocation that controls for unknown and unmeasured differences as well as those that are known and measured. Unfortunately it can rarely, if ever, be assumed that all the important prognostic factors are known, and for those that are known difficulties can arise in measuring and accounting for them in analyses. Empirical evidence supports these logical concerns (see tables).

There is consistent evidence from comparisons of randomised and non-randomised trials of the same intervention (table 4.1). These studies indicate important differences in the apparent effects of care in relation to how patients were allocated. It seems that these differences are primarily due to a poorer prognosis in non-randomly selected controls compared with randomly selected controls.

The evidence from comparisons across different interventions (table 4.2) is less consistent. This can best be explained by the fact that there are many other factors that could distort or mask an association between randomisation and estimates of the effects of care—that is, there is so much "noise" in these heterogeneous samples of studies that the observed impact of randomisation and other factors on the observed treatment effects is uncertain and difficult to interpret.

Finally, empirical studies that have addressed "allocation concealment" (to prevent foreknowledge of treatment assignment) indicate that it is most likely this feature of random allocation that is crucial in achieving similar comparison groups (table 4.3). When assessing a potential participant's eligibility for a trial, those who are recruiting participants and the participants themselves should remain unaware of the next assignment in the sequence until after the decision about eligibility has been made. Then, after it has been revealed, neither the assignment nor the decision about eligibility should be altered.

It is important to recognise that differences between comparison groups in prognosis, responsiveness to treatment, or exposure to other factors that affect outcomes can distort the apparent effects of care in either direction, causing them to appear either larger or smaller than they are. It is generally not possible to predict the magnitude, and often not even the direction of this bias in specific studies. However, on average, these differences tend to exaggerate treatment effects and the size of these distortions can be as large or larger than the size of the effects that it is hoped to detect.

What isn't special about randomised controlled trials?

In no respects other than the abolition of bias at the moment of assignment to treatment comparison groups do randomised controlled trials—of necessity—differ from alternative study designs for assessing the effects of health and social care. As with other study designs, the comparison groups in randomised trials may, after the actual moment of assignment to one or other comparison group, differ in ways other than the contrasting forms of care which the study has been designed to compare, and some of these differences may be important in interpreting differences or similarities in the subsequent experiences of the comparison groups. Researchers using other research designs must also consider eligibility criteria, the size of the comparison groups, outcome measures, subgroup analyses, duration of follow up, blinding of treatment and outcome assessment (whether or not using placebos), and the generalisability of the results of the comparisons. There are no necessary or inevitable differences between randomised trials and other forms of treatment comparisons in any of these respects.

What shouldn't be special about randomised trials?

"If you can believe fervently in your treatment, even though controlled tests show that it is quite useless, then your results are much better, your patients are much better, and your income is much better too. I

19

Table 1

Studies of randomised controlled trials compared with non-randomised controlled trials within specific interventions

Study	Sample	Comparison	Results
Chalmers et al[39]	32 controlled studies of anticoagulation in acute myocardial infarction identified through a systematic search	Randomised controlled trials were compared with CCTs and HCTs on case-fatality rate, thromboembolism rate, and rate of haemorrhages	The largest relative risk reduction for mortality was observed in HCTs (0.42), compared with randomised controlled trials (0.31) and CCTs (0.33). The case-fatality rate was highest in HCs (38.3), compared with RCs (19.6) and CCs (29.2). A similar pattern was found for thromboembolism
Sacks et al[40]	Convenience sample of 50 randomised controlled trials and 56 HCTs assessing 6 interventions (treatment of oesophageal varices, coronary artery surgery, anticoagulation in myocardial infarction, chemotherapy in colon cancer, chemotherapy in melanoma, and DES for recurrent miscarriage)	Randomised controlled trials and HCTs were compared on the frequency of detecting statistically significant results (P £ 0.05) of the primary outcome and reduction of mortality	20% of the randomised controlled trials found a statistically significant benefit from the new therapy, compared with 79% of HCTs. The relative risk reduction of mortality in HCTs v randomised controlled trials (HCT/randomised controlled trials) was 0.49/0.27 (1.8) for cirrhosis, 0.68/0.26 (2.6) for coronary artery surgery at 3 years, 0.49/0.22 (2.2) for anticoagulation in myocardial infarction, 0.67/−0.02 for DES in recurrent miscarriage. Outcomes in the treatment groups were similar in both designs, but outcomes in the control groups were worse among historical controls
Diehl and Perry[41]	19 randomised controlled trials and 17 HCTs for 6 types of cancer (breast, colon, stomach, lung, melanoma, soft tissue sarcoma) identified from the reference lists of two textbooks	RCs and HCs matched for disease, stage, and follow up were compared on survival and relapse free survival	In 43 matched control groups 18 (42%) varied by more than 10% (absolute difference in either outcome), 9 (21%) by more than 20%, and 2 (5%) by more than 30%. Survival or relapse free survival was better in RCs compared with HCs in 17/18 matches

Tables 4.1–4.3 are adapted from Kunz RA, Oxman AD. Empirical evidence of selection bias in studies of the effects of health care: a systematic review. Presented at the Cochrane Colloquium, Oslo, 5–8 October, 1995.
CC = concurrent control; CCT = trial using concurrent controls; HC = historical control; HCT = trial using historical controls; RC = randomised control.

19

Table 2

Studies of randomised controlled trials compared with non-randomised controlled trials across different interventions

Study	Sample	Comparison	Results
Colditz *et al*[42]	113 studies published in 1980 comparing new interventions with old, identified in leading cardiology, neurology, psychiatry, and respiratory journals through a systematic literature search	36 parallel randomised controlled trials, 29 randomised COTS, 3 parallel CCTs, 46 nonrandom COTS, 5 ECSs, and 9 RRSs were compared on treatment gain (measured by the Mann-Whitney statistic). The relation between quality scores and treatment gains was also examined. The Mann-Whitney statistic is the probability that a patient receiving the new therapy would do better than a patient receiving the old. 0.5 indicates no difference between comparison groups	All but one design had, on average, similar estimates of treatment gain (0.56–0.65). Overall 87% of new treatments were rated as improvements over old, but only in the nonrandom COTS were patients, on average, significantly more likely to suggest benefit from the new treatment (0.94; $P = 0.004$). Non-double-blinded randomised controlled trials were more likely to suggest a benefit from the new treatment (0.69) than double blinded randomised controlled trials (0.58; $P = 0.02$). Within randomised controlled trials there was not a significant correlation between quality scores and treatment gains ($R = -0.16$; $P = 0.18$)
Miller *et al*[43]	188 studies published in 1983 comparing new interventions in surgery with old, identified in leading surgical journals through a systematic literature search	81 randomised controlled trials, 15 CCTs, 27 ECSs, 91 RRSs, and 7 BASs were compared on treatment gain (measured by the Mann-Whitney statistic). Differences in proportions of treatment success associated with each study design for primary therapy (aimed at the patient's principal disease) and secondary therapy (aimed at complications of therapy) and the relation between quality score and treatment gains were also examined	There was a statistically non-significant trend towards larger treatment gains on new primary therapies in non-randomised controlled trials (0.78 for BASs, 0.63 for ECSs, 0.62 for CCTs, 0.56 for RRSs) compared with randomised controlled trials (0.56). For secondary therapies the treatment gain was similar across all study designs (0.54–0.55) except BASs (0.90). Within randomised controlled trials, there was not a significant correlation between quality scores and treatment gains ($r = 0.04$; $P = 0.7$)
Ottenbacher[44]	Sample of randomised controlled trials and non-randomised controlled trials from a systematic search of *N Engl J Med* and *JAMA* (30 articles from each journal, with 50% randomised controlled trials and 50% non-randomised controlled trials) across a variety of medical specialties	Randomised controlled trials were compared with non-randomised controlled trials on treatment effects (measured by standardised mean differences). The standardised mean difference (Cohen's *d* index) estimates the difference between comparison groups in terms of their average standard deviation; for example, a *d* of 0.50 means that 1/2 standard deviation separates the average subject in the two groups	No significant difference was found in standardised mean differences for non-randomised controlled trials (0.23) compared with randomised controlled trials (0.21)

COT = cross over trial; ECS = studies using external controls (from previously published material, often equivalent to historical controls); RRS = study using retrospective review of records ("observational" study); BAS = before and after study. For other abbreviations see table 4.1

19

Table 3

Study	Sample	Comparison	Results
Chalmers *et al*[45]	145 controlled trials of the treatment of acute myocardial infarction, identified through a systematic search	Studies with treatment allocation through non-random assignment, non-concealed random allocation, and concealed random allocation were compared on the frequency of statistically significant (P £0.05) maldistribution of prognostic variables, statistically significant (P£0.05) results, and case fatality rates	There was a 34% maldistribution of prognostic factors in non-randomised controlled trials, 7% in randomised controlled trials with non-concealed allocation, and 3.5% in randomised controlled trials with concealed allocation. 25% of results were statistically significant in non-randomised controlled trials, 11% in randomised controlled trials without concealment of allocation, and 5% in randomised controlled trials with concealed allocation. The average relative risk reduction for mortality was 33% in non-randomised controlled trials, 23% in non-concealed randomised controlled trials, and 3% in randomised controlled trials with concealed allocation. The case fatality rate for the control group was 32% in non-randomised controlled trials; 23% in non-concealed randomised controlled trials, and 16% in randomised controlled trials with concealed allocation. The case fatality rate for treatment groups was 21% in non-randomised controlled trials, 18% in non-concealed randomised controlled trials, and 16% in randomised controlled trials with concealed allocation
Schulz *et al*[34]	250 randomised controlled trials from 33 meta analyses from The Cochrane Pregnancy and Childbirth Database	The association between four methodological features of randomised controlled trials (allocation concealment, sequence generation, complete follow up after randomisation and double blinding), and treatment effects (measured by the odds ratio) was examined	The treatment effect (odds ratio) was exaggerated by 41% in "randomised controlled trials" with inadequate allocation concealment and by 30% in "randomised controlled trials" in which the adequacy of allocation concealment was unclear (P<0.001, after adjustment for other methodological features). The odds ratio was exaggerated by 17% in studies without double blinding compared with studies with adequate double blinding (P = 0.01). The difference in odds ratios for randomised controlled trials that excluded patients from the analysis compared with randomised controlled trials that did not exclude patients was non-significant (7%, 95% confidence interval –6% to 21%)

For abbreviations see tables 4.1 and 4.2.

19

believe this accounts for the remarkable success of some of the less gifted, but more credulous members of our profession, and also for the violent dislike of statistics and controlled tests which fashionable and successful doctors are accustomed to display"[16]

Aspects of the style and content of communication between those providing and those receiving care can influence the effects of care.[17] Over the past three decades, there have been changes in the nature and the content of the interaction between those providing and those receiving care.[18] One of these changes has resulted from externally imposed requirements of professionals to admit their uncertainty about the effects of treatment to their patients, and to provide them with uniform, detailed, and unsolicited information about the alternative forms of care concerned, including details of possible side effects. These requirements about informed consent have been applied selectively, such that they are far more likely to accompany treatments prescribed within the context of randomised trials than they are to accompany prescription of identical forms of care in other kinds of formal treatment comparisons— for example, comparisons using concurrent but non-randomised controls, or care given outside the context of formal comparisons.

Differential imposition of these requirements may result in the psychological effects of care within randomised comparisons being different from those made within other kinds of formal comparisons, particularly if these "setting variables" are effect modifiers of the specific treatments being evaluated.[19,20] In some circumstances, and for some outcomes, a feeling of "specialness" may result from knowing that one is participating in a formal treatment evaluation. This may have beneficial psychological effects, and these, in turn, may be reflected in improved outcome of treatment, even expressed in terms of physical outcomes.[21] In other circumstances, explicit acknowledgement of uncertainty may result in the loss of potentially important placebo effects; indeed, adverse effects of treatment may result from symptom suggestion.

These *de facto* characteristics of treatment comparisons based on randomised groups are not associated with random allocation *per se*. Rather, they reflect an illogical, externally imposed double standard which results in some patients receiving less information and in different ways than others about the relative merits, demerits, and uncertainties about alternative forms of care.[22] But they may have consequences for the interpretation of the results of formal treatment comparisons. For many people the confident professional certainty which is typical of everyday practice constitutes a more effective form of care than the explicit admission of professional uncertainty that is required of those who are providing care within the context of a randomised trial. The operation of this irrational double standard may result in the psychological effects of care within randomised

controlled comparisons being atypical, and thus less generalisable than they might otherwise be.

Limited generalisability due to selected patient populations participating in randomised controlled trials has long been considered an important problem, but the effects on generalisability of different information given to patients in the context of randomised controlled trials compared with daily practice and effects on generalisability of other "setting" factors which influence the expectancy of patients have not received much attention. However, empirical evidence exists demonstrating these phenomena,[20] illustrated by the following examples:

In a randomised trial in general practice, patients presenting with symptoms but no abnormal physical signs, in whom no firm diagnosis could be made, were more satisfied with care and more likely to experience symptomatic improvement after a "positive" consultation (with a confident assurance that the symptoms would disappear in a few days), than control patients who received a "neutral" consultation (in which the doctor admitted that he could not be certain what was wrong or whether his prescribed treatment would have any effect).[23] In another trial, involving women undergoing termination of pregnancy, it was found that, compared with an egalitarian style of consultation, a paternalistic approach not only prompted women to have greater confidence in the physician, but also resulted in them reporting less discomfort during the procedure.[24] Other evidence confirms the importance of psychological and educational factors in mediating the effects of care.[25] The presence of a support person during childbirth, for example, has dramatic effects on the need for analgesics, anaesthetics, episiotomy, caesarian section, and on maternal depression after childbirth.[26]

The extent to which these phenomena compromise the generalisability of results of randomised controlled trials is unknown; but this is certainly an issue which needs to be addressed more actively than hitherto. We believe this should occur at two levels. Firstly, the public must discuss whether continued acquiescence in the double standard currently operated on informed consent to treatment is defensible. We believe that there should be a single standard across the board. Secondly, researchers must decide how best to design empirical research to assess the effects of the double standard, and of other setting characteristics. This would require, as a first step, more detailed description and reporting of setting and information characteristics in reports of randomised controlled trials.

Discussion

We were prompted to write this article because we were concerned about unfruitful polarisation in current debates on evaluation of interventions, illustrated, on the one hand, by the view that "randomised trials are the only effective way to validate treatment options",[27] and on the other, the rejection of randomised controlled

19

trials, both by social scientists[28–31] and by some medical scientists.[32–33] These polarised viewpoints provide good theatre but a poor basis for making decisions about health and social care. The particular strength of randomisation is the ability to generate unbiased comparison groups. Other research designs are also important, including qualitative research to help elucidate the mechanisms through which interventions may have or fail to have their effects.[34] Those who promote the naive view that randomised trials provide the only secure way of detecting important effects of interventions also overlook the fact that other study designs are often needed to detect rare but important adverse effects of interventions.[35–36] Polemics about the perceived limitations or strengths of randomised experiments are as unhelpful as polemics about the perceived limitations or strengths of any other of the variety of methodological approaches which should be deployed by people seeking valid estimates of the differential effects of health and social care.

We believe that the quality of debate about how to generate reliable comparison groups to assess the relative merits of alternative forms of social and medical care would improve if those involved made greater efforts to seek relevant empirical evidence. We are certainly willing to make a contribution to these efforts. What is clear from empirical investigations is that different ways of generating comparison groups tend to yield different results, and thus different conclusions about the value and safety of health care and social interventions. Studies using strict randomisation to generate comparison groups tend to yield less dramatic estimates of the effects of care than studies using non-randomised control groups.[11,37]

As Susser has pointed out, "Our many errors show that the practice of causal inference … remains an art. Although to assist us we have acquired analytical techniques, statistical methods and conventions, and logical criteria, ultimately the conclusions we reach are a matter of judgement."[38] Given that one will always be faced with the need to make judgements in making causal inferences about the effects of health and social care, which logical criteria should we deploy in our attempts to maximise the potential benefits and minimise the potential harm done to people who look to professionals for help?

We are not aware of any empirical evidence which would lead us to reject the hierarchy—with randomised experiments at the top—which has been proposed repeatedly by social and medical scientists over the past three decades. Most drug regulatory authorities established to protect the public interest require evidence from studies which have used random allocation to generate the comparison groups. We endorse the judgement upon which this is based and we believe that those who promote any relaxation of this standard in respect of other forms of health and social care should be required to show how their proposals are more likely to increase the beneficial effects and decrease the harmful effects of well intentioned health and social care. A great deal is at stake—the health and welfare of people who have looked to health professionals and social workers for help.

Acknowledgements

We thank Doug Altman, Clare Bradley, Ann Oakley, and William Silverman for comments on draft versions of this chapter. This does not necessarily mean that they endorse all elements of our analysis and conclusions.

References

1 Silverman WA. Human experimentation: a guided step into the unknown. Oxford: Oxford University Press, 1980.

2 Fischer J. Is casework effective? A review. *Social Work* 1973;**17**:1–5.

3 Macdonald G, Sheldon B. Contemporary studies of the effectiveness of social work. *British Journal of Social Work* 1992;**22**:615–43.

4 Office of Technology Assessment. *Identifying health technologies that work*. Washington DC: Congress of the United States, 1994:1–308.

5 McCord J. A thirty year follow-up of treatment effects. *Am Psychol* 1978;**33**:284–9.

6 Moore AJ. *Deadly medicine*. New York: Simon and Schuster, 1995.

7 Black N. Why we need observational studies to evaluate the effectiveness of health care. *BMJ* 1996;**312**:1215–18.

8 Ellenberg JH. Cohort studies. Selection bias in observational and experimental studies. *Stat Med* 1994;**13**:557–67.

9 Segelov E, Tattersall MHN, Coates AS. Redressing the balance—The ethics of *not* entering an eligible patient on a randomised clinical trial. *Ann Oncol* 1992;**3**:103–5.

10 Campbell DR, Stanley JC. *Experimental and quasi-experimental designs for research*. Chicago: Rand McNally, 1963.

11 Soumerai SB, McLaughlin TJ, Avorn J. Improving drug prescribing in primary care: a critical analysis of the experimental literature. *Milbank Q* 1989;**67**:268–317.

12 Canadian Task Force on the Periodic Health Examination. The periodic health examination. *Can Med Assoc J* 1979;**121**:1193–254.

13 US Department of Health and Human Services, Public Health Service, Office of the Assistant Secretary for Health, Office of Disease Prevention and Health Promotion, Preventive Services Task Force. *Guide to clinical preventive services*. Baltimore MD: Williams and Wilkins, 1989.

14 Guyatt GH, Sackett DL, Sinclair JC, Hayward R, Cook DJ, Cook RJ, for the Evidence-Based Medicine Working Group. User's guides to the medical literature. IX. A method for grading health care recommendations. *JAMA* 1995;**274**:1800–4.

15 Commonwealth Department of Human Services and Health. *Guidelines for the pharmaceutical industry on preparation of submissions to the pharmaceutical benefits advisory committee*. Canberra, Australia: Commonwealth Department of Human Services and Health, 1995.

16 Asher R. *Talking sense*. London: Pitman Medical, 1972.

17 Luborsky L, McLellan T, Woody GE, O'Brien CP. Therapist success and its determinants. *Arch Gen Psychiatry* 1985;**42**:602–11.

18 Silverman WA, Altman DG. Patients' preferences and randomised trials. *Lancet* 1996;**347**:171–4.

19 Bradley C. Clinical trials—time for a paradigm shift? *Diabet Med* 1988;**5**:107–9.

20 Kleijnen J, de Craen AJM, van Everdingen J, Krol L. Placebo effect in double-blind clinical trials: a review of interactions with medications. *Lancet* 1994;**344**:1347–9.

21 Kramer MS, Shapiro SH. Scientific challenges in the application of randomized controlled trials. *JAMA* 1984;**252**:2739–45.

22 Chalmers I, Silverman WA. Professional and public double standards on clinical experimentation. *Control Clin Trials* 1987;**8**:388–91.

23 Thomas KB. General practice consultations: is there any point in being positive? *BMJ* 1987;**294**:1200–2.

24 LeBaron S, Reyher J, Stack JM. Paternalistic vs egalitarian physician styles: the treatment of patients in crisis. *J Fam Pract* 1985;**21**:56–62.

25 Devine EC, Cook TD. A meta-analytic analysis of effects of psychoeducational interventions on length of postsurgical hospital stay. *Nurs Res* 1983;**32**:267–74.

26 Hodnett ED. Support from caregivers during childbirth. In: Enkin MW, Keirse MJNC, Renfrew MJ, Neilson JP, Crowther C, eds. *Pregnancy and childbirth module of the Cochrane database of systematic reviews*, 1996 [updated 29 February 1996] . Available in the Cochrane Library from BMJ Publishing Group: London.

27 British Medical Association. *Medical ethics today*. London: BMA, 1993:209.

28 Cheetham J, Fuller R, McIvor G, Petch A. *Evaluating social work effectiveness*. Buckingham: Open University Press, 1992.

29 Hunter D. Let's hear it for R&D. *Health Service Journal* 1993;**15**:17.

30 Nutbeam D, Smith C, Calford J. Evaluation in health education: a review of progress, possibilities and problems. *J Epidemiol Community Health* 1990;**44**:83–9.

31 Stecher BM, Davis WA. *How to focus an evaluation*. Newbury Park, CA: Sage Publications, 1987.

32 Charlton BG. Randomised clinical trials: the worst kind of epidemiology? *Nat Med* 1995;**1**:1101–2.

33 Herman J. The demise of the randomised controlled trial. *J Clin Epidemiol* 1995;**48**:985–8.

34 Oakley A. *Social support and motherhood*. Oxford: Blackwell, 1991.

35 Venning GR. The validity of anecdotal reports of suspected adverse drug reactions—the problem of false alarms. *BMJ* 1982;**284**:249–52.

36 Chalmers I. Evaluating the effects of care during pregnancy and childbirth. In: Chalmers I, Enkin M, Keirse MJNC, eds. *Effective care in pregnancy and childbirth*. Oxford: Oxford University Press, 1989:3–38.

37 Schulz KF, Chalmers I, Hayes RJ, Altman DG. Empirical evidence of bias: dimensions of methodological quality associated with estimates of treatment effects in controlled trials. *JAMA* 1995;**273**:408–12.

38 Susser M. Causal thinking in practice: strengths and weaknesses of the clinical vantage point. *Pediatrics* 1984;**74**:842–9.

39 Chalmers TC, Matta RJ, Smith H, Jr., Kunzler AM. Evidence favoring the use of anticoagulants in the hospital phase of acute myocardial infarction. *N Engl J Med* 1977; **297**:1091–6.

40 Sacks H, Chalmers TC, Smith HJ. Randomized versus historical controls for clinical trials. *Am J Med* 1982;**72**:233–40.

41 Diehl LF, Perry DJ. A comparison of randomized concurrent control groups with matched historical control groups: are historical controls valid? *J Clin Oncol* 1986;**4**:1114–20.

42 Colditz GA, Miller JN, Mosteller F. How study design affects outcomes in comparisons of therapy. I: Medical. *Stat Med* 1989;**8**:441–54.

43 Miller JN, Colditz GA, Mosteller F. How study design affects outcomes in comparisons of therapy. II: Surgical. *Stat Med* 1989;**8**:455–66.

44 Ottenbacher K. Impact of random assignment on study outcome: an empirical examination. *Control Clin Trials* 1992;**13**:50–61.

45 Chalmers TC, Celano P, Sacks HS, Smith H, Jr. Bias in treatment assignment in controlled clinical trials. *N Engl J Med* 1983;**309**:1358–61.

19

These guidelines were first published by the Medical Research Council and are reproduced by permission of the MRC

MRC GUIDELINES FOR GOOD CLINICAL PRACTICE IN CLINICAL TRIALS

This document provides guidelines for good clinical practice (GCP) in MRC trials. During 1998 it will be sent to all the Principal Investigators of MRC trials. The guidelines will be re-issued during 1999 incorporating necessary modifications from feedback received.

Trials sponsored by industry are required to follow the International Conference on Harmonisation's Good Clinical Practice Guideline (ICH GCP). However, there are many other funders of clinical trials in the public and charity sectors who will have an interest in maintaining standards of GCP in their trials. Clearly there is an opportunity to produce a single set of guidelines for this purpose and during 1998 the MRC will consult widely with these organisations with a view to agreeing a unified approach. The present document has already been drafted in close consultation with the NHS Research and Development Programme.

Medical Research Council
20 Park Crescent
London
W1N 4AL

March 1998

CONTENTS

INTRODUCTION

About the medical research council (MRC)

The MRC is the largest public sector organisation in the UK responsible for directly funding research relating to human health. It is funded mainly by the UK government, but is independent in its choice of which research to support. The aim of the MRC is to improve health by funding research across the spectrum of biomedical science. It supports research in three main ways: through its research establishments, via response-mode awards to universities and through training and career development awards. The competition for funds is vigorous and the portfolio of research supported, which has all been the subject of rigorous independent peer review, is therefore of high quality.

The MRC recognises the importance of the randomised controlled trial as the optimum methodology for assessing the effects of particular interventions on defined outcome measures. Its portfolio includes a large number of trials aimed at the assessment of health interventions used in the promotion of health, the prevention and/or treatment of disease and in rehabilitation or long-term care.

Aim of these guidelines

As a funder of research, the MRC needs to be assured that those who conduct research it has funded involving human participants agree to adhere to guidelines that safeguard study participants and ensure that the data gathered are of high quality. This needs to be done without destroying the essential element of trust that underpins all research funding, or adding a cumbersome layer of bureaucracy that stifles legitimate research activity. The guidelines are based on the thirteen principles laid down in the ICH Harmonised Tripartite Guideline for Good Clinical Practice agreed in May 1996[1].

The scientific integrity of the trial and the credibility of the data produced depend primarily on the trial design and not solely on the accuracy of the data collected. A properly randomised trial will ensure no foreknowledge of the random treatment allocations, no bias in patient management, unbiased outcome assessment, and no post-randomisation exclusions. The appropriateness and quality of the trial design will be carefully considered at the peer-review stage and this document does not attempt to provide detailed guidelines on trial design. However, it does provide guidelines on appropriate conduct of a trial to ensure the accuracy of the data gathered.

The Council expects that this framework for good practice will be implemented in all MRC-funded trials that involve human participants, including all trials involving medicinal products. MRC trials involving investigational medicinal products in which the resulting data are likely to be pivotal in a subsequent licensing application may also need to follow the ICH Guideline. Under these circumstances it is expected that there will be an industrial partner who will fund the extra costs involved.

Scope of these guidelines

Most MRC trials are large comparative studies of established therapies, but these guidelines are designed to be used in any prospective study involving human participants and the administration of a treatment or type of management, including diagnosis or the provision of lifestyle (eg, dietary) advice. However, the MRC also funds non-trial-research involving human participants and the detailed guidance contained in this document may be overly complex for the methodologies used in this type of research. The MRC is therefore drafting separate guidelines for this type of non-trial-research and decisions on which guidelines to follow will be made at the peer-review stage.

Responsibility for the conduct of MRC-funded trials

Most MRC trials are funded through grants awarded to host institutions (universities, medical schools, hospital trusts) in response to applications submitted by a principal investigator(s) (PIs) who has(ve) designed and will ultimately run the trial. This document details the responsibilities of those involved in MRC-funded trials, and provides guidelines on appropriate mechanisms to oversee the trial. A brief summary of their roles is given below.

The MRC Role – Before awarding a grant to support a trial, the MRC will ensure that: the proposed trial design is of the highest scientific quality; due consideration has been given to ethical and safety issues; the PI and Host Institution agree to conduct the trial to the standard of GCP; and appropriate arrangements for the day-to-day management and independent supervision of the study have been proposed. Once the trial is underway the MRC will monitor progress of the trial through consideration of annual reports and may wish to carry out random audits of individual studies.

The Host Institution Role – When a trial is funded through a grant, the organisation receiving the grant is known as the Host Institution. As the organisation in receipt of the funds for conducting the trial and as the employer of the PI, the Host Institution has a responsibility for ensuring that the trial is run to the highest standards as laid out in these guidelines. This responsibility is accepted by the Host Institution when it accepts the terms and conditions of the MRC award. Although the exact level of involvement will depend on the trial and the institution involved, it is expected that Department Heads and Deans of Medicine should ensure that the arrangements for trial management include an element of independent advice. In addition, and as a minimum, they should: a) be aware of trials run through their departments; b) be aware of progress in each of these trials; c) be aware of any problems and complaints associated with these trials; and d) work with the PIs and MRC to resolve these problems and complaints. For trials funded through MRC Units or Trials Offices, the MRC is the Host Institution.

The Principal Investigator's Role – The Principal Investigator has overall responsibility for the design, conduct, analyses and reporting of the trial.

The Investigator's Role – The Investigator has responsibility for the conduct of the trial in his/her participating centre.

Independent Supervision of the Trial – Arrangements for the management of trials will vary according to the nature of the study proposed. However, all should include an element of expert advice that is entirely independent of the Principal Investigators and the Host Institution involved. This will normally take the form of a Trial Steering Committee (TSC) and an independent Data and Monitoring and Ethics Committee (DMEC). It is recognised that these arrangements may not always be appropriate and structures may need to vary according to the nature of the study and the Host Institution involved. Thus, the arrangements for supervision should be detailed and justified in the trial proposal and the MRC should satisfy itself that these are appropriate in the light of the risks involved.

When TSCs and DMECs are appropriate:

The Trial Steering Committee Role –
The role of the TSC is to provide overall supervision for the trial. It should also provide advice through its independent Chairman to the PI(s), the MRC and the

20

Host Institution on all aspects of the trial. Involvement of independent members who are not directly involved in other aspects of the trial provides protection for both trial participants and PIs.

The Data and Ethics Monitoring Committee Role – The DMEC is the only body involved in the trial that has access to the unblinded comparative data. The role of its members is to monitor these data and make recommendations to the Steering Committee on whether there are any ethical or safety reasons why the trial should not continue. In addition, the DMEC may be asked by the TSC or MRC to consider data emerging from other related studies. If funding is required above the level originally requested, the DMEC may be asked by the PI, TSC or MRC to provide advice and where appropriate information on the data gathered to date in a way that will not unblind the trial. Membership of the DMEC should be completely independent of the PIs, TSC and Host Institution.

These guidelines are designed to be used by: MRC Officers and members of their Boards; Host Institutions in receipt of funding for clinical trials; members of Trial Steering and Data Monitoring and ethics committees; Principal Investigators and those involved in MRC-funded trials. They provide details of where responsibility for different aspects of trial conduct lie.

A statement acknowledging receipt of these guidelines and accepting the responsibilities laid out in them must be signed by a representative of the Host Institution and by the Principal Investigator before funds are made available.

1. GLOSSARY

1.1 Applicable Regulatory Requirements
Any law(s) and regulation(s) addressing the conduct of clinical trials of investigational products.

1.2 Audit
A systematic and independent examination of trial-related activities and documents to determine whether the evaluated trial-related activities were conducted, and the data were recorded, analysed and accurately reported according to the protocol, standard operating procedures (SOPs), Good Clinical Practice (GCP), and the applicable regulatory requirement(s).

1.3 Case Report Form (CRF)
A printed, optical, or electronic document designed to record all of the protocol required information to be reported to the Principal Investigator/co-ordinating centre on each trial participant.

1.4 Confidentiality
Prevention of disclosure, to other than authorised individuals, of a participant's identity.

1.5 Host Institution
University or hospital that is in receipt of a grant from the MRC for the purposes of running a trial. In the case of trials funded through MRC Units or Trials Offices the Host Institution will be the MRC itself.

1.6 Investigator
The person responsible for conducting a trial at one of the trial sites.

1.7 Monitoring
The act of overseeing the progress of a clinical trial, and of ensuring that it is conducted and recorded in accordance with the protocol, Standard Operating Procedures (SOPs), Good Clinical Practice (GCP), and the applicable regulatory requirement(s).

1.8 Multicentre Trial
A clinical trial conducted according to a single protocol but at more than one site, and therefor, carried out by more than one investigator.

1.9 Principal Investigator(s)
The person(s) who is/are responsible for: a) initiating the trial by applying to the MRC for support; and b) conduct of the trial on a daily basis.

1.10 Protocol
A document that describes the objective(s), design, methodology, statistical considerations, and organisation of a trial. The protocol usually also gives the background and rationale for the trial, but these could be provided in other protocol referenced documents. Throughout these Guidelines the term protocol refers to protocol and protocol amendments.

1.11 Protocol Amendment
A written description of a change(s) to or formal clarification of a protocol.

1.12 Quality Assurance (QA)
All those actions that are established to ensure that the trial is performed and the data are generated, documented (recorded), and reported in compliance with these guidelines for Good Clinical Practice (GCP) and the applicable regulatory requirements.

1.13 Quality Control (QC)
The operational techniques and activities undertaken within the quality assurance system to verify that the requirements for quality of the trial-related activities have been fulfilled.

1.14 Randomisation
The process of assigning trial participants to treatment or control groups using an element of chance to determine the assignments in order to reduce bias.

1.15 Serious Adverse Event (SAE)

Any untoward medical occurrence that at any dose:
- results in death,
- is life-threatening,
- requires inpatient hospitalisation or prolongation of existing hospitalisation,
- results in persistent or significant disability/incapacity, **or**
- is a congenital anomaly/birth defect.

1.16 Sponsor

That person/organisation taking responsibility for the initiation, management and financing of a trial. Sponsorship of MRC trials is shared between the Principal Investigator (initiation and management) and the MRC (finance).

1.17 Participant/Trial Participant

An individual who participates in a clinical trial, either as a recipient of the investigational procedure or product(s) or as a control.

1.18 Trial Management Group

A group set up by the PIs to manage the trial on a day-to-day basis

1.19 Trial Site

The location(s) where trial-related activities are actually conducted.

1.20 Trial Steering Committee

A Committee formed to provide overall supervision for the trial. Membership should include one or two PIs, one or two independent experts and an independent Chair as well as observers from the MRC and Host Institution

2. THE PRINCIPLES OF GOOD CLINICAL PRACTICE FOR MRC-FUNDED TRIALS

The principles for Good Clinical Practice in MRC-funded trials are the same as those laid down in the ICH Harmonised Tripartite Guideline for Good Clinical Practice agreed in May 1996[1]. However, the principles have been qualified to allow for exceptional circumstances pertaining to the nature of publicly funded research and the health system in the UK.

2.1. Clinical trials should be conducted in accordance with the ethical principles that have their origin in the Declaration of Helsinki (appendix 1) and are consistent with GCP and the applicable regulatory requirement(s).

2.2. Before a trial is initiated, foreseeable risks and inconveniences should be weighed against the anticipated benefit for the individual trial participant and society. A trial should be initiated and continued only if the benefits justify the risks.

2.3. The rights, safety and well-being of the trial participants are the most important consideration and should prevail over interests of science and society.

2.4. The available non-clinical and clinical information on an investigational product should be adequate to support the proposed trial.

2.5. Clinical trials should be scientifically sound and described in a clear detailed protocol.

2.6. A trial should be conducted in compliance with the protocol that has received prior Ethical Committee favourable opinion.

2.7. The medical care given to, and medical decisions made on behalf of, participants should always be the responsibility of a qualified physician or, when appropriate, a qualified dentist.*

2.8. Each individual involved in conducting a trial should be qualified by education, training, and experience to perform his or her respective task(s).

2.9. Freely given informed consent should be obtained from every participant prior to clinical trial participation**.

2.10. All clinical trial information should be recorded, handled, and stored in a way that allows its accurate reporting, interpretation and verification.

2.11. The confidentiality of records that could identify participants should be protected, respecting the privacy and confidentiality rules in accordance with the applicable regulatory requirement(s).

2.12. Investigational products should be manufactured, handled, and stored in accordance with Good Manufacturing Practice (GMP)***. They should be used in accordance with the approved protocol.

2.13. Systems with procedures that ensure the quality of every aspect of the trial should be implemented.

In the UK there may be situations where it would be appropriate for other qualified health care professionals, such as midwives etc to be responsible for patient care.

** *Situations do exist in which fully informed consent may not possible (eg emergency settings). In these cases, procedures agreed in existing guidelines (see text) should be followed, provided favourable opinion has been given by the appropriate independent ethics committee.*

*** *Or the appropriate guidelines for the manufacture of medicinal products.*

3. THE MEDICAL RESEARCH COUNCIL

3.1 Peer Review of scientific, ethical and management arrangements

3.1.1 The MRC procedures for peer-review of proposals for trials require that an application is submitted in a structured format (see Appendix 2) that ensures that all the information required to judge whether a trial will be conducted according to the principles detailed in 2 above will be provided. In peer reviewing the proposals for a new trial the MRC should satisfy itself based on the information available that:

20

3.1.2 The proposed trial is scientifically sound, designed to produce results which are sufficiently reliable for the purposes of the trial, clearly described and feasible.

3.1.3 Any foreseeable risks and inconveniences have been weighed against the anticipated benefit for the individual trial participant and society and the benefits of the proposed trial justify the risks;

3.1.4 The principal investigator(s) are competent to undertake the proposed trial. The applicants for any proposed trial should be able to demonstrate an adequate track record appropriate to their role in the trial;

3.1.5 The proposals include details of the trial team that includes the key disciplines necessary for all aspects of the design and implementation of the trial, as well as the clear allocation of responsibilities within the trial;

3.1.6 Arrangements for the management of trials should include an element of expert advice that is entirely independent from the Principal Investigator(s) and the Host Institution. The model presented in these guidelines is for a Trial Steering Committee with an independent Chair and an independent Data Monitoring and Ethics Committee. However, it is recognised that the exact arrangements for supervision may need to vary according to the nature of the study, the Host Institution and the risks involved. Therefore, detailed arrangements for trial management should be presented as part of the proposal for funding and the MRC should satisfy itself that these are appropriate to the trial proposed;

3.1.7 The proposals include appropriate resources (including facilities) to conduct and complete (including adequate follow up) the research according to the trial protocol, and the monitoring of resource use during the trial;

3.1.8 The proposal details the availability of adequate and competent support staff and appropriate facilities for the duration of the trial;

3.1.9 The proposal states that all potential trial participants will be informed whenever possible of the possible benefits and known risks of the intervention (or of no intervention or a placebo) and of the possibility that there are unknown risks;

3.1.10 The proposal states that freely given informed consent will be sought from every participant prior to clinical trial participation whenever possible. When fully informed consent is not possible (eg, emergency settings), consent procedures should be fully justified, existing guidelines (referred to in 5.4.3) should be followed, and a favourable opinion from the appropriate ethics committee should be supplied;

3.1.11 Any necessary approval has been, or will be, obtained from the relevant ethical and regulatory bodies before the trial's implementation (see Note 1);

3.1.12 The publication policy proposed will report the results of the trial within an appropriate time scale of the findings being available and that adequate plans are in place to disseminate and implement the results of the proposed trial;

3.1.13 The time period proposed by the PI for retention of relevant trial documentation is appropriate.

3.2 Award of funds

If funding is agreed in principle by the MRC, the MRC ensures that the award will be contingent on:

3.2.1 A written undertaking being given by the Host Institution and Principal Investigator that they will conduct the trial in accordance with the general MRC terms and conditions of an award and these GCP guidelines.

3.3 Monitoring and audit of progress

Once the trial has started the MRC may:

3.3.1 consider reports from the Host Institution, TSC and DMEC when appropriate;

3.3.2 carry out a random audit of a number of randomly selected MRC-funded trials annually.

4. THE HOST INSTITUTION

4.1 As the organisation in receipt of the funds for conducting the trial and as the employer of the PI, the Host Institution has a responsibility to ensure that the trial is run to the highest standards as laid out in these guidelines. This responsibility is accepted by the Host Institution when it agrees to accept the terms and conditions of the MRC award. In particular the Host Institution must:

4.1.2 ensure that the trial is conducted in accordance with the general MRC terms and conditions, these GCP guidelines and with the specified protocol, and according to the proposed schedule of resource use and the requirements of other relevant regulatory bodies;

4.1.3 ensure that appropriate arrangements for the management of the research are in place. These should include an element of expert advice that is entirely independent from the PIs and the Host Institution itself. These arrangements will have been proposed by the PI and approved by the MRC. If these arrangements include a TSC, the MRC regards it as good practice for a representative of the Host Institution to be appointed as an observer on the TSC;

4.1.4 make a commitment to maintain, for the trial's duration, the key disciplines for all aspects of the design and implementation of the trial;

4.1.5 permit monitoring, auditing and inspection (see section 8 below);

4.1.6 provide appropriate facilities for all the relevant documentation as laid out in section 7, to be kept for the appropriate period;

4.1.7 ensure that a Report is submitted to the MRC annually.

4.1.8 It is expected that Department Heads and Deans of Medicine should as a minimum requirement: a) be aware of trials run through their departments; b) be aware of progress in each of these trials; c) be aware of any problems, complaints or claims associated with these trials; and d) work with the PIs and MRC to resolve these problems, complaints or claims. However, the level of direct involvement required from the Host Institution in any one trial may vary and will depend on the type of trial and the institution involved.

4.1.9 In the case of trials funded through MRC Units or Trials Offices the Host Institution will be the MRC itself.

5. THE PRINCIPAL INVESTIGATOR AND PARTICIPATING INVESTIGATORS

This section details the responsibilities of those involved in the running of the trial on a day-to-day basis. The practices detailed here should be followed by all those involved in the recruitment and follow-up of trial participants. With respect to multicentre trials, the Principal Investigator has overall responsibility for the conduct of the trial and this role is specified accordingly.

The Principal Investigator has overall responsibility for design of the proposed trial and co-ordination and the day-to-day management of the trial. The PI must ensure that: 1) the trial is run in accordance with these guidelines; and 2) all the investigators involved are aware and adhere to these guidelines.

5.1 Trial management

5.1.1 The PI is responsible for the day-to-day running of all aspects of the trial and for managing the trial budget

5.1.2 The PI should ensure that all the investigators involved in the trial conduct the trial in accordance with the proposal funded by the MRC and the specified final protocol (as approved by the TSC), and according to the proposed schedule of resource use as submitted in the original application.

5.1.3 The PI should ensure that all Participating Investigators are aware of their responsibilities as laid out in these guidelines and that the trial follows these guidelines in all the participating centres.

5.1.4 The PI should ensure that appropriate systems and procedures that assure the appropriate quality of every aspect of the trial are in place.

5.1.5 The PI should ensure that all the persons involved in implementing the protocol are adequately informed about the protocol, the nature of the intervention and their trial-related duties.

5.1.6 The PI should ensure that all trial-related functions are clearly defined, allocated and documented and that the responsibilities of participating investigators are clearly understood. It is good practice for the PI to produce a standard investigator agreement that lays out the terms and conditions of centre participation and is signed by the Participating Investigator.

5.1.7 The PI should ensure that clear lines of communication are established between investigators.

5.1.8 It is good practice for the PI to nominate a dedicated trial co-ordinator with clearly defined duties, in particular to ensure that recruitment targets are met.

5.1 9 The PI should manage the resources for the trial in a way that maximises the chances of the trial finishing within the available funding.

5.1.10 The PI should call meetings of the TSC (or the agreed alternative source of independent advice) when there are any matters arising from the conduct or management of the trial that might require their advice.

5.1.11 The PI should submit an annual report to the MRC. This should be endorsed by the TSC (or alternative source of independent advice).

5.1.12 The PI should ensure that, on completion of the study, the results are analysed, written up, reported and disseminated. All MRC trials should be registered at the time of approval and publication with a current trial register. Trials should be submitted to a peer-reviewed journal irrespective of the result of the trial.

5.2 Compliance with protocol

5.2.1 The trial should be conducted in accordance with the proposal funded by the MRC (and the protocol approved by the TSC) and favourably reviewed by the relevant ethics committees. It is the ultimate responsibility of the Principal Investigator to ensure that this happens. Any material amendments or alterations to or deviations from the protocol which affect the scientific or ethical basis of the trial, which could affect the personal integrity and/or welfare of trial participants, or which could have resource implications must have approval of the relevant ethics committees and the Trial Steering Committee (or the agreed alternative source of independent advice) before their implementation. The MRC should be notified of all material changes.

5.3 Medical care of trial participants

5.3.1 The current revision of the Declaration of Helsinki (Appendix 1) is the accepted basis for clinical trial ethics and must be known and implemented by those engaged in research involving human participants. The personal integrity and welfare of the trial participants is the ultimate responsibility of the doctor responsible for their care.

5.3.2 The medical care given to, and medical decisions made on behalf of, participants should always be the responsibility of a qualified doctor or, when appropriate, a qualified dentist or other qualified health care professional. It is the responsibility of the PI to ensure that the trial is organised in a way that ensures that appropriately qualified staff are responsible for patient care.

5.4 Respect for trial participants and informed consent

5.4.1 The principles of informed consent in the current revision of the Helsinki Declaration (Appendix 1) and those laid out in the 13 principles at the beginning of this document should be implemented in all RCTs.

5.4.2 Whenever possible, all participants, or their representative(s), must give their consent to participate in the trial on the basis of appropriate information and with adequate time to consider this information and ask questions. The participant's consent to participate should be obtained through signing an appropriate consent form and should be available, if necessary, for verification. Situations do exist in which fully informed consent is not possible (eg, emergency settings). In these cases, procedures agreed in the guidelines referred to in 5.4.3 should be followed after favourable opinion from the appropriate ethics committee. If any changes

20

to the protocol are made (ref 5.2.1 above), then the need for changes to the patient information leaflet should be considered and, if appropriate, implemented without delay.

5.4.3 In the case of children up to the age of 18, mentally incapacitated individuals who cannot give full informed consent and the unconscious, particular considerations apply. The Council's guidance on these is set out in the relevant MRC Ethic Series publications[2]. The Health Department, LREC and Royal College of Physicians Guidelines also cover these topics.

5.4.4 If the investigators are aware that participant samples or information for the trial may be used subsequently for other specific purposes beyond the aims of the current study, the participants' consent should also be obtained for such uses.

5.4.5 The participants, (or their representative(s)) must be made aware before consenting to participate that they are free to withdraw without obligation at any time and that such an action will not adversely affect any aspect of their care.

5.4.6 Appropriate information should be provided in a form which is readily accessible (see Note 2) and at a level which will enable an **informed** decision by the trial participants or their representative(s) regarding participation in the trial. It is good practice and can prove helpful to seek advice from consumers/lay people when drafting this information.

5.4.7 The written information about the trial that is to be provided to the participants will usually have been considered by the MRC as part of the overall assessment of the trial, and always by relevant ethics committees, and it is the responsibility of the Principal Investigator(s) to ensure that it is used as approved and that any necessary amendments are made without delay.

5.4.8 During the course of the trial results from related studies or interim results from the trial may become available. If these have implications for the ongoing trial, and following consultation with the TSC, the patient information should be changed and trial participants and collaborating investigators should be notified where appropriate. Where feasible, trial participants should also be notified of progress with the trial and the eventual outcome of the trial.

5.4.9 Participants and their GPs should be given a long-term contact point/ source of information about the trial.

5.4.10 It may be appropriate for the Principal Investigator(s) and/or the responsible clinician to inform other clinicians in contact with the participant of their participation in the trial, with appropriate information about relevant aspects of the study.

5.4.11 Participants should have access to information on the complaints procedure outlined in 6.10.1.

5.4.12 The participant should have access to information about the procedures for obtaining compensation and treatment following harm through negligence or non-negligence as a direct result of participating in the trial.

5.5 Communication with LREC/MREC

5.5.1 The MRC has published its own ethics guidelines on aspects of research involving human participants and these should be applied generally in the context of all randomised controlled trials[2]. The following publications are of particular relevance:

- Responsibility in investigations on human participants and material and on personal information
- The ethical conduct of research on the mentally incapacitated
- Responsibility in the use of personal medical information for research – principles and guide to practice
- The ethical conduct of research on children
- The ethical conduct of AIDS vaccine trials
- Principles in the assessment and conduct of medical research and publicising results

5.5.2 All MRC support is contingent on approval being obtained from the relevant Multicentre Research Ethics Committee (MREC), where appropriate, and all Local Research Ethics Committees (LREC) from all Health Authorities in which the trial will be implemented. Centres can only begin recruiting when both the MREC and LREC approvals have been obtained.

5.5.3 Documentation of MREC approval should be submitted to MRC Head Office, and for multicentre trials should also always be available, along with LREC approval, for verification at the co-ordinating centre for the trial.

5.5.4 During the trial the PI should notify, and where necessary seek favourable opinion of, the appropriate MREC/LRECs and the MRC of any material modifications to the trial protocol and patient information leaflet.

5.6 Investigational products

5.6.1 If investigational products are part of the trial intervention they should be manufactured, handled, and stored in accordance with the appropriate guidelines for the manufacture of medicinal products. They should be used in accordance with the approved protocol. Where appropriate, the PIs should seek advice from a suitably experienced pharmacist when planning the trial.

5.7 Randomisation procedures

5.7.1 The PI should ensure that any randomisation procedures are rigorously designed, and identify any possible sources of bias. He/she should ensure that the randomisation procedures are rigorous and strictly controlled and adhered to by all the investigators. If the trial is blinded, investigators should promptly document and explain any premature unblinding.

5.8 Safety reporting

5.8.1 All serious adverse events (SAEs) should be reported to the trial co-ordinating centre in a timely manner in accordance with the protocol and reported regularly to the TSC and DMEC. Where appropriate, and in keeping with the applicable regulatory requirement(s) related to the reporting of serious adverse reactions, these should be reported to the regulatory authorities and, as appropriate, to ethics committees.

5.8.2 Clear procedures should be developed and implemented for the purpose of SAE reporting.

5.9 Data handling and record keeping

5.9.1 The primary objective of good data handling and record keeping is to ensure that data collected on participants in the trial are accurate and complete and unbiased with respect to the study treatment allocation. The procedures and documentation used to ensure that the data contained in the final clinical trial report agree with original observations should be made explicit by, and are the responsibility of, the PI and would normally require some degree of monitoring at the clinical site by the PI.

5.9.2 The PI should ensure that the Case Report Forms (CRF) are designed to capture the required data at all multicentre trial sites and that the information gathered is appropriate to the aims of the trial and will not adversely affect recruitment.

5.9.3 The PI should ensure that the procedures to be followed to ensure that the data are of high quality and accuracy at the point of collection and the integrity of the data during processing are set out. The level of clinical site monitoring necessary will vary from trial to trial and should be agreed between the PI and TSC.

5.9.4 All data and documentation associated with the trial should be readily accessible for independent inspection and validation (see below, Section 8). Ensuring such availability is the responsibility of the Principal Investigator.

5.9.5 The PI should take responsibility for drafting the annual report to the MRC in the format requested for approval by the TSC. The PI and Chairman of the TSC should approve and sign the final report of the trial.

5.9.6 It is essential that data on personal health are treated confidentially and held securely. Where such data are held on computer, the Data Protection Act places legal obligations on those who 'control' such data (eg, the local and principal investigators). In 1995 the EC issued a Directive[3] which will be incorporated into UK law as a new Data Protection Act. The Council has issued guidance on the use of personal information in its Ethics Series.[2] For NHS patients, DH guidance was updated in 1996[4] and there is guidance from the DH and others (eg, the BMA[5]) on computer security systems[6]. These references give further information in a complex area, and new guidelines may follow new legislation in 1997/98.

5.9.7 The PI should ensure that data are recorded and stored in a way that ensures that they are: a) secure and cannot be tampered with, (eg, limited access, lock and key); and b) unlikely to be damaged (eg, appropriate environmental conditions).

5.9.8 The appropriate time period for which patient identification codes should be retained will vary depending on the nature of the study. The PI should justify the proposed retention period in the proposal to the MRC for agreement by the Board.

6. INDEPENDENT SUPERVISION OF THE TRIAL

6.1 Independent advice

6.1.1 Arrangements for the management of trials will vary according to the nature of the study proposed. However, all should include an element of expert advice that is entirely independent from the Principal Investigators and the Host Institution involved. This will normally take the form of a Trial Steering Committee and an independent Data and Monitoring and Ethics Committee. It is recognised that these arrangements may not always be appropriate and structures may need to vary according to the nature of the study and the Host Institution involved. Thus, the arrangements for supervision should be detailed and justified in the trial proposal and the MRC should satisfy itself that these are appropriate to the risks involved.

6.2 The trial steering committee

6.2.1 Membership of Trial Steering Committee Applicants should submit a proposal for membership for the TSC with their full application to the MRC who will agree the final membership. The membership should be limited and include an independent Chairman (not involved directly in the trial other than as a member of the TSC), not less than two other independent members plus one or two Principal Investigators. Trial co-ordinators, statisticians etc. should attend meetings as appropriate. An observer from the MRC and Host Institution should be invited to attend all Steering Committee meetings.

6.3 Steering Committee Meetings

6.3.1 A meeting of the TSC should be organised by the PI before the start of the trial to approve the final protocol, which should then be sent to the MRC. After that the TSC should meet at least annually although there may be periods when more frequent meetings are necessary and maybe called either by the Chairman of the TSC or the PI. Responsibility for calling for and organising Steering Committee meetings lies with the Principal Investigators. However, there may be occasions when the MRC will wish to organise and administer these meetings for particular trials. Papers for meetings should be circulated well in advance of the meeting rather than tabled and an accurate minute of the meeting should be prepared by the PI and agreed by all members.

6.4 Data Monitoring

6.4.1 Applicants should submit their proposed arrangements for overseeing of the trial and for membership for the DMEC with their full application to the MRC, who will consider whether the proposed arrangements are appropriate to the trial and approve membership proposed. The Data Monitoring and Ethics Committee (DMEC) should be established to report to the TSC and when appropriate the MRC. Membership of the DMEC should be completely independent of the trial. Detailed terms of reference and guidance notes are

20

given at annex 3. DMEC meetings should be called for and organised by the PIs with the DMEC Chair. However, attendance by Investigators or Principal Investigators at these meetings should only be at the invitation of the DMEC Chair.

6.5 Trial Steering and Management

6.5.1 The role of the TSC is to provide overall supervision of the trial and ensure that the trial is conducted to the rigorous standards set out in these MRC Guidelines for Good Clinical Practice. In particular, the TSC should concentrate on progress of the trial, adherence to the protocol, patient safety and the consideration of new information. Day-to-day **management** of the trial is the responsibility of the investigators. The PI(s) may wish to set up a separate Trial Management Group to assist with this function.

6.6 Patient Safety

6.6.1 In all the deliberations of the TSC the rights, safety and well-being of the trial participants are the most important considerations and should prevail over the interests of science and society. The TSC should ensure that the protocol demands freely given informed consent from every trial participant. The TSC should look closely at the patient information provided and advise the investigators on its completeness and suitability.

6.7 Progress of the Trial

6.7.1 It is the role of the TSC to monitor the progress of the trial and to maximise the chances of completing it within the time scale agreed by the MRC. At the first TSC meeting, targets for recruitment, data collection, compliance etc. should be agreed with the PIs. These targets should not be "set in stone" but are designed to permit adequate monitoring of trial progress. The TSC should agree which data, based on the targets set, should be presented at each TSC meeting (template attached at appendix 3).

6.7.2 The PI is required to submit an annual report to MRC based on the template provided. This report should be endorsed by the TSC and should be stand alone and contain sufficient data to allow the relevant MRC Board to judge progress in the trial without the need to refer back to the original grant proposal, and inform the MRC of any new information that has a bearing on safety or ethical acceptability of the trial or any significant complaints arising, with a justification of any decisions taken on the matter.

6.6.3 In exceptional circumstances, Council will consider proposals for the extension of grants for clinical trials. In these cases, the Boards will require evidence from TSCs that all practicable steps have been taken to achieve targets and keep within the agreed tenure of the grant. In these cases an analysis of the data collected to date that does not unblind the trial may be requested. If progress of the trial suggests that an extension may be necessary, the TSC should notify MRC officers at the earliest opportunity.

6.8 Adherence to Protocol

6.8.1 The TSC should ensure that there are no major deviations from the trial protocol. A full protocol should be presented as an agenda item at the first TSC meeting. If the PIs need to make any material changes to the protocol during the course of the trial, approval should be sought from the TSC and the LREC/MREC and the MRC should be informed.

6.9 Consideration of New Information

6.9.1 The TSC should consider new information relevant to the trial including reports from the DMEC and the results of other studies. It is the responsibility of the PIs, the TSC Chairman and independent members of the TSC to bring to the attention of the TSC any results from other studies of which they are aware that may have a direct bearing on future conduct of the trial.

6.9.2 On consideration of this information, the TSC should recommend appropriate action, such as changes to the trial protocol, additional patient information, or stopping or extending the study. The rights, safety and well-being of the trial participants (present and future) should be the most important considerations in these deliberations.

6.9.3 It is the responsibility of the investigators to report regularly the extent of serious adverse events to the TSC and DMEC. In the case of unexpected SAEs, the Chairman of the TSC should be notified and, where appropriate, the regulatory authority.

6.10 Dissemination and Implementation of Results

6.10.1 The TSC should ensure that appropriate efforts are made to ensure that the results of the trial are adequately disseminated and due consideration is given to the implementation of the results into clinical practice.

6.11 Complaints Procedure and Compensation for Participants

6.11.1 The TSC should ensure that participants in a trial should have access to information that clearly explains that if they are unhappy with any aspect of the conduct of the trial they can pursue their grievance by taking the matter up with the clinician responsible for their care. Following this, if the problem remains unresolved, they should take it up with the authority responsible for their care. In some circumstances they may wish to take it up with the Chairman of the Trial Steering Committee and, if there is still no resolution, the Chief Executive of the MRC.

6.11.2 The MRC as funder of a trial accepts responsibility for its sponsorship of the trial, and as such would give sympathetic consideration to claims for any non-negligent harm suffered by individuals as a result of participating in the trial. (This would not extend to non-negligent harm arising from conventional treatment where this is one arm of a trial.) Like other publicly funded bodies, the Council is unable to insure and thus cannot offer advance indemnity cover for participants in MRC-funded studies.

6.11.3 Where studies are carried out in a hospital, the hospital continues to have a duty of care to the patient being treated within that hospital, whether or not that patient is participating in an MRC-supported study. Therefore the MRC does not accept liability for negligence on the part of employees of, or staff engaged by, hospitals. This applies whether the hospital is an NHS Trust or not. The MRC cannot be held liable for any breach in the hospital's duty of care.

7. DOCUMENTATION

7.1 The documentation for the trial relates to all records in any form describing the methods and conduct of the trial, factors affecting the trial and action taken. These include, as appropriate, all versions of the protocol and agreed amendments, copies of submissions and approvals from relevant authorities and ethics committees, consent forms, monitor reports, audit reports, relevant letters, reference ranges, raw data such as laboratory reports etc, completed case report forms and the final report. Documentation of the ethics committee approval for the conduct of the trial should be retained by the PIs. In multicentre trials, this may be co-ordinated centrally. Similarly, evidence of informed consent should be available for verification. Written procedures for the scientific basis, design, conduct, organisation and verification of all trials are required. This should be the ultimate responsibility of the Principal Investigator. For those trials using medicinal products where it is clear at the start of the trial that the data may be required for a licensing application, the documentary requirements outlined in the ICH GCP Guideline should be followed. In the majority of MRC trials, in which this is not the case, the actual requirements will vary according to the trial, the type of intervention and whether or not medicinal products are involved. Appendix 4 provides guidance on the retention of key documentation under these circumstances.

7.2 The scientific basis of the trial will usually be in the form of a clear and concise protocol which will also include information on the design, conduct and organisation of the trial. Many of these issues will have been considered in the original proposal for the trial which was submitted for funding. The application procedure for MRC funding for trials now requires submission of full proposals in a structured proforma. Full details are given at appendix 2

7.3 The case report form is the record of the relevant information and data collected during the trial on each participant in the trial as defined by the protocol. The level of detail of information recorded will be defined by the trial in question, with the fundamental principle being to ensure the collection of adequate, relevant and accurate data which are not excessive in quantity and/or detail. Often data are collected on each patient unnecessarily and the quality of the recorded data can be adversely affected as a consequence. In addition, particularly for multicentre trials, collection of excessive data can seriously discourage collaboration and jeopardise the trial overall by undue complication of the trial procedures (while also wasting limited resources). Copies of case report forms after completion should be stored centrally and, if required, should be available for verification. This is the responsibility of the Principal Investigator, who should ensure that these records are retained for the period agreed by the MRC.

8. QUALITY ASSURANCE AND AUDIT

8.1 In order to reassure itself of the reliability of the data gathered and the ethical conduct of its trials, the MRC may audit a randomly selected number of MRC-funded trials.

8.2 Audits will be carried out by individual(s) entirely independent of the trial and the MRC will define the level of audit required on a case-by-case basis depending on the nature of the trial concerned.

8.3 Reports of the audits will be reviewed by the MRC and, if necessary, by the relevant Research Board. Principal Investigators will be given the opportunity to comment on the audit before it is passed on to the relevant Board or TSC. Copies of the reports, together with the comments of the PIs and assessment by the MRC/Board, will be made available to the Principal Investigator and, where relevant, Chairmen of the Steering and Data Monitoring Committees.

20

References

1. International Conference on Harmonisation (ICH) guideline (1996)
2. MRC Ethics Series: Grants and Training Awards: Terms and Conditions of Award
   - Responsibility in investigations on human participants and material and on personal information
   - The ethical conduct of research on the mentally incapacitated
   - Responsibility in the use of personal medical information for research – principles and guide to practice
   - The ethical conduct of research on children
   - The ethical conduct of AIDS vaccine trials
   - Principles in the assessment and conduct of medical research and publicising results
3. EC Directive on Data Protection (1995)
4. The Protection and Use of Patient Information. Department of Health (1996)
5. Security in Clinical Information Systems. British Medical Association (1996)
6. The NHS Security Reference Manual. NHS (1996)

Appendix 1

Declaration of Helsinki

Recommendations Guiding Physicians in Biomedical Research Involving Human Subjects.

Adopted by the 18th World Medical Assembly, Helsinki, Finland, 1964 and amended by the 29th World Medical Assembly, Tokyo, Japan October 1975, the 35th World Medical Assembly, Venice, Italy, October 1983 and the 41st World Medical Assembly, Hong Kong, September 1989 and in South Africa, October 1996.

INTRODUCTION

It is the mission of the physician to safeguard the health of the people. His or her knowledge and conscience are dedicated to the fulfilment of this mission.

The Declaration of Geneva of the World Medical Association binds the physician with the words, "The health of my patient will be my first consideration", and the International Code of Medical Ethics declares that, "A physician shall act only in the patient's interest when providing medical care which might have the effect of weakening the physical and mental condition of the patient".

The purpose of biomedical research involving human subjects must be to improve diagnostic, therapeutic and prophylactic procedures and the understanding of the aetiology and pathogenesis of disease.

In current medical practice most diagnostic, therapeutic or prophylactic procedures involve hazards. This applies especially to biomedical research.

Medical progress is based on research which ultimately must rest in part on experimentation involving human subjects.

In the field of biomedical research a fundamental distinction must be recognised between medical research in which the aim is essentially diagnostic or therapeutic for a patient, and medical research, the essential object of which is purelyscientific and without implying direct diagnostic or therapeutic value to the person subjected to the research.

Special caution must be exercised in the conduct of research which may affect the environment, and the welfare of animals used for research must be respected.

Because it is essential that the results of laboratory experiments be applied to human beings to further scientific knowledge and to help suffering humanity, the World Medical Association has prepared the following recommendations as a guide to every physician in biomedical research involving human subjects. They should be kept under review in the future. It must be stressed that the standards as drafted are only a guide to physicians all over the world. Physicians are not relieved from criminal, civil and ethical responsibilities under the laws of their own countries.

I. BASIC PRINCIPLES

1. Biomedical research involving human subjects must conform to generally accepted scientific principles and should be based on adequately performed laboratory and animal experimentation and on a thorough knowledge of the scientific literature.

2. The design and performance of each experimental procedure involving human subjects should be clearly formulated in an experimental protocol which should be transmitted for consideration, comment and guidance to a specially appointed committee independent of the investigator and the sponsor provided that this independent committee is in conformity with the laws and regulations of the country in which the research experiment is performed.

3. Biomedical research involving human subjects should be conducted only by scientifically qualified persons and under the supervision of a clinically competent medical person. The responsibility for the human subjects must always rest with a medically qualified person and never rest on the subject of the research, even though the subject has given his or her consent.

4. Biomedical research involving human subjects cannot legitimately be carried out unless the importance of the objective is in proportion to the inherent risk to the subject.

5. Every biomedical research project involving human subjects should be preceded by careful assessment of predictable risks in comparison with foreseeable benefits to the subject or to others. Concern for the interests of the subject must always prevail over the interests of science and society.

6. The right of the research subject to safeguard his or her integrity must always be respected. Every precaution should be taken to respect the privacy of the subject and to minimise the impact of the study on the subject's physical and mental integrity and on the personality of the subject.

7. Physicians should abstain from engaging in research projects involving human subjects unless they are satisfied that the hazards involved are believed to be predictable. Physicians should cease any investigation if the hazards are found to outweigh the potential benefits.

8. In publication of the results of his or her research, the physician is obliged to preserve the accuracy of the results. Reports of experimentation not in accordance with the principles laid down in this Declaration should not be accepted for publication.

9. In any research on human beings, each potential subject must be adequately informed of the aims, methods, anticipated benefits and potential hazards of the study and the discomfort it may entail. He or she should be informed that he or she is at liberty to abstain from participation in the study and that he or she is free to withdraw his or her consent to participation at any

20

time. The physician should then obtain the subject's freely-given informed consent, preferably in writing.

10. When obtaining informed consent for the research project the physician should be particularly cautious if the subject is in a dependent relationship to him or her or may consent under duress. In that case the informed consent should be obtained by a physician who is not engaged in the investigation and who is completely independent of his official relationship.

11. In case of legal incompetence, informed consent should be obtained from the legal guardian in accordance with national legislation. Where physical or mental incapacity makes it impossible to obtain informed consent, or when the subject is a minor, permission form the responsible relative replaces that of the subject in accordance with the national legislation.

Whenever the minor child is in fact able to give a consent, the minor's consent must be obtained in addition to the consent of the minor's legal guardian.

12. The research protocol should always contain a statement of the ethical considerations involved and should indicate that the principles enunciated in the present Declaration are complied with.

II. MEDICAL RESEARCH COMBINED WITH PROFESSIONAL CARE (CLINICAL RESEARCH)

1. In the treatment of the sick person, the physician must be free to use a new diagnostic and therapeutic measure, if in his or her judgement it offers hope of saving life, re-establishing health or alleviating suffering.

2. The potential benefits, hazards and discomfort of a new method should be weighed against the advantages of the best current diagnostic and therapeutic methods.

3. In any medical study, every patient – including those of a control group, if any – should be assured of the best proven diagnostic and therapeutic method. This does not exclude the use of inert placebo in studies where no proven diagnostic or therapeutic method exists.

4. The refusal of the patient to participate in a study must never interfere with the physician-patient relationship.

5. If the physician considers it essential not to obtain informed consent, the specific reasons for this proposal should be stated in the experimental protocol for transmission to the independent committee (I.2.).

6. The physician can combine medical research with professional care, the objective being the acquisition of new medical knowledge, only to the extent that medical research is justified by its potential diagnostic or therapeutic value for the patient.

III. NON-THERAPEUTIC BIOMEDICAL RESEARCH INVOLVING HUMAN SUBJECTS (NON-CLINICAL BIOMEDICAL RESEARCH)

1. In the purely scientific application of medical research carried out on a human being, it is the duty of the physician to remain the protector of the life and health of that person on whom biomedical research is being carried out.

2. The subjects should be volunteers – either healthy persons or patients for whom the experimental design is not related to the patient's illness.

3. The investigator or the investigating team should discontinue the research if in his/her or their judgement it may, if continued, be harmful to the individual.

4. In research on man, the interest of science and society should never take precedence over considerations related to the well-being of the subject.

Appendix 2
MRC PROFORMA APPLICATION FORM

MRC Controlled Trials 1997-1998

Proforma for full proposals
Please structure Annex 1 of your application form using the headings listed below
- Please make an entry under every heading
- Do not exceed 9 sides of A4 (10 point)

1 Full title of trial
1.1 ACRONYM (only if applicable – this is not a requirement)
1.2 CONTACT APPLICANT (name, address, tel, fax, e-mail)

2 The need for a trial
2.1 WHAT IS THE PROBLEM TO BE ADDRESSED?
2.2 WHAT IS THE HYPOTHESIS TO BE TESTED?
2.3 WHY IS A TRIAL NEEDED NOW?

2.4 HAS A SYSTEMATIC REVIEW BEEN CARRIED OUT AND WHAT WERE THE FINDINGS?
2.5 HOW WILL THE RESULTS OF THIS TRIAL BE USED?
(eg, inform clinical decision making /improve understanding)
2.6 PLEASE DETAIL ANY RISKS TO THE SAFETY OF PARTICIPANTS INVOLVED IN THE TRIAL

3 The proposed trial
3.1 WHAT IS THE PROPOSED TRIAL DESIGN?
(eg, randomised or observational, open, double or single blinded, etc)
3.2 WHAT ARE THE PLANNED TRIAL INTERVENTIONS?
(both experimental and control)

3.3 WHAT IS THE PROPOSED DURATION OF TREATMENT PERIOD?

3.4 WHAT ARE THE PLANNED INCLUSION/EXCLUSION CRITERIA?

3.5 WHAT ARE THE PROPOSED OUTCOME MEASURES?

PRIMARY:

SECONDARY:

3.6 WILL HEALTH SERVICE RESEARCH ISSUES BE ADDRESSED?
(Please justify inclusion/exclusion of health economics and quality of life measures. If these measures are to be included full details should be given including power calculations)

3.7 WHAT IS THE PROPOSED FREQUENCY /DURATION OF FOLLOW-UP?

3.8 HOW WILL THE OUTCOME MEASURES BE MEASURED AT FOLLOW-UP?

3.9 WHAT ARE THE PROPOSED PRACTICAL ARRANGEMENTS FOR ALLOCATING PARTICIPANTS TO TRIAL GROUPS?
(eg, Randomisation Method)

3.10 WHAT ARE THE PROPOSED METHODS FOR PROTECTING AGAINST OTHER SOURCES OF BIAS? (eg, blinding or masking)

3.11 WHAT IS THE PROPOSED SAMPLE SIZE AND WHAT IS THE JUSTIFICATION FOR THE ASSUMPTIONS UNDERLYING THE POWER CALCULATIONS? (include both control and treatment groups, a brief description of the power calculations detailing the outcome measures on which these have been based, and give event rates, means and medians etc as appropriate)

3.12 WHAT IS THE PLANNED RECRUITMENT RATE?

3.13 ARE THERE LIKELY TO BE ANY PROBLEMS WITH COMPLIANCE?

3.14 WHAT IS THE LIKELY RATE OF LOSS TO FOLLOW-UP?

3.15 HOW MANY CENTRES WILL BE INVOLVED?
(details can be given on the final sheet)

3.16 WHAT IS THE PROPOSED TYPE OF ANALYSES?

3.17 WHAT IS THE PROPOSED FREQUENCY OF ANALYSES?

3.18 ARE THERE ANY PLANNED SUBGROUP ANALYSES?

3.19 HAS ANY PILOT STUDY BEEN CARRIED OUT USING THIS DESIGN?

4 Trial management

4.1 WHAT ARE THE ARRANGEMENTS FOR DAY-TO-DAY MANAGEMENT OF THE TRIAL? (eg, randomisation, data handling, and who will be responsible for co-ordination)

4.2 WHAT WILL BE THE RESPONSIBILITIES OF THE APPLICANTS? (Please give below details of the roles of the named applicants).

4.3 WHAT WILL BE THE RESPONSIBILITIES OF THE STAFF EMPLOYED ON THE GRANT? (Please give below details of the roles of the staff requested on the grant).

4.4 WHAT WILL BE THE ROLES OF THE NAMED COLLABORATORS?
(Please give below details of the roles of the named collaborators).

4.5 WHO IS THE TRIAL STATISTICIAN?

4.6 TRIAL STEERING COMMITTEE (Please give names and affiliations of the proposed trial steering committee to include – independent Chairman, independent members, principal investigators – see guidance notes)

5 Financial details of the trial?
Please complete the financial sections of the application form as normal.

In addition in the body of the application form please provide the following information:

5.1 Financial Summary
(please summarise the total cost of the trial in a table)

	Year	1997/98	1998/99	1999/2000[etc]	TOTAL
Research Costs					
Treatment Costs					
Service Support Costs					
TOTAL					

NB Please see the note on NHS service support in the attached guidelines and the summary of definitions

5.2 Justification for support requested (Please give full justification for the resources requested (excluding those described under 4.3 above).

APPENDIX 3

Trial steering committee (TSC)

It is MRC policy that for all its trials a Trial Steering Committee (TSC)
should be set up with the following terms of reference:

A) TERMS OF REFERENCE

1. to monitor and supervise the progress of the trial
["title of trial"] towards its interim and overall objectives;
2. to review at regular intervals relevant information
from other sources (eg, other related trials);
3. to consider the recommendations of the Data
Monitoring and Ethics Committee;
4. in the light of 1, 2 & 3, to inform the Council and
relevant Research Boards on the progress of the trial;
5. to advise Council on publicity and the presentation of
all aspects of the trial.

B) MEMBERSHIP

Applicants should submit a suggested membership with
their full application. The relevant Board(s) will decide
on the final membership of the TSC. The membership
should be limited and include an **independent**
Chairman (not involved directly in the trial other than
as a member of the TSC), not less than two other
independent members and one or two Principal
Investigators. Where possible membership should
include a lay/consumer representative. Trial co-
ordinators, statisticians etc should attend meetings as
appropriate. Observers from the MRC and Host
Institution should be invited to all meetings.

C) GUIDANCE NOTES

Meetings

A meeting of the TSC should be organised by the PI before
the start of the trial to finalise the protocol, which should
then be sent to the MRC. After that the TSC should meet
at least annually although there may be periods when more
frequent meetings are necessary. Meetings should be called
for organised by the PI. Papers for meetings should be
circulated well in advance of the meeting rather than tabled
and an accurate minute of the meeting should be prepared
by the PI and agreed by all members.

Trial Steering and Management

The role of the TSC is to provide overall supervision of
the trial on behalf of the MRC. In particular, the TSC
should concentrate on progress of the trial, adherence to
the protocol, patient safety and the consideration of new
information. Day-to-day **management** of the trial is the
responsibility of the Principal Investigators. The Principal
Investigators may wish to set up a separate Trial
Management Committee to assist with this function.

Patient Safety

In all the deliberations of the TSC the rights, safety and
well-being of the trial participants are the most
important considerations and should prevail over the
interests of science and society. The TSC should ensure
that the protocol demands freely given informed
consent from every trial participant. The TSC should
look closely at the patient information provided and
advise the investigators on its completeness and
suitability.

Progress of the Trials

It is the role of the TSC to monitor the progress of the
trial and to maximise the chances of completing the
study within the time scale agreed by the Board. At the
first TSC meeting, targets for recruitment, data
collection, compliance etc. should be agreed with the
investigators. These targets should not be "set in stone"
but are designed to act as a gauge of trial progress. The
TSC should agree a set of data, based on the targets set,
that should be presented to each TSC (template
attached).

The PI is required to submit an annual report to
Council based on the standard template attached. This
report should be endorsed by the TSC and should be
stand alone and contain sufficient data to allow the
relevant Research Board to judge progress in a trial
without the need to refer back to the original grant
proposa,l and inform the MRC of any new information
that has a bearing on safety or ethical acceptability of the
trial or any significant complaints arising, with a
justification of any decisions taken on the matter.

In exceptional circumstances, Council will consider
proposals for the extension of grants for clinical trials. If
progress on the trial suggests that an extension may be
necessary, the TSC should notify MRC officers at the
earliest opportunity (for a large study it may take a year
before approval of further funding can be given). In
these cases, the Boards will require evidence from TSCs
that all practicable steps have been taken to improve
recruitment and keep within the agreed duration of the
grant. In these circumstances the DMEC should be
asked to advise the TSC and may be required to provide
information on the availability of data collected to date
(from this and other studies) and advice on the
likelihood that continuation of the trial will allow
detection of an important effect. This should be done
using methods that do not unblind the trial.

Adherence to Protocol

The full protocol should be presented as an agenda item
at the first TSC meeting to be agreed. If the
investigators need to make any changes to the protocol
during the course of the trial, approval should be sought
from the TSC, LREC/MREC and, if necessary, the
MRC.

20

Consideration of New Information

The TSC should consider new information relevant to the trial including reports from the DMEC and the results of other studies. It is the responsibility of the PI and the Chairman and other independent members of the TSC to bring to he attention of the TSC any results from other studies that may have a direct bearing on future conduct of the trial.

On consideration of this information the TSC should recommend appropriate action, such as changes to the trial protocol, additional patient information or stopping of the study. The rights, safety and well-being of the trial participants should be the most important considerations in these deliberations.

It is the responsibility of the investigators to notify the TSC and DMEC and relevant regulatory authority (if applicable) of any unexpected serious adverse events during the course of the study.

Data Monitoring and Ethics Committee

The TSC should, at its first meeting, establish a Data Monitoring and Ethics Committee (DMEC) that meets regularly to view the data and the results of any interim analyses. The terms of reference and guidelines for DMECs are attached. Members should be independent of both the trial and TSC.

MRC GCP

The TSC should endeavour to ensure that the trial is conducted at all times to the rigorous standards set out in the MRC Guidelines for Good Clinical Practice.

CLINICAL TRIALS FUNDED BY THE MRC

DRAFT TEMPLATE FOR STEERING COMMITTEE AGENDAS AND REPORTS

The Medical Research Council requires that independent Steering Committees are set up for every major trial it funds and that these committees should meet at least once a year and submit a report to the relevant Research Board. Presented below are guidelines on the information that should be provided by triallists for discussion at Steering Committee meetings and included in the Steering Committee's annual report. It is suggested that the headings listed below should provide a basis for the agenda of the meetings and form the template for the report. These headings may not be appropriate at every stage of an individual trial or for all trials.

	Target (date target set)	**Achieved** (date achieved)
1) Name of Trial		
2) Grant No.		
3) Sample size sought		
4) Date recruitment started		
5) Proposed date for recruitment end		
6) Actual recruitment rate versus target rate (by month/quarter)		
7) Acceptance rate, as a proportion of		
i) those invited to participate and		
ii) if known all eligible participants		
8) Quarterly/monthly forecasts of recruitment for the planned remainder of the trial		
9) Losses to follow-up,		
i) as a proportion of those entered, and ii) per month/quarter		
10) No. for whom follow-up has been completed successfully (or still being successfully followed-up)		
11) Completeness of data collected		
12) Any available results (pooled)		
13) Any organisational problems		
14) Issues specific to individual trials (to be specified by the Steering Committee)		

20

DATA MONITORING & ETHICS COMMITTEE (DMEC)

a) Terms of reference
1. to determine if additional interim analyses of trial data should be undertaken
2. to consider the data from interim analyses, unblinded if considered appropriate, plus any additional safety issues for the trial ["title of trial"] and relevant information from other sources
3. in the light of 2., and ensuring that ethical considerations are of prime importance, to report (following each DMEC meeting) to the Trial Steering Committee and to recommend on the continuation of the trial
4. to consider any requests for release of interim trial data and to recommend to the TSC on the advisability of this
5. in the event of further funding being required, to provide to the TSC and MRC appropriate information and advice on the data gathered to date that will not jeopardise the integrity of the study.

b) Membership
The membership should be proposed as part of the proposal to the MRC and approved by the Board.

Members	Invited to attend
The membership of the DMEC will usually be small: *3-4 members and the members will be independent; * expert(s) in the field (eg, clinician with experience in the relevant area) *expert trial statistician(s)	The trial statistician may be invited to attend for part of the DMEC meeting to present the most current data from the trial, unblinded if appropriate.

c) Guidance notes
• The DMEC should meet at least annually, or more often as appropriate, and meetings should be timed so that reports can be fed into the Trial Steering Committee (TSC) meetings. Meetings should be called for and organised by the Principal Investigator of the trial in association with the Chairman of the DMEC. Dates for DMEC meetings should be agreed in advance and only altered with agreement of all members. All significant communications between the Principal Investigators and the DMEC should be in writing, or if they have to be oral, they should be backed up by written records.

• The role of the DMEC is to look at the [unblinded] data from an ethical standpoint, the safety, rights and well being of the trial participants being paramount
• The PIs (normally the trial statistician) should prepare a comprehensive report for the DMEC. This should be prepared and circulated well in advance of the meeting to allow DMEC members time to study the data. Content of the report should be agreed in advance with the DMEC Chairman. The trial statistician may be invited by the Chairman to attend part of the meeting to present the data; otherwise, no one involved with the trial or TSC should be present to see the unblinded data.
• A full confidential report should be made in writing by the Chairman of the DMEC providing advice to the Trial Steering Committee (and PI) on whether the trial should continue or not. If the the DMEC recommends that the trial should be stopped at any point, the funding body should be notified. It will be the responsibility of the TSC to decide whether or not to act upon the information received from the DMEC.
• If at any stage an extension to the grant is needed the DMEC may be requested by the Board to provide information on the data gathered to date (from this and other studies) and advice on the likelihood that continuation of the trial will allow detection of an important effect. This should be done using methods that do not unblind the trial.

Before reporting on the results of the trial the DMEC will consider not only the interim results as presented by the trial statistician, but also any major new information from other sources thought to be relevant to the trial. It follows that the DMEC will not automatically follow pre-assigned statistical rules, although it will be guided by statistical considerations.
• Information provided by the DMEC is likely to fall into the following categories:
  (a) Information that might lead to the TSC stopping the trial prematurely in the event of a clear outcome, if this is deemed to be appropriate in the light of the accumulating data from the study, or on the basis of information available from other sources;
  (b) Information that might lead to the TSC modifying the design of the trial, if this is deemed to be appropriate in the light of the accumulating data from the study, or on the basis of information available from other sources.

20

Appendix 4a

ESSENTIAL DOCUMENTS THAT SHOULD BE HELD BEFORE THE CLINICAL PHASE OF THE STUDY BEGINS

For those trials using medicinal products where it is clear at the start of the trial that the data may be required for a licensing application, the documentary requirements outlined in the ICH GCP Guideline should be followed. In the majority of MRC trials in which this is not the case the actual requirements will vary according to the trial, the type of intervention and whether or not medicinal products are involved. The table below provides guidance on the retention of key documentation under these circumstances.

Document	Principal investigator/ coordinating centre	Participating investigator	MRC
Final protocol, including • Patient information • Consent form • Case record forms • Instructions on handling trial product	Yes	Yes	Yes
Investigator agreement on final protocol (Participation form or Agreement)	Yes	–	–
Investigator's Brochure	If applicable	If applicable	–
Local variation on • Patient information • Consent form • Advertising	yes	yes	–
Ethics approval and composition of committee	Yes (MREC)	Yes (LREC)	Yes (MREC)
CTX approval	If applicable	If applicable	–
Investigator's qualifications (CV)	Yes (known consultant/GP post acceptable)	Yes	–
List of Investigators	Yes	Yes	
List of pharmacy contacts	If applicable	If applicable	–
Normal Ranges	If applicable	If applicable	–
List of signatures	If applicable	If applicable	–
Sample label	If applicable	If applicable	–

Appendix 4b

ESSENTIAL DOCUMENTS THAT SHOULD BE HELD ONCE CLINICAL PHASE OF THE STUDY HAS BEGUN

For those trials using medicinal products where it is clear at the start of the trial that the data may be required for a licensing application, the documentary requirements outlined in the ICH GCP Guideline should be followed. In the majority of MRC trials, in which this is not the case, the actual requirements will vary according to the trial, the type of intervention and whether or not medicinal products are involved. The table below provides guidance on the retention of key documentation under these circumstances.

Document	Principal investigator/ coordinating centre	Participating investigator	MRC
Protocol revisions: ● Amendments ● Case record forms ● Patient information ● Case record forms	Yes	Yes	Yes
Ethics approvals necessary for any protocol revision	Yes	Yes	Yes
Investigator's Brochure: ● Any updates	Yes	Yes	–
New investigator's qualifications (CV)	Yes (known consultant/GP post acceptable)	Yes	–
List of new investigators	Yes	–	–
Changes to normal ranges	If applicable	If applicable	–
Changes to list of signatures	If applicable	If applicable	–
Monitor visit reports	Yes	Yes	–
Record of communications with sites: letters, telephone calls	Yes	Yes	–
Signed consent forms	–	Yes	–
Completed CRFs: ● includes SAE reports from that site	Yes (original)	Yes (copy)	–
CRF corrections	Yes	Yes	–
SAE reports of unexpected events from pharmaceutical company	Yes	Yes	–
Annual reports to ethics committees if required	Yes, if required	Yes	–
Screening log/Trial register	–	Yes	–
Record of stored blood or tissue samples, if any	Yes	Yes	–

For further information and comments contact:
Liam O'Toole
Clinical Trials Manager
Medical Research Council
20 Park Crescent
London W1N 4AL
Telephone: 0171 636 5422
Facsimile: 0171 436 6179
Email: liam.otoole@headoffice.mrc.ac.uk

Design and Production
Medical Research Council
Publications Department
Print
Aldridge Print Group
Mitcham, Surrey
Telephone: 0181 239 4100

© Medical Research Council 1998

20

This information is reproduced by permission of the NHS Executive South East Research and Development Directorate

MULTI-CENTRE RESEARCH ETHICS COMMITTEES

APPLICATION FORM

For official MREC Use Only **MREC/ / /**	*For official MREC Use Only*

INSTRUCTIONS: Please complete in type. Please place a circle around Yes/No options as appropriate. A version of this form is available on disc from the administrator of the MREC.

It is essential that this form is completed fully and sent with relevant enclosures. **You should not simply refer to the protocol but complete the form with the information requested.** Please refer to the accompanying Guidance Notes when completing the form and complete the checklist before sending. Where a question is not applicable it is important to make this clear and not to leave it blank. **It is important that the language used in this application is clear and understandable to lay members.** All abbreviations should be explained.

Applicant's Checklist

Please indicate if the following have been enclosed by underlining or placing a circle round Yes/No/Not applicable options.

Application Form (one copy only)	Yes	No	
Full protocol with reference details (**six** copies)	Yes	No	Not applicable
Application Fee of £1000	Yes	No	Not applicable
Research subject consent form with version number and date	Yes	No	Not applicable
Research subject information sheet with version number and date	Yes	No	Not applicable
Advertisement for research subjects	Yes	No	Not applicable
GP/consultant information sheet or letter	Yes	No	Not applicable
Interview schedules for research subjects	Yes	No	Not applicable
Letters of invitation to research subjects	Yes	No	Not applicable
Questionnaire* Finalised/Not yet finalised	Yes	No	Not applicable
Researchers brochure or data sheet for all drugs (**six** copies)	Yes	No	Not applicable
Statement regarding compensation arrangements (one copy only)	Yes	No	Not applicable
Principal Researcher c.v. (one copy only)	Yes	No	Not applicable
CTX/CTC/DDX (one copy only)	Yes	No	Not applicable
Annexe A**	Yes	No	Not applicable
Annexe B***	Yes	No	Not applicable
Annexe C****	Yes	No	Not applicable

*	*Please indicate whether or not this is the final version*
**	*Required if the study involves the use of a new medicinal product or medical device, or the use of an existing product outside the terms of its product licence. Annexe A is attached to the Application Form.*
***	*Required if the study includes the use of ionising, radioactive substances or X-Rays. Annexe B is attached to the Application Form.*
****	*Information concerning local researchers should always be given where possible at this stage. Annexe C is attached to the Application Form. Please make additional copies as necessary.*

Instructions for the application form for ethical approval

There are eight other documents with this one:
- **guide.doc** is the guidance notes to assist in the completion of the application form and should be read before completing the form.
- **appform.doc** is the standard application form for ethical approval used by all MRECs. Answers should be typed into the appropriate frame provided.
- **contacts.doc** is the details of names, addresses and contact numbers for MREC Administrators together with the arrangements for cheques and dates and deadlines for meetings.
- **standord.doc** contains the Standing Orders (Constitution) for the Multi Centre Research Ethics Committees in compliance with the International Conference on Harmonisation's Good Clinical Practice Guidelines as they relate to the conduct of Independent Ethics Committees.
- **statemnt.doc** is a Statement of Compliance with these guidelines as required by Sponsor Companies.
- **helsinki.doc** contains the current version of the Declaration of Helsinki
- **pis.doc** is the Patient Information Sheet and Consent Form guidelines
- **consent.doc** is the model Consent Form

Information should be entered into the frames provided and the page breaks between sections in the application form should be retained.

Once the form has been completed you should save it, print it out and obtain all the necessary signatures before submitting a printed original to the MREC. You should also ensure that you have submitted the correct enclosures and completed the check list on the front of the form. Forms received without the necessary signatures or on disk will not be accepted. You are advised to retain a copy of the completed form in an electronic format as any amendments required by the MREC will need to be made before a submission can be made to the relevant LRECs for local approval.

If you have any queries about any of these documents or with our compliance with the ICH Guidelines, please contact the relevant MREC Administrator shown in **contacts.doc**.

The MREC documentation is also available on the Internet at:: **http://dspace.dial.pipex.com/mrec**

21

SECTION 1	Details of applicant(s)

---

1. **Short title of project (including any version dates):**

    Full title:

---

2. **Principal researcher (who will be responsible for dealing with the MREC)**

    Surname:

    Forename:

    Title:

    Present appointment of applicant:

    Qualifications:

    Address:

    Tel:

    Fax:

    E-Mail:

3. Senior researcher at LEAD centre (if different from above)

Surname:

Forename:

Title:

Present appointment:

Qualifications:

4. **Who is sponsoring the study?**

Contact name:

Organisation:

Address:

Tel:

Fax:

21

E-Mail:

5. **Drug Company Reference Number**

6. **Will researchers be paid for taking part in the study?**   *Yes*   *No*

   If so, will BMA guidelines (*Manual* II.47 – see Guidelines) **be followed?**   *Yes*   *No*

   If not, why not?

7. **Proposed start date and duration of the study**

8. **What other researchers are/do you intend to be involved in this project?**
   (Details of researchers added subsequently must be notified to the MREC)
   Please use the form attached at Annexe C

21

SECTION 2	Details of project

*This section must be completed fully. A copy of the protocol should be enclosed with the application form, but it is **not** sufficient to complete questions by referring to the protocol.*

9. **Aims and objectives of project** *(Approx. 250 words)*

10. **Scientific background of study** *(Approx. 250 words)*

11. **Brief outline of project** *(Approx. 250 words)*

12. **Study design** (e.g. RCT, cohort, case control, epidemiological analysis)

13. **Size of the study (including controls)**

    Will the study involve:

(a) Human Subjects   *Yes*   *No*

   i)   How many patients will be recruited?

   ii)   How many controls will be recruited?

   iii)   What is the primary end point?

   iv)   How was the size of the study determined?

   v)   What is the statistical power of the study?

21

(b)   Patient Records   *Yes*   *No*

    i)   How many records will be examined?

    ii)   How many control records will be examined?

    iii)   What is the primary end point?

    iv)   How was the size of the study determined?

    v)   What is the statistical power of the study?

---

14. Scientific critique

Has the protocol been subject to scientific critique? If so, please give the following information:

If the critique formed part of the process of obtaining funding, please give the name and address of the funding organisation:

If the critique took place as part of an internal process, please give brief details:

If no critique has taken place, please explain why, and offer justification for this:

If you are in possession of any referees' or other scientific critique reports relevant to your proposed research, please forward copies with your application form.

SECTION 3	Recruitment od subjects

15. How will the subjects in the study be:

    i)   selected?

    ii)   recruited?

    iii) what inclusion criteria will be used?

    iv) what exclusion criteria will be used?

16. How will the control subjects group (if used) be: *(Type N/A if no controls)*

    i)   selected?

    ii)   recruited?

    iii) what inclusion criteria will be used?

    iv) what exclusion criteria will be used?

21

17. Will there be payment to research subjects of any sort?   *Yes*   *No*

    If yes, how much per subject and for what?

SECTION 4	Consent

18. Is *written* consent to be obtained?   Yes   No

  If yes, please attach a copy of the consent form to be used.

  If no written consent is to be obtained, please justify.

19. How long will the subject have to decide whether to take part in the study?

  If less than 24 hours please justify.

20. Please attach a copy of the written information sheet or letter to be given to the subject.

  (See Guidelines page 3 and Appendix A.)

  If no Information Sheet is to be given, please justify.

21. Have any special arrangements been made for subjects for whom English is not a first language?   Yes   No   N/A

  If yes, give details.

  If no, please justify.

22. Will any of the subjects or controls be from one of the following vulnerable groups?

  Children under 18 (16 in Scotland)
  People with learning difficulties
  Unconscious or severely ill
  Other vulnerable groups e.g. mental illness, dementia

  Yes   No

  If yes, please specify and justify:

23. What special arrangements have been made to deal with the issues of consent for the subjects above? *(Please see Guidelines.)*

21

SECTION 5	Details of interventions

24. Does the study involve the use of a new medicinal product
   or medical device, or the use of an existing product outside
   the terms of its product licence? *(Please see Guidelines.)*   *Yes*   *No*

   If yes, please complete Annexe A of the Application Form.

25. Will any ionising or radioactive substances or X-Rays be administered?   *Yes*   *No*

   (NB Please ensure information in Question 14 includes exclusion criteria with regard to ionising radiation if appropriate.)

   If yes, please complete Annexe B of the Application Form.

26. Please list those procedures in the study to which subjects will be exposed indicating those
   which will be part of normal care and those that will be additional (e.g. taking more samples
   than would otherwise be necessary). Please also indicate where treatment is withheld as a
   result of taking part in the project.

21

SECTION 6	Risks and ethical problems

27. Are there any potential hazards?   *Yes   No*

If yes, please give details, and give the likelihood and details of precautions taken to meet them, and arrangements to deal with adverse events.

28. Is this study likely to cause any discomfort or distress?   *Yes   No*

If yes, please give details and justify.

29. What particular ethical problems or considerations do you consider to be important or difficult with the proposed study?

Please give details.

30. Will information be given to the patient's General Practitioner?   *Yes   No*

Please note: permission should always be sought from research subjects before doing this.

If yes, please enclose an information sheet/letter for the GP.

If no, please justify:

21

31. If the study is on hospital patients, will consent of all consultants whose patients are involved in this research be sought?   *Yes   No*

If no, please justify:

SECTION 7	Compensation and confidentiality

Product liability and consumer protection legislation make the supplier and producer (manufacturer) or any person changing the nature of a substance, e.g. by dilution, strictly liable for any harm resulting from a consumer's (subject or patient) use of a licensed product.

---

32. Have arrangements been made to provide indemnity and/or compensation in the event of a claim by, or on behalf of, a subject for non negligent harm?

(Please indicate N/A if not applicable)

Yes   No   N/A

If yes, please give details of compensation arrangements with this application.

For NHS-sponsored research, HSG(96)48 reference no. 2 refers.

For pharmaceutical company sponsored research, the company should confirm that it will abide by the most recent ABPI guidelines *(Manual V.14.1.1)*

---

33. In cases of equipment or medical devices, have appropriate arrangements been made with the manufacturer to provide indemnity?

(Please indicate N/A if not applicable)   Yes   No   N/A

If yes, please give details and enclose a copy of the relevant correspondence with this application.

---

34. Will the study include the use of any of the following?

Audio/video recording	Yes	No
Observation of patients	Yes	No

If yes to either:

i) How are confidentiality and anonymity to be ensured?

ii) What arrangements have been made to obtain consent for these procedures?

---

35. Will medical records be examined by research worker(s) outside the employment of the NHS?   Yes   No

If yes, please see Guidelines.

21

36. What steps will be taken to safeguard confidentiality of personal records?

37. What steps will be taken to safeguard the information relating to specimens and the specimens themselves?

PLEASE ENSURE THAT YOU COMPLETE THE CHECKLIST ON THE FRONT COVER OF THE APPLICATION FORM AND ENCLOSE ALL RELEVANT ADDITIONAL DOCUMENTS.

SECTION 8	Declaration

DECLARATION

The information in this form is accurate to the best of my knowledge and belief and I take full responsibility for it.

I understand it is my responsibility to obtain management approval where appropriate from the relevant NHS body before the project takes place.

I agree to supply interim and final reports on the pro forma provided, and to advise my sponsor, the MREC from which approval was granted for this proposal and any local researchers taking part in the project of any adverse or unexpected events that may occur during this project.

Signature of Principal Researcher: ....…...................................   Date:...............................

21

Annexe A	Drugs and Devices

This form is to be used if the study involves the use of a new medical product or medical device, or the use of an existing product outside the terms of its produce licence.

i)   Is a pharmaceutical or other commercial company arranging this trial?   *Yes*   *No*

    If no, has approval of the licensing authority been obtained by means of a DDX?   *Yes*   *No*

ii)   Does the drug(s) or device have a product licence(s) for
the purpose for which it is to be used?   *Yes*   *No*

    If yes, please attach data sheet or equivalent.

iii)   Is any drug or medical device being supplied by a company
with a Clinical Trial Certificate or Clinical Trial Exemption?   *Yes*   *No*

    Please attach CTC, CTX, or DDX.

iv)   Has a CTC, CTX or DDX been applied for but not yet received?   *Yes*   *No*

    If so, the application can be made but a valid CTX must be provided to the MREC before the research can proceed

v)   **Details of drugs to be used** *(Please complete the table below for each drug making additional copies of this page as necessary)*

    Approved Name(s):

    Generic Name:

    Trade Name:

Strength	Dosage and Frequency	Route	Duration of Course

vi)   When Drugs not listed in the British National Formulary are being used, applicants should provide the following information on not more than 3 sides of A4 paper :

a)   What is the formulation, purity and source of the Drug ?

b)   What are the pharmacological actions of the Drug – including those not relevant to the proposed therapeutic indications ?

c)   Toxicology – including details of species, number of animals, doses, duration of treatment and route(s) of administration. Important findings should be summarised.

21

d) **Clinical pharmacology in Man including :**

- Extent of Use in Man
- Dosage schedules used – dose, route, duration
- Side effects and their frequency
- Information on duration of action and mechanism of elimination, if known.

e) **Applicant's experience with this drug in man. Give brief information on previous studies, number and type of subjects and nature and incidence of side effects.**

vi) **Details of Medical Device**

vii) **If an electrical device, has the device been through acceptance and safety testing?**   *Yes*   *No*

Give details:

| Annexe B | Radiation |

This form is to be used if the study involves the use of additional ionising or radioactive substances or X-Rays.

a) RADIOACTIVE SUBSTANCES

i) **Details of substances to be administered** *(Please complete the table below)*

Investigation:

Radionucleide

Chemical form

Quantity of radio-activity to be administered (MBq)   Route   Frequency

ii) **Estimated Effective Dose (Effective Dose Equivalent) (mSv):**
(Please supply source of reference or attach calculation)

iii) **Absorbed dose to organ or tissues concentrating radioactivity (mGy)**
(Specify dose and organ)
(Please supply source of reference or attach calculation)

b) X-RAYS

i) **Details of radiographic procedures**

Investigation   Organ(s)   Frequency

ii) **Estimated Effective Dose (Effective Dose Equivalent) (mSv):**
(Please supply source of reference or attach calculation)

21

Annexe C	Local Researchers

OTHER RESEARCHERS INVOLVED IN THIS STUDY

Please provide the name and contact details of other researchers involved in this study. Please include your own name and centre if you are also a local researcher.

(Please copy and complete this page for each researcher. You must inform the MREC Administrator by means of a copy of this form as each new researcher is recruited.)

MREC Reference Number:

Name

Contact Address:

Location of research
(if different):

Telephone:

Fax:

E-Mail:

Please retain a blank copy of this form, complete it and send to the MREC Administrator whenever other local researchers become involved in the future.

21

Annexe D	Supplementary Form for LRECs

SUPPLEMENTARY FORM FOR LOCAL ARRANGEMENTS

To be completed by the local researcher or principal researcher if appropriate (please see guidelines) <u>once MREC approval has been obtained</u>.

Please send this signed and completed form to the appropriate LREC administrator together with the **appropriate number** of copies of::

> the MREC application form
> the MREC letter of approval
> the signed MREC response form.
> the local researcher's c.v.
> the consent form and information sheet
>
> together with **one** copy of the protocol

If you require help with the address of your appropriate LREC please seek advice from the MREC Administrator.

1   **MREC Reference Number:**

2.   **Short title of project**

3.   **Details of lead of local investigator:**

Surname:

Forename:

Title:

Present Appointment:

Qualifications:

Please give an approximate figure for the number of trials/studies in which the principal researcher has been involved over the past year

5.   **Proposed start date and duration of project**

6.   Names, titles and qualifications of other local researchers working on this project

7.   Location of project

8.   Funding

Please give full details where applicable of:

a)   Payment to subjects

b)   Payment to Trust/practice/research funds

c)   Personal payment or personal benefit to researcher

   Is payment:

   i)   A block grant   *Yes*   *No*

   ii) Based on the number of research subjects recruited?   *Yes*   *No*

        If yes, how much per patient:

   d)   Details of other benefits, e.g. equipment

   e)   Will the costs incurred by the institution be
        covered by the payment?   *Yes*   *No*

9.   Local Recruitment of Subjects

   a)   How many subjects are being studied locally?

   b)   Are any of these subjects involved in existing research
        or have been involved in any recent research in the
        last six months?   *Yes*   *No*

        If yes, please justify their use in this project

   c)   Will any of the subjects involved be in a dependent
        relationship with the researcher?   *Yes*   *No*

        If yes, please ensure you comply with local recruitment arrangements

   d) Will any of the subjects involved be medical students?   *Yes*   *No*

       If yes, please obtain signed agreement of the Principal of the Medical School:

Signature of Principal of Medical School: ....

10. Local Safety Requirements

   a) Are you going to administer radioisotopes?   *Yes*   *No*

      i) If yes, do you have an ARSAC certificate?   *Yes*   *No*

      ii) Have you informed the local radiation officer?   *Yes*   *No*

Signature of Radiation Safety Officer: ....

   b) If you are going to administer drugs what arrangements have you made to store, code and administer them?

Signature of Hospital Pharmaceutical Officer: ....

   c) Local emergency contact details:

   d) Local independent adviser details:

DECLARATION

I have read and understood the MREC form and the supplementary form for LRECs, the protocol, guidelines and all documents pertaining to this research approved by the MREC that I now enclose. The information therein and above is accurate to the best of my knowledge and belief and I take full responsibility for it.

I understand it is my responsibility to obtain management approval where appropriate from the relevant NHS body before the project takes place.

I confirm that this research will comply with all relevant UK legislation, including the Data Protection Act and the Access to Medical Records Act.

I agree to supply interim and final reports to my LREC as required.

I agree to advise my sponsor, the LREC and MREC from which approval was granted for this proposal of any adverse or unexpected events that may occur during this project. I also agree to advise the LREC if this is withdrawn or not completed.

Signature of Local Investigator: …………..………... Date: ………..........................

21

MULTI-CENTRE RESEARCH ETHICS COMMITTEES

GENERAL GUIDANCE FOR RESEARCHERS

INTRODUCTION

Medical research is important and the National Health Service (NHS) has a role in enabling such research to take place. While approval for a research project is a management decision, advice on ethical issues comes from a Local Research Ethics Committee (LREC). When research is to take place within five or more LREC geographical boundaries anywhere in the UK (i.e. where application to five or more LRECs would previously have been required), ethical appraisal must be carried out by a Multi-Centre Research Ethics Committee (MREC). There are MRECs in each of the eight English Regions, one in Scotland and one in Wales. It is intended that one will also be established in Northern Ireland but until that time, such applications will be co-ordinated by the South Thames MREC. The MRECs have been established in accordance with Health Service Guidance HSG(97)23 (Management Executive Letter MEL[1997]8 in Scotland) taking effect on 1 April 1997 in Scotland and 1 July 1997 in the rest of the United Kingdom. MRECs will operate within the framework of guidance from the Departments of Health, the Royal College of Physicians and other professional bodies and the principles contained in the Declaration of Helsinki.

REMIT OF THE MRECs

An MREC must be consulted about any multi-centre research within five or more LREC geographical boundaries anywhere in the UK which is health related involving:

(a) Human subjects including NHS patients, i.e. those subjects recruited by virtue of their past or present treatment by the NHS, fetal material, in vitro fertilisation and the recently dead. (This includes those treated under contract with private sector providers.)

(b) Access to records and names of past and present NHS patients.

(c) The use of, or potential access to, NHS premises or facilities.

Where research in fewer than five such LREC geographical boundaries that has received local ethical approval is subsequently extended to include additional centres bringing the total to five or more, MREC approval **will** need to be obtained, although the LREC approval will remain valid for those specific centres for which it had already been obtained. It is therefore recommended that MREC approval be sought for research which is thought **likely** to be carried out within five or more LREC geographical boundaries.

WHO SHOULD APPLY?

It is necessary to obtain ethical approval from only **one** of these MRECs, normally the one for the area in which the principal researcher is based. The principal researcher is the person (often, but not necessarily, a clinician) with day-to-day contact with the project and an overall knowledge of the research, who will take on the overall responsibility for ethical issues. For drug company sponsored research it is possible for this person to be an employee or contractor, as long as they have recourse to the necessary clinical expertise, although for drug trials it is expected that the principal researcher would be a clinician. For research funded by a grant, the principal researcher is likely to be the grant-holder. The individual named as the principal researcher, and who submits the application, should be based in the United Kingdom.

HOW TO APPLY TO AN MREC

The principal researcher can obtain copies of the MREC application form and notes for guidance from any MREC Administrator, although specific enquiries should be made to the administrator of the MREC to which the application will be made. A list of information about the Committees is attached. Researchers applying to the MREC for ethical approval are strongly advised to read the notes for guidance carefully before completing an application form, and should ensure that **all** the required enclosures and the correct number of protocols are included with the application. Failure to do so could lead to delay. The application form and information are also available on disc and on the Internet at **http://dspace.dial.pipex.com/mrec**. The application form is standard for all MRECs.

When an application is submitted the committee normally expects to receive a protocol which has already been subjected to scientific critique (although exceptions will be permitted if there is a satisfactory explanation). The MREC is required to take account of such critiques and where possible they should be provided. It is understood that this may not be possible in the case of some commercial research. In such cases the names and professions of those conducting the critique should be provided. If it is thought to be necessary the MREC may obtain an independent scientific critique, following consultation with the principal researcher.

The MREC would also like to see as complete a list as possible of local researchers on Annexe C of the application form. Where the full number of local sites has not been identified at the time the proposal is submitted for ethical approval the names should be sent to the appropriate MREC, using a copy of Annexe C, as soon as sites are recruited. It is essential that the MREC has this information, both to review the research it has approved and to undertake an evaluation of the process. Where there is no local researcher the principal researcher (i.e. the person who is conducting research in all areas) should, where appropriate, seek approval from the relevant LRECs.

WHAT DOCUMENTATION SHOULD BE SENT TO THE MREC?

One copy of the completed application form together with any relevant accompanying information (i.e. consent form, information sheet, etc.) and **six** copies of the protocol (and investigator's brochure if relevant) should be returned to the administrator at least **three** weeks before the meeting date that is being targeted. All documentation should be supplied in a form that can be easily copied i.e. unbound. Applications sponsored by a commercial company should also be submitted with a cheque for the application fee of one thousand pounds (£1000) (For Scotland and Wales. Applicants to English MRECs will be invoiced by the Department of Health.) Dates of future meetings are to be found in the attached MREC details.

The International Conference on Harmonisation (ICH) Tripartite Guideline for Good Clinical Practice states that the following documents should be submitted:

- Trial protocol(s)/amendment(s)
- Written informed consent form(s) and consent form updates that the investigator proposes for use in the trial
- Subject recruitment procedures (e.g. advertisements)
- Written information to be provided to subjects
- Investigator's brochure
- Available safety information
- Information about payments and compensation available to subjects
- The principal investigator's current c.v. and/or other documentation evidencing qualifications
- Any other documents that the MREC may need to fulfil its responsibilities

WHAT HAPPENS WHEN YOUR APPLICATION IS RECEIVED?

An acknowledgement letter from the administrator will be sent confirming the date on which the application will be considered and allocating an MREC reference number which should be quoted on all correspondence. An invitation **may** be extended to you to attend the meeting of MREC to give you the opportunity to explain the proposal to the committee. In such cases every effort will be made to give a precise time to attend. The committee will advise of its decision in writing within 10 working days of the meeting at which the proposal was considered. The committee will always give reasons for asking for changes to the project, or for rejecting it. It should be noted that ethical approval is always given to a named principal researcher and any change in personnel should be notified to the MREC.

21

CRITERIA FOR JUDGING RESEARCH PROPOSALS

Once your application has been considered by an MREC you will receive written comments under the following headings:

(a) The applicant (Section 1).

(b) The scientific merit of the proposal (Section 2).

(c) The health and welfare of the research subject (Sections 3, 5 and 6).

(d) Compensation and confidentiality (Section 7).

(e) Consent of the research subject (Section 4).

(f) General comments.

OBTAINING LREC APPROVAL

MREC approval must always be received **before** contacting any LREC to gain local approval. The following documentation should be forwarded to local researchers:

One copy of:

- the protocol, incorporating any amendments required by the MREC and including the Information Sheet

Appropriate numbers of copies of:

- the information sheet

- the MREC application form

- the MREC response form

- the supplementary form for LRECs (Annexe D of the Application Form)

The local researcher is required to complete Annexe D and submit it to the appropriate LREC along with the other documents listed above in the quantities required by the respective LRECs. The LREC will be primarily concerned with the suitability of the local researcher, local research locations and the welfare of patients or research subjects recruited within their boundaries. The LREC cannot amend the protocol but may occasionally need to seek locally applicable amendments, when essential, which do not affect the integrity of the protocol, for example information sheets and consent forms in minority languages. The LREC can, however, raise issues of general concern with the MREC if it has concerns or issues it feels will affect the validity of the research and other sites. The LREC will advise the researcher and the MREC of its decision by sending a copy of the completed and endorsed supplementary form. **The local researcher must obtain the approval of the relevant LREC before recruiting any research subjects.**

MANAGEMENT APPROVAL

The MREC and LRECs advise the NHS bodies under the auspices of which the research is intended to take place. It is these NHS bodies who have the responsibility of deciding whether or not the project should go ahead, taking account of this advice. **The local researcher must obtain relevant management approval before recruiting any research subjects.**

LEGAL REQUIREMENTS

Principal and local researchers must comply with all relevant UK legislation, such as the Data Protection Act, Access to Medical Records Act, etc. MREC approval is conditional upon all legal requirements being observed.

APPLICATION FEE

The Departments of Health has determined that the MREC will charge a fee of one thousand pounds (£1000) for each application sponsored by a commercial company. A cheque should be included with your application, crossed "A/C Payee" and made payable to the relevant Health Authority/Health Board. Please see the information in the MREC details. This revenue will be used to help meet the cost of training for members of both MRECs and LRECs. This fee is in addition to any fees or charges made subsequently by Local Research Ethics Committees. Payment of the fee does not affect the outcome of the ethical consideration but failure to enclose the fee will result in a delay in the processing of the application.

COMMUNICATION WITH MRECs

All application forms and correspondence concerning applications should be sent to the relevant MREC Administrator shown in the MREC details.

21

MREC APPLICATION FORM GUIDANCE NOTES

GENERAL

Reference is made in these notes to various` publications. They will be listed with a reference number or relevant page number of the *Manual for Research Ethics Committees (ISBN I 898484 00 7 – published by and available from the Centre of Medical Law and Ethics, King's College, Strand, London, WC2R 2LS.).* The references and contents list of the *Manual* are given at the end of these Guidelines. Copies of the *Manual* and other publications are also held by MREC Administrators.

The application form should be completed in plain English understandable to lay members and all abbreviations should be explained. It should contain sufficient information to enable a thorough ethical review to take place. **The applicant should always complete the application form and not simply refer to the protocol.** Copies of the protocol are required, however, so that members to refer to it in cases of uncertainty.

The application form should be self explanatory and notes have not been provided for every question. If you are unsure about any aspect, please ask the relevant MREC Administrator for help.

POLICY REGARDING PATIENTS/HEALTHY VOLUNTEERS

1. Recruitment *(Section 3)*

No-one should be asked to participate in a research project against his/her will. Those recruiting participants should avoid exerting undue influence. This is particularly important when volunteers are recruited from the researcher's own students or patients. Participation in a research project should be entirely voluntary. No sanctions should be enacted if the volunteer decides to leave the project at any time. It is essential when the volunteers are students or employees of the researcher that local recruitment policies are followed. These points should be made clear in the Patient Information Sheet.

Payment in cash or kind to participants should only be for expense, time and inconvenience reasonably incurred. It should not be set at a level of inducement which would encourage people to take part in studies against their better judgement, or which would encourage them to take part in multiple studies.

If an advertisement or letter is to be used to recruit volunteers please enclose a copy, or the form of words to be used if the recruitment is via other media.

2. State of Health of Research Subjects

The MREC regards it as the responsibility of the researcher to ensure that at the time of recruitment and during the study the health of the research subject is appropriate to the demands of the study. Volunteers for non-therapeutic research need not be in perfect health providing that their participation will not adversely affect their underlying condition. Researchers should seek permission to contact the GP of volunteers to ensure the acceptability of participation in a study; and refusal by them to permit such communication should lead to their rejection as a participant. Where an exception to this requirement is sought it must be fully justified to the MREC. Where a GP indicates that participation is unacceptable, the volunteer should not participate in the study. If the research subject is a hospital patient the permission of the consultant responsible for the patient should also be sought. When the research subject is an inpatient who is discharged into the care of the community services it is the responsibility of the principal researcher to advise the patient's GP. Similarly, where it is a GP who is the principal researcher it is his responsibility to inform the consultant should the subject be admitted to hospital.

3 Consent *(Section 4)*

The MREC regards the issue of consent to be extremely important. For consent to be valid in law the patient must be competent to consent. Consent must be based on adequate information and must be voluntary. When it is intended not to seek written consent this should always be justified. The MREC usually requires that written consent be gained for all but the most trivial procedures. When seeking a patient's consent and providing information on a study the MREC asks that the Checklist attached to these Notes of Guidance (see Appendix A) is used. Adequate time and appropriate circumstances should be available to enable the potential subject to consider fully and rationally the implications of taking part in the study (ideally at least 24 hours). It must be made clear to research subjects that it is possible to withdraw at any time from a study without hindrance or detriment to their future treatment.

The consent to take part in a study should always be recorded in a patient's notes and research documents.

21

4 Patient/Healthy Volunteer Information Sheet

An Information Sheet should be given to and retained by the research subject. A checklist for producing an Information Sheet is attached to the application form (Appendix A) and it is strongly recommended that this is followed. Where detailed information is required by ICH or other guidelines and may not be easily understood, a simplified summary sheet should also be included at the front as informed consent is not possible if the subject is unable to understand what the research involves.

The MREC expects that adequate steps will be taken to ensure valid consent is obtained when the research subjects do not speak English. LRECs are likely to pay particular attention to this, and are entitled to request provision of suitable translations of Patient Information Sheets in languages relevant to the locality. Ethnicity is a sensitive issue and researchers may wish to make use of the attached guidelines (Appendix B).

5 Research on Children (Manual II.17 and V.27.1)

Research on children should only take place where it is absolutely essential and the information cannot be gained by using an adult patient.

In Scotland a young person aged 16 or over has full capacity to consent to medical procedures or treatment (Age of Legal Capacity(Scotland) Act 1991 section 2(4)). The consent of the young person's parent or guardian is irrelevant and unnecessary. Under the Children (Scotland) Act 1995 (section 15(5)(b)) a parent's right to act as a child's legal representative in relation to giving of consent applies only where a child is incapable of consenting on his or her own behalf. Where children are under the age of 16 the researcher should be qualified to administer whatever procedure is involved and should form a view regarding whether each child understands the nature and possible consequences of the procedure. Where the child clearly does not understand, then the consent of the parent should be sought. Where the child clearly does understand, then the consent of the child should be accepted. If the medical practitioner is in doubt, the best advice is to take the consent of both.

In England and Wales, when seeking consent to participate in therapeutic research, young people aged over 16-18 with sufficient understanding are able to give their full consent independently of their parents and guardians. Children under 16 are able to give their full consent providing they satisfy the Gillick criteria of competence, namely:

(1) They have been counselled and do not wish to involve their parents.

(2) They have sufficient maturity to understand the nature, purpose and likely outcome of the proposed research.

(3) It is in the best interest of the child to participate. It is the responsibility of the health professional attending the child to make this judgement.

It should be noted that while the law allows a child under 16 to consent to treatment without the supporting consent of their parent or guardian providing the Gillick criteria is fulfilled, the MREC would regard it as unwise for a researcher to allow the participation of a child in a project where parental consent was not forthcoming. Where it is viewed that a child is incapable of understanding the implications of taking part in a study, the child is regarded as incompetent to consent. The power to consent, in law, is that of his/her parents or legal guardian. The child's refusal to participate in research must always be respected unless according to the protocol the child would receive therapy for which there is no medically accepted alternative. Those acting for a child are only acting legally if participation in the project is of benefit to the child. If it is not, the parent or guardian could be said to be acting illegally. However, most guidelines acknowledge the need for some non-therapeutic research and regard it as acceptable if the risk and discomfort are no greater than minimal and the research could be done in no other people. The MREC will judge such research on its own merits in each case.

6 Research on Women

Where women are included as research subjects, the possibility of their being or becoming pregnant should always be considered. The implications of involving a woman who is breast feeding should also be carefully assessed.

7 Research on Prisoners

Where a research subject is a prisoner, the permission of the Director of Prison's Health Care as well as the consent of the subject is required.

8 Research on all People whose Capacity to Consent may be Impaired

Research on all people whose capacity to consent may be impaired either permanently or temporarily, e.g. a person with learning difficulties, a stroke patient or unconscious patient, is a particularly sensitive area because of the level of vulnerability of this group and the fact that some may be unable to give consent. Where possible, consent must still be freely given based on information which is provided in a form that is understandable to each individual. When a mentally disordered or temporarily incapacitated person is unable to consent to take part in a research project, there is no provision in law for another person to give consent on his/her behalf. The MREC will judge any research where consent cannot be obtained on its own merits. When there is any doubt about the patient's ability to consent, ideally the services of an independent assessor or witness should be sought to help assess whether the consent is valid. When the researcher is also the person who normally provides health care for the patient, ideally an independent advisor should be used when gaining the patient's consent.

9 Research Involving Fetuses and Fetal Material (Manual V.5.23)

The researcher should be aware of the code of practice in The Polkinghorne Report (CM 762 HMSO 1989) and the DoH guidance on the supply of Fetal Tissue for Research, Diagnosis and Therapy.

10 Gene Research (Manual V.29.1)

Researchers should consider guidelines issued by the Gene Therapy Advisory Committee.

11 Confidentiality *(Section 7)* (Manual V2.1.1 and13.1.1)

Any initial approach to a subject should usually be from a person whom the subject knows. In any case, when informing GPs that their patients are to be in a study, the patient's permission should be sought first. If patients do not give their consent to this, they should not participate in the trial unless a specific exemption has been obtained from the MREC.

Everyone working for or on behalf of the NHS is under a legal duty to keep patient information confidential. Information, anonymised or aggregated whenever possible, may be used for research purposes by or on behalf of the NHS, without the express consent of the patient. If, however, a patient refuses consent for the use of his/her information, this must be respected unless exceptionally, there is an overriding public interest in using it. Any research activity which involves the patient personally will require his/her express consent.

The use of patient information by other than NHS Bodies is addressed in *The Protection and Use of Patient Information HSG(96)18* – (*ref:* Manual V.2.1.1). The MREC will consider each application in the light of current policy. Confidential information given or obtained for one purpose must not be used for another. Arrangements must be made to safeguard confidentiality and data should be secured against unauthorised access.

Identifiable information may only be used when it can be fully justified. No individual should be identifiable from published results without his/her explicit consent. Research data from which an individual can be identified should be destroyed after the duration of the project. In a case where an investigator wishes to keep identifiable information after the project has ended, the MREC, the relevant NHS body and the research subject should be informed of the reason for retaining the information and the circumstances in which it might be disclosed.

In the case of sponsored drug trials the MREC is aware that some drug companies' regulatory bodies now request access to the patient's clinical notes to verify or cross check data. There is concern that this may represent breach of confidentiality, but on the other hand the MREC does realise that there have been cases of fraudulent data handling in some institutions, in various parts of the world. There is a duty to ensure that research data is recorded and reported accurately. The committee will approve protocols which incorporate such agreements provided that the following guidelines are observed:

21

(a) The information sheet must include a statement about company access to records.

(b) The subject is told in the information sheet that: their trial record form may be inspected by a company representative; the representative will also check the accuracy of the doctor's records.

(c) In some circumstances it may be appropriate to add that the data in anonymous form may be used for preparation of the trial report, and for submission to Government agencies as part of the procedures for marketing any new medicine.

(d) The company representative must have an appropriate professional background.

Certain enquiries and surveys involving only access to patients records do not require MREC approval (see Appendix C for a list).

12 Data Protection Act

The MREC wishes to make clear that when a researcher is using a patient's medical records, all current codes of practice and data protection legislation must be complied with.

13 Clinical Photography and Video Recordings

Obtain consent and specify the uses to which the material might be put. It should be noted that videos should not be used for commercial purposes.

It may also be advisable to state how long the photographs or video recordings might be kept and whether or not they would be destroyed at some time in the future. These considerations are particularly important when the material is required for research purposes. Consult the Medical Defence Union, Medical Protection Society or Royal College of General Practitioners for advice if in doubt.

14 Safety *(Sections 5 and 6)*

In cases of research involving the use of drugs, medicines, appliances or medical devices, the MREC will require proof or very clear indication of safety, quality and stability of any substance administered.

15 Compensation Arrangements *(Section 7)* (ref. no.3, Manual II.31-46 and V.2.2.1)

The MREC requires that the subject is aware of the arrangements for the compensation before agreeing to take part as indicated on the Checklist provided (Appendix A). Compensation for harm arising from negligence is normally the responsibility of the employer of the local researcher.

When research is sponsored by the NHS there is no provision to offer advance indemnity to participants. A person suffering injury as a result of having taken part in research will need to pursue a claim for negligence through litigation or may be offered an ex gratia payment by the Trust or Medical School. Each case will be considered on its merits. It is essential that the researcher gains management approval before starting a project to ensure that the Trust or Medical School is aware of the possibility of a compensation claim should a problem occur. In the case of healthy volunteers it will be necessary for the management body to take out separate insurance.

Separate cover for non-negligent harm for subjects may be required in some circumstances. This will usually be covered by the ABPI guidelines in a drug trial, and by Health Service Guidance in NHS sponsored research.

FINANCIAL CONSIDERATIONS (Sections 1, 3 & Annexe D of the MREC Application Form)

The MREC will require information on aspects of finances connected with the study. The MREC will wish to be reassured that the researcher(s) is not being unduly influenced by financial reward for conducting the study, and that research subjects, if they are to be paid, are not being paid for taking risks. Payment to research subjects, apart from travel expenses, is only appropriate in some non-therapeutic research, but must come only in the form which covers their expenses, including loss of earnings and inconvenience, and should not be enough to influence his/her judgement

The MREC will be concerned should there be wide variations in payments between different sites.

EC DIRECTIVES (Annexe A of the MREC Application Form) (Manual V.1-4)

1 Active Implantable Medical Devices
It should be noted that the Active Implantable Medical Devices Directives became effective on 1 January 1993. Therefore, if your research involves the use of active implantable medical devices, e.g. pacemakers, implantable defibrillators, it is essential that you, or the manufacturer sponsoring the research, contact the Medical Devices Agency of the Department of Health*. The Medical Devices Agency, acting as the Competent Authority under this Directive, must assess all clinical investigations of active implantable medical devices prior to commencement of the investigation, providing the device in question has not yet obtained the CE marking.

The Directorate will only authorise this research if approval has been obtained from the relevant ethics committee.

It should be emphasised that it is the responsibility of the researcher to meet the requirements of the Active Implantable Medical Devices Directive.

* Advice on the provisions of the Active Implantable Medical Devices Directive and how it affects clinical investigation can be obtained from:

Dr S Ludgate
Senior Medical Officer
Medical Devices Agency
Hannibal House
Elephant & Castle   Tel: 0171 972 8123
LONDON SE1 6TE   Fax: 0171 972 8103

2 Medical Devices Directive
The MDD came into effect from early 1995. The advice is the same as for the Active Implantable Medical Devices Directive.

3 In Vitro Diagnostic Devices
This Directive is currently subject to EC confirmation.

21

LIFE SPAN OF APPROVAL
Approval will expire if the project is not started within three years after the date MREC approval is given. An extension to this period can be applied for.

PUBLICATION
Publication arrangements should be agreed with the sponsor before starting research. The results of the research should be publicly accessible.

AMENDMENTS
Any change to the research protocol should be drawn up as an amendment and the approval of the MREC obtained.

MONITORING (ref. no. 1)

1 Research Register

Researchers should note that the MREC will keep a register of all research projects that come before it. The information contained on the register includes the title of the research project, the name of the principal researcher, a brief description of what is required of the research subjects and confirmation of compliance with guidelines, the local researchers involved in the project and record of LREC approval. This information is not normally available to the public, but can be used by NHS bodies for management purposes.

2 Progress

Once ethical approval is given by the MREC, the principal researcher is required to advise the MREC of progress in the form of regular updates and the outcome of the research in the form of a final report using the report forms supplied by the MREC Administrator. The MREC will also send out forms annually to review progress until the research is concluded.

3 Untoward Events

The researcher is also required to advise the MREC, LRECs involved in the project and the sponsor of the research of any unusual or unexpected events which raise questions about the safety of the research. The MREC would wish to know any case of difficulties experienced in recruiting subjects. The MREC would also like to know of cases where the research is withdrawn or cancelled.

4 Notification of Serious, Unexpected, Adverse Drug Reactions

It is the responsibility of the principal researcher to report any unexpected serious adverse event is reported immediately to the MREC that approved their application, the local researchers involved in the project and the research sponsor, together with advice on its relevance to the study.

The principal researcher should advise the Chairman or Vice Chairman or, if neither is available the Administrator, immediately the incident occurs. Any appropriate additional action will be advised at this time. The Chairman may, if the incident is serious enough, call an emergency meeting of the MREC. The principal researcher will be asked to attend this meeting. The Committee will expect to receive full details of the incident. The Committee will consider:

(a) Was it right to approve the research?

(b) Was it conducted in accordance with the approved protocol?

(c) Has the subject's family been informed and advised of the appropriate further action regarding legal advice?

(d) Should the research proceed or should it be suspended or discontinued and are there implications for other related research projects or centres?

A written record of this meeting will be kept.

REFERENCES

The following publications may be of use to researchers and are available from the Department of Health in London:

1. Department of Health <u>Standards for LRECs</u> (1995)

2. Department of Health <u>The Protection and Use of Patient Information</u> HSG (96) 18

3. Department of Health <u>NHS Indemnity: Arrangements for Handling Clinical Negligence Claims against NHS Staff</u>

Relevant guidance may also be found in the Manual for Research Ethics Committees (ISBN I 898484 00 7) which may be obtained from the Centre of Medical Law and Ethics, King's College, Strand, London, WC2R 2LS. The contents pages of the Manual are reproduced here:

MANUAL FOR RESEARCH ETHICS COMMITTEES

VOLUME I
Page   Item

21

V.10-13
Medical Research Council Guidelines

V.10.1   Responsibility in Investigations on Human Participants and Materials and on Personal Information

V.11.1   The Ethical Conduct of Research on the Mentally Incapacitated

V.12.1   The Ethical Conduct of Research on Children

V.13.1   The Ethical Conduct of AIDS Vaccine Trials

V.13.1.1   Responsibility in the use of Personal Medical Information for Research

V.14-22 *Association of the British Pharmaceutical Industry Guidelines*

V.14.1   Good Clinical (Research) Practice

V.14.1.1   Clinical Trials Compensation Guidelines

V.14.3   Good Clinical Trial Practice

V.15.1   Relationships between the Medical Profession and the Pharmaceutical Industry

V.16.1   Guidelines for Phase IV Clinical Trials

V.17.1   Guidelines for Ethical Approval of Human Pharmacology Studies carried out by Pharmaceutical Companies

V.18.1   Guidelines for Research Ethics Committees considering Studies conducted in Healthy Volunteers by
           Pharmaceutical Companies

V.19.1   Guidelines for Medical Experiments in Non-Patient Human Volunteers

V.20.1   Facilities for Non-Patient Volunteer Studies

V.21.1   Guidelines on the Conduct of Investigator Site Audits

V.22.2   Guidelines for Company-Sponsored Safety Assessment of Marketed Medicines (SAMM)

V.23-24 *Council for International Organisations of Medical Science Guidelines*

V.23.1   International Ethical Guidelines for Biomedical Research involving Human Subjects

V.24.1   International Guidelines for Ethical Review of Epidemiological Studies

V.25-32 *Other Guidelines*

21

V.25.1   Guidelines for Research Ethics Committees on Psychiatric   Royal College of Psychiatrists
           Research involving Human Subjects

V.26.1   Ethical Principles for Conducting Research with   British Psychological Society
           Human Participants

V.27.1   Guidelines for the Ethical Conduct of Medical Research   British Paediatric Association
           involving Children

V.28.1   Statement of Ethical Practice   British Sociological Association)

V.29.1   Guidance on Making Proposals to Conduct Gene Therapy   Gene Therapy Advisory Committee
           Research on Human Subjects

SECTION VI: FURTHER READING

Annexe A	Suggested guidelines for the consent procedure

The MREC requires that all subjects who are involved in a research project are provided with a written information sheet. This information sheet should be submitted with the application for approval. The MREC also requires care is taken when obtaining consent from a research subject and the following issues should be considered:

(1) Have you allowed the subject sufficient time to consider the matter on his/her own, discuss with others if wished, and to ask you questions?

(2) In your opinion, has the subject understood and consented to take part in this research?

(3) Has the patient signed and dated the consent form?

(4) Has the consent form been signed by a parent or guardian where the research subject is a child (see Notes for Guidance).

(5) If no written consent is being obtained, has consent been documented?

THE INFORMATION SHEET CHECKLIST

(6) The information sheet should be printed on appropriately headed paper and should avoid being too long. Where detailed information is required by ICH or other guidelines a simplified summary sheet should also be included at the front as informed consent is not possible if the subject is unable to understand what the research involves.

(7) The project should be given a simplified title if there is any likelihood that the full title will confuse the research subjects involved.

(8) The purpose of the project and the fact that it is a research project should be explained in plain, concise English. The nature of the project and all technical terms and abbreviations should be clearly explained. A translation should be provided where needed. It should also be made clear whether the research is therapeutic or non-therapeutic.

(9) When undertaking a randomised trial, an explanation of randomisation should be given along with an explanation of how the subjects are assigned and in what proportions to the control and intervention groups.

(10) The alternative forms of diagnosis and treatment being assessed should be explained clearly, including the expected benefits to the subject and/or others.

(11) Any serious risks and possible side effects and discomforts should be clearly indicated.

(12) The length of the trial and any extra attendances and procedures involved, nature of the drug or devices being tested should be explained.

(13) A careful explanation, with assurances, should be given if the project involves withholding effective treatment for a short time.

(14) It should be made clear that involvement in a research project is entirely voluntary.

(15) The right to withdraw at any time from the project without influencing current or future treatment should be made clear.

(16) A statement should be made assuring subjects of the confidentiality of health information and the protection of their identity when publishing results unless their consent is obtained.

(17) A clear statement should be made offering refund of expenses such as travel costs. Where payments to healthy volunteers are being made it should be stated these may be liable to tax.

21

(18) Clear information about indemnity arrangements should be given.

(19) A statement may need to be included if the participation in a trial affects health related insurance.

(20) The subject's permission should be sought to contact his/her GP about his/her involvement in the trial.

(21) A name and contact number should be given to enable the subject to obtain advice and information.

(22) The researcher should indicate on the information sheet if he/she is to receive any funding in the form of a personal payment. It is not necessary to give details of any amounts involved.

(23) Any subject involved in research which could harm a fetus should be advised of this and be given advice about contraception. This could apply to both men and women.

(24) Patients should be advised when trial medication may be withdrawn at the end of a trial.

(25) It should be made clear to the subject that the monitor(s), the auditor(s), the ethics committee and the regulatory authority(ies) will be granted direct access to the subject's original medical records for verification of clinical trials procedures and/or data without violating the confidentiality of the subject to the extent permitted by the applicable laws and regulations and that, by signing a written informed consent form, the subject or the subject's legally acceptable representative is authorising such access.

Appendix B	Ethnic origin

If you propose to enquire about the ethnic origin of your subjects in the/a questionnaire, then you should consider the following breakdown of categories which follows that used in the National Census. These categories are known to be acceptable to the ethnic minorities concerned; and data are available for the composition of the whole UK population based on these categories.

COUNTRY OF BIRTH

Please tick as appropriate

England ....

Scotland ....

Wales ....

Northern Ireland ....

Irish Republic ....

Elsewhere ....

If elsewhere, please write
in the present names
of the country ....

ETHNIC GROUP

Please tick as appropriate

If the person is descended from more than one ethnic or racial group, please tick the group to which the person considers he/she belongs, or tick the 'Any other ethnic group' ancestry in the space provided.

White ....

Black-Caribbean ....

Black-African ....

Black-other ....

Please describe ....

Indian ....

Pakistani ....

Bangladeshi ....

Chinese ....

Any other ethnic group ....

Please describe ....

21

Appendix C

EXAMPLES OF ENQUIRIES AND SURVEYS IN THE PUBLIC INTEREST WHERE NO REFERENCE TO A RESEARCH ETHICS COMMITTEE IS NECESSARY

THE NATIONAL UK SPONTANEOUS REACTION REPORTING SCHEME (YELLOW CARD SCHEME OF CSM)

This is a scheme under which doctors, dentists and coroners use yellow card report forms voluntarily to report adverse drug reactions to the Committee on Safety of Medicines. (Pharmaceutical companies are obliged to make reports.) It is a vital early warning mechanism for identifying adverse reactions not evident from clinical trials and enables CSM to monitor drug safety and keep prescribers' informed.

PRESCRIPTION EVENT MONITORING (PEM)

This is an established method of post marketing surveillance carried out by the Drug Safety Research Unit in Southampton. Patients treated with new medicines are identified from prescriptions and prescribers are contracted to provide information (on green forms). This is used to identify possible adverse drug reactions.

NATIONAL MORBIDITY SURVEYS

There have been four National Morbidity Surveys undertaken since 1956. The studies have provided the most comprehensive description of illness in the community and have been of great value in planning health care resources. The studies examine the prevalence of reported disease provide an indication of the care given to patients in general practice, and the fourth study will also relate disease and care to socio-economic factors.

COMPANY SPONSORED POST MARKETING SURVEILLANCE STUDIES

The Committee on Safety of Medicines has recommended that pharmaceutical companies carry out PMS studies on new drugs intended for widespread long term use using cohorts of at least 10,000 patients. Guidelines on these studies were published in the British Medical Journal 1988; vol 296 pp 399-400 and can be found in the Manual for Research Ethics Committees, (V.22.2) It is imperative that they include adequate numbers of patients to monitor drug safety and that their design and methods are appropriate for their stated scientific and medical objectives.

This article was first published in the Lancet *and is reproduced by permission of the* Lancet

PATIENTS' PREFERENCES AND RANDOMISED TRIALS

William A Silverman, Douglas G Altman

Lancet 1996; **347**: 171–74

90 La Cuesta Drive Greenbrae, CA 94904, USA (W A Silverman MD); and
ICRF Medical Statistics Group, Centre for Statistics in Medicine, PO Box 777, Oxford OX3 7LF, UK (D G Altman HEAD)
Correspondence to: Dr W A Silverman

The physician's first duty is to his patient—to do all in his power to save the patient's life and restore him, as rapidly as possible, to health. That fundamental and ethical duty must never be overlooked—though with the introduction of brighter, better and ever more toxic drugs … the onlooker may perhaps with good reason sometimes ask the clinician, "Are you sure you know where that duty lies?" It seems to me sometimes to be unethical not to experiment.

Sir Austin Bradford Hill

The randomised clinical trial (notably the famous streptomycin RCT reported in 1948[1]) arrived at a time when patients indicated their preferences for treatment, as they had for countless centuries, by voting with their feet. Patients simply appeared at doctor's surgeries, outpatient clinics, and hospitals. In the silent world of doctor and patient,[2] voluntary submission was taken as evidence of consent for treatment. The overriding issue in the healer–supplicant relationship was one of trust; patients needed to have faith in their doctor's ability to choose the best treatment. Physicians felt duty-bound to reinforce this belief by suppressing all doubt when discussing the choice of treatment. Therapeutic decisions were imperious: doctors felt no obligation to discuss the details with their patients.

In the streptomycin trial, patients with pulmonary tuberculosis were enrolled by their physicians who believed they were making the best treatment decision possible under conditions of uncertainty. But enrolees were not told about the doubts. They were not told they were participating in a parallel treatment trial, nor were they told that the comparative treatments were to be allotted by random sampling numbers. Many doctors believed it would be cruel to undermine the relationship of trust under these bewildering and paralysing circumstances (the magnitudes of benefit and risk of the new antibiotic were unknown). It seemed cowardly to shift the responsibility for the decision to enrol on to the shoulders of frightened patients.

The longstanding paternalistic attitude of doctors continued to dominate medical research during the first 20 years of increasing experience with RCTs. And, in these first two decades, participating doctors were expected to enrol all of their eligible patients in a given trial.

INFORMED CONSENT

In the USA, this paternalistic stance was outlawed in the mid-1960s, when the requirement for formal consent was introduced by fiat.[3] For the past quarter of a century, in most countries of the world, only patients who had given informed consent could be enrolled in RCTs. As a result of this shift from enrolment decisions made by doctors to the freely exercised choice of individual patients, the composition of populations in clinical trials changed. Many patients, when told about the randomisation requirement, now refused to take part. For example, MacIntyre noted[4] that "poor recruitment [in RCTs] is hampering research", and he cited instances of the difficulty in the UK and the USA.

In the hope of overcoming these problems, Zelen proposed[5] that the consent-before-randomisation sequence be reversed. When randomisation of eligible patients is completed, he argued, patients allotted to standard care can be treated immediately; there is no need for informed consent, since they will receive the accepted form of care. In Zelen's original plan only those allotted to the experimental arm of the trial are informed; they receive the experimental treatment if they give formal consent and standard care otherwise. Some critics saw the plan as an unfair way to circumvent the requirement that all patients enrolled in a trial must give their fully informed consent. Later, a double randomised consent design was proposed; here, formal permission is also obtained from patients allocated to standard treatment. But questions about full disclosure are still debated,[6] and there are serious statistical drawbacks with the design.[7]

When agreement to enrol is based on patients' preferences for individual treatments, the group assembled is unlikely to mirror the target population of all eligible patients. There is ample opportunity for sampling distortion, and extrapolation from results obtained in treatments of the non-random cohorts in RCTs must, at the very least, be questioned. Ellenberg[8] has recently pointed out that "the scientific community has not … yet accepted the necessity for critical assessment of the method of sample selection in the planning and execution of [medical] studies as a fundamental underpinning of [these investigations]". He then cites several examples of non-compliance with the strict requirements of random sampling in studies involving free-willing patients.

A telling example of the extrapolation problem surfaced, Ellenberg notes, after the results of the International Extracranial/Intracranial Anastomosis trial were published. Many eligible patients had not been enrolled. Moreover, some of those excluded received the experimental treatment outside the trial.[9] A committee convened to examine the question of whether the trial results should be generalised concluded[10] that "the issue cannot be resolved, because the data on the patients operated on outside the trial are so limited".

PSYCHOSOCIAL INFLUENCES

An estimate of the size of the beneficial effect expected may be unreliable when that projection is based on trials in which the intervention was prescribed arbitrarily and covertly (random allotment of masked treatments). These trials, the critics point out, do not reproduce the situations found in everyday life in which there is open use of the treatment by individualised prescription according to the free choice of doctors and their patients. For instance, these views have given rise to a proposal for clinician-preferred treatment trial formats;[11] proponents argue that "a clinician who prefers [a] treatment for a particular patient may impart his enthusiasm and obtain better compliance than one who does not".

Although systematic efforts to dissect out and measure the size of such non-specific effects have not been made, the critics are quite right to raise these questions. The long history of the efficacy of placebos in medicine suggests that psychosocial influences cannot be ignored; they may either augment or repress the purely biological responses to a treatment when patients do or do not receive the treatments they prefer. But the argument overlooks an antecedent need to protect patients from exploitation by overblown claims of efficacy, and from unlimited exposure to unexpected dangers of innovation.

PROTECTION OF PATIENTS

In the present era of powerful medical weaponry, clinical researchers must assume, in the patient's best interest, that in addition to the hoped for effect, every new treatment does have some, as yet unknown, effect on the expected course of disease. The dark suspicion is based on past experience: there are no "magic bullets" (therapeutic agents are rarely, if ever, so specific that they strike only the intended target of action). Since all treatments are expected to produce some unintended effects, there is ample justification for insisting on a rigorous experimental format to obtain an estimate of the expected size of the hoped for benefit and size of any serious risk, before the untested intervention is introduced for general use. (Once the genie escapes from the bottle, it is extremely difficult, and usually impossible to put him back in.)

The sulfisoxazole lesson

Soon after RCTs were introduced, a dreadful experience showed the need for rigorous evaluation early in the life of a medical innovation. In the 1950s, favourable anecdotal reports from hospitals throughout the world provided the rationale for giving penicillin plus sulfisoxazole to all very small neonates transferred from outside hospitals to the Babies Hospital premature infant station in New York City. This prophylactic antibiotic treatment was used to reduce the risk of fatal sepsis in these highly susceptible babies. In 1954, a new prophylactic regimen was proposed (subcutaneous oxytetracycline); this provided an opportunity to begin a systematic programme to test all unevaluated treatments used in this special care nursery.

The RCT undertaken[12] to compare the two prophylactic antibacterial regimens revealed a startling effect. Although the number of fatal infections was lower among infants receiving standard treatment (penicillin plus sulfisoxazole), this outcome of interest, specified before the trial began, became irrelevant. The mortality was strikingly higher in infants treated with this widely used regimen (60/95 deaths in penicillin and sulfisoxazole treated infants vs 27/97 deaths in oxytetracycline-treated babies). The necropsy findings were also shocking: kernicterus (a highly lethal form of brain damage) occurred almost entirely in infants who received standard treatment (19 instances of kernicterus among 46 necropies of infants who received penicillin plus sulfisoxazole vs one example of kernicterus among 22 necropsies of infants in the oxytetracycline-treated group). A retrospective review of the pathological findings in necropsies of infants who died before the RCT in 1954 revealed a sharp rise in the occurrence of kernicterus coincident with the introduction of penicillin plus sulfisoxazole. The damning association had been completely overlooked among the myriad of abnormal conditions found at necropsy in these marginally viable infants with a very high mortality rate. (5 years after this trial, the mechanism underlying the disastrous effect was uncovered by in-vitro studies[13] and in laboratory animals.[14])

The clinical trialists took some comfort in the knowledge that the RCT saved half the enrolled babies from exposure to the unrecognised hazard of a treatment that was used very confidently throughout the world. They were sobered, however, by the realisation that if a controlled trial had been conducted originally, when the new regimen was first introduced, the overall size of this therapeutic disaster could have been reduced substantially.

The lesson learned from this and other experiences during the past four decades is clear. First, clinical researchers must protect their patients by conducting rigorous RCTs of medical and surgical innovations. And the protection afforded by the hedging strategy of randomisation should begin, Chalmers has advised,[15] with the very first patient treated with an untested intervention.

OUTCOMES OF NON-RANDOMISED PATIENTS

When only a relatively small and self-selected proportion of eligible patients agreed to enrol in an RCT, the call for additional information about the fate of all patients not enrolled—all ineligible patients plus eligible "refusers"—should not be ignored. Ellenberg argues[8] that this information (obtained at each stage of selection, beginning with the screening of patients with the target disorder to the final enrolment of those who consent) will provide information about the impact of the selection process. This insight may establish some basis for judging limits when generalising results obtained in an intervention trial. However, as Ellenberg points out, strict quantification of the effect of selection is difficult if not impossible.

Comprehensive cohort design

Olschewski and Scheurlen[16] described a partly randomised trial design, which they called a "comprehensive cohort study" (a prospective cohort follow-up study with a randomised subcohort). The approach should be reserved, they suggested, for trials in which a relatively large proportion of eligible patients refuse randomisation because they or their doctors have a definite preference and when the a priori probability of no treatment difference is high. The challenge to the analyst is to determine the extent to which the results observed in the relatively small number of randomised patients can be extrapolated to the target population of interest.

Olschewski's group has suggested that this can be approached by comparing the outcomes in the randomised and non-randomised groups (taking randomisation status into account, as one of the indicator variables included in the usual covariates for treatment, and the important prognostic factors). They showed the use of this approach in the analysis of a trial of radiotherapy versus mastectomy for treatment of nonmetastatic breast cancer (less than 10% of eligible patients agreed to randomisation) and in the Coronary Artery Surgery Study[17] (only a third of eligible patients accepted randomisation).

These attempts to quantify the external validity of trials (based on follow-up of all patients irrespective of randomisation status) are interesting, but the results are not conclusive. Moreover, the warning sounded by Olschewski's group should be emphasised: the approach cannot substitute for a randomised comparison and the randomised cohort itself must be large enough to assure a reliable estimate of the treatment effect.

Patient-preference design

Bradley and co-workers[18–20] have noted the special difficulties that turn up when evaluating participative interventions (those requiring self-monitoring, diet, self-medication, and the like). In these situations, study formats in which patients make their own choice of the treatments on offer provide information about the feasibility of the proposed interventions. Here, they have argued, patients' preferences are relevant variables.

Bradley's group has also pointed to the difficulty in interpreting results after randomised allocations, when some patients agree to enrol only because a new treatment is unavailable outside the study. If these patients with preferences are allotted to what they

regard as the wrong treatment arm of the trial, their disappointment may lead to poor cooperation and to drop out after randomisation.

Bradley's group has emphasised that the goal of "self-choice" alternatives to randomised design is to enrol all eligible patients. (For example, in a partly randomised scheme, patients with no preference are assigned to treatments in random order, creating sets of randomised groups and a set of other patients with a specific preference who have their treatment of choice, the same design as that of Olschewski and co-workers noted above.) These adaptive approaches, determined by the aims of the investigation and the characteristics of treatment, Bradley's group suggests, have made it possible to explore the association of psychosocial factors and outcomes in several disorders. Further evidence, in the form of independent replications, is needed to support the claim.

Wennberg has emphasised[21] the importance of patients' preferences for various "soft outcomes" (quality of life) when evaluating proposed treatments in, for example benign prostatic hypertrophy. When informed of the uncertainties about probabilities of symptom relief, few patients, he finds, are willing to accept randomisation. Wennberg proposed a trial design in which patients would be randomly assigned to a "preference arm" or to an "RCT arm" (the same interventions would be compared in both arms). The aim of the exercise would be that of comparing the probabilities for symptom relief after the same treatment in the two modes of assignment. Wennberg makes the hopeful prediction that a treatment chosen by patients who believe it will help them will experience more relief than after random assignment of this same treatment.

Till and colleagues[22] have also been interested in evaluating interventions that have an impact on quality of life. They make a distinction between "preference studies" (surveys of patients or their surrogates to assess their intentions concerning proposed interventions) and "preference trials" (assess consequences when a prospective cohort of trial-eligible patients actually choose their own preferred treatment from among the options on offer, the results from previous RCTs having been equivocal). Till's group views preference trials as supplemental to RCTs, rather than as an alternative to them.

An example of a partly randomised trial to examine the relation between patients' preferences and acceptability of treatment was conducted by Henshaw and co-workers.[23] Pregnant women eligible for abortion in the first trimester were asked to choose between two methods to terminate the pregnancy (mifepristone/gemeprost or vacuum aspiration). Almost half of the women (168/363) expressed a preference; the remainder (195/363) were willing to undergo either method, and were randomly allocated to one of the alternatives under test. On follow-up questionnaires, no important differences in acceptability were found among women allocated to the method of their choice. However, this was not true of women in the randomised group: only two women allocated to surgical termination indicated they would, in future, opt for a different method; 21 women assigned to the medical method of abortion said they would choose another method next time. This trial format, the authors suggest, provided information that would not have been unearthed without allowance for a patient-preference arm in the study design.

In some instances the information needed cannot be obtained when a patient-preference is offered. For example, Hickish and others[24] treated patients with lung cancer with a fixed course of chemotherapy. Then they began a trial in which patients who had symptomatic improvement were offered randomisation either to continue with a further fixed course or to stop. 17 patients were eligible for this new trial, but only four consented to randomisation; 13 wished to continue with chemotherapy. The researchers were convinced that duration of palliative chemotherapy was an important question, but the brief experience suggested that a conventional pretreatment randomisation design will be necessary to look for an answer in a future trial.

It does seem reasonable to assume that patients who are given treatments they prefer do better than others who are unhappy about treatments prescribed for them. But the difficulties of making causal inferences on the basis of comparisons between randomised and non-randomised groups should not be minimised. There are always questions about the validity of comparing outcomes of self-selected treatment with any other experience. The dependability of these evaluations is crippled by the potential influence of uncontrolled confounders in non-randomised comparisons.

FUTURE STUDIES

Participants in a recent workshop[25] recommended further study of the question of how patients' preferences affect outcomes in clinical trials. There is also a need for continued study of the influences that determine patients' preferences.

A distinction needs to be drawn between informed choice (in which patients rely on the estimates of the size of risks and benefits of proposed interventions, as reported in reliable overviews[26]) and subjective preference (in which patients ignore the available evidence and prefer to rely on prayer, on a hunch, or the advice of friends, relatives, or seers for a decision). The large amount of research on how judgments under uncertainty are made in everyday life[27] is relevant here. What emerges from these studies is a blemished portrait of human capabilities: people's judgmental biases are found to be large and persistent. There is simply no evidence to support the notion that in a given set of circumstances in medicine the preferences of rational persons are in any way uniform.

For instance, Kassirer[28] points to at least seven situations in which patients' preferences are expected to vary widely (he uses the term utility-sensitive for these circumstances): (a) when there are major differences in the kinds of possible outcomes (for example, death and disability); (b) when there are major differences between treatments in the likelihood and impact of complications; (c) when choices involve trade-offs between near-term and long-term outcomes; (d) when one of the choices can result in a small chance of a grave outcome; (e) when the apparent difference between options is marginal; (f) when a patient is particularly averse to taking risks; and (g) when a patient attaches unusual importance to certain possible outcomes.

While there is wide agreement that the RCT is the only reliable way to compare therapies, there is no clear view of how best to proceed when randomisation is either impossible or unacceptable to most patients. Perhaps ongoing studies, by psychologists and decision theorists, will help decipher the complex interaction between doctors and their patients when faced with the need to act under conditions of uncertainty. We suspect that the most difficult hurdles are the widespread misconceptions about probability. Paulos[29] observed that many notions are as primitive as that of the barber who revealed his lottery strategy: "The way I figure it, I can either win or lose, so I've got a 50–50 shot at it".

The grant to WAS by the Nuffield Provincial Hospitals Trust of a Cochrane Fellowship at the UK Cochrane Center is gratefully acknowledged. We are grateful to Iain Chalmers for many helpful discussions.

References

1   Hill AB. Suspended judgment. Memories of the British streptomycin trial in tuberculosis. *Controlled Clin Trials* 1990; **11**: 77–79.

2   Katz J. *The silent world of doctor and patient.* New York: The Free Press, 1982.

3   Faden R, Beauchamp TL. *A history and theory of informed consent.* Oxford: Oxford University Press, 1986.

4   MacIntyre IMC. Tribulations for clinical trials. Poor recruitment is hampering research. *BMJ* 1991; **302**: 1099–100.

5   Zelen M. A new design for randomized clinical trials. *N Engl J Med* 1979; **300**: 1242–45.

6   Editorial. Your baby is in a trial. *Lancet* 1995; **345**: 805–06.

7   Altman DG, Whitehead J, Parmar MKB, Stenning SP, Fayers PM, Machin D. Randomised consent designs in cancer clinical trials. *Eur J Cancer* (in press).

8   Ellenberg JH. Cohort studies: selection bias in observational and experimental studies. *Stat Med* 1994; **13**: 557–67.

9   Sundt TM Jr. Special reports: was the international randomized trial of extracranial-intracranial arterial bypass representative of the population at risk? *N Engl J Med* 1987; **316**: 814–16.

10 Barnett HJM, Sackett D, Taylor DW. Are the results of the extracranial-intracranial bypass trial generalizable? *N Engl J Med* 1987; **316**: 820–24.

11 Korn EL, Baumrind S. Randomised clinical trials with clinician-preferred treatment. *Lancet* 1991; **337**: 149–52.

12 Silverman WA, Andersen DH, Blanc WA, Crozier DN. A difference in mortality rate and incidence of kernicterus among premature infants allotted to two prophylactic antibacterial regimens. *Pediatrics* 1956; **18**: 614–25.

13 Odell GB. Studies in kernicterus, I: the protein binding of bilirubin. *J Clin Invest* 1959; **38**: 823–33.

14 Johnson L, Sarmiento F, Blanc WA, Day R. Kernicterus in rats with an inherited deficiency of glucuronyl transferase. *Am J Dis Child* 1959; **97**: 591–608.

15 Chalmers TC. Randomization of the first patient. *Med Clin North Am* 1975; **59**: 1035–38.

16 Olschewski M, Scheurlen H. Comprehensive cohort study: an alternative to randomized consent design in a breast preservation trial. *Methods Information Med* 1985; **24**: 131–34.

17 Olschewski M, Schumacher M, Davis KB. Analysis of randomized and nonrandomized patients in clinical trials using the comprehensive cohort follow-up study design. *Controlled Clin Trials* 1992; **13**: 226–39.

18 Bradley C. Clinical trials: time for a paradigm shift? *Diab Med* 1988; **5**: 107–09.

19 Brewin CR, Bradley C. Patients' preferences and randomised clinical trials. *BMJ* 1989; **299**: 313–15.

20 Bradley C. Designing medical and education intervention studies: a review of some alternatives to conventional randomised controlled trials. *Diab Care* 1993; **2**: 509–18.

21 Wennberg JE. What is outcomes research? Institute of Medicine. Medical Innovation at the Crossroads. Vol I. Modern methods of clinical investigation. Washington: National Academy Press, 1990.

22 Till JE, Sutherland HJ, Meslin EM. Is there a role for preference assessments in research on quality of life in oncology? *Qual Life Res* 1992; **1**: 31–40.

23 Henshaw RC, Naji SA, Russell IT, Templeton AA. Comparison of medical abortion with surgical vacuum aspiration: women's preferences and acceptibility of treatment. *BMJ* 1993; **307**: 714–17.

24 Hickish TF, Smith IE, Middleton G, Nicolson M. Patient preference for palliative chemotherapy for non-small cell lung cancer. *Lancet* 1995; **345**: 857–58.

25 Silverman WA. Patients' preferences and randomised trials. *Lancet* 1994; **343**: 1586.

26 Cochrane Database of Systematic Reviews (database on disk and CD ROM). The Cochrane Collaboration. London: BMJ Publishing Group, 1995.

27 Kahneman D, Slovic P, Tversky A, eds. Judgment under uncertainty. Heuristics and biases. Cambridge: Cambridge University Press, 1982.

28 Kassirer JP. Incorporating patients' preferencs into medical decisions. *N Engl J Med* 1994; **330**: 1895–96.

29 Paulos JA. Beyond numeracy. New York: Vintage Books, 1992.

This information is reproduced by permission of the NHS Executive South East Research and Development Directorate

GUIDELINES FOR RESEARCHERS

Patient Information Sheet & Consent Form

The guidance which follows applies primarily to multi-centre pharmaceutical studies and encompasses the ICH Good Clinical Practice guidelines. However, the principles and much of the content will be of use to researchers writing information sheets in their particular fields, for trials involving patients, patient volunteers and healthy volunteers. You will find it helpful to refer also to other guidelines produced for writing patient information sheets.

Potential recruits to your research study must be given sufficient information to allow them to decide whether or not they want to take part. An Information Sheet should contain information under the headings given below where appropriate, and in the order specified. It should be written in simple, non-technical terms and be easily understood by a lay person. Use short words, sentences and paragraphs. 'The readability' of any text can be roughly estimated by the application of standard formulae. Checks on readability are provided in most word processing packages.

Use headed paper of the hospital/institution where the research is being carried out. Patient Information Sheets submitted to an MREC should be headed simply 'Hospital/Institution/GP Practice headed paper'. **If you are a local researcher for an MREC approved study, the Patient Information Sheet should be printed on local hospital/surgery paper with local contact names and telephone numbers before it is submitted to the LREC.** Unheaded paper is not acceptable.

1. STUDY TITLE

Is the title self explanatory to a lay person? If not, a simplified title should be included.

2. INVITATION PARAGRAPH

This should explain that the patient is being asked to take part in a research study. The following is a suitable example:

'You are being invited to take part in a research study. Before you decide it is important for you to understand why the research is being done and what it will involve. Please take time to read the following information carefully and discuss it with friends, relatives and your GP if you wish. Ask us if there is anything that is not clear or if you would like more information. Take time to decide whether or not you wish to take part.

Consumers for Ethics in Research (CERES) publish a leaflet entitled. 'Medical Research and You'. This leaflet gives more information about medical research and looks at some questions you may want to ask. A copy may be obtained from CERES, PO Box 1365, London N16 0BW.

Thank you for reading this.'

3. WHAT IS THE PURPOSE OF THE STUDY?

The background and aim of the study should be given here. Also mention the duration of the study.

4. WHY HAVE I BEEN CHOSEN?

You should explain how the patient was chosen and how many other patients will be studied.

5. DO I HAVE TO TAKE PART?

You should explain that taking part in the research is entirely voluntary. You could use the following paragraph:-

'It is up to you to decide whether or not to take part. If you do decide to take part you will be given this information sheet to keep and be asked to sign a consent form. If you decide to take part you are still free to withdraw at any time and without giving a reason. This will not affect the standard of care you receive.'

6. WHAT WILL HAPPEN TO ME IF I TAKE PART?

You should say how long the patient will be involved in the research, how long the research will last (if this is different), how often they will need to visit a clinic (if this is appropriate) and how long these visits will be. You should explain if the patient will need to visit the GP (or clinic) more often than for his/her usual treatment and if travel expenses are available. What exactly will happen e.g. blood tests, x-rays, interviews etc.? Whenever possible you should draw a simple flowchart or plan indicating what will happen at each visit. What are the patient's responsibilities? Set down clearly what you expect of them.

You should set out simply the research methods you intend to use – the following simple definitions may help:-

Randomised Trial:

Sometimes because we do not know which way of treating patients is best, we need to make comparisons. People will be put into groups and then compared. The groups are selected by a computer which has no information about the individual – i.e. by chance. Patients in each group then have a different treatment and these are compared.

You should tell the patients what chance they have of getting the study drug/treatment e.g. a one in four chance.

Blind trial:

In a blind trial you will not know which treatment group you are in. If the trial is a double blind trial, neither you nor your doctor will know in which treatment group you are (although, if your doctor needs to find out he/she can do so).

Cross-over trial:

In a cross-over trial the groups each have the different treatments in turn. There may be a break between treatments so that the first drugs are cleared from your body before you start the new treatment.

Placebo:

A placebo is a dummy treatment such as a pill which looks like the real thing but is not. It contains no active ingredient.

7. What do I have to do?

Are there any lifestyle restrictions? You should tell the patient if there are any dietary restrictions. Can the patient drive?, drink?, take part in sport? Can the patient continue to take their regular medication? Should the patient refrain from giving blood? What happens if the patient becomes pregnant?

Explain (if appropriate) that the patient should take the medication regularly.

8. What is the drug or procedure that is being tested?

You should include a short description of the drug or device and give the stage of development.
You should also state the dosage of the drug and method of administration. Patients entered into drug trials should be given a card (similar to a credit card) with details of the trial they are in. They should be asked to carry it at all times.

9. What are the alternatives for diagnosis or treatment?

For therapeutic research the patient should be told what other treatments are available.

10. What are the side effects of taking part?

For any new drug or procedure you should explain to the patients the possible side effects. If they suffer these or any other symptoms they should report them next time you meet. You should also give them a contact

name and number to phone if they become in any way concerned.

The known side effects should be listed in terms the patient will clearly understand (e.g. 'damage to the heart' rather than 'cardiotoxicity'; 'abnormalities of liver tests' rather than 'raised liver enzymes'). For any relatively new drug it should be explained that there may be unknown side effects.

11. What are the possible disadvantages and risks of taking part?

For studies where there could be harm to an unborn child if the patient were pregnant or became pregnant during the study, the following (or similar) should be said:

> It is possible that if the treatment is given to a pregnant woman it will harm the unborn child. Pregnant women must not therefore take part in this study, neither should women who plan to become pregnant during the study. Women who are at risk of pregnancy may be asked to have a pregnancy test before taking part to exclude the possibility of pregnancy. Women who could become pregnant must use an effective contraceptive during the course of this study. Any woman who finds that she has become pregnant while taking part in the study should immediately tell her research doctor.'

Use the pregnancy statement carefully. In certain circumstances (e.g. terminal illness) it would be inappropriate and insensitive to bring up pregnancy.

There should also be an appropriate warning and advice for men if the treatment could damage sperm which might therefore lead to a risk of a damaged fetus.

If future insurance status e.g. for life insurance or private medical insurance, could be affected by taking part this should be stated (if e.g. high blood pressure is detected.) If the patients have private medical insurance you should ask them to check with the company before agreeing to take part in the trial. They will need to do this to ensure that their participation will not affect their medical insurance.

You should state what happens if you find a condition of which the patient was unaware. Is it treatable? What are you going to do with this information? What might be uncovered? E.g. high blood pressure, HIV status.

12. What are the possible benefits of taking part?

Where there is no intended clinical benefit to the patient from taking part in the trial this should be stated clearly. It is important not to exaggerate the possible benefits to the particular patient during the course of the study, e.g. by saying they will be given extra attention. This could be seen as coercive. It would be reasonable to say something similar to:

> 'We hope that both (all) the treatments will help you. However, this cannot be guaranteed. The information we get from this study may help us to treat future patients with (name of condition) better.'

23

13. What if new information becomes available?

If additional information becomes available during the course of the research you will need to tell the patient about this. You could use the following:-

> 'Sometimes during the course of a research project, new information becomes available about the treatment/drug that is being studied. If this happens, your research doctor will tell you about it and discuss with you whether you want to continue in the study. If you decide to withdraw your research doctor will make arrangements for your care to continue. If you decide to continue in the study you will be asked to sign an updated consent form.
>
> Also, on receiving new information your research doctor might consider it to be in your best interests to withdraw you from the study. He/she will explain the reasons and arrange for your care to continue.'

14. What happens when the research study stops?

If the treatment will not be available after the research finishes this should be explained to the patient. You should also explain to them what treatment will be available instead. Occasionally the company sponsoring the research may stop it. If this is the case the reasons should be explained to the patient.

15. What if something goes wrong?

You should inform patients how complaints will be handled and what redress may be available. Is there a procedure in place? You will need to distinguish between complaints from patients as to their treatment by members of staff (doctors, nurses etc.) and something serious happening during or following their participation in the trial i.e. a reportable serious adverse event.

Where there are no Association of the British Pharmaceutical Industry (ABPI) or other no-fault compensation arrangements, and the study carries risk of physical or significant psychological harm, the following (or similar) should be said:

> 'If you are harmed by taking part in this research project, there are no special compensation arrangements. If you are harmed due to someone's negligence, then you may have grounds for a legal action but you may have to pay for it. Regardless of this, if you wish to complain about any aspect of the way you have been approached or treated during the course of this study, the normal National Health Service complaints mechanisms may be available to you.'

Where there are ABPI or other no-fault compensation arrangements the following (or similar) should be included:

> 'Compensation for any injury caused by taking part in this study will be in accordance with the guidelines of the Association of the British Pharmaceutical Industry (ABPI). Broadly speaking the ABPI guidelines recommend that the sponsor, without legal commitment, should compensate you without you having to prove that it is at fault. This applies in cases where it is likely that such injury results from giving any new drug or any other procedure carried out in accordance with the protocol for the study. The sponsor` will not compensate you where such injury results from any procedure carried out which is not in accordance with the protocol for the study. Your right at law to claim compensation for injury where you can prove negligence is not affected. Copies of these guidelines are available on request.'

16. Will my taking part in this study be kept confidential?

You will need to obtain the patient's permission to allow restricted access to their medical records and to the information collected about them in the course of the study. You should explain that all information collected about them will be kept strictly confidential. A suggested form of words for drug company sponsored research is:

> 'If you consent to take part in the research any of your medical records may be inspected by the company sponsoring (and/or the company organising) the research for purposes of analysing the results. They may also be looked at by people from the company and from regulatory authorities to check that the study is being carried out correctly. Your name, however, will not be disclosed outside the hospital/GP surgery.'

or for other research:-

> 'All information which is collected about you during the course of the research will be kept strictly confidential, Any information about you which leaves the hospital/surgery will have your name and address removed so that you cannot be recognised from it.'

You should explain that for studies not being conducted by a GP, the patient's own GP will be notified of their participation in the trial. This should include other medical practitioners not involved in the research who may be treating the patient. You should seek the patient's agreement to this. In some instances agreement from the patient that their GP can be informed is a precondition of entering the trial.

17. What will happen to the results of the research study?

You should be able to tell the patients what will happen to the results of the research. When are the results likely to be published? Where can they obtain a copy of the published results? Will they be told which arm of the study they were in? You might add that they will not be identified in any report/publication.

This article was first published in the *Journal of the American Medical Association* and is reproduced by permission of the American Medical Association

A PROPOSAL FOR STRUCTURED REPORTING OF RANDOMIZED CONTROLLED TRIALS

The Standards of Reporting Trials Group

Reprint requests to the Clinical Epidemiology Unit, Loeb Medical Research Institute, Ottawa Civic Hospital, 1053 Carling Ave, Ottawa, Ontario, Canada K1Y 4E9 (Mr Moher).

A randomized controlled trial (RCT) is the most reliable method of assessing the efficacy of health care interventions.[1,2] Reports of RCTs should provide readers with adequate information about what went on in the design, execution, analysis, and interpretation of the trial. Such reports will help readers judge the validity of the trial.

There have been several investigations evaluating how RCTs are reported. In an early study, Mahon and Daniel[3] reviewed 203 reports of drug trials published between 1956 and 1960 in the Canadian Medical Association Journal. Only 11 reports (5.4%) fulfilled their criteria of a valid report. In a review of 45 trials published during 1985 in three leading general medical journals, Pocock and colleagues[4] reported that a statement about sample size was only mentioned in five (11.1%) of the reports, that only six (13.3%) made use of confidence intervals, and that the statistical analyses tended to exaggerate intervention efficacy. Altman and Doré[5] reviewed 80 reports of trials published in 1987 and 1988 and found that information about the type of randomization was only reported in 32 (40%) of the trials. Schulz and colleague[6] reviewed 206 reports of trials published during 1990 and 1991 in two British and two US obstetries and gynecology journals. Only 66 (32%) of the trials reported on how the randomization sequence was generated and only 47 (22.8%) reported on how intervention assignment was concealed until the allocation of therapy. Gøtzsche[7] has suggested the quality of RCT reports in rheumatology may be so weak that it may be impossible to place any confidence in the statistical analyses or conclusions.

A few years ago, to improve the quality of reporting of clinical research, more informative abstracts were developed.[8] Such abstracts provide readers with a series of headings pertaining to the design, conduct, and analysis of a trial and standardized information within each heading. Evidence to date indicates that more informative abstracts have had a positive impact on how the results of abstracts are communicated.[9] More recently, there has been a call to extend more informative abstracts to include structured reporting of the text of each RCT.[10]

A workshop was held in Ottawa, Ontario, on October 7 and 8, 1993, with the aim of developing a new scale to assess the quality of RCT reports. However, during preliminary discussions, participants felt that many of the suggested scale items were irrelevant because they were not regularly reported by authors. There was unanimous agreement that the remainder of the workshop should focus on ways to improve the reporting of RCTs. This report provides a summary of that workshop.

METHODS

Based on prior research,[11] we identified investigators who had published or were developing a scale to assess quality. We also identified researchers who had experience in the design, conduct, and analysis of RCTs, as well as those who had made several contributions to the methodology of RCTs. Our intent was to keep the number of invitees small while comprehensive in scope. Once all potential participants were identified, invitations to participate in the workshop were sent to 32 individuals, of whom 30 agreed to participate.

A 144-item questionnaire was sent to invitees (n=19) primarily responsible for the development of a scale. The questionnaire asked participants to rate which content areas and items they thought important to include when assessing the quality of an RCT. These content areas focused on general characteristics (ie, sample size, informed consent, description of patients, interventions, and outcomes) and internal validity (ie, participant assignment, masking, participant follow-up, and approaches to statistical analysis) of a trial. Based in part on the questionnaire responses, four content areas were identified (participant assignment, masking, participant follow-up, and statistical analysis) for discussion during the workshop.

Once the content areas were decided all participants were sent a questionnaire asking them to indicate the content area groups in which they would like to participate. Based in part on these responses, participants were divided into one of the groups. We attempted to balance each small group with a scale developer, a clinical trialist, and a content specialist. The workshop comprised small group and plenary sessions. Each small group had an invited chair and a rapporteur, and each plenary session had an invited chair.

24

The group as a whole was first asked to agree on definitions of "quality" and "structured reporting." Each small group was asked to identify items they thought should be included in a structured report of an RCT. To identify items and decide whether they were considered essential or not, the small groups used a modified Delphi process. It was emphasized that this selection of items should be based on elements of trial design and conduct relevant to internal validity. For each item chosen, the small groups were asked to state whether its importance was based on conviction alone or on empirical research, and failure to clearly report, such information was associated with systematically different estimates of intervention effects. For example, Schulz and colleagues[12,13] reviewed 250 reports of RCTs and found the odds ratios in the unclearly concealed trials were on average 30% (95% confidence interval, 21% to 38%) lower than in the adequately concealed trials (ie, they estimated the intervention to be more effective than it really was). Items not based on empirical evidence were identified to generate a research agenda for the future.

The small groups were also asked to identify which items should be included in a checklist to be used by readers when reviewing an RCT. The chair and rapporteur of each small group made a short presentation of the results of their session at the plenary sessions, and these were followed by discussions with all workshop participants. As this article was going through its revisions, the group reemphasized that this is an evolutionary process. This process will be continued within the Cochrane Collaboration[14] and its Methods Working Groups as well as with others.

RESULTS

We defined structured reporting as "providing sufficiently detailed information about the design, conduct and analysis of the trial for the reader to have confidence that the report is an accurate reflection of what occurred during the various stages of the trial." We defined trial quality as "the confidence that the trial design, conduct, analysis, and presentation has minimized or avoided biases in its intervention comparisons," thus focusing on the internal validity of a trial. Assessing trial quality is based on a desire to estimate the likelihood that the trial results provide a valid (unbiased) estimate of the "truth" — something we cannot observe.

There were 32 items proposed for inclusion in the checklist to be used when preparing a report of an RCT (Table). This article elaborates on 24 items (numbered to correspond to the Table) the group felt to be essential. The results are divided into the four content areas.

CONTENT AREA 1—PARTICIPANT ASSIGNMENT

1. State the Unit of Assignment (eg, Individual, Cluster, or Geographic Region).—If the unit of assignment is not at the individual participant level, but a group, a rationale and description must be provided. Trials that use cluster randomization and are analyzed using standard statistical techniques applied to individual participants can lead, without appropriate adjustment, to invalid results.[18] Appropriate ways of analyzing and reporting group or cluster assignments are provided elsewhere.[19]

2. State the Method Used to Generate the Intervention Assignment Schedule (eg, Random Numbers Table, Computer Random Number Generator, or Random Permuted Blocks Stratified by What Factor).—If random allocation is not used, the alternative method (eg, day of the week) needs to be justified and described. Many trial reports do not provide essential information about assignment.[20] One of the principal advantages of randomization, noted by Hill,[21] is to ensure unpredictability of the intervention group to which the next participant will be assigned. Randomization is also essential to ensure balance for any unknown as well as known confounders, permitting unbiased comparisons between intervention groups.[2,20]

3. Describe the Method Used to Conceal the Intervention Assignment Schedule From Participants and Clinicians Until Recruitment Was Complete and Irrevocable.—To avoid selection bias in participant assignment to intervention, concealment is essential and should be feasible in all trials. Chalmers and colleagues[22] reviewed 145 reports of RCTs in the intervention for acute myocardial infarction to assess whether concealment of participant assignment was associated with estimates of intervention effects. Their results showed that trials that reported concealed assignment yielded smaller differences in case-fatality rates than trials in which assignment was unconcealed (ie, the latter were biased). This empirical work has been supported by Schulz.[12,13]

4. Describe the Method(s) Used to Separate the Generator and Executor of the Assignment.—We have defined generator as "the individual(s) who, using some bias-free method (eg, central randomization, numbered containers, or sealed opaque envelopes), generated the listing that identified the intervention assignment for every participant," and executor as "the individual(s) who, having determined a participant's eligibility, consults the assignment system for that participant's intervention designation." The person(s) who prepared the randomization scheme ideally should not be involved in determining eligibility, administering intervention, or assessing outcome. That, is obviously important because regardless of the methodological quality of the randomization process, such an individual would always have access to the allocation schedule and, thus, the opportunity to introduce bias.

5. Describe an Auditable Process of Executing the Assignment Method.—It should be possible for a review body to reconstruct, from trial records, exactly how each assignment was made. If the process of participant assignment to intervention cannot be

24

Checklist to Be Used by Authors When Preparing or by Readers When Analyzing a Report of a Randomized Controlled Trial

Item		Yes	No	Unable to Determine
1.	State the unit of assignment.	[ ]	[ ]	[ ]
2.	State the method used to generate the intervention assignment schedule.	[ ]	[ ]	[ ]
3.	Describe the method used to conceal the intervention assignment schedule from participants and clinicians until recruitment was complete and irrevocable.	[ ]	[ ]	[ ]
4.	Describe the method(s) used to separate the generator and executor of the assignment.	[ ]	[ ]	[ ]
5.	Describe an auditable process of executing the assignment method.	[ ]	[ ]	[ ]
6.	Identify and compare the distributions of important prognostic characteristics and demographics at baseline.	[ ]	[ ]	[ ]
7.	State the method of masking.	[ ]	[ ]	[ ]
8.	State how frequently care providers were aware of the intervention allocation, by intervention group.	[ ]	[ ]	[ ]
9.	State how frequently participants were aware of the intervention allocation, by intervention group.	[ ]	[ ]	[ ]
10.	State whether (and how) outcome assessors were aware of the intervention allocation, by intervention group.	[ ]	[ ]	[ ]
11.	State whether the investigator was unaware of trends in the study at the time of participant assignment.	[ ]	[ ]	[ ]
12.	State whether masking was successfully achieved for the trial.	[ ]	[ ]	[ ]
13.	State whether the data analyst was aware of intervention allocation.*	[ ]	[ ]	[ ]
14.	State whether individual participant data were entered into the trial database without awareness of intervention allocation.	[ ]	[ ]	[ ]
15.	State whether the data analyst was masked to intervention allocation.	[ ]	[ ]	[ ]
16.	Describe fully the numbers and flow of participants, by intervention group, throughout the trial.	[ ]	[ ]	[ ]
17.	State clearly the average duration of the trial, by intervention group, and the start and closure dates for the trial.†	[ ]	[ ]	[ ]
18.	Report the reason for dropout clearly, by intervention group.	[ ]	[ ]	[ ]
19.	Describe the actual timing of measurements, by intervention group.	[ ]	[ ]	[ ]
20.	State the predefined primary outcome(s) and analyses clearly.	[ ]	[ ]	[ ]
21.	Describe clearly whether the primary analysis has used the intention-to-treat principle.	[ ]	[ ]	[ ]
22.	State the intended sample size and its justification.	[ ]	[ ]	[ ]
23.	State and explain why the trial is being reported now.	[ ]	[ ]	[ ]
24.	Describe and/or compare trial dropouts and completers.	[ ]	[ ]	[ ]
25.	State or reference the reliability, validity, and standardization of the primary outcome.‡	[ ]	[ ]	[ ]
26.	Define what constituted adverse events and how they were monitored by intervention group.	[ ]	[ ]	[ ]
27.	State the appropriate analytical techniques applied to the primary outcome measure(s).	[ ]	[ ]	[ ]
28.	Present appropriate measures of variability (eg, confidence intervals for primary outcome measures).	[ ]	[ ]	[ ]
29.	Present sufficient simple (unadjusted) summary data on primary outcome measures and important side effects so that the reader can reproduce the results.	[ ]	[ ]	[ ]
30.	State the actual probability value and the nature of the significance test.	[ ]	[ ]	[ ]
31.	Present appropriate interpretations (eg, NS ≠ no effect; P<.05 ≠ proof).	[ ]	[ ]	[ ]
32.	Present the appropriate emphasis in displaying and interpreting the statistical analysis, in particular controlling for unplanned comparisons.	[ ]	[ ]	[ ]

* If the data analyst is not masked as to the interventions, new treatments may be grossly favored over standard treatments.[6,15]

† This information may sometimes reveal duplicate publication rather than two separate trials by the same author(s).

‡ Many trials are longitudinal and require several follow-up assessments. These assessments may be subjective based on the responses of questionnaires or scales. There is wide variation in how scales and questionnaires are constructed,[16,17] which may influence the assessment, reliability, validity, and responsiveness of the treatment outcome of interest. Providing information or references about the development of these outcome measures will enable readers to judge how confident they should be about the results.

reconstructed, the validity of the methodology, and, thus, trial results may be in question. Investigators should indicate that adequate trial records have been kept.

6. Identify and Compare the Distributions of Important Prognostic Characteristics and Demographics at Baseline.

—We have defined distribution as "the complete summary of the frequencies of the values or categories of a measurement made on a group of persons."[23] When reporting the results of any trial, it is important to present information regarding the comparability of intervention groups. This can best be achieved by presenting data on the distributions of measured baseline variables (other than intervention) thought to affect the outcome. Although *P* values are often used to compare the characteristics of the intervention groups, these statistical comparisons are inappropriate, unless the investigators suspect that the randomization schedule has not been adhered to. A discussion of appropriate ways to present comparability between intervention groups can be found elsewhere.[24]

24

CONTENT AREA 2—MASKING

7. State the Method of Masking (eg, Physical Characteristics [Whether the Interventions Look and Taste the Same] or Route of Administration).—If masking has not been used, sufficient justification should be provided. Many trial reports do not provide detailed information as to how masking was carried out,[7] whether single, double, or triple, and evidence indicates that masking can affect, estimates of intervention effects on subjective outcomes.[12,13,25,26]

8. State How Frequently Care Providers Were Aware of the Intervention Allocation, by Intervention Group.—To reduce bias, it, is important that caregivers be unaware of intervention group assignment.[27] For example, contamination bias, in which participants assigned to the control group receive the experimental intervention, and cointervention bias, in which participants assigned to either the control or the experimental group receive additional therapy, can influence intervention results.[28,29] Investigators should also report on how they assessed whether caregivers knew the intervention group to which the participants were being assigned.

9. State How Frequently Participants Were Aware of the Intervention Allocation, by Intervention Group.—To reduce bias, it is important that participants be unaware of their intervention group assignment. Otherwise, participants may become more aware of and may report more symptoms, leading to biased results.[26] Investigators should also report on how they assessed whether participants knew their assignment group.

10. State Whether (and How) Outcome Assessors Were Aware of the Intervention Allocation, by Intervention Group.—We recognize that the outcome assessor as described here may be the caregiver as described in item 7 (indeed, we use the latter only when we cannot, assure the former). When study clinicians guess intervention allocations at levels greater than chance, it need not be due to code-breaking, but may merely represent their suspicion about efficacy. For example, before the Canadian aspirin trial,[29] sulfinpyrazone (but not aspirin) was thought to be efficacious for transient ischemic attacks, whereas the trial found that the reverse was true. An end-of study polling of study clinicians found them to be statistically significantly wrong about intervention allocations; when participants fared well, their clinicians tended to believe that they had been on sulfinpyrazone.

**14. State Whether Individual Participant Data Were Entered Into the Trial Database Without Awareness of Intervention Allocation, and 15. Whether Data

Analyst Was Masked to Intervention Allocation.—When changes in the measurement scale are made, such as from a continuous to a binomial scale, results can be altered from statistically not significant to significant and vice versa depending on the cutoff points used.[30] Gøtzsche[7] has shown that unmasked data analysis can favor new interventions over standard interventions. To prevent this, cutoff points should be declared a priori, or rationale and cutoff points should be described.

CONTENT AREA 3—PARTICIPANT FOLLOW-UP

16. Describe Fully the Numbers and Flow of Participants, by Intervention Group, Throughout the Trial.—It is important to know how participants were followed up from the time of their randomization until they completed the trial. Unfortunately, it is often difficult to ascertain from reports whether participants were unavailable for follow-up during the course of a trial.[12,13] Without knowledge of this information, readers can make false conclusions about the efficacy of therapy. In a trial that, compared medical vs surgical therapy for carotid stenosis,[31] an analysis limited to those participants available for follow-up was statistically in favor of surgical intervention to reduce transient ischemic attacks, stroke, or death. However, when all participants had been accounted for and added to the analysis, the advantage of surgery was no longer statistically significant. Similar, less dramatic examples can be found elsewhere.[32]

Information on the flow of participants should include the number of participants eligible, randomized, treated, completing, and failing to complete the trial, by intervention group. Readers are likely to be in a better position to make decisions if the report documents what happened to all participants from the time they were initially asked to participate to when they were included in the analysis. The flow of participants through a trial can best be represented in a simple flow diagram (Figure).

18. Report the Reason for Dropout Clearly, by Intervention Group.—Participant dropout can be due to a host of factors (such as relocation or adverse reactions), some of which may be related to outcome. Information on dropouts should include reasons for dropout. Providing this information to readers will enable them to judge how confident they should feel about the results.[33] Information about participant dropout can often be best represented in a simple flow diagram (Figure).

19. Describe the Actual Timing of Measurements by Intervention Group.—If intervention groups are followed up with different intensity, this may lead to unmasking, cointervention, and distortion of outcome measurements. This information can best be represented in a simple flow diagram (Figure).

CONTENT AREA 4—APPROACHES TO STATISTICAL ANALYSIS

Methods Section

20. State the Predefined Primary Outcome(s) and Analyses Clearly.—The primary outcome(s), the main event or condition that the trial is designed to evaluate, differs from the secondary outcome(s), which is considered less important. If the primary outcome is not specified a priori and all outcomes are treated alike, there is an increased risk that multiple analyses mill result in false-positive, statistically significant results merely by chance.[34] There is a need for consistency between the predefined primary outcome and the actual primary, analysis.

21. Describe Clearly Whether the Primary Analysis Has Used the Intention-to-Treat Principle.—For the majority of trials, the preferred analysis is based on including all participants and their follow-up results in the intervention groups as initially assigned (intention to treat), although there may be important exceptions to this.[27,35] Analysis based on the intervention participants actually received, rather than the intervention.to which they were initially assigned (efficacy analysis), may produce invalid results.[36,37] If such efficacy analysis is used, it should be clearly reported and justified.

22. State the Intended Sample Size and Its Justification.—Surveys have shown that most trials do not report their intended sample size.[4,5,7,38,39] Describing and justifying, a priori, the size of a trial gives the reader a clear idea of what potential intervention differences the investigators were interested in detecting. Trials with insufficient sample size may result in potentially useful new therapies being ignored and/or therapies with significant toxicity being accepted. Recommendations on including sample size justification in a structured report have been made elsewhere.[10]

23. State and Explain Why the Trial Is Being Reported Now.—When a trial is being reported, it is important to know whether the trial has gone its intended course or has been terminated early (or late). The reasons for early (or late) termination, such as the discovery of large differences in outcome between intervention groups, unacceptably high adverse events in one group, or slow recruitment, should be specified.[40,41]

RESULTS SECTION

27. State the Appropriate Analytic Techniques Applied to the Primary Outcome Measure(s).—Evans and Pollock[42] reviewed the statistical methods reported in 45 trials in the antibiotic literature. In 31 reports (68.9%), the statistical methods were considered incorrect. In 11 reports (24.4%), the conclusions were not supported by the data. Similarly, in a survey of 20 trials submitted to the *British Medical Journal*, inappropriate analyses were reported in 12 trials (60%).[43] When comparing outcomes between three or more intervention groups, multiple pairwise tests will inflate the overall type I error, increasing the risks of a false-positive result.[34] Several solutions exist, including the following: specifying the primary contrasts beforehand, correcting for multiple comparisons, using another statistical test (such as an analysis of variance), or declaring openly that multiple comparisons have been made. Statistical methods are also likely to be improved by incorporating a statistician in the project,[44] particularly at the beginning.[32]

28. Present Appropriate Measures of Variability (eg, Confidence Intervals) for Primary Outcomes.— Appropriate measures of statistical uncertain should be reported along with the measure of central tendency. The standard error and confidence intervals are two closely related ways to describe such uncertainty. Presenting confidence intervals for any key estimate enables the reader to see the range within which the true effect or association may plausibly lie, rather than simply assessing whether it is statistically significant.[45]

29. Present Sufficient Simple (Unadjusted) Summary Data on Primary Outcome Measures and Important Side Effects so That the Reader Can Reproduce the Results (eg, Both Numbers of Participants and Numbers of Events, Such as p^1, p^2, n^1, and n^2).— Such presentations allow the reader to make a basic assessment of the intervention(s) and its potential risks.

30. State the Actual Probability Value and the Nature of the Significance Test. — Reporting the actual probability value provides the reader with a precise statement as to the significance of the trial result (eg, $P=.02$ rather than $P<.05$; $P=.20$ rather than "not significant" or NS). Although the probability value $P=.06$ is not statistically significant at the 5% level and $P=.04$ is, readers should not interpret these results as substantially different. A statement of the obtained values from the primary statistical test(s) should also be considered when reporting actual probability values (eg, $P=.02$, $z=2.33$). It is also important to state (preferably a priori) whether significance testing is onesided or two-sided. The one-sided approach only assesses whether the experimental therapy is better than the standard under consideration, but because one should always also consider that the experimental intervention may instead be inferior,[46] we recommend use of a two-sided P value. If on rare occasions the one-sided approach is used, it should be described and justified clearly.

There is often particular excitement when a P value falls into the <.05 category, but such an obsession with an arbitrary cutoff is entirely inappropriate. Unfortunately, P values do not express many important attributes of a trial's result: the overall magnitude and consistency of direction in the intervention difference and its range of uncertainty. The confidence interval addresses many of these issues, incorporating statistical as well as clinical significance.[45,47]

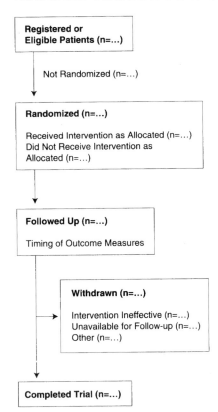

Flow diagram of how participants can be represented passing through the various stages of a trial, including withdrawals and timing of outcome measurements.

31. Present Appropriate Interpretations (eg, NS ≠ No Effect; *P*<.05 ≠ Proof).—Trials that report no statistically significant differences between intervention groups may conceal clinically important differences that could not be detected because of small sample size.[39,48] That is, small trials with apparently negative results may be erroneously reported as proof of no intervention benefit. Less commonly, a large trial that reports statistically significant results could have clinical differences that are too small to be of practical importance.[49]

32. Present the Appropriate Emphasis in Displaying and Interpreting the Statistical Analysis, in Particular Controlling for Unplanned Comparisons (eg, Subgroups, Multiple Outcome Measures, or Multiple Analyses).—Many trials report several outcome measures, repeated measures over time or subgroups, without appropriate adjustment for the consequent inflation of the type I error (risk of rejecting the null hypothesis of no intervention effect when in fact it is true). It is important to report all the challenges to the data, how many times they have been evaluated for statistical significance. If there is no statistical adjustment, this needs to be stated and justified. It is also important to report what methods (if any) have been used to control type I errors.[50]

Subgroup analysis is commonly conducted and inappropriately interpreted in many RCTs. Such analyses are more credible[51] when they have a rationale, are stated a priori, have sufficient statistical power, and appropriately carried out and interpreted cautiously,

with appropriate use of statistical tests of interaction. There is evidence that subgroup analyses can inappropriately affect intervention recommendations.[52] Oxman and Guyatt[52] and Yusuf and colleagues[53] provide valuable guidelines to the analysis and interpretation of subgroup analyses. Statistical presentation is not only providing factual information, but also relying on a judicious selection of appropriate presentation of data.

COMMENT

Clinical trialists have had at least four decades in which to improve the reporting of RCTs. Several guidelines have been published,[54-57] to facilitate this process, describing what needs to be included when reporting a trial. In addition, some journals[58] have published checklists of items for assessing RCTs to be used by authors, referees, and readers. Other journals[59] have published their policy on the statistical assessment of trials. With the possible exception of the British Journal of Obstetrics and Gynaecology,[6] these efforts have not had their intended impact.[60] We believe our proposal for structured reporting will improve the quality of reporting of RCTs. Our proposal may be unique in that it identifies which items should be included, why they should be included (empirical evidence, when available), and how they can be included (discussed hereinafter).

Structured reporting requires the reporting of what actually took place during the trial. We have provided a checklist of items that a group of trialists believe should be included in a structured report of a trial as well as why they need to be presented. Using this checklist, investigators will provide precise details about the design, conduct, and analysis of their trial. A principal advantage of such reporting is that all readers will have uniform and standardized information to review, unaffected by the writing nuances of authors and the policies of editors. This will give readers essential information about what happened during the trial, especially around issues affecting a trial's internal validity.

Some observers may argue that we have only included items, in particular those concerned with masking, that are more relevant to specific interventions, such as pharmacologic ones. Whether authors are reporting a triple-masked trial or a surgical trial in which it may be impractical or unethical to double-mask,[61] we believe it is important to report all the relevant items and justification if these were not carried out. In proposing structured reporting, our objective is not to pass judgment on the quality of the trial itself, but to improve on how it is reported to the reader.

Critics may view our proposal for structured reporting as rigid with a subsequent loss of the "creative process." On the contrary, our intent is not to discourage creativity in the research design process, but to encourage trial reports that provide readers with sufficient information. We believe there are several parts of a trial report, such as the introduction and discussion, where originality is needed. However, internal validity has little to do with the creative process and everything to do with providing accurate information to the reader about how the trial was performed. Describing the rationale for an intervention is just as important as describing how the participants were assigned to that intervention.

Where structured reporting will require inventiveness is in the style in which authors use it (ie, its format). One suggestion is for authors to report the methods and results section of their trial using the 24 essential items discussed above in a style similar to that of more informative abstracts. Each content area would be a separate heading with subheadings for each item within the content area. The number of items and subsequent text may vary slightly from report to report, especially for unmasked trials. What matters most when reporting trials using this approach is maintaining the structured report format.

Structured reporting, at least during the initial phase of its introduction, may increase the size of the trial report. It is also possible that structured reporting, with its focus on reporting issues relating to a trial's internal validity, may decrease the length of reports because other information, such as stating whether a trial was double-masked, can be removed as authors become more proficient in writing a structured report. Similar experiences were noted when more informative abstracts were first introduced.[62]

Our discussions indicated support for 24 recommendations and several areas where there is little or no evidence regarding the effects certain items have on estimates of intervention effects. There are important reasons to continue pursuing such methodologic investigations. The results of these studies will help to clarify which items should be added or deleted from a structured report and may influence which items should be included in any instrument developed to assess trial quality.

Although this report specifically addresses issues related to internal validity, several other items have been recommended to improve the reporting of RCTs. Laupacis and colleagues[63] have provided reasons for reporting results as absolute risk differences rather than relative risk reductions. Rochon et al[64] have recommended that age information be better reported, and Baar and Tannock[65] have encouraged the assessment and reporting of costs of therapy.

If structured reporting is to be successful, journal editors need to be involved to help refine the items to be included and to help with implementation and evaluation. This article documents the rationale for structured reporting of RCTs and suggests items to be included. We invite journal editors to review this article,

join us in making it more suitable for "instructions to authors," and implement structured reporting of RCTs in their journals. We will continue to carry out discussions and empirical studies of the relations between trial reporting, trial quality, and trial results.

The Standards of Reporting Trials Group consisted of the following: Erik Andrew, PhD, Nycomed Imaging, Oslo, Norway; Aslam Anis, PhD, Clinical Epidemiology Unit, Ottawa (Ontario) Civic Hospital; Tom Chalmers, MD, New England Medical Center for Health Services Research and Study Design, Boston, Mass; Mildred Cho, PhD, Institute for Health Policy Studies, University of California, San Francisco; Mike Clarke, PhD, Clinical Trial Service Unit, Radcliffe Infirmary, Oxford, England; David Felson, MD (member of writing committee), Boston (Mass) University School of Medicine; Peter Gøtzsche, MD (member of writing committee), The Nordic Cochrane Centre, Research and Development Secretariat, Copenhagen, Denmark; Richard Greene, MD, PhD, Agency for Health Care Policy and Research, Rockville, Md; Alejandro Jadad, MD, Oxford Regional Pain Relief Unit, Headington, Oxford, England; Wayne Jonas, MD, Medical Research Fellowship, Walter Reed Army Institute of Research, Washington, DC; Terry Klassen, MD, Division of Emergency Medicine, Children's Hospital of Eastern Ontario, Ottawa; Paul Knipschild, MD, Ryksuniversiteit Limburg, Vakgoep Epidemiologie, Limburg, the Netherlands; Andreas Laupacis, MD, MSc (member of writing committee), Clinical Epidemiology Unit, Ottawa (Ontario) Civic Hospital; Curtis L. Meinert, PhD, Department of Epidemiology, The Johns Hopkins University, Baltimore, Md; David Moher, MSc (chair and member of writing committee), Clinical Epidemiology Unit, Ottawa (Ontario); Civic Hospital; Graham Nichol, MD, Clinical Epidemiology Unit, Brigham and Women's Hospital, Boston, Mass; Andy Oxman, MD, Department of Health Services, National Institute of Public Health, Oslo, Norway; Marie-France Penman, BSeN, Multiple Sclerosis Clinic, Ottawa (Ontario) General Hospital; Stuart Pocock, PhD (member of writing committee), Medical Statistics Unit, London School of Hygiene and Tropical Medicine, University of London, (England); Joan Reisch, PhD, Department of Pediatries and Medical Computer Science, University of Texas Health Science Center, Dallas; David Sackett, MD (member of writing committee), Nuffield Department of Clinical Medicine, University of Oxford (England); Kenneth Schulz, Division of STD/HIV Prevention, National Center for Prevention Services, Centers for Disease Control and Prevention, Atlanta, Ga; Judy Snider, Department, of Epidemiology and Community Medicine, University of Ottawa (Ontario); Peter Tugwell, MD (member of writing committee), Department of Medicine, University of Ottawa (Ontario); Jon Tyson, MD, Department of Pediatries, University of Texas Southwestern Medical Center, Dallas; France Varin, PhD, Faculty of Pharmacy, University of Montreal (Quebec); Wikke Walop, PhD, Biometries Division, Drugs Directorie, Health Canada, Ottawa, Ontario; Sharon Walsh, MD, Deaprtment of Medicine, Ottawa (Ontario) Civic Hospital; and George Wells, PhD (member of writing committee), Clinical Epidemiology Unit, Ottawa (Ontario) Civic Hospital.

We would like to thank Du Pont Pharma, the National Health Research and Development Program, Health Canada, the Medical Research Council of Canada, Ortho-McNeil, and Rhône-Poulenc-Rorer for their financial support in convening the workshop. We would also like to thank Francis Rolleston for his encouragement, Carol Reichert for reviewing an earlier draft of the manuscript, and Iain Chalmers for his support in this process and his thoughtful comments on the manuscript.

References

1. Cook DJ, Guyatt GH, Laupacis A, Sackett DL. Rules of evidence and clinical recommendations on the use of antithrombotic agents. *Chest.* 1992;102:305S-311S.
2. Sacks H, Chalmers TC, Smith H. Randomized versus historical controls for clinical trials. *Am J Med.* 1982;72:233-240.
3. Mahon WA, Daniel EE. A method for the assessment of reports of drug trials. *Can Med Assoc J.* 1964;90:565-0!69.
4. Pocock SJ, Hughes MD, Lee RJ. Statistical problems in the reporting of clinical trials. *N Engl J Med.* 1987;317:426-432.
5. Altman DG, Doré CJ. Randomization and baseline comparisons in clinical trials. *Lancet.* 1990;335:149-153.
6. Schulz KF, Chalmers I, Grimes DA, Altman DG. Assessing the quality of randomization from reports of controlled trials published in obstetrics and gynecology journals. *JAMA.* 1994;272:125-128.
7. Gøtzsche PC. Methodology, and overt and hidden bias in reports of 196 double-blind trials of nonsteroidal anti-inflammatory drugs in rheumatoid arthritis. *Control Clin Trials.* 1989;10:31-56. Correction. 1989;10:356.

24

8. Ad Hoc Working Group for Critical Appraisal of the Medical Literature. A proposal for more informative abstracts of clinical articles. *Ann Intern Med*. 1987;106:598-604.

9. Haynes RB, Mulrow CD, Huth EJ, Altman DG, Gardner MJ. More informative abstracts revisited. *Ann Intern Med*. 1990;113:69-76.

10. Moher D, Dulberg CS, Wells GA. Statistical power, sample size, and their reporting in randomized controlled trials. *JAMA*. 1994;272:122-124.

11. Moher D, Jadad AR, Nichol. G, Penman M, Tugwell P, Walsh S. Assessing the quality of randomized controlled trials: an annotated bibliography of scales and checklists. *Control Clin. Trials*. In press.

12. Schulz KF, Chalmers I, Hayes RJ, Altman DG. Emperical evidence of bias: dimensions of methodologic quality associated with estimates of treatment effects in controlled trials. *JAMA*. In press.

13. Schulz KF. *Methodological Quality and Bias in Randomized Controlled Trials*. London, England: University of London; 1994. Thesis.

14. Chalmers I. The Cochrane Collaboration: preparing, maintaining, and disseminating systematic reviews of the effects of health care. *Ann N Y Acad Sci*. 1993;703:156-165.

15. Gøtzsche PC. Bias in double-blind trials. *Dan Med Bull*. 1990;37:329-336.

16. McDowell I, Newell C. *Measuring Health: A Guide to Rating Scales and Questionnaires*. New York, NY: Oxford University Press; 1987.

17. Steiner DL, Norman GR. *Health measurement Scales: A Practical Guide to Their Development and Use*. Oxford, England: Oxford University Press; 1989.

18. Donner A, Brown KS, Brasher P. A methodologic review of nontherapeutic intervention trials employing cluster randomization, 1979-1989. *Int J Epidemiol*. 1990;19:795-800.

19. Donner A. Statistical methodology for paired cluster designs. *Am J Epidemiol*. 1987;126:972-979.

20. Altman DG. Randomization: essential for reducing bias. *BMJ*. 1991;302:1481-1482.

21. Hill AB. The clinical trial. *N Engl J Med*. 1952;247:113-119.

22. Chalmers TC, Celano P, Sachs HS, Smith H. Bias in treatment assignment in controlled clinical trials. *N EngI J Med*. 1983;309:1358-1361.

23. Last JM, ed. *A Dictionary of Epidemiology*. 2nd ed. New York, NY: Oxford University Press; 1988:38.

24. Altman DG. Comparability of randomized groups. *Statistician*. 1985;34:125-136.

25. Colditz GA, Miller JN, Mosteller F. How study design affects outcomes in comparisons of therapy, I: medical. *Stat Med*. 1989;8:441-454.

26. Karlowski TR, Chalmers TC, Frenkel LD, Kapikian AZ, Lewis TL, Lynch JM. Ascorbic acid for the common cold: a prophylactic and therapeutie trial. *JAMA*. 1975;231:1038-1042.

27. Sackett DL, Gent M. Controversy in counting and attributing events in clinical trials. *N Engl J Med*. 1979;301:1410-1412.

28. Sackett DL. Bias in analytic research. *J Chronic Dis*. 1979;32:51-63.

29. The Canadian Cooperative Study Group. The Canadian trial of aspirin and sulfinpyrazone in threatened stroke. *N Engl J Med*. 1978;299:53-59.

30. Moses LE, Emerson JD, Hosseini H. Analyzing data from ordered categories. *N Engl J Med*. 1984; 311:442-448

31. Fields WS, Maslenikov V, Mayer JS, Hass WK, Remington R D, Macdonald M. Joint study of extracranial arterial occlusion, V: progress report of prognosis following surgery or nonsurgical treatment for transient cerebral ischemic attacks and cervical carotid artery lesions. *JAMA*. 1970;211:1993-2003.

32. Pocock SJ *Clinical. Trials: A Practical Approach*. Chichester, England: John Wiley & Sons Inc; 1983:182-186.

33. Laupacis A. The validity of survivorship analysis in total joint arthroplasty. *J Bone Joint Surg Am*. 1989;71:1111-1112.

34. Godfrey K. Comparing the means of several groups. In: Bailer JC III, Mosteller F, eds. *Medical Uses of Statistics*. 2nd ed. Boston, Mass: NEJM Books; 1992:233-257.

35. Makuch R, Johnson M. Issues in planning and interpreting active control equivalence studies. *J Clin Epidemiol*. 1989;42:503-511.

36. The Coronary Drug Project Research Group. Influence of adherence to treatment and response of cholesterol on mortality in the Coronary Drug Project. *N Engl J Med*. 1980;303:1038-1041.

37. Lee YJ, Ellenberg JH, Hirtz DG, Nelson KB. Analysis of clinical trials by treatment actually received: is it really an option? *Stat Med*. 1991;10:1595-1605.

38. DerSimonian R, Charette W, McPeek B, Mosteller F. Reporting on methods in clinical trials. In: Bailer JC III, Mosteller F, eds. *Medical Uses of Statistics*. 2nd ed. Boston, Mass: NEJM Books; 1992: 333-347.

39. Freiman JA, Chalmers TC, Smith H, Kuebler RR. The importance of beta, the type II error, and sample size in the design and interpretation of the randomized controlled trial: survey of 71 'negative' trials. *N Engl J Med*. 1978;299:690-694.

40. Laupacis A, Connolly SJ, Gent M, Roberts RS, Cairns JA, Joyner C, for the CAFA Study Group. How should results from completed studies influence ongoing clinical trials? the CAFA Study experience. *Ann Intern Med*. 1991;115:818-822.

41. Pocock SJ. When to stop a clinical trial. *BMJ*. 1992;305:235-240.

42. Evans M, Pollack AV. Trials on trial: a review of trials of antibiotic prophylaxis. *Arch Surg*. 1984;119:109-113.

43. Gardner MJ, Bond J. An exploratory study of statistical assessment of papers published in the British Medical Journal. *JAMA*. 1990;1263:1355-1357.

44. McKinney WP, Young MJ, Hartz A, Bi-Fong Lee M. The inexact use of Fisher's Exact Test in six major medical journals. *JAMA*. 1989;261:3430-3433.

45. Gardner MJ, Altman DG. Estimation rather than hypothesis testing: confidence intervals rather than P values. In: Gardner MJ, Altman DG, eds. Statistics With Confidence: Confidence Intervals and Statistical Guidelines. London, England: BMJ; 1989:6-19.

46. Echt DS, Liebson PR, Mitchell LB, et al. Mortality and morbidity in participants receiving encainide, flecainide, or placebo: the Cardiac Arrhythmia Suppression Trial. *N Engl J Med*. 1991;324:781-788.

47. Braitman LE. Confidence intervals assess both clinical significance and statistical significance. *Ann Intern Med*. 1991;114:515-517.

48. Amen, A, Roeber G, Vermeulen HJ, Verstraete M. Single-blind randomized multicentre trial comparing heparin and streptokinase treatment in recent myocardial infaretion. *Acta Med Scand*. 1969;505:1-35.

49. Steering Committee of the Physicians' Health Research Group. Final report on the aspirin component of the ongoing Physicians' Health Study. *N Engl J Med*. 1989;321:129-135.

50. Bauer P. Multiple testing in clinical trials. *Stat Med*. 1991;10:871-890.

51. Bulpitt CJ. Subgroup analysis. *Lancet*. 1988;2:31-34.

52. Oxman AD, Guyatt GH. A consumer's guide to subgroup analyses. *Ann Intern Med*. 1992;116:78-84.

53. Yusuf S, Wittes J, Probstfield J, Tyroler HA. Analysis and interpretation of treatment effects in subgroups of patients in randomized clinical trials. *JAMA*. 1991;266:93-98.

54. Simon R, Wittes RE. Methodologic guidelines for reports of clinical trials. *Can Treat Rep*. 1985;69:1-3.

55. Grant A. Reporting controlled trials. *Br J Obstet Gynaecol*. 1989;96:397-400.

56. Zelen M. Guidelines for publishing papers on cancer clinical trials: responsibilities of editors and authors. *J Clin Oncol*. 1983;1:164-169.

57. Mosteller F, Gilbert JP, McPeek B. Reporting standards and research strategies for controlled trials. *Control Clin Trials*. 1980;1:37-58.

58. Gardner MJ, Machin D, Campbell MJ. Use of checklists in assessing the statistical content of medical studies. *BMJ*. 1986;292:810-812.

59. Gore SM, Jones G, Thompson SG. The Lancet's statistical review process: areas for improvement by authors. *Lancet*. 1992;340:100-102.

60. Altman DG. Statistics in medical journals: developments in the 1980s. *Stat Med*. 1991;10:1897-1913.

61. Turner JA, Deyo RA, Loesel. JD, Von Korff M, Fordyee WE. The importance of placebo effects in pain treatment and research. *JAMA*. 1994;271:1609-1614.

62. Comans ML, Overbeke AJ. The structured summary: a tool for reader and author. *Ned Tijdschr Geneeskd*. 1990;134:2338-2343.

63. Laupacis A, Naylor CD, Sackett DL. How should the results of clinical trials be presented to clinicians? ACP *Journal Club*. 1992;A12-A14.

64. Rochon PA, Fortin PR, Dear KBG, Minaker KL, Chalmers TC. Reporting of age data in clinical trials of arthritis: deficiencies and solutions. *Arch Intern Med*. 1993;153:243-248.

65. Baar J, Tannock I. Analyzing the same data in two ways: a demonstration model to illustrate the reporting and misreporting of clinical trials. *J Clin Oncol*. 1989;7:969-978.

This article was first published in the BMJ *and is reproduced by permission of the* BMJ

Understanding controlled trials
WHAT IS ZELEN'S DESIGN?
David J Torgerson, Martin Roland

This is the fourth of an occasional series on the methods of randomised controlled trials   *BMJ* 1998;**316**:606

When patients do not receive their preferred treatment in randomised trials there may be difficulties with patient recruitment and scientific problems with bias.[1] For example, bias may occur when patients are aware of a new treatment not available to them and comply poorly with the standard treatment.

Zelen's design can address these difficulties[2][3] by randomising patients *before* consent to participate has been sought. Two types of the design exist: double and single consent. In the double consent version patients are initially offered the treatment to which they were randomised; however, if they decline the randomised treatment, they can then be offered alternative therapies—including the experimental treatment. In the single consent version only patients offered the experimental treatment are told there is an alternative treatment (the control) available. Patients randomised to the control treatment are not allowed the experimental treatment (although they are given unhindered access to any usual treatment facilities). Analysis is undertaken with patients retaining their original assignment.

Zelen's design has been much discussed and for most therapeutic trials is probably unethical. Occasionally, however, it has been chosen on ethical grounds. For example, in a trial of extracorporeal membrane oxygenation for infants with pulmonary hypertension Zelen's design was used as it was considered preferable not to raise false hopes among half the parents that there was a novel treatment available for their child only to have it denied them through the randomisation.[4]

Zelen's design may be particularly useful for evaluating population based interventions such as screening, where it is important to estimate the effects on a whole population. However, if the presence of the trial is known to the non-screened group this may artificially induce changes in that group which may influence the results (a Hawthorne effect). For example, in a randomised trial of bone density screening[5] the non-screened group were not contacted at baseline as this might have artificially increased their use of hormone replacement therapy. Had the trialists not used Zelen's design the investigators could not have been sure of the full unbiased impact of screening on uptake of hormone replacement therapy.

If bias due to patients knowing they are in the "usual care" group is to be avoided patients usually need to be followed up for key events at a distance so as not to alert them to the study. For example, in a randomised trial of colorectal cancer screening cancer events for both groups of patients were ascertained through medical records and a cancer registry.[6] By using Zelen's design in screening trials it is possible to achieve more accurate estimates of population outcomes such as cancer reduction[6][7] compared with the conventional trial designs.

There are obvious ethical problems in using Zelen's design to randomise patients without their consent[8] (though treatment consent is always sought). For some interventions, however, such as screening, this may be the only practical design For example, if all patients in the colorectal cancer screening trials had been screened but only a random half had been offered intervention, there would have been an ethical dilemma of not offering further investigation and treatment to control patients who appeared to be at high risk.

Zelen's design can have other disadvantages. If the trial requires intrusive data collection or monitoring then Zelen's design as control patients will be aware of the study. Given that intrusive data collection is not feasible, it may not be possible to use restrictive inclusive or exclusive patient recruitment criteria. Furthermore, if many patients refuse their original treatment, this will lead to a reduction in study power. Both these factors will lead to the need for a large sample size.[9]

National Primary Care Research and Development Centre, Centre for Health Economics, University of York, York YO1 5DD
David Torgerson, *senior research fellow*
National Primary Care Research and Development Centre, University of Manchester, Manchester M13 9PL
Martin Roland, *director of research and development*
Correspondence to: Dr Torgerson.

References

1   Torgerson DJ, Sibbald B. What is a patient preference design? *BMJ* 1998;**316**:360.
2   Zelen M. A new design for randomized clinical trials. *N Engl J Med* 1979;**300**:1242–5.
3   Zelen M. Randomized consent designs for clinical trials: An update. *Stats in Med* 1990;**9**:645–56.

4   O'Rourke PP, Crone RK, Vacanti JP, Ware JH, Lillehli CW, Parad RB et al. Extracorporeal membrane oxygenation and conventional medical therapy in neonates with persistent pulmonary hypertension of the new born: A prospective randomized study. *Pediatrics* 1989;**84**:957–63.

5   Torgerson DJ, Thomas RE, Campbell MK, Reid DM. Randomised trial of osteoporosis screening: HRT uptake and quality of life results. *Arch Intern Med* 1997;**157**:2121–5.

6   Hardcastle JD, Chamberlain JO, Robertson MHE, Moss SM, Amar SS, Balfour TW, et al. Randomised controlled trial of faecal-occult-blood screening for colorectal cancer. *Lancet* 1996;**348**:1472–7.

7   Kronborg O, Fenger C, Olsen J, Jorgensen OD, Sondergaard O. Randomised study of screening for colorectal cancer by faecal occult blood test. *Lancet* 1996;**348**:1467–71.

8   Smith R. Informed consent: the intricacies. *BMJ* 1997;**314**:1059–60.

9   Altman DG, Whitehead J, Parmar MKB, Stenning SP, Fayers PM, Machin D. Randomised consent designs in cancer clinical trials. *Eur J Cancer* 1995;**31A**;1934–44.

This article was first published in the BMJ *and is reproduced by permission of the* BMJ

Understanding controlled trials

WHAT IS A PATIENT PREFERENCE TRIAL?

David J Torgerson, Bonnie Sibbald

This is the third of an occasional series on the methods of randomised controlled trials *BMJ* 1998;**316**:360

A common problem in randomised controlled trials arises when patients (or their clinicians) have such strong treatment preferences that they refuse randomisation.[1] The absence of these patients from trials may restrict generalisation of the results, as participants may not be representative. A further potential source of bias exists when patients with strong treatment preferences are recruited and randomised. When it is not possible to blind patients to their treatment allocation they may suffer resentful demoralisation[2] if they do not receive their preferred treatment and may comply poorly. On the other hand, patients receiving their preferred treatment may comply better than average. There may therefore be a treatment effect which results from patient preferences and not from therapeutic efficacy. The effects of resentful demoralisation are so far a theoretical concern which have yet to be shown in practice, in part because they are difficult to evaluate.

Patients may be placed in one of three groups according to preference and willingness to be randomised: (*a*) patients who have no strong preferences and therefore consent to randomisation; (*b*) patients with a preference who still consent to randomisation; and (*c*) patients who refuse randomisation and opt for their treatment of choice.

To cope with patient preferences the use of a comprehensive cohort design[3] or the patient preference trial has been suggested.[4] Patients with treatment preferences are allowed their desired treatment; those who do not have strong views are randomised conventionally. Hence, in a trial of two interventions, A and B, we end up with four groups: randomised to A; prefer A; randomised to B; prefer B. The analysis of such a trial is uncertain. Any comparison using the nonrandomised groups is unreliable because of the presence of unknown and uncontrolled confounders.[5] At least one analysis should therefore be a comparison between the two randomised arms alone. Analyses which include the unrandomised groups should be treated as observational studies with known confounding factors adjusted for in the analysis. Olschewski and Scheurlen have suggested that an analysis using randomisation status as a covariate might

be helpful.[3] A further limitation of the patient preference approach is that it may increase the size and cost of trials.

An alternative to the partially randomised approach has been proposed whereby the strength and direction of patient preferences are elicited before randomisation, with all consenting patients randomised.[6] This approach combines the advantage of the partially randomised design—that is, gathering information on the effect of preference on outcome—but retains the rigour of a full randomised design.[6] The design has been used in a randomised trial of physiotherapy treatment for back pain and, despite most patients expressing a preference, no patient refused randomisation.[6] The practical advantages of establishing and including patient preferences in trials has not been fully established. However, using a patient preference design, Henshaw et al in a comparison of medical versus surgical abortion produced important additional information on the acceptability of the two treatments in different preference groups which would not have been be available in the usual trial.[7] In addition, a recent preference trial of early amniocentesis versus chorionic villus sampling for diagnosing fetal abnormalities showed that rate of pregnancy loss did not differ between the preference group and their randomised equivalent.[8] This trial is important in that only 38% of patients accepted randomisation. Thus, including the unrandomised patients in the trial offered some reassurance that the results could be extrapolated to a wider group of patients.

Patient preference designs complement, but do not replace randomised trials. However, measuring patient preferences within a fully randomised design deserves further use as this conserves all the advantages of a fully randomised design with the additional benefit of allowing for the interaction between preference and outcome to be assessed.

National Primary Care Research and Development Centre, Centre for Health Economics, University of York, York YO1 5DD
David Torgerson, *senior research fellow*
National Primary Care Research and Development Centre, University of Manchester, Manchester M13 9PL
Bonnie Sibbald, *reader in health services research*
Correspondence to: Dr Torgerson.

References

1   Fairhurst K, Dowrick C. Problems with recruitment in a randomized controlled trial of counselling in general practice: causes and implications. *J Health Serv Res Policy* 1996;**1**:77–80.

2   Bradley C. Designing medical and educational intervention studies. *Diabetes Care* 1993;**16**:509–18.

3   Olschewski M, Scheurlen H. Comprehensive cohort study: An alternative to randomised consent design in a breast preservation trial. *Meth Inform Med* 1985;**24**:131–4.

4   Brewin CR, Bradley C. Patient preferences and randomised clinical trials. *BMJ* 1989;**299**:313–5.

5   Silverman WA, Altman DG. Patient preferences and randomised dials. *Lancet* 1996;**347**:171–4.

6   Torgerson DJ, Klaber-Moffett J, Russell IT. Patient preferences in randomised trials: threat or opportunity? *J Health Serv Res Policy* 1996;**1**:194–7.

7   Henshaw RC, Naji SA, Russell TI, Templeton AA. Comparison of medical abortion with surgical vacuum aspiration: women's preferences and acceptability of treatment *BMJ* 1993;**307**:714–7.

8   Nicolaides K, de Lourdes Brizot M, Patel F, Snijers R. Comparison of chorionic villus sampling and amniocentesis for fetal karyotyping at 10–13 weeks gestation. *Lancet* 1994;**344**:935–9.

26

This article was first published by the British Journal of General Practice *and is reproduced by permission of the* British Journal of General Practice

BJGP 1998;**48**:1089-90

CLUSTER RANDOMIZATION: A TRAP FOR THE UNWARY

Martin Underwood, Adrian Barnett, Steven Hajioff

SUMMARY

Controlled trials that randomize by practice can provide robust evidence to inform patient care. However, compared with randomizing by each individual patient, this approach may have substantial implications for sample size calculations and the interpretation of results. An increased awareness of these effects will improve the quality of research based on randomization by practice.

Keywords: randomized controlled trials; statistical method; primary care; survey design.

INTRODUCTION

Both the current fashion for evidence-based medicine and the move towards a primary care led National Health Service mean that there is an increased requirement for scientifically robust data from general practice on which to base clinical and administrative decisions. Randomized controlled trials (RCTs) based in general practice are one of the best sources of such data.

A conventional RCT, randomizing by individual patient, does not always lend itself to hypothesis testing within general practice. There are situations in which it is appropriate to randomize the intervention by practice rather than by individual. Examples of these situations arise when:

- It would be difficult or inappropriate to randomize to deny access to some patients within a practice; e.g. for a health promotion initiative when waiting room gossip or promotional material in the waiting room could affect the control group.

- The intervention or resource is expensive and therefore would need to be used fully to be cost-effective; e.g. if specialist diagnostic or computer equipment was being used.

- The intervention is, by necessity, practice or clinician based; e.g. an education programme aimed at general practitioners or other members of the primary health care team.

CLUSTER RANDOMIZATION

Randomization by practice (cluster randomization) can have a large effect on sample size requirements for, and

analysis of, RCTs. This has not always been taken into account in published trials. Donner found that only three out of 16 trials randomizing by cluster produced a sample size justification based on cluster randomization.[1] More recently, Butler found that only three out of 10 trials of smoking cessation, based in primary care, had corrected for the effect of randomizing by cluster.[2]

The usual requirements for calculating a sample size for an RCT include the following:

- that the subjects are expected to behave independently

- that a principal outcome measure has been defined that will be sensitive to differences between the two groups

- that a clinically significant difference between intervention and control groups is defined, and

- that the required probabilities of a Type I error (rejecting the null hypothesis when it is in fact true) and a Type II error (accepting the null hypothesis when it is in fact false) have been defined.

The impact on sample size of cluster randomization is caused by the tendency for patients from the same practice to behave similarly owing to factors within the practice. Thus, individual patients cannot be said to react with total independence, thereby invalidating one of the basic assumptions of most statistical analyses.

Differences between practices that are measurable, such as the age or social class of patients, can, to some extent, be corrected for in the analysis. However, other factors that are not quantifiable, such as the physical environment of the practice, the personal characteristics of the care providers, or the type of person attracted to a particular practice, cannot be corrected for in the same way.

INTRA-CLUSTER CORRELATION COEFFICIENT

The magnitude of the effect of cluster randomization is quantified by the intra-cluster correlation coefficient (ICC), which is a statistical measure derived from the 'between' cluster and the 'within' cluster variation of the subjects.[3,4,5] If each individual's behaviour is unaffected by membership of the cluster, it will have no effect on the sample size calculation and the ICC will be zero. If all the individuals in one cluster behave in an identical manner, no statistical advantage will be gained from entering more than one individual from each cluster and the ICC will be one. So the ICC is a measure of the similarity of individuals (patients) within a cluster.

Assuming that the clusters are of similar sizes, the amount by which the overall sample size requirement has to be multiplied can be calculated from the equation $1+(ñ-1)\rho$, where ρ is the value of the ICC and $ñ$ is the average number of individuals in each cluster.[1] Primary care studies that have taken cluster effects into account in the analysis do not always state the value of the ICC in the final text.[6,7] Hence, calculating sample size can be difficult and estimates may be based on guesswork rather than genuine figures. In the North of England Study of Standards and Performance in General Practice, the value of ρ was greater than 0.1; for some intermediate outcomes, such as recording of general practitioner activity, and for some final outcome measures, such as prescribing rates, ρ was less than 0.01 (L Russell, personal communication, 1996). Values from general practice studies are commonly between 0.01 and 0.05 (M Campbell, personal communication, 1996).

The effect of cluster randomization can be demonstrated by two examples:
1. If there is a small ICC of 0.01 (i.e. individual behaviour is only affected to a minor degree by cluster membership) in a study that plans to recruit 10 patients in each of 10 practices, the inflation factor will be 1.09. This will have little overall effect on the study design, only increasing the numbers required from 100 to 109 compared with randomization by individual.
2. If there is an ICC larger than 0.05 in a trial that plans to recruit 50 patients in each of 10 practices, then the inflation factor will be 3.45. This will have a major effect on study design, increasing the numbers required from 500 to 1725.

The most efficient results will be obtained from cluster randomization where the size of each cluster is small. Taken to its extreme, if each cluster has only one individual, then the statistical power is the same as for individual randomization. There is little advantage in increasing the size of each cluster above 50. If, in the second example, a sample size of 1000 was required using randomization by individual, the extra number of patients required could be achieved either by doubling the size of each cluster to 100 (which would mean that 5950 individuals would be required), or by keeping the size of each cluster at 50 and doubling the number of clusters (which would mean that 3450 individuals would be required).

TRIAL FINDINGS

Even if the number of patients in each cluster is large, scientifically robust trials are possible. In a trial of the effectiveness of dietary advice by practice nurses in lowering coronary heart disease risk, which recruited 956 patients from eight practices, a modest reduction in serum cholesterol was shown.[8] The statistical section explicitly states that cluster effects were taken into consideration in both trial design and analysis. It is therefore possible to be confident that the findings are scientifically robust. However, the values of ρ used in the sample size calculation and in the final analysis were not stated.

A study of a computer-based, active clinical decision support system in the care of patients with diabetes, which was performed by one of the authors (SH), required significant redesign. Because computerized Hb_{A1C} results were easily available, all patients known to have diabetes were studied. Twenty-four practices, each with an average of 200 diabetic patients, were randomly allocated to intervention or control. To show a difference of 0.5% in Hb_{A1C} between the two groups, with a significance of 5% and a power of 90%, assuming a standard deviation of 3%, randomizing by individual, and using a standard t-test, a total of 1514 diabetic patients was required. The 4800 patients available to the study comfortably exceeded this. However, in another study[9] of diabetes in primary care, the value of ρ for Hb_{A1C} was 0.018 (A-L Kinmonth, personal communication, 1996). This suggests that the required inflation factor is 24.5. Thus, to be confident of an adequate sample, 37 093 patients with diabetes from 186 practices would be required. Alternative outcome measures are now being used for this study.

When, as in this example, a whole practice intervention is used and the cluster size cannot be controlled, then outcomes that are less susceptible to changes at a practice level are to be preferred. It might be expected that different practices would be affected differently by the intervention. There might be large cluster effects with some outcome measures that could be influenced by individual doctor behaviour, such as the proportion of patients who had had their lipids measured or a retinal examination performed. The effect on Hb_{A1C} levels, which could be affected by many aspects of the improved care, would be expected to be smaller.

CONCLUSION

The case will arise where an important question can only be answered using cluster randomization where there is a high ICC. Researchers and funding bodies need to be prepared for the possibly large increase in study size required to obtain meaningful results.

Randomization by practice can give valuable unbiased data that may not be accessible using a conventional randomization; if the possible effects of cluster randomization are not taken into account, there is a potentially serious trap for the unwary researcher. We would reiterate Donner's suggestions[4] that all studies using cluster randomization state clearly that corrections have been made to account for this effect, and that when the value of ρ has been calculated it is included in the results to help other workers in designing their studies.

References

1   Donner A, Brown KS, Brasher P. A methodological review of non-therapeutic intervention trials employing cluster randomization 1979-89. *Int J Epidemiol* 1990; **19**: 795-800.

2   Butler C, Bachmann M. Design and analysis of studies evaluating smoking cessation interventions where effects vary between practices or practitioners. *Fam Pract* 1996; **13**: 402-407.

3   Cornfield J. Randomization by group: a formal analysis. *Am J Epidemiol* 1978; **108**: 100-102.

4   Donner A, Birkett N, Buck C. Randomization by cluster: sample size requirements and analysis. *Am J Epidemiol* 1981; **114**: 906-114.

5   Hsieh FY. Sample size formulae for intervention studies with the cluster as unit of randomization. *Stat Med* 1988; **8**: 1195-1201.

6   Wood DA, Kinmonth A-L, Davies GA, *et al*. Randomized controlled trial evaluating cardiovascular screening and intervention in general practice: principal results of the British Family Heart Study. *BMJ* 1994; **308**: 313-320.

7   North of England Study of standards and performance in general practice. Medical audit in general practice I: effects on doctors' clinical behaviour for common childhood conditions. *BMJ* 1992; **304**: 1480-1484.

8   Roderick P, Ruddock V, Hunt P, Miller G. A randomized trial to evaluate the effectiveness of dietary advice by practice nurses in lowering diet-related coronary heart disease risk. *Br J Gen Pract* 1997; **47**: 7-11.

9   Kinmonth A-L, Woodcock A, Griffen S, *et al*. *Diabetes care from diagnosis: the achievement of successful recruitment in a multipractice randomized control trial (RCT)*. Proceedings of the AUDGP 25th Annual Scientific Meeting, Newcastle, 17-19 July, 1996.

Address for correspondence
Dr M Underwood, Medical Research Council Epidemiology and Medical Care Unit, Wolfson Institute of Preventive Medicine, St Bartholemew's and the Royal London School of Medicine and Dentistry, Queen Mary and Westfield College, Charterhouse Square, London EC1M 6BQ.

27

This article was first published in the British Journal of General Practice *and is reproduced by permission of the* Royal College of General Practitioners

CONDUCTING RANDOMIZED TRIALS IN GENERAL PRACTICE: METHODOLOGICAL AND PRACTICAL ISSUES

Elaine Ward, Michael King, Margaret Lloyd, Peter Bower, Karin Friedli

© *British Journal of General Practice*, 1999, **49**, 919–922

SUMMARY

The evaluation of the outcome of health services technologies is a requirement for their efficient provision in clinical practice. The most reliable evidence for treatment efficacy comes from randomized trials. Randomized trials in general practice pose particular methodological and practical difficulties. In this paper, we discuss how best to plan and manage a clinical trial in this setting. We base our discussion on our experience of conducting randomized trials to evaluate the effectiveness of brief psychotherapy in general practice.

Keywords: randomized controlled trial; randomization; family practice; patient preference; recruitment; treatment.

INTRODUCTION

Research in general practice is expanding rapidly to meet the need for evidence-based health care. The results of randomized trials in secondary care settings may not be applicable to primary care. For example, while most antidepressants are prescribed in primary care, their efficacy has been assessed almost entirely within secondary care. The changes to research funding within the National Health Service (NHS) that stem from the recommendations of Culyer and Mant[1,2] will increase pressure for the involvement of general practice, and currently primary care networks are being established to foster the development of research in this setting.[2] Randomized trials in general practice are used to evaluate a broad range of treatment, including musculoskeletal manipulation, psychotherapy, and self-help packages.[3] In this article, we discuss the practicalities involved in conducting randomized trials in general practice. Although there has been considerable debate about the theory of randomized trials, we draw on our experiences of mental health research in this setting to suggest practical issues to consider in the planning stages. We aim this article at all practitioners involved in randomized trials in general practice, be they a part of the research or practice teams. We aim specifically to debate:

- methodological issues in trials in general practice,
- ethical and practical considerations in the evaluation of complex interventions,
- establishing and managing such trials,
- research collaboration in general practice, and
- funding issues.

Inevitably, much of our discussion focuses on the difficulties that may be encountered. This is not to suggest that running randomized trials in general practice is not worth attempting. In fact, we believe that general practice will take an increasing role in clinical trials in the United Kingdom (UK).

METHODS: SCIENTIFIC ISSUES VERSUS PATIENT AUTONOMY

Randomization and patient choice

People are better informed than ever about medical research and clinical trials.[4] They may not accept randomization when considerable differences exist between the arms of the trial, and therefore blindness cannot be maintained. This is particularly true of psychological interventions when patients must provide time, attention, and concentration, and disclose personal facts about themselves. People who refuse to participate in trials desire more participation in decision-making and cite aversion to randomization as the chief reason for their refusal.[5] Patients may prefer one treatment arm of a trial. Their doctors will also have views and may influence their patients' decisions. Patients who do not receive the treatment arm of their choice may become resentful or drop out of the trial. Cooke and Campbell[6] have described the 'resentful demoralization' that ensues when subjects are not randomized to their preferred treatment. Demoralization may reduce compliance with treatment, affect motivation, and influence outcome. For example, in a trial comparing brief psychotherapy with usual general practice care, patients may feel they can progress no further with their doctors and resent randomization back to their care. Disappointment with allocation may lead to a worsening of symptoms or objections to follow-up. Paradoxically, patients allocated to their less preferred option may make a special effort to get better, thus reducing the expected difference.[6] Our experience provides some endorsement for this latter possibility. In a trial of brief psychotherapies compared with usual care, patients allocated back to their doctor for treatment complied as well with follow-up as those in the active treatment groups, but several admitted to feeling they had drawn the 'short straw' and so tried harder to overcome their problems themselves.

Patient preference trials

Trials with partial randomization or patient preference have developed as an attempt to cope with the difficulties posed by standard randomization.[7] Only patients with no strong preference for a treatment arm are randomized. All patients (randomized or not) remain involved in the research assessments and doctors feel less concerned that patients will receive treatments they do not want or trust. External validity is ensured in that all eligible patients take part. Internal validity is maintained by the randomized group.

Although evidence suggests that results are little different in the randomized and non-randomized cohorts,[8] there are statistical objections to including non-randomized patients in the analysis of data from such trials.[9] Although there are a number of patient preference designs to choose from,[10] the trials are more costly to run and it is difficult to elicit treatment preference without influencing participants. The proportion of participants agreeing to full randomization is often difficult to predict; which, in turn, affects power calculations and target recruitment. However, recruitment can be optimized by including a preference option in the study design.

Maximizing validity

Validity is important in any pragmatic or explanatory trial. In pragmatic trials in primary care, scientific rigour is balanced against the flexibility expected by professionals and participants in a naturalistic setting. Strict adherence to protocol and the use of standardized questionnaires will aid internal validity. External validity will be affected by the representativeness of participating sites and subjects. In addition, the doctor's approach to treatment, and consequently outcome, may be affected by participation in a trial that carries with it a confirmation of diagnosis.[11] External validity will also be affected if subjects who refuse or drop out are systematically different from those who complete the trial. It is unclear what effects it will have on representativeness if payments to patients in trials becomes commonplace in general practice research. In our experience, small payments to cover expenses are appreciated by participants and may increase compliance with follow-up assessments.

RECRUITMENT OF PATIENTS

Explanations to patients

Even in randomized trials that take account of patient preference, it may be difficult to explain the nature of each treatment option to participants. Patients who are stressed or depressed only retain a limited amount of information. While it is crucial to avoid bias by providing a careful description of each treatment arm, explaining the differences between complex interventions, such as counselling or cognitive behaviour therapy, may be misleading. Who provides the information, at what point patients receive it, and how to avoid influencing their decisions are important strategies that must be planned before the trial begins.

General practitioners (GPs) may feel uncomfortable or lack the time needed to explain the treatments in the trial or to randomize patients. Trialists, who are independent of the doctor-patient relationship, can more readily carry out allocation to treatment. GPs may also bias allocation by implying the superiority of one or more treatment options.[12] This can be avoided by convincing them that genuine clinical equipoise exists and that there are ethical dangers in treating patients with unproven remedies in these situations. However, if family doctors lack confidence about the treatments under evaluation, they may not refer patients.[13,14] One solution is to randomize only those patients in whom clinicians disagree on the most appropriate treatment.[15] However, this introduces as many problems as it solves and raises the same statistical objections as in patient preference randomized trials. Alternatively, cluster randomization may be considered, where the unit of the randomization is the general practice. However, this also creates difficulties in that the unit of analysis in the trial becomes the practice rather than the patient. This has important knock-on effects in terms of the power of the study and the sample size required to show evidence of efficacy for the treatments under evaluation.

PROVISION OF TREATMENT

When evaluating services such as physiotherapy or practice nurse interventions, a choice may exist between using established providers or recruiting *de novo*. Using established providers means the trial may not have to fund the service. However, quality control of the service may be lost. For example, in a randomized trial of counselling versus GP management for patients with depression, it might seem pragmatic to use counsellors already attached to the practices. However, the trial team cannot control the quality of the intervention so easily and the doctors may question the advisability of *not* using their practice counsellor for patients randomized to usual care.[12]

Ethical issues

Participants must be informed of all aspects of a trial, be competent to give consent, and give it voluntarily. Another prerequisite is clinical equipoise.[16] This means that doctors recruiting patients should be genuinely uncertain about the efficacy of the interventions. Doctors must act in patients' best interests by taking account of their values and preferences when deciding on their care. This can cause conflict if the doctor believes that one arm of the trial would be preferable. Equipoise would thus not exist, and entering that patient could be considered unethical. Doctors may simply be uninformed, and it is important that they understand the need for the trial in the first place. Doctors' concerns about equipoise do not arise in patient preference trials, or in trials where only patients for whom clinicians cannot agree on the best treatment are randomized. A further issue is who should obtain consent: patients may hesitate to refuse their doctor's request and it may be more appropriate for trialists to seek consent.

Managing the intervention under study in the trial
Providers of the intervention

Introducing a new service as part of the trial offers greater incentive to practices to take part and is easier for the research team to manage. However, the providers brought in for the trial may be less integrated into the practices and the costs for the research will be greater.[17] When an established service is evaluated, the trial team will need to persuade the providers to take part. The providers of the intervention should be flexible to respond to the changing needs of the research, whether they are already practice-based or are brought in for the trial. It is essential to convey to them the benefits of participation. These include reports on their patients' progress, liaison with professional colleagues, and opportunities for professional development. Regular meetings provide team support, a forum for developing professional links, and time to discuss issues that arise during the research. Good morale in the providers reduces loss of staff from the study: a particular problem where a skill is in short supply, such as cognitive behaviour therapy or physiotherapy.

Financial issues

Where the intervention under study is financed by the research, a failure to predict service use can jeopardize the budget. In a multicentre trial, there may be geographical variations in cost. A patient preference design may produce greater demand for one treatment arm with a resultant increase in costs.

Whether payment for the intervention(s) is made to individuals or to a service provider, all parties must be clear about session payments, arrangements regarding non-attendance of patients, and travel and incidental costs.

Recruiting practices

General practitioners are likely to agree to a trial because of local contacts with the trialists and the attraction or relevance of the research. Practice staff may not wish, however, to remain in the background or merely refer patients. They may desire an active role; for example, as part of research networks of practices centred on academic departments of primary care (e.g. the North Central Thames Primary Care Research Network, NoCTeN). Besides trials funded by the pharmaceutical industry, payment to practices for their participation is unusual in the UK. Targeted financial incentives might, however, be an effective approach if other means of involving general practitioners fail.[18] Redirection of the NHS levy for research and development from hospital and community trusts will also ease the underfunding of infrastructure for randomized trials in general practice.[1,2]

Making the approach

Practices are most likely to be recruited if they lack the service that the trial will provide (such as counselling or physiotherapy). We introduce the trial in a letter, inviting the practice staff to meet with the research team to discuss it. Soon after sending the letter, it is advisable for the trialist to telephone the practice to gauge interest in the study and arrange a meeting. A GP who is associated with the research team should be present at this meeting. This is of obvious practical value and assists the credibility of the project. It is essential to prepare an attractive and accessible information pack that includes a summary of the study and a flowchart for the wall of each office in the practice. The meeting needs to include the practice manager and lead receptionist. It is helpful for the research team to allow practice staff several days after the meeting to decide whether they wish to participate.

Reluctance to be involved

Practices may not wish to participate for the following reasons:

- They perceive they are already over-committed to research or feel pressurized by time. The constant bombardment with postal questionnaires experienced by most GPs may create this impression, rather than actual research that is underway. Payments for practice staff time[1,2] may alleviate this difficulty.

- Staff are concerned about lack of space, particularly if this involves treatments taking place on the premises. Payments for research infrastructure that will allow practices to create space may help to ameliorate this difficulty in future.[1,2]

- Doctors may not see how their working practices can accommodate the study. Although this is a common objection,[19] it usually stems from a misunderstanding of what the trial involves. Trials that depend on lengthy participation by clinicians will founder in any setting.

- Practices may be undergoing structural or personnel change.

Advantages for the practices

There may be competition to recruit general practices into trials. Thus, the potential benefits of participation must be highlighted. These might include:
- ready access to a new treatment under evaluation;
- a free, or highly professional, service;
- a reduced patient load;
- closer links with a university department;
- feedback about their own practice;
- acquisition of new knowledge about the treatments being tested; and
- an opportunity for practice staff to participate and learn about research.

The research team should emphasize how benefits can offset the costs of participation, such as time or space, in the practice. Even if one of the doctors is a member of the trial team, the research needs to appeal to the remainder of the practice staff.

ROLE OF THE RESEARCHER
Coordination of practices
One GP or practice manager needs to coordinate the study within each practice; the practice manager usually assumes this role. Linking research assistants to specific general practices helps them to develop relationships with the practice staff. The same applies to the providers of services under evaluation. Maintaining a good relationship between the research and practice teams requires effective channels of communication. Poor communication may have led to the collapse of at least one large multicentre trial.[20]

Keeping in touch
Regular contact with practices serves to detect problems and check that the presence of the study personnel is acceptable. It is not clear whether it boosts referrals but it does have the effect of enhancing relations as well as monitoring actual participation and referrals to the study. We have rarely found that regular telephone calls or informal visits are unwelcome. The research team can become aware of obstacles in advance and decide whether to withdraw from a practice at any time. This can occur, for example, when building works threaten the availability of space.

Providing regular, one-page 'news flashes' will remind practice staff about the project, update them on the progress of all the practices involved, make them feel part of the study, and remind them of the inclusion and exclusion criteria. News flashes can display the recruitment rates of all practices in the trial and introduce a competitive element. Most practitioners value the updates as useful reminders to avoid protocol deviations and maintain recruitment.

Maintaining momentum
Even enthusiastic practitioners become fatigued after recruiting for many months, and staff may wish to phase their involvement. We find it helpful to suggest that practices recruit for one month at a time. This on-off approach is welcome where participation of a doctor or practice nurse is required in one treatment arm. However, it may have cost implications when the trialists provide the intervention.

Recruitment early in the trial predicts the pattern for the practice. Once the protocol is fully understood, it is rare that slow practices can be encouraged to recruit greater numbers. Persistently low recruiting practices may have to leave the study. It usually proves cost-effective to limit the number of practices and maximize cooperation from each of them. Withdrawal may, however, jeopardize randomization if this is by practice or by therapist. Once decided upon, it requires diplomacy if practice staff are to avoid regarding it as a failure. Withdrawal is even more sensitive if one of the GPs is a member of the trial team. A reserve list of interested general practices is necessary for replacements. Equally, it is vital to have alternative service providers available if the need arises. This is indispensable where a service is limited in supply, as with cognitive behaviour therapists or community pharmacists.

FUNDING ARRANGEMENTS
Multicentre trials
Randomized trials in more than one general practice are, by definition, multicentre. When the trial involves multiple academic centres, however, the difficulties compound. It is important to build in flexible funding that is not centralized but can follow high recruiting academic centres. Research staff will have contracts that provide them with job security during the study. However, in multicentre trials, they may need to move the base in response to fluctuating recruitment. This can pose logistical problems if the centres are dispersed, and requires forward planning.

Payment of practice staff is likely to expand with the establishment of general practice research networks. Just as academic institutions and some hospital trusts receive overheads for the infrastructural costs of research, so should participating general practices receive funding for the cost the research entails. This cost must ultimately be borne by the organizations funding the trial, or by the NHS funding levy for research and development.[1]

DISCUSSION
In this paper, we have discussed a number of methodological and practical ideas, many of which stem from our own experience. In order to run a successful randomized controlled trial to evaluate a complex intervention in primary care, it is vital to use effective and practical research strategies. This type of project requires a tailored, workable design. Success is likely as a result of prudent planning and depends on cooperative, well-informed health professionals. It can be achieved by addressing factors likely to affect recruitment and follow-up, by sensitive management, and by payments to practices for the use of their time and infrastructure as required by the project.

E Ward, MSc, research fellow, Department of Psychiatry and Behavioural Sciences; M King, MD, professor, Department of Psychiatry and Behavioural Sciences; and M Lloyd, MD, reader, Department of Primary Care and Population Sciences, Royal Free and University College Medical School. P Bower, PhD, research associate, National Primary Care Research and Development Centre, University of Manchester. K Freidli, PhD, formerly project co-ordinator, PRiSM, Institute of Psychiatry, London.
Submitted: 6 August 1998; final acceptance: 24 February 1999.

References

1. Culyer A. *Supporting Research and Development in the NHS*. London: HMSO, 1994.
2. Mant D. *R&D in Primary Care: National Working Group report for the NHS*. London: HMSO, 1997.
3. Silagy CA, Jewell D. Review of 39 years of randomised controlled trials in the *British Journal of General Practice*. *Br J Gen Pract* 1994; **44**: 359–363.
4. Mattson ME, Curb JD, McArdle R, AMIS and BHAT Research Groups. Participation in a clinical trial: the patients' point of view. *Controlled Clinical Trials* 1985; **6**: 156–167.
5. Llewellyn-Thomas HA, McGreal MJ, Thiel EC, *et al*. Patients' willingness to enter clinical trials: measuring the association with perceived benefit and preference for decision participation. *Soc Sci Med* 1991; **32**: 35–42.
6. Cooke TD, Campbell DT. *Quasi-experimentation: Design and analysis issues for field settings*. Chicago: Rand McNally Co, 1979.
7. Brewin CR, Bradley C. Patient preferences and randomised clinical trials. *BMJ* 1989; **299**: 313–315.
8. McKay JR, Alterman AI, McLellan AT, *et al*. Effect of random versus non-random assignment in a comparison of inpatient and day hospital rehabilitation for male alcoholics. *J Consult Clin Psychol* 1995; **63**: 70–78.
9. Silverman WA, Altman DG. Patients' preferences and randomised trials. *Lancet* 1996; **347**: 171–174.
10. Torgerson D, Sibbald B. Understanding controlled trials: What is a patient preference trial? *BMJ* 1998; **316**: 360.
11. Scott J, Moon CAL, Blacker CVR, *et al*. Edinburgh Primary Care Depression Study. *Br J Psychiatry* 1994; **164**: 410–415.
12. King M, Broster G, Lloyd M, Horder J. Controlled trials in the evaluation of counselling in general practice. *Br J Gen Pract* 1994; **44**: 229–232.
13. Fairhurst K, Dowrick C. Problems with recruitment in a randomized controlled trial of counselling in general practice: causes and implications. *J Health Services Res Policy* 1996; **1**: 77–80.
14. Hancock BW, Aitken M, Radstone C. Hudson CV. Why don't cancer patients get entered into clinical trials? Experience of the Sheffield Lymphoma Group's collaboration in British National Lymphoma Investigation studies. *BMJ* 1997; **314**: 36–37.
15. Kom EL, Baumrind S. Randomised clinical trials with clinician-preferred treatment. *Lancet* 1991; **337**: 149–152.
16. British Medical Association. *Medical ethics today: its practice and philosophy*. London: BMJ Publishing Group, 1993.
17. Friedli K, King MB, Lloyd M, Horder J. Randomised controlled assessment of non-directive psychotherapy versus routine general practice care. *Lancet* 1997; **350**: 1662–1643.
18. Foy R, Parry J, McAvoy B. Clinical trials in primary care. *BMJ* 1998; **317**: 1168–1169.
19. Pringle M, Churchill R. Randomised controlled trials in general practice. *BMJ* 1995; **311**: 1382–1383.
20. Tognoni G, Alli C, Avanzini F, *et al*. Randomised clinical trials in general practice: lessons from a failure. *BMJ* 1991; **303**: 969–971.

Acknowledgement

The authors gratefully acknowledge Bonnie Sibbald and Sharon Farrelly who advised on penultimate drafts.

Address for correspondence

Professor Michael King, Department of Psychiatry and Behavioural Sciences, Royal Free and University College Medical School, Royal Free Campus, Rowland Hill Street, London NW3 2PF.